W9-BUP-187

50X1   6.75

YALE CO-OP
USED BOOK

THE
RANDOM HOUSE
HANDBOOK

second edition

Frederick Crews

UNIVERSITY OF CALIFORNIA, BERKELEY

RANDOM HOUSE • NEW YORK

THE RANDOM HOUSE
HANDBOOK

second edition

Copyright © 1977, 1974 by Random House, Inc.

All rights reserved under International and Pan-American Copyright Conventions.
No part of this book may be reproduced in any form or by any means, electronic or
mechanical, including photocopying, without permission in writing from the publisher. All inquiries should be addressed to Random House, Inc., 201 East 50th Street,
New York, N.Y. 10022. Published in the United States by Random House, Inc., and
simultaneously in Canada by Random House of Canada Limited, Toronto.

Library of Congress Cataloging in Publication Data

Crews, Frederick B
  The Random House handbook.

  Includes index.
  1. English language—Rhetoric. 2. English language—
Grammar—1950–   I. Title.
PE1408.C715 1977   808'.042   76-46538
ISBN 0-394-31211-2

Manufactured in the United States of America
Second Edition
98765432

Since this page cannot legibly accommodate all the copyright notices, the pages following constitute an extension of the copyright page.

PERMISSIONS ACKNOWLEDGMENTS

PHILIP H. ABELSON and ALLEN L. HAMMOND, excerpt from "The New World of Materials," *Science*, 191 (20 Feb. 1976), 663. Copyright 1976 by the American Association for the Advancement of Science. Reprinted by permission of the author and publisher.

HARVEY ARDEN, excerpt from "In Search of Moses," *National Geographic*, Jan. 1976, p. 36. Reprinted by permission.

JAMES BALDWIN, excerpt from *Nobody Knows My Name*. Copyright © 1961 by James Baldwin. Reprinted by permission of The Dial Press.

JACQUES BARZUN, excerpt from "In Favor of Capital Punishment," *The American Scholar*, Spring 1962, p. 182. Copyright © 1962 by the United Chapters of Phi Beta Kappa. Reprinted by permission of the publisher.

SAUL BELLOW, excerpt from *Herzog*. Copyright © 1964, 1967. Reprinted by permission of The Viking Press, Inc.

LEWIS M. BRANSCOMB, excerpt from "Taming Technology," *Science*, 171 (12 Mar. 1971), 973. Copyright 1971 by the American Association for the Advancement of Science. Reprinted by permission of the author and publisher.

KINGMAN BREWSTER, excerpt from *The Report of the President*, Yale University, 1974–1975. Reprinted by permission of Yale University.

PAUL A. CARTER, excerpt from "Of Towns and Roads, Three Novelists, and George McGovern," *The Columbia Forum*, Spring 1973, pp. 10–11. Copyright © 1973 by the Trustees of Columbia University in the City of New York. Reprinted by permission of the publisher.

SHARON CURTIN, excerpt from "Aging in the Land of the Young," *Atlantic*, July 1973, p. 68. Copyright © 1973 The Atlantic Monthly Company, Boston, Massachusetts. Reprinted by permission.

J. A. DEUTSCH and H. S. KOOPMANS, excerpt from "Preference Enhancement for Alcohol by Passive Exposure," *Science*, 179 (23 Mar. 1973), 1242. Copyright 1973 by the American Association for the Advancement of Science. Reprinted by permission of the authors and publisher.

GEORGE DEVEREUX, excerpt from *From Anxiety to Method in the Behavioral Sciences*. Reprinted by permission of Mouton & Co., The Hague, The Netherlands.

DOUG DOWD, excerpt from "Watch Out: Prosperity Is Just Around the Corner (Again)," *Ramparts*, Mar. 1971, p. 36. Copyright 1971 by Noah's Ark, Inc. (for Ramparts Magazine). Reprinted by permission.

RALPH ELLISON, excerpt from "The World and the Jug," *Shadow and Act*. Copyright © 1953, 1964 by Random House, Inc. Reprinted by permission of Random House, Inc.

AMITAI ETZIONI, excerpt from "Grade Inflation," *Science*, 190 (10 Oct. 1975), 101. Copyright 1975 by the American Association for the Advancement of Science. Reprinted by permission of the author and publisher.

MICHAEL FIELD, excerpt adapted from *All Manner of Food*. Copyright © 1965, 1966, 1967, 1968, 1970 by Michael Field. Reprinted by permission of Alfred A. Knopf, Inc.

RON FIMRITE, excerpt from "Kings of the Hill Again," *Sports Illustrated*, 21 July 1975, p. 15. © Time Inc., 1975. Reprinted by permission of *Sports Illustrated*.

MILTON FRIEDMAN, excerpt from "Monumental Folly," *Newsweek*, 25 June 1973, p. 64. Copyright 1973 by Newsweek, Inc. All rights reserved. Reprinted by permission.

RICHARD GAMBINO, excerpt from "Watergate Lingo: A Language of Non-Responsibility," *Freedom at Issue*, Nov./Dec. 1973, pp. 15–16. Copyright *Freedom at Issue*, published by Freedom House, New York. Reprinted by permission.

ALBERT GOLDMAN, excerpt from "The Emergence of Rock," *New American Review*, No. 3, p. 119. Copyright © 1968 by Albert Goldman. Reprinted by permission of Sterling Lord Agency, Inc.

ARTHUR GOLDSMITH, excerpt from "Ralph Gibson Quadrants," *Popular Photography*, Mar. 1976, p. 100. © Ziff-Davis Publishing Co. Reprinted by permission of the publisher.

PAUL GOODMAN, excerpt from "The Psychology of Being Powerless," *Like a Conquered Province*. Copyright © 1967 by Random House, Inc. Reprinted by permission of Random House, Inc., Canadian Broadcasting Corporation, and Sally Goodman for the Estate of Paul Goodman.

NOEL GROVE, excerpt from "Mark Twain: Mirror of America," *National Geographic*, 148, Sept. 1975, p. 300. Reprinted by permission.

NORMAN HACKERMAN, excerpt from "The Future of Graduate Education, If Any," *Science*, 175 (4 Feb. 1972), 475. Copyright 1972 by the American Association for the Advancement of Science. Reprinted by permission of the author and publisher.

AMOS H. HAWLEY, excerpt from "Ecology and Population," *Science*, 179 (23 Mar. 1973), 1196. Copyright 1973 by the American Association for the Advancement of Science. Reprinted by permission of the author and publisher.

TIMOTHY E. HEAD, excerpt from *Going Native in Hawaii: A Poor Man's Guide to Paradise*. Reprinted by permission of Charles E. Tuttle Co., Inc.

ERNEST HEMINGWAY, excerpt from *A Moveable Feast*. Copyright © 1964 Ernest Hemingway, Ltd. Reprinted by permission of Charles Scribner's Sons.

NANCY JO HOFFMAN, excerpt from "Sexism in Letters of Recommendation," *MLA Newsletter*, Sept. 1972, p. 5. Copyright © 1972 by The Modern Language Association of America. Reprinted by permission of the publisher.

CONSTANCE HOLDEN, excerpt from "Community Mental Health Centers: Storefront Therapy and More," *Science*, 174 (17 Dec. 1971), 1221. Copyright 1971 by the American Association for the Advancement of Science. Reprinted by permission of the publisher.

JOSEPH F. JOHNSTON, JR. excerpt from "The Leader as Mass Man," *National Review*, 28 (19 Mar. 1976), 272. Reprinted by permission of the publisher.

LEROI JONES, excerpt from *Home: Social Essays*. Copyright © 1963, 1966 by LeRoi Jones. Reprinted by permission of William Morrow and Company, Inc.

PAULINE KAEL, excerpt from *Kiss Kiss Bang Bang*. Copyright © 1967 by Pauline Kael. Reprinted by permission of Little, Brown and Company in association with The Atlantic Monthly Press.

MARSHALL KOUGHAN, excerpt from "Goodbye, San Francisco," *Harper's*, Sept. 1975, p. 30. Copyright © 1975 Harper's Magazine. Reprinted by permission of the publisher.

JONATHAN KOZOL, excerpt from "The Open Schoolroom: New Words for Old Deceptions," *Ramparts*, July 1972, p. 41. Copyright 1972 by Noah's Ark, Inc. (for Ramparts Magazine). Reprinted by permission.

DIANA LOERCHER, excerpt from "The Cat: Friend, Villain, Enigma?" *The Christian Science Monitor*, 16 Mar. 1976, p. 14. © 1976 The Christian Science Publishing Society. Reprinted by permission of the publisher.

SAMUEL MCCRACKEN, excerpt from "The Scandal of 'Britannica 3,'" *Commentary*, Feb. 1976, p. 68. Copyright © 1976 by the American Jewish Committee. Reprinted by permission.

RAYMOND S. MOORE and DENNIS R. MOORE, excerpt from "The Dangers of Early Schooling," *Harper's*, July 1972, pp. 58–62. Copyright © 1972 by Harper's Magazine. Reprinted by permission.

ROBERT A. NISBET, excerpt from "Crisis in the University?" *The Public Interest*, Winter, 1968, p. 64. Copyright © 1968 by National Affairs, Inc. Reprinted by permission of the author.

GEORGE ORWELL, excerpt from "Politics and the English Language," from *Shooting an Elephant and Other Essays*. Copyright 1945, 1946, 1949, 1950, by Sonia Brownell Orwell. Reprinted by permission of Harcourt Brace Jovanovich, Inc., Mrs. Sonia Brownell Orwell, & Secker Warburg.

SONYA O'SULLIVAN, excerpt from "Single Life in a Double Bed," *Harper's*, Nov. 1975, p. 45. Copyright by Sonya O'Sullivan. Reprinted by permission of the author.

TALCOTT PARSONS, excerpt from "The Kinship System of the Contemporary United States," *Essays in Sociological Theory* (rev. ed.). Copyright 1949, 1954 by The Free Press, Inc. Reprinted by permission of Macmillan Publishing Co., Inc.

TERENCE DES PRES, excerpt from *The Survivor: An Anatomy of Life in the Death Camps*. Reprinted by permission of Oxford University Press.

PAUL ROAZEN, excerpt from *Freud and His Followers*. Copyright © 1975 by Alfred A. Knopf, Inc. Reprinted by permission of Alfred A. Knopf, Inc.

FRANK ROWSOME, excerpt from "Apple & Beech, Birch & Oak," from *The Bright and Glowing Place*. Copyright © 1975 by Frank Rowsome, Jr. Reprinted by permission of The Stephen Greene Press.

SONYA RUDIKOFF, excerpt from "Marriage and Household," *Commentary*, June 1973, p. 59. Copyright © 1973 by the American Jewish Committee. Reprinted by permission of the publisher.

ALAN H. SCHOENFELD, excerpt from "Exploiting the Job Market," *Chronicle of Higher Education*, 26 Jan. 1976, p. 24. Reprinted by permission of the author and publisher.

ALIX KATES SHULMAN, excerpt from "The War in the Back Seat," *Atlantic*, July 1972, p. 50. Copyright © 1972 by Alix Kates Shulman. Reprinted by permission of Curtis Brown, Ltd.

HENRY NASH SMITH, excerpt from "Some Patterns of Transcendence in Hawthorne and Howells," from *English Studies Today*, 1975, p. 437. Reprinted by permission.

THEODORE SOLOTAROFF, excerpt from "World of Our Fathers," *New York Times Book Review*, 1 Feb. 1976, p. 1. © 1976 by The New York Times Company. Reprinted by permission.

KENNETH M. STAMPP, excerpt from *The Era of Reconstruction, 1865–1877*. Copyright © 1965 by Alfred A. Knopf, Inc. Reprinted by permission of Alfred A. Knopf, Inc.

JOHN WALSH, excerpt from "Brigham Young University: Challenging the Federal Patron," *Science*, 191 (16 Jan. 1976), 160–163. Copyright 1976 by the American Association for the Advancement of Science. Reprinted by permission of the author and publisher.

MANFRED WEIDHORN, excerpt from "Blood, Toil, Tears and 8,000,000 Words: Churchill Writing," *The Columbia Forum*, Spring 1975, p. 19. Copyright © 1975 by The Trustees of Columbia University in the City of New York. Reprinted by permission.

ELLEN WILLIS, excerpt from "The Fantasy of the Perfect Lover," *New York Review of Books*, 31 Aug. 1972, p. 7. Copyright © 1972 Nyrev, Inc. Reprinted with permission from *The New York Review of Books*.

TOM WOLFE, excerpt from *The Pump House Gang*. Copyright © 1968 by Tom Wolfe. Copyright © 1966 by the World Journal. Reprinted by permission of Farrar, Straus & Giroux, Inc.

ANTHONY WOLFF, excerpt from "We Shall Fight Them on the Beaches . . . ," *Harper's*, Aug. 1973, p. 55. Copyright © 1973 Harper's Magazine. Reprinted by permission of the publisher.

SHELDON S. WOLIN, excerpt from "The New Conservatives," *New York Review of Books*, 5 Feb. 1976, p. 6. Copyright © 1976 Nyrev, Inc. Reprinted with permission from *The New York Review of Books*.

VIRGINIA WOOLF, excerpt from "Life and the Novelist," from *Granite and Rainbow*. Reprinted by permission of Harcourt Brace Jovanovich, Inc., the Author's Literary Estate, and The Hogarth Press.

WILLIAM ZINSSER, "Frankly, Miss Dodds," *Atlantic*, Apr. 1973, p. 94. Copyright © 1973 by William K. Zinsser. Reprinted by permission of the author.

ABIGAIL ZUGER, "Acrophobia in the Ivory Tower," *Harper's*, Oct. 1975, pp. 4–5. Copyright © 1975 Harper's Magazine. Reprinted by permission.

Excerpt from "D is for Dodo," *Newsweek*, 9 Feb. 1976, p. 84. Copyright 1976 by Newsweek, Inc. All rights reserved. Reprinted by permission.

Excerpt from "Food: The New Wave," *Newsweek*, 11 Aug. 1975, p. 50. Copyright 1975 by Newsweek, Inc. All rights reserved. Reprinted by permission.

Excerpt from "Making Babies," *Newsweek*, 11 Aug. 1975, p. 13. Copyright 1975 by Newsweek, Inc. All rights reserved. Reprinted by permission.

Excerpt from "The Matador," *Newsweek*, 22 Sept. 1975, p. 61. Copyright 1975 by Newsweek, Inc. All rights reserved. Reprinted by permission.

Excerpt from "The President's Palace Guard," *Newsweek*, 19 Mar. 1973, p. 24. Copyright 1973 by Newsweek, Inc. All rights reserved. Reprinted by permission.

Excerpt from "The Quantum Mechanic," *Newsweek*, 16 Feb. 1976, p. 90. Copyright 1976 by Newsweek, Inc. All rights reserved. Reprinted by permission.

FOR BETTY
again and always

PREFACE

The first edition of this book won many friends, who saw in it a reflection of their hopes for a candid and humane approach to English composition. I think they will find that the second edition meets such hopes more fully than its predecessor. It is, in fact, precisely the friends of my book who are responsible for its improvement; literally thousands of practical comments from students and instructors have shown me how to make the *Handbook* a more effective classroom instrument.

Among other changes, this edition offers:

1. a reorganization that places all the "rhetoric" chapters in one sequence and all the "handbook" chapters in another;
2. fuller explanations of types of essays, stages of composition, and methods of paragraph development;
3. many more exercises, with clearer instructions;
4. more definitions and cross-references, plus a Glossary of Terms;
5. more positive (less cautionary) advice on the building of successful arguments;

6. more examples, especially from student prose;
7. more emphasis on major points of usage, and less on disagreements among the authorities; and
8. a brief Appendix on the writing of essays in examinations.

Since most composition students are asked to produce essays in the early weeks of a course, the *Handbook* begins by considering what essays are, how they get composed, and what strategic and stylistic resources can make them succeed. Chapters One through Nine, leading to the writing of a documented research essay, can be read in order, with detours as necessary to the later, "handbook," chapters and the Glossary. Many students and instructors, however, will want to begin with Chapters Ten, Eleven, and Twelve, which review the fundamentals of grammar, usage, and punctuation. Those chapters lay the groundwork for much that is said elsewhere.

Professor Jule Kaufman of the University of Cincinnati has written an extensive manual—available to instructors on request—which offers answers to my exercises and much down-to-earth advice about the teaching of composition. She has also prepared a companion text, *The Random House Workbook*, with exercises keyed to chapters of the *Handbook*. A separate diagnostic test by Robert Atwan, linked to both the *Handbook* and the *Workbook*, is designed to measure students' writing proficiency.

Among the printed sources behind this book, I would once again like to single out Roy H. Copperud's *American Usage: The Consensus*; it has spared me many a misconception. Correspondents who have suggested changes are too numerous to mention; they have already been told how grateful I am to them. Alan Hager, Miriam Spongberg, Beverly Voloshin, and other members of the Berkeley English 1A-B staff have supplied me with useful examples of student prose. I have received important guidance and criticism from Nadean Bishop, Nicholas P. Carlucci, Murray Curtin, F. A. Ehmann, Carol Flechner, Matthew J. Holdreith, Charles W. Johnson, George Kearns, Josephine Miles, Carol J. Russett, Kay Scully, Teoman Sipahigil, Rita Speicher, and Theodore Whyland. And eight people have sustained me not only with detailed critiques, but also with extraordinary kindness and dedication: Elizabeth Crews, David Follmer, Jule Kaufman, Richard Larson, Helen D. Litton, Robert T. Mundhenk, Donald A. McQuade, and June Smith. I hope that all of them realize how impoverished this book would be without their guiding influence.

Frederick Crews

CONTENTS

PART II STYLE 99

6 PARAGRAPHS   156

PART III SOURCES

12 PUNCTUATION   328

PART V   FOR REFERENCE

13 SPELLING

PART I
A WRITER'S WORK

1 THE ESSAY

YOU AND YOUR READER

If you're like most students entering a composition course, you arrive with a mixture of hope and worry. The hope is that the course will help you to put your thoughts into written words with greater precision and effect. The worry is that nothing of the sort will happen and that you'll have to go through a painful, humiliating ordeal. Essays, you know, will be required of you on short notice. Will you be able to write them at all? Looking ahead, perhaps you experience a feeling that assails every writer from time to time—the suspicion that words may fail you. (And if words fail you, the instructor may fail you, too.)

It may seem odd at first that "putting your thoughts into words" should be so challenging. Since childhood, after all, you've been speaking intelligible English. When you talk about things that matter to you, the right words often come to your lips without forethought. Again, in writing letters to friends you scribble away with confidence that you'll be understood. But in writing essays you find yourself at a disadvantage. You know that your prose is expected to carry your reader along with a developing idea, but you don't have a clear

2

notion of who that reader is. Instead of exchanging views with some-one who can see your face, interpret your gestures, and tell you when a certain point needs explanation or support, you have to assume a nonexistent relationship and keep on writing. It's almost like com-posing love letters "to whom it may concern" and mailing them off to "Occupant" or "Boxholder."

This is the normal situation of every writer, but it is humanized a bit in a composition course. There you do get to know your reader, the instructor, in a certain limited way, and you can gradually devel-op some ease as you become familiar with his or her judgment. Un-like the mythical "general reader," this one will talk back to you, and even keep on reading when bored. Nowhere else are you likely to get the systematic, prolonged encouragement and criticism your instruc-tor will offer. Thus the composition course gives you a unique oppor-tunity to test how other readers, the silent ones, would receive your writing.

But the course holds a risk as well as an opportunity. The risk comes directly from that first anxiety about having nothing to say. You'll quickly learn that there *are* ways of getting words onto paper even when you're confused, and if you're not careful you may begin writing mechanically. Instead of exploring your mind and trying to communicate what you believe, you may begin serving up ingredi-ents you think the instructor wants to see. An essay, you tell yourself, has to have an introduction, a body, and a conclusion (pp. 36–37)—and you forget that it's supposed to be interesting. You allot one prominent topic sentence (pp. 158–161) to every paragraph, but the paragraphs, instead of moving forward, just stand there like abandoned temples to the god of the essay. Your prose acquires unity, coherence, emphasis—and acid indigestion. You've simply stopped trying to say what you mean.

The irony about "giving the teacher what he wants" is that this isn't what he wants at all. No teacher I've ever met has preferred an imitation essay to the real thing. Teachers often dwell on technical aspects of the essay because these are important and discussible, but what they want above all is that you develop a strong, persuasive way of presenting *your* ideas, not theirs. They know that a writer's willingness to explore and expose his feelings often makes the differ-ence between a passable but drab essay and one that commands at-tention.

This is not to say, however, that anything goes. Some students want to believe that any way of expressing their thoughts is all right so long as it comes from the heart. *To be true to myself, I have to use my very own words*—and your very own spelling and punctuation as well. But spelling, punctuation, and correct usage aren't private mat-ters. They are established by *convention*, or longstanding agreement. Writers who master the conventions haven't sacrificed any original-ity; they have simply removed an obstacle to being seriously read.

So, too, "exploring your feelings" needn't be confused with putting forward the first thoughts that occur to you, or certain pet notions that you've never bothered to question. It means presenting ideas *about a topic that you've found suitable for treatment within the scope of an essay;* ideas that are *neither too obvious nor too outrageous* to catch a reader's sympathetic attention; and ideas *for which you can offer convincing support.* For an essay isn't a blunt announcement of your opinions. It's rather an act of communication—an establishing of a common ground on which two strangers, you and your reader, can agree to meet. The private ground of your feelings is only your starting place as you head toward that public encounter.

It is, in fact, the essay's unavoidably public character that justifies your instructor's role. If the essay were merely a means of self-display, you could write as thoughtlessly as you pleased. But the proper audience of an essay is neither yourself nor your instructor as one unique individual. It is rather a general *audience of reasonable people.* What reasonable people share, in their better moments, is precisely a willingness to listen to reason. Their minds are open to persuasion, but only if certain standards of intelligibility, consistency, and evidential support (see Chapter Three) have been observed. Your instructor intends to apply those same standards in reading your work. He or she is, in effect, a stand-in for the anonymous public. By writing for the wider audience that the instructor represents, you can use the course as a workshop for developing your persuasive and communicative skills.

In this time of massively manipulated opinion, when the arts of advertising and propaganda have joined forces with the hypnotic medium of television, many students wonder whether there isn't something hopelessly old-fashioned about the essay's appeal to cool judgment and patient reasoning. Aren't people really persuaded by an incessant repetition of slogans? Indeed they are—unless they have learned how to form opinions on a rational basis. Lacking that capacity, they are only consumers of products, images, and official half-truths. Possessing it, they have a precious and continuing source of independence. If you think of the essay, not as a quaint literary mode, but as an instrument for the sharpening of reasoned personal judgment, you will realize why essay-writing forms the backbone of your composition course. The essay is useful exactly because the values it entails are so hard to acquire in any other way.

WHAT AN ESSAY DOES

Most of the other writing you will do in college—exams, reports, term papers, perhaps a senior thesis—resembles the essay in some respects and calls on identical techniques of persuasion. The same is true of much "postgraduate" prose, from business letters and petitions to technical and scientific reports, newsletters, lawyers' briefs, even campaign speeches. If you can write an effective essay, you will be able to master any of these modes after a little practice. But so long as you are writing essays proper, you should be aware of their distinctive features. What sets an essay apart from other modes of verbal reasoning is a characteristic blend of opinion and demonstration, of intimacy and objectivity.

An *essay* can be defined as a *fairly brief piece of nonfiction that tries to make a point in an interesting way:*

1. *It's fairly brief.* Some of the classic essays by Montaigne and Bacon occupy only a few paragraphs, but essays generally fall between about three and twenty typed pages. Under that minimum, the development of thought that typifies an essay would be difficult to manage. Above that maximum, people might be tempted to read the essay in installments, like a book. A good essay makes an unbroken experience.

2. *It's nonfiction.* The essayist tries to tell the truth; if he describes a scene or tells a story, we presume that he is doing his best to capture reality or illustrate an idea.

3. *It tries to make a point . . .* An essay characteristically tells or explains something, or expresses an attitude toward something, or supports or criticizes something — an opinion, a person, an institution, a movement. A poem or a novel may also do these things, but it does them incidentally. An essay is directly *about* something called its *topic* (see p. 28), and its usual aim is to win sympathy or agreement to the point or *thesis* (see p. 28) it is maintaining.

4. *. . . in an interesting way.* When you write an answer to an "essay question" on an exam, you don't pause to wonder if the reader actually *wants* to pursue your answer to the end; you know you'll succeed if you concisely and coherently satisfy the terms of the question. But a full-fledged essay tends to be read in another way. Its reader could agree with every sentence and still be displeased. What that reader wants isn't just true statements, but a feeling that those statements *matter.* In both cases, to be sure, you have to employ *rhetoric* — that is, you have to *choose and arrange your words for their maximum effect on the reader.* But the rhetoric counts for more in a genuine essay, where maintaining the reader's involvement has to be a central consideration.

This point may leave you uneasy if you think of *rhetoric* in its casual meaning of insincere, windy deception, as in *Oh, that's just a lot of rhetoric.* But in this book the term is used only in its primary sense as *the effective placement of ideas and choice of language.* Rhetoric and sincerity needn't work at cross-purposes; and whenever they do the rhetoric comes out sounding all wrong. Your job isn't to deceive your readers, but merely to draw them toward accepting your thesis by making dramatic use of the steps that led you to accept it yourself. Insincerity enters the picture only if you don't believe what you're saying.

The essayist, then, harmonizes reason and rhetoric, trying to be at once lively, fair, and convincing. He must:

tell the truth ⟶ but first make people interested in hearing it;

write with conviction ⟶ but consider whether the ideas will stand up under criticism;

supply evidence ⟶ but not become a bore about it;

be purposeful ⟶ but not follow such a predictable pattern that the reader's attention slackens.

HOW AN ESSAY SOUNDS

The way an essay sounds — the quality of feeling it conveys — is called its *tone*. Depending on your personality and the effect you want to create, you can be formal or informal, sober or whimsical, assertive or pleading, straightforward or sly. But the essay's general function, to present and support opinion, tends to rule out certain tones. Consider these three passages:

A. Yes, you CAN stop drinking! I tell you it's really possible! The fact that you're reading these words means that you have the MOTIVATION, the WILL POWER, to make the change now — *today!* — and to STAY ON THE WAGON *FOREVER!!* Think and believe, *I am just as good as everybody else! I don't NEED that bottle!* It's really true. You have more potential than the HYDROGEN BOMB! Just take yourself in hand *today*, and by tomorrow you'll start feeling like a NEW PERSON — the person that you really are inside!

B. While it has seemed probable that addiction to alcohol is at least in part due to the development of physiological tolerance to the drug, there have been to date no clear demonstrations that alterations in the blood level of alcohol alone (without concomitant experiential factors of taste and ingestion) were sufficient to produce a lasting enhancement of alcohol preference subsequent to treatment. Here we report a method capable of producing a lasting enhancement of alcohol preference without concomitant oral stimulation. . . .

This enhancement of preference has been achieved by prolonged passive infusion of alcohol into the stomach of rats. After recovery from surgical preparation, the rats were placed in a Bowman restrainer cage to adapt for 24 hours. After this initial period each rat was connected to a pump. . . .[1]

C. A man who once developed printed circuits for computers begs on street corners for enough coins to buy another bottle of cheap port. A woman whose husband walked out when she couldn't stop drinking at home sits stupefied on a park bench, nodding senselessly at passers-by. An anxious teenager raids her parents' liquor closet at every opportunity. These people, though they have never met, suffer from the same misfortune. If they were placed together in a room, each of them might recognize the others as alcoholics. Yet what they have most in common is their inability to see *themselves* as alcoholics — and this is the very worst symptom of their disease. For until the alcoholic's self-deception can be broken down, not even the most drastic cure has a chance of success.

You can see at once that passage A wasn't taken from an essay. It seizes us and gives us a series of hysterical jolts, as if we had no minds of our own and had to be bullied into obeying the writer's will. This prose simply gives orders — reminding us that essays, even impassioned ones, tend to be less direct and blaring than this. Something must be placed between writer and reader: a subject they both can contemplate while each party retains a certain independence.

Passage B is a scientific report. Here we have nothing *but* objectivity — reminding us that essays deal in personal opinion. As a presentation of findings this excerpt is competent and efficient. An essayist, however, would have stepped forward and expressed an attitude of some sort. *Facts are facts*, says the report. *Take an interest in this*, says the essay.

Only passage C, a student writer's prose, can be called fully essayistic. Unlike A, it is *about* something that can be regarded with a degree of detachment. In this respect C resembles B. But a reading of B and C together reveals a new element, the felt presence of the writer as a mind at work. While B flatly reports data, C draws us into its subject, develops a certain dramatic momentum and emphasis, and takes a stand. Consider how the paragraph begins with particular images of people and then gradually moves into broad reflections about alcoholism. We feel a build-up of tension and curiosity through the first three sentences, followed by an increasing sense of understanding. Notice, too, that the sentences in C "hang together." Their demonstratives (*These* people, *this* . . . symptom), their terms of logical relationship *(Yet, For)*, and their repeated structures *(A man . . . begs, A woman . . . sits, An anxious teenager raids)* hinge each sentence to its neighbor, making the paragraph read like a continuous flow of thought.

Because every essay communicates something about the writer's character, two equally good essays may be very different in tone. Your own essays, for example, needn't match the rather urgent and sober tone of passage C. But neither should you expect that your tone will be automatically right if you give no thought to it. Like other aspects of the essay, tone has to be considered in relation to the *topic*, your *attitude* toward that topic, and the *reader* you hope to influence. When tone is neglected, the most usual result is inconsistency, not naturalness; readers are hurtled erratically from "high" to "low" effects and back again. And this makes them unsympathetic, not just toward the writer's manner, but toward the substance of the essay as well. Who can concentrate on ideas while being taken on a roller-coaster ride?

One determining element of tone is *diction* or word choice (pp. 100–121). Words that are plain or fancy, formal or informal, particular or general, intimate or distant, vivid or colorless lend their character to an entire essay. Then, too, there is *sentence structure* (pp. 128–151—the writer's preference for short or long sentences, simple or intricate ones, straightforward or "poetical" placement of subjects and verbs, one standard sentence pattern or a variety of them. The length, complexity, and structure of *paragraphs* (pp. 156–196) also influence tone. Yet an essay's tone isn't the sum of all these technical features. Rather, it is a general mood or attitude lying behind them. Most people, even if they've had little practice describing and explaining differences of tone, easily register those differences as they read.

Consider, for example, two paragraphs, each by a well-known essayist. The first is from Tom Wolfe's portrait of surfers in southern California:

> Well, actually there is a kind of back-and-forth thing with some of the older guys, the old heroes of surfing, like Bruce Brown, John Severson, Hobie Alter and Phil Edwards. Bruce Brown will do one of those incredible surfing movies and he is out in the surf himself filming Phil Edwards coming down a 20-footer in Hawaii, and Phil has on a pair of nylon swimming trunks, which he has had made in Hawaii, because they dry out fast—and it is like a grapevine. Everybody's got to have a pair of nylon swimming trunks, and then the manufacturers move in, and pretty soon every kid in Utica, N.Y., is buying a pair of them, with the competition stripe and the whole thing, and they never heard of Phil Edwards. So it works back and forth—but so what? Phil Edwards is part of it. He may be an old guy, he is 28 years old, but he and Bruce Brown, who is even older, 30, and John Severson, 32, and Hobie Alter, 29, never haired out to the square world even though they make thousands. Hair refers to courage. A guy who "has a lot of hair" is courageous; a guy who "hairs out" is yellow.[2]

This essayist borrows his tone and even his vocabulary from what he is describing. The surfers' mentality as Wolfe understands it is restless, action-oriented, one-dimensional, and so is Wolfe's prose. Note the flat, slangy sentences, studded with terms like *back-and-forth thing, guys, incredible, so what,* and *haired out.* The key word seems to be *and:* instead of *subordinating* one idea to another by words like *although* or *because* or *unless* (see pp. 135–141), Wolfe turns his sentences into strings of *coordinate clauses* (pp. 131–135), as if every thought were just as important or unimportant as the last. The offhand tone is keyed to the surfers' odd combination of prolonged adolescence and effortless genius for making money.

This contrasting paragraph is by James Baldwin, reflecting on a conference of black writers and artists:

> And yet it became clear as the debate wore on that there *was* something which all black men held in common, something which cut across opposing points of view, and placed in the same context their widely dissimilar experience. What they held in common was their precarious, their unutterably painful relation to the white world. What they held in common was the necessity to remake the world in their own image, to impose this image on the world, and no longer be controlled by the vision of the world, and of themselves, held by other people. What, in sum, black men held in common was their ache to come into the world as men. And this ache united people who might otherwise have been divided as to what a man should be.[3]

Here the tone is distinctly formal. Unlike Wolfe, who attempts a prose equivalent of his surfers' loose and fast-paced style of life, Baldwin draws back from the people he has been describing and solemnly discloses his own insight into their shared concern. The paragraph is stylistically all of a piece; we read it as the continuous, patient unfolding of an idea that has been fully conceived beforehand. Whereas Wolfe sounds deliberately random, chatty, and impressionable, here the air is one of dignity and heroic control; we know that at least one black writer has determined to cease being a victim and to "impose [his] image on the world."

What has made Baldwin's paragraph so different in tone from Wolfe's? The most obvious contrast lies in their diction. In place of Wolfe's slangy and *concrete* language (pp. 114–115), picturing physical things like *a 20-footer in Hawaii,* Baldwin gives us general and *abstract* words (pp. 115–116) like *experience, relation, image,* and *vision*—words that convey thoughts without affecting our senses. Slang is altogether missing from his paragraph, and certain words— *precarious, unutterably, ache* in the sense of "desire"—are notably "high-toned." Baldwin's choice of words puts us on notice that his subject is nothing to joke about or skip over quickly.

More important than diction in this instance, however, is sentence structure. You have seen that Wolfe's sentences lurch from one hurried remark to the next, with a minimum of subordination. Baldwin's sentences, by contrast, show logical forethought and a high degree of internal order. One component of that order is *parallelism* (pp. 319–321), the placing of similar terms or ideas in syntactically equivalent positions:

- *their precarious, their unutterably painful* relation
- something which *cut across . . . and placed . . .*
- the necessity *to remake . . ., to impose . . .,* and no longer [*to*] *be controlled*
- vision *of the world,* and *of themselves*

Another related factor is the "symphonic" repetition of certain words and phrases, making each sentence echo into the rest of the passage. Note the recurrence of *something, black men, held in common, world,* and *ache.* And a final component of order is Baldwin's use of "delaying tactics" to postpone the main idea within each sentence and throughout the whole paragraph: not *Black men held in common such-and-such,* but *And yet it became clear as the debate wore on that there* was *something which all black men held in common, something . . .;* not *They held in common their painful relation to the white world,* but *What they held in common was their precarious, their unutterably painful relation . . .;* etc. These tactics lend a heavy finality, a sense of fulfillment, to the one sentence in which they aren't used — the last one.

Wolfe's and Baldwin's paragraphs represent two extremes of formality and informality, each appropriate to its subject and audience. Most essay prose, however, is neither as casual as Wolfe's nor as ceremonious as Baldwin's. Rather, it strikes a "middle" tone, an air of speaking in a normal, unhurried voice to an intelligent but nonspecialized reader. Such a tone still allows plenty of room for the writer's individuality to come through. Look, for example, at the following complete essay by a college senior, Abigail Zuger:

My father, who has not set foot in a college classroom in almost fifty years, occasionally wakes up in the middle of the night in a cold sweat, shouting loud and unintelligible phrases into the darkness. At breakfast he tells us that he was somewhere on his college campus, racing blindly up a walk, two hours late for an exam and stark naked. Someone has taken all the knobs off his bureau drawers, and he has spent two frantic hours looking for his clothes. Stomach churning, he pounds on the door of the exam building. His advisor has told him that the outcome of this exam is crucial to his professional career. The door remains locked, however; the jeers of the passersby resound in his ears, and his professor peers out of an upstairs window, face convulsed in laughter. Fifty years have done nothing to quell the horror of this dream.

In 1973 *Harvard Magazine,* a bulletin for Harvard alumni, published a short article on pre-exam nightmares and received a staggering number of congratulatory letters. Harvard men of all ages wrote in that their subconscious minds still regularly treated them to these dreams. Graying businessmen found themselves seated for an art-history exam without ever having taken the course. Feeble doctors habitually galloped across the campus searching for a Bio. 1 exam no one seemed to have heard of. Lawyers by the score showed up for freshman English and found the exam written in Chinese. To a man they seemed to be saying that to live through these dreams was a thousand times more grueling than anything they had experienced since leaving college.

The ivory tower, as college students — and psychiatrists — across the country will testify, is not nearly so pleasant an abode as it appears from the outside. It shelters its inhabitants from some of life's pedestrian difficulties, but at the same time creates new traumas and problems, which take on, in such closed quarters, an importance of which the real world cannot conceive. The legendary tower of learning is not a stable structure: it is buffeted by the high winds of exam periods, by the gales of preprofessional competition; it shakes with the constant underground rumblings of adolescent crises. What shall I be? What shall I do? Will I succeed? At times it sways so forebodingly that the unfortunate standing on top sees his future in a heap of broken bones and ivory rubble.

Every student has his own mechanism for coping with the panic which invades even the most sedate college existence. It is a kind of panic difficult to describe except by example, a panic of which there is no real equivalent in the nonacademic world. It comes after forty-eight hours of sleepless labor, with the realization that the paper must be completely reorganized; or on the day before the exam, with the realization that a human being cannot read 5,000 pages in one day; or on the Friday before the Monday, with the realization that an academically respectable job on the given topic is the work of a lifetime, and not a weekend. It is the lucky student who can internalize his worries and convert them into an occasional nightmare. Others resort to desperate means.

When the federal law giving students the right to see their own records went into effect last fall, colleges across the country began to sort painstakingly through student files for confidential letters of recommendation, which must be returned to the writer for a signature before being released to the student. At Harvard, several professors received letters of recommendation they had never written, urging that a student named [deleted] be considered for admission to various medical schools, for Phi Beta Kappa, for a highly desirable scholarship. Admitting to the forgeries, ——— was requested to leave the school.

His saddened coworkers in the lab announced they were forced to question the validity of experimental work he had done; his friends were baffled. He had been an enormously talented, straight-A student, had celebrated promising lab results over champagne with Dr. James D. Watson, could probably have gotten into any medical school in the country. The recommendations he had written for himself, it was whispered across Harvard, were couched in far less glowing terms than the recommendations other professors had written for him.

———, accounting for his "highly regrettable acts," explained that he had lost all perspective on his life and his work. "Almost constant pressure . . ., spending excessive time in the laboratory, and a demanding course load," he admitted, "caused me to see events in desperate terms."

———'s desperation is only an ironic exaggeration of the desperation that pervades college campuses in other forms. It is at the root of the notorious pre-med gangsterism, of the flourishing term-paper companies, of the waiting lists in college psychiatric facilities, of the occasional sad college suicide that never makes the front page. Some students survive their college traumas with enough equanimity to mold it all, under the benign influence of time, into part of the best years of their lives. The others wince as they remember, and dream unsettling dreams.[4]

This writer, you may notice, doesn't feel required to use dead-center "middle" diction in every phrase. A few of her terms are rather casual (*Bio. 1 exam, lab, pre-med*), while some others strike a distinctly formal note (*abode, buffeted, pedestrian* in the sense of "humdrum"). Some of her sentences are brief and plain in structure— *What shall I be? What shall I do? Will I succeed?* —while quite a few others are long and complex. Yet one consistent tone is struck throughout this essay. It is the tone of an observant, humorous, sympathetic person, involved but not upset, appealing to her readers' intelligence without false chumminess or gimmicky effects. This writing, even as it deals with the theme of academic panic, is poised and quietly assertive from first to last.

At this point in your own career, with many college writing assignments ahead of you, it would be wise to steer away from extremes of tone. For your audience is a sober one; it's that serious, sensible reader (alias your instructor) who expects you to influence him or her by marshaling good reasons for your views. Those reasons will be less convincing if presented in a tone as jumpy and self-consciously "hip" as Wolfe's. And Baldwin's high tone assumes something that you'd better not take for granted, namely the reader's prior interest in the state of the writer's soul. Aim instead for a tone that conveys earnestness without pressing your own importance on the reader. The *middle tone*, illustrated by all the passages examined in the next section of this chapter, is the one that can carry you successfully through any essay required in college.

MODES OF THE ESSAY

It is traditional and useful to think of essays as falling into four types, corresponding to four basic functions of prose: *description*, or picturing; *narration*, or telling; *exposition*, or explaining; and *argument*, or convincing.

Description

A *descriptive* essay aims to *make vivid* a place, an object, a character, or a group. The writer tries, not simply to convey facts about the object, but to give readers a direct impression of that object, as if they were standing in its presence. The descriptive writer's task, we might say, is one of translation: he wants to find words to capture the way his five senses have registered the item, so that a reader of those words will have a mental picture of it.

In its simplest form the descriptive essay treats one provocatively simple thing, such as an apple or a pencil. If you are asked to write such an essay, you will quickly realize how challenging it is. The plainer and more familiar the object, the harder the task. This is because both you and your reader have long taken the object for granted as a single, recognized thing requiring no further consideration: an apple is, well, just an apple.

The first part of your business must be to unlearn this attitude — to put aside the object's name and open your senses to its physical characteristics. As soon as you do, you'll be surprised by its endless particularity: the lopsidedness of the apple, its creases and scars and speckles, the fuzziness of its stem, and so forth. And you will begin to appreciate the real lesson your instructor has in mind, namely the value of language that is both *concrete* and *specific*.

A *concrete* word or phrase denotes an actual, observable thing or quality such as *skin* or *crunchy*. Words of the opposite sort, like *nutrition* or *impossible assignment*, are called *abstract*; they address the mind without making any appeal to the senses. And *specific* language, unlike *general* language, gets down to particulars: not *colored* but *greenish-red*, not *too soft* but *dented by my thumb print*. Concrete and specific terms are the only ones that can bring the object to life in your reader's imagination.

Perhaps the best way to generate good observations is to *act upon* the object, or at least to move around it and see it from various angles. Don't let that apple just sit there taunting you with its indescribable appleness. Pick it up, feel its weight in your palm, scratch its skin, turn it in the light, smell it, bite it, twirl it by the stem — and be alert for all the changes of impression you've produced. Your reader, too, wants to have a sense of active control and play. Instead of forcing him to gaze straight at your apple as if he were handcuffed to his chair, let him participate in your freedom of movement and perspective.

Narration

A *narrative* essay *recounts something that has happened.* That something can be as small as a minor personal experience or as large as a war, and the narrator's tone can be either intimate and casual or neutrally objective and solemn. Inevitably, a good part of narration is taken up with describing. But a narrative essay differs from a descriptive one in its emphasis on *time* and *sequence.* The essayist turns storyteller, establishing when and in what order a series of related events occurred.

This doesn't mean, though, that a narrative essay must begin with the earliest event in its sequence and march straight through to the end. That pattern is the exception, not the rule, and it tends to muffle dramatic effects. Good writers know that some incidents will naturally appear more important than others. Just as their individual sentences *subordinate* minor to major elements (pp. 135–141), so they build their whole essays around certain key developments to which all others contribute. One common strategy is to open the essay with a crucial piece of action, narrated only in part; then, when the reader's attention is secured, to skip back in time to establish the causes or issues that gave the action its significance; and finally to return to that action and its outcome. By breaking the ordinary chronological order, you can spare your reader the deadly monotony of having to push through a thicket of equivalent items: "and then . . . and then . . . and then . . . ."

Essays whose governing intent is descriptive or narrative are relatively uncommon in college writing. *Exposition* and *argument* tend to prevail.

Exposition

An *expository* essay is one whose chief aim is to present information or to explain something. To *expound* is to set forth in detail, so that a reader will learn some facts about a given subject: the climate of Australia, sewage treatment by evaporation ponds, the style of Beethoven's late sonatas, your goals in life, the decay of inner cities. As we have seen, however, no essay is merely a set of facts. Behind all the details lies an attitude, a *point of view*. In exposition, as in all the other modes, details must be selected and ordered according to the writer's sense of their importance and interest. Though the expository writer isn't primarily taking a stand on an issue, he can't—and shouldn't try to—keep his opinions completely hidden. Think of expository essays on American grain exports to Communist countries, or the renewed controversy over abortion, or the effect of natural-gas pipelines on the Alaskan tundra. There is no interesting way of expounding those subjects without at least implying a position.

Argument

When the writer's position is not implied but openly and centrally maintained, the essay is *argumentative*. This word may be startling to readers who think of an argument as a quarrel, often involving raised voices and frazzled tempers. That is one common meaning, but not the one that applies to discussions of writing. An argument is simply *a reasoned attempt to have one's opinions accepted*. Quarrelsomeness needn't enter an argumentative essay at all. On the contrary, the essayist who appears to be losing his temper will also appear to be losing the argument. The ideal is to present *supporting evidence* which points so plainly to the correctness of your stand that you can afford to be civil and even generous toward those who believe otherwise. Much of that supporting evidence will inevitably consist of exposition: you want to show that *facts* a, b, c, and d oblige any reasonable person to agree with *conclusion* x. But if you give any of those facts more emphasis than the idea they were meant to prove, you are losing track of the fundamental purpose of argumentation.

In one vital respect argument stands alone among the four modes: it is the only one in which there are *technically* right and wrong methods of proceeding. Quite apart from its truth or falsity, an argument is either *valid* or *invalid* ("logical" or "illogical") according to whether or not the rules of reasoning have been properly observed. If the writer's *conclusion* necessarily follows from his or her *premises* or supporting statements, the argument is *valid*—whether or not it contains errors of fact. And the argument is *invalid* if a rule of reasoning has been broken in the process of getting from premises to conclusion. This is not a point of interest to logicians only. An invalid argument will be recognized by ordinary readers as weak, even if by good fortune its wrongly derived conclusion happens to be true.

This may sound disheartening, even forbidding. But the logic that applies to essay writing falls entirely within the common sense we all possess. There is no need to memorize a great many abstract rules in order to undertake an argument. The argument should *be* logical, but it shouldn't *display* its logic in an arid, self-consciously rule-abiding way. You need only sharpen your awareness of the most usual mistakes in reasoning (pp. 66–92), and you will be able to compose essays that *withstand logical criticism* without sounding as if they had been written by a computer.

Mixed Modes

In practice it would be difficult to write an essay that drew on just one of the four basic modes. Nor would there be much point in trying, since each of the four functions—to picture, to tell, to explain, and to convince—can help to serve any of the others. A typical essay might describe something in order to narrate its part in a historical episode (what Hiroshima looked like just before it was leveled by the Bomb), tell a story to enliven an exposition (how people reacted to one showing of a movie you are analyzing), or expound something (the mechanism of the catalytic converter) in order to back an argument (that the catalytic converter should be abandoned as a fire hazard).

Here, for example, is the first paragraph of an essay that will be mainly expository:

> Shortly after dawn, at the Saint-Antoine produce market in the ancient French city of Lyons, a white pickup truck screeches around a corner, double-parks impatiently and disgorges a rugged man wearing a rumpled windbreaker. As if by prearranged signal, prize raspberries, dewy spinach and pristine baby carrots suddenly emerge from hiding places below the trestle tables where they've been saved for inspection by this very special customer. *"Viens ici*, Paul," shouts a fruit vendor. "I've got some melons you won't believe." Slicing a sample in half, the man in the windbreaker rejects the melons and some string beans as well ("too fat"). But thirty-five minutes later, he has sniffed, nibbled, pinched, prodded, and fondled his way through the choicest fruits and vegetables, loaded fifteen crates of produce into his van and hummed off toward his next quarry: plump chickens from Bresse, Charolais beef and fresh red mullet. Paul Bocuse, the most visible, the most influential—and possibly the best—chef in the world, has begun another working day.[5]

The key sentence in this paragraph is the final one, for it establishes the importance of the man whose new philosophy of cooking will be *expounded* in the rest of the essay. Yet the paragraph itself is one of *narrative*, enlivened with precise *description*. By allowing us to share some thirty-five minutes of Paul Bocuse's day, and only then revealing how eminent "this very special customer" is, the writer keeps us from saying to ourselves, "What do *I* have to do with the world's greatest chef?" We've been "hooked"—involved in the writer's subject—before having any chance to resist. Think how much more effective this paragraph is than one beginning *Paul Bocuse is the most visible, the most influential — and possibly the best — chef in the world.*

Storytelling can also be a means of *argument,* as you can see from this paragraph about the importance of precise language:

> What to us has become so deeply questionable was a certainty for Confucius. When once his disciples asked him what he would do first if he had to administer a country, he answered: "The first would be to correct language." "Surely," they said, "this has nothing to do with the matter. Why should language be corrected?" The Master's answer was: "If language is not correct, then what is said is not what is meant; if what is said is not what is meant, then what ought to be done remains undone; if this remains undone, morals and arts will decay; if morals and arts decay, justice will go astray; if justice goes astray, the people will stand about in helpless confusion. Hence language must not be allowed to deteriorate. This matters above everything." What a grand definition of the writer's social responsibility, and what confident faith in the very correspondence between language and reality, and therefore between literature and life! Shall we ever regain the confidence of both this definition and this faith? It is the very condition of literary responsibility, and on it depends the future of our liberal education.[6]

The story about Confucius, to be sure, doesn't *prove* the writer's point. Yet it does lend authority to that point, thanks to Confucius's great reputation for wisdom. Without this anecdotal support, the three emphatic sentences that follow it would have sounded hollow.

Here is a more extended example from a piece entitled "Abraham Lincoln: The Politics of a Practical Whig." The title leads us to anticipate *exposition,* and we get it. But at times Kenneth Stampp's exposition is framed by *argument,* as indicated in the notes at the left:

1. The writer sets up a view of Lincoln contrary to his own.

> Unfortunately Lincoln's admirers have often operated on the assumption that to call him a politician is somehow to degrade him; they reserve that label for his congressional critics.
>
> This attitude toward Lincoln reflects a curious American attitude toward politics. As Richard N. Current has observed: "Among Americans the words *politics* and *politician* long have been terms of reproach. Politics generally means 'dirty' politics, whether the adjective is used or not. Politicians, then, are dirty politicians unless they happen to be statesmen, and in that case they are not politicians at all." Lincoln himself contributed to this unpleasant image when, early in his career, he described politicians as "a set of men

who have interests aside from the interests of the people, and who . . . are, taken as a class, at least one long step removed from honest men."

2. He then expounds Lincoln's political ambitions and talents.

And yet Lincoln's own much-admired statesmanship was based on a solid foundation of political talent and experience. He ranked loyalty to party high among human virtues; he understood the techniques of party management; he knew when to concede and when to hold firm; and he had a most sensitive feeling for trends in public opinion. Lincoln was an ambitious man—his ambition, said his former law partner, "was a little engine that knew no rest"—and he thoroughly understood that public office does not seek the man, but the man seeks the office. Accordingly, Lincoln was, from his early manhood, openly available, unblushingly eager for any office to which he could win appointment or election. Early in 1860, when the greatest prize of all seemed within reach, he confessed to a friend with disarming candor, "The taste *is* in my mouth a little." He won the prize, and his masterful performance during his years as President has rarely been equaled and never surpassed. Under the most trying circumstances he presided over a Cabinet of prima donnas, held together his loosely organized party, and repeatedly outmaneuvered a dangerously powerful opposition party. "If Abraham Lincoln was not a master politician," wrote one of his admiring contemporaries who knew the meaning of the word, "I am entirely ignorant of the qualities which make up such a character. . . . No man knew better . . . how to summon and dispose of political ability to attain great political ends."

3. Finally, he contrasts the reality with the appearance; his point has been secured.

This is the man, it has often been made to appear, who approached the problem of postwar reconstruction without giving a thought to the political consequences of his plans. It was his innate generosity, his inner tenderness, and nothing else, that impelled him to extend to the South his generous terms, while selfish, scheming politicians in Congress cried out for vengeance. Nothing could be farther from the truth; nothing could more distort the character of the man.[7]

The author throws out a challenge to Lincoln's "admirers," whose discomfort with politics has made them sentimentalize their hero. By pausing over the meaning of *politics* and *politician*, producing evidence that Lincoln was a politician even in his best moments, he disputes the cliché that may have warped our own idea of Lincoln. He is simultaneously giving information, winning a debate, and fostering a new attitude toward his subject.

Even "pure" narrative is bound to have aspects of exposition and argument. Here, as a final example, is a paper written for a freshman English course. It appears at first to be sheer story and not an essay at all, but the last two paragraphs, without directly stating the point, bring everything into focus:

"You should fix everyone's coffee or tea. You know, add the sugar, etc., and pour it. If the meat is hard to handle, you should cut it for the patient," instructed my predecessor. "After you've passed out the trays, you feed Irene and Molly."

"That's Granny Post in there. She's 106. Even though she's not particularly senile, she's lost her teeth and must be fed with a giant eyedropper." I discovered just how clear Granny Post's mind was when I tried to feed her. The dear old lady wasn't hungry and spat it back at me.

After that first day at the convalescent hospital, I was on my own. Irene was eager to please and partially fed herself, but I dreaded feeding Molly. She was blind and pitifully thin. "I'm sick. I'm sick," she'd cry. "Don't make me eat any more. Please, I'm sick."

"But Molly, you've got to eat so you can get well. Come on, one more bite. Here, hold my hand. It's not so bad." And I'd coach one more bite down her before gathering the sixty trays onto their racks and wheeling them back to the safety of the kitchen. The rest of the evening I cleaned the coffee pot, set up the breakfast trays, scoured sinks, and mopped the floors. I didn't mind sitting on the floor scrubbing at the oven or making the juices and sandwiches for the evening nourishment. It was when I confronted the elderly people on the other side of that kitchen door that I became nervous and awkward.

In a few weeks I mastered the hospital routine, the names of most of the patients, and their idiosyncrasies.

Opposite the kitchen was what was fondly called "the ward." Dora, a small, white-haired woman who was continually nearly slipping out of the bottom of the wheelchair to which she was tied, was the ringleader of this group. She cussed up a storm at anyone who came near her and perpetually monotoned, "What can I do? Tell me, what can I do?" May accompanied her with "Put me to bed. I want to go to bed." One evening as I entered with dinner, the woman across from Dora was gaily slinging her waste matter about the room, especially at anyone who threatened to come near her. A nurse and some aides calmed her down.

As far as the two sisters in room twelve were concerned, they were traveling on a huge ocean liner. When I brought their trays, they always asked, "How long till we get to port?" or "I'm sorry. We can't eat today because we're seasick."

John mumbled perpetually about the batty ladies in the TV room. He liked his smokes and his sports magazine.

Mr. Harrison fed a stray cat that stayed outside his sliding-glass door.

He loved his cat and I gave him leftovers to feed it. One day a car rushed down the hill and struck his cat. Mr. Harrison told me his cat ran away, but it would come back as always. He stood at his door watching for it.

There were two Irenes. Dora advanced to feeding herself so I began feeding Ethel Irene. Ethel Irene was small, roly-poly, and had gray-black hair cut short like a little boy's. She liked to joke and use large words. Sometimes when she grasped for a word, it just wouldn't come and great big tears would form in her eyes. She liked sunshiny days and the sound of birds singing. She liked me to sing to her, too. Always clamped tightly in her hand was the buzzer to call the nurse. It was Ethel Irene's lifeline. Occasionally it fell out of her hand and she became so frantic she couldn't speak, only pointing and crying.

I tried to regard the other Ethel as just one of the many patients to whom I delivered food. When I brought dinner, I fixed Ethel's tea, cut her meat, and tucked in her napkin. Then I'd clearly shout, "Enjoy your dinner." But instead of letting me leave, she'd pull me down to her and in a low, halting voice struggle out, "I like you. Can I kiss you?"

It became increasingly difficult to leave Ethel. She'd refuse to release my arm, purposely eat slowly so I was forced to return just to retrieve her tray, and cry when I succeeded in making my exit. To avoid upsetting her, I began sneaking into the room to take her tray or sending someone else. If she realized the deception, she'd let out an anguished cry and begin sobbing. I couldn't bear to pass Ethel's room and see her arms reaching out for me.

Many of the patients were lonely like Ethel and starved for attention. Some were on welfare and had few or no relatives. Most were just forgotten.

Ethel's son visited one day. Roaring drunk, he first tried to get fresh with me and then stomped into the kitchen demanding food.

Molly had visitors once, too. When I reached work and dropped by to see Molly, two or three of her relatives were standing about her. Molly was breathing laboriously, her nose and mouth were attached to an oxygen tank. She'd often pleaded with me to leave her in peace to die. She was dying now. The relatives left shortly. Molly's bed was empty when I returned the next day.

I worked in the convalescent hospital only sixteen hours a week for eight months. The old people remained there twenty-four hours a day for months or years, depending on how "lucky" they were. They were fed, diapered at night, and sponge-bathed in the morning. But what they needed most . . .

The age is gone when three generations occupy the same house. Young people want a life of their own.

My parents are nearly fifty now.

The other members of the class were hard on this paper when it was shown to them. They commented:

"She hasn't told us the context."
"Dick and Jane dialogue . . . choppy sentences."
". . . weak transitions."
"It's too detached — just a lot of facts, and then she changes the subject at the end."
"The paragraphs are too short."
"What is it supposed to be about, anyway?"
"She says *coach* when she means *coax*."
"*Monotone* isn't a verb."
"I found a run-on sentence in paragraph 14."

There is much truth in these objections; undoubtedly the writer could have made minor improvements at her classmates' urging. But the small defects of this essay are outweighed by its compassion and control. The memorable description of Ethel Irene with her "lifeline" buzzer and the understated recounting of Molly's death seem like reality itself. And the apparent disorganization covers a subtle and effective movement engaging the reader in the writer's own ordeal of first learning her chores, then coping with the patients' oddities, then facing the ultimate fact of death, and finally turning her thoughts to her own parents, who "are nearly fifty now" and may someday be like Molly and Mr. Harrison. Will she look after them in their senility? The abrupt ending leaves us troubled, not only by grotesque and tender images from the convalescent hospital, but also by conflicting feelings toward parents who deserve our care but who threaten to invade "a life of [our] own."

In later chapters you will have further opportunities to see how a successful writer meets the first requirement of an essay, that it seize and hold a reader's interest. You will learn, for example, numerous ways of developing the basic unit of composition, the paragraph. But by now you already know that your goal will not be to turn out a routine description, narration, exposition, or argument. Your goal will be quite simply to write essays that have authority. The sign of a good writer's work is that it makes its readers set aside their expectations and *listen*, lending themselves to a confident voice.

How can that confident voice be acquired? Inborn talent is a blessing, but determination and practice count for more. Even the most gifted writers will stumble if they imagine that their first drafts are perfect just as they stand, while writers who struggle with draft after draft can give their prose a strong, tight eloquence. Confidence is largely a matter of critical rewriting, of refusing to be satisfied with the clichés and awkward phrases that crowd your mind when you're facing a blank page. A composition course and a handbook can show you the general difference between successful and unsuccessful prose, but only you know what is clamoring for expression in your mind. The essential thing is to keep pressing toward clarity, trying both to sharpen your ideas and to put them into the most convincing form you can devise.

EXERCISES

I. Look through available newspapers and magazines for an advertisement that strikes you as being markedly different in tone from a carefully reasoned essay. Clip out or copy down the advertisement and then write a few sentences commenting on specific ways in which this passage is not "essayistic" (pp. 4–13).

II. Imagine the following sentences as having been spoken by an angry citizen. Writing *in a middle tone* (pp. 6–13), suitable for a typical college essay, compose a paragraph that expresses some of the same grievances:

> Supermarket prices are a damn ripoff! The middleman and store managers take us consumers for a bunch of suckers! Hamburger "extended" with soybeans but labeled as pure meat costs more than steak did a few years ago! Hey, man, don't try to tell me it's just inflation! The filthy con artists shake you down for all you're worth! "Specials" in bins turn out to cost more per item than the cans on the shelves, for God's sake! I've *had* it with those dudes! Have you seen the way they put candy right by the checkout counter, where your kid will grab it and throw a tantrum if you don't buy it?

III. Taking the *dangers of city life* as a general subject, explain in a few sentences how those dangers could be made the topic of four distinct essays, by turns mainly *descriptive, narrative, expository,* and *argumentative* (pp. 13–16).

IV. Reread the essay on pages 19–20. Explain, in a brief paragraph or two, how the writer, without significantly adding to the narrative material she presented, could have used the same experience to write essays consisting mainly of (a) *exposition* and (b) *argument* (pp. 14–16).

V. Study the following five paragraphs. Then explain, in a brief paragraph or two, how the writer has (a) caught his reader's interest and (b) shifted between different modes of the essay form (pp. 13–21).

> For five nights in a row, the same dream. It begins when I see tree branches stirring, as though slipping by. *"We're adrift!"* I bolt upright, sensing the slate-gray river gliding alongside, carrying our raft crazily downstream in the midnight gloom. The mind races with it: *"Our tie-up came loose—we're out of control . . . we'll hit a barge, a dike, overturn on a snag. . . ."*
>
> Then I awaken. The river vanishes, dissolved into the pavement outside my suburban Washington home. The raft, a ragtag lot of logs

and driftwood, remains tied up where I left it—on a riverbank hundreds of miles away, below Ste. Genevieve, Missouri.

Always, oddly enough, I feel myself closer than ever to the man whom I have pursued into the past and across the United States for more than a year—Mark Twain. For Twain also had a nightmare about the river he immortalized.

He would see himself in the pilothouse of a stern-wheeler, on a barely recognizable stretch of the Mississippi, headed for some vague disaster: ". . . usually in my dream I am just about to start into a black shadow without being able to tell whether it is Selma bluff, or Hat Island, or only a black wall of night."

Our shared nightmare became for me an apt symbol for the great author's life. Most Americans remember Mark Twain as the father of Huck Finn's idyllic cruise through eternal boyhood and Tom Sawyer's endless summer of freedom and adventure. Indeed, this nation's best-loved author was every bit as adventurous, patriotic, romantic, and humorous as anyone has ever imagined. I found another Twain as well—one who grew cynical, bitter, saddened by the profound personal tragedies life dealt him, a man who became obsessed with the frailties of the human race, who saw clearly ahead a black wall of night.[8]

VI. Write an imaginary letter to a friend, reeling off miscellaneous things or thoughts that have occurred to you lately. Don't pause over the phrasing; though this free writing is to be handed in, it will *not* be graded. When you have finished, look through the "letter" for ideas that might become the basis for an essay of any sort. Compose *one paragraph* of that essay, loosely imitating the form of any passage reproduced in this chapter. (Indicate which passage you have chosen as a model.)

VII. Here is a set of facts about solar heating, presented without any particular emphasis. Using some of these facts, along with some reflections of your own, write an "essayistic" paragraph about solar heating—a paragraph, that is, revealing an attitude and seeking to involve the reader's feelings (pp. 5–13). Use your own words, making *new* sentences.

About one-fourth of American energy is used for the heating of buildings.

Heat from the sun, as it strikes most buildings, could easily supply the energy necessary to heat them.

The relative cost of solar heating, as compared to the costs of conventional fuels, has been rapidly dropping.

Oil and gas shortages have focused a new interest in solar heating.

Government inducements, such as subsidies and tax incentives, could make solar energy more attractive than it is today.

The future of nuclear power has become clouded by controversy in recent years.

American dependence on foreign sources of energy is widely recognized as undesirable.

VIII. Study the sample paragraph on page 16. Then think of someone you know who might be made the subject of an interesting essay. Write an opening paragraph which, like the paragraph about Paul Bocuse, *introduces* that person *by first narrating or describing one of his or her activities,* and *then* revealing who the person is.

NOTES

[1]J. A. Deutsch and H. S. Koopmans, "Preference Enhancement for Alcohol by Passive Exposure," *Science,* 179 (23 Mar. 1973), 1242.

[2]Tom Wolfe, *The Pump House Gang* (New York: Farrar, Straus & Giroux, 1968), pp. 33–34.

[3]James Baldwin, *Nobody Knows My Name* (New York: Dial, 1961), pp. 28–29.

[4]Abigail Zuger, "Acrophobia in the Ivory Tower," *Harper's,* Oct. 1975, pp. 4–5.

[5]"Food: The New Wave," *Newsweek,* 11 Aug. 1975, p. 50.

[6]Erich Heller, "Literature and Political Responsibility: Apropos the 'Letters of Thomas Mann,' " *Commentary,* July 1971, p. 54.

[7]Kenneth M. Stampp, *The Era of Reconstruction, 1865–1877* (1965; rpt. New York: Vintage, n.d.), pp. 29–30.

[8]Noel Grove, "Mark Twain: Mirror of America," *National Geographic,* 148 (Sept. 1975), 300.

COMPOSING

From time to time every essayist has the pleasant sense of knowing from the first moment exactly what to write about, what to say, and how to say it. When this mood arrives, you don't want to pause for advice about method; you just begin writing. If you can keep going until a whole draft is finished, *then* you can look back and see whether you really did have an inspiration. Even if something is gravely wrong with the draft, at least it has cost you little effort and is likely to be salvageable in some way.

More often, however, the feeling of inspiration leaks away after a paragraph or two, and you wonder how you could have been so confident about a project that has scarcely begun. And still more often, you have no such illusion in the first place. Especially if you're being asked to write one essay after another on topics that you haven't previously considered, you need to have some procedures for getting your bearings and ensuring that your very limited time won't be wasted on false leads and unworkable plans.

As a relatively inexperienced writer, you may envy the practiced writer's "stenographic" knack of feeding ideas directly into well-formed sentences and paragraphs. But almost nobody, even after years of patient effort, actually has such a knack. In all but the rarest cases, the successful writer isn't simply writing but *composing*—that is, carrying out the steps of a total process from the first hesitant grasping at a subject to the checking of a final draft.

This should be a cause for optimism. If you realize that the whole business doesn't have to be undertaken at once, and if you see that a misstep at any stage can be retracted before it has caused much trouble, you needn't feel dependent on luck or genius to see you through. To be sure, the best means of gaining confidence is to write with frequency until the activity becomes familiar and (almost) enjoyable. But you will write more easily if you consider writing as just one aspect of a task whose other parts are already within your competence.

The stages of composing, once identified, may themselves look discouragingly complex. You should understand, however, that the headings below are only the formal names for ordinary mental activities, some of which can be pressed into a few minutes of reflection. (For example: as soon as you decide what your main point will be, you have immediately taken care of "subject area," "topic," and "thesis.") The stages are worth listing only because you may find yourself stuck at one of them and wondering what to do about it. You may realize, for example, that you've tried to write a first draft without settling on a thesis, or with no clear organizational plan. Acquaintance with the usual stages can help you to spot the problem and solve it without further wasted effort.

Here in schematic form, then, is the total work of composing:

1. Getting Started:
overlapping activities {
choosing a subject area
focusing on a topic
finding a thesis
taking notes
exploratory writing
}

3. Revising:
critical rereading
writing further drafts

2. Completing a Draft:
organizing and outlining
writing the first draft
choosing a title

4. Preparing the Final Copy:
typing the completed essay
checking and proofreading

GETTING STARTED

The first requirement of every essayist is to have something to write about. In a composition class the problem is often solved by executive order: "Describe x," "Narrate y," "Defend or oppose z." Even then, however, you have to choose an appropriate focus. That choice becomes urgent if the topic is broadly stated or left completely free. Then especially, you must be alert to the difference between three things that are often confused, a *subject area*, a *topic*, and a *thesis:*

1. A *subject area* consists of a wide range of possible ideas; it defines the boundaries within which you will find your actual topic. Assignments in a composition course are typically stated in terms of subject areas. Thus, if you're asked to "describe a personal experience," or "discuss an issue of civil liberties," or "write a paper about Book Four of *Gulliver's Travels*," you've been given subject areas, not topics. A subject area is usually much too large to be taken as a topic in itself.

2. The *topic* of an essay is its specific subject, the ground to be covered or the question to be answered. In fact, it is often useful to state a topic in question form so as to prevent any possible confusion between topic and thesis (below). Within the subject area of civil liberties, for example, you might choose one of the following topics:

a. How sacred is the right to privacy?
b. Should criminals go free on technicalities?
c. What did I learn from my night in jail?
d. Are civil liberties threatened by government spying?
e. How did civil liberties fare at the hands of Earl Warren's Supreme Court?

Each of these topics would be narrow enough to permit you to say something meaningful; the question form reminds you that they *are* topics and not theses.

3. The *thesis* is the point of the essay, the one main idea to which all others should be subordinated. If the topic is a question, the thesis is the answer. It ought to lend itself to statement in *one clear sentence, making one point.* Thus, in the five sample essays about civil liberties, the theses might be:

a. The right to privacy, broadly conceived, is the most fundamental of civil liberties in a democracy.
b. Known criminals shouldn't be excused from punishment because of technical errors in the way they were arrested and tried.
c. After my night in jail I will have more respect for prisoners' rights.

   d. When government officials place innocent citizens under observation and routinely tap one another's phones, everyone's civil
liberties are threatened.

   e. Civil liberties were significantly expanded under the Warren
Court.

Moving from Subject Area to Topic

Choosing a subject area *within which* to locate a topic isn't usually a
major problem. Often the subject area has been named by your instructor. When it hasn't, you need only ask yourself what general
problems or activities or events have captured your interest; somewhere among them you ought to be able to find a more specific question that will interest your reader.

    Many students, however, take a misstep as soon as they've been
assigned a subject area. They conceive the time- and effort-saving
plan of *turning the subject area directly into a topic, thesis, and title.*
Asked to write about civil liberties, they immediately pull out a sheet
of paper and christen it with their title:

CIVIL LIBERTIES

Well, that's settled, they think; *I'm two words closer to being finished.*
But in fact such students have wandered into a maze. How is their
brief essay going to say something conclusive about civil liberties in
general? In their haste they have dodged exactly those steps of
thought that would have made for real efficiency of composition.

    The narrower your topic is, the better your chance of providing
enough supporting material to make a convincing case for your thesis. Of course you don't want to shrink the topic until it becomes
trivial. Temptation, however, usually lies on the other side. Remember that huge questions can be settled only in a format that allows for
very extensive discussion and a sweeping array of evidence.

    If you have trouble deciding whether a certain theme is already a
topic or only a subject area, consider that a subject area is just "material," lacking shape or definition; if you try to formulate a *thesis*
directly about it without any narrowing, you usually find that you've
taken on much too vast a problem. Thus, for example, "Education" is
a subject area, not a topic; you couldn't write an effective essay "for"
or "against" or "about" education as a whole. In contrast, you *could*
write any number of essays about the attempt by certain public uni-
versities to eliminate all admissions standards. Some workable topics
might be:

Has the experiment of open admissions proved successful?
Can open admissions bring about social equality?

Are "high potential" students held back by open admissions?

What do I owe to the policy of open admissions?

Why did open admissions become popular in the late sixties?

Notice that these topics, though far from wordy, take up considerably more words than "Education." Potential "topics" of one or two words are probably subject areas in disguise. A topic is *definite,* and definiteness means spelling something out.

Once in a while you may find yourself desperately unsure of how to locate a topic; the assigned subject area "means nothing" to you. When this happens, bear in mind that meaning is always a matter of *establishing connections*—associations, comparisons, contrasts—between one thing and others. How can the subject area be divided? What terms does it suggest to you? Check the definitions of those terms in your dictionary, looking for clues to new paths of thought. Start listing *particular instances* you might feel comfortable writing about, and ask yourself what broad ideas are illustrated by those instances. Discuss the subject area with a friend, hoping to pick up a promising lead. In short, don't allow the subject area to remain a large, indivisible thing; break it up and see where the pieces fall.

Finding a Thesis

Just as some writers never get a subject area adequately funneled to a topic, others neglect the essential next move and begin writing *as if the topic were a thesis*. That is, they fail to ask, "What *about* my topic?" The result is inevitably a wishy-washy essay, one that meanders in the territory marked by the topic, exhausting the reader's patience and good will.

Choosing a thesis is without doubt the most crucial step in planning an essay. Lacking a thesis, all you have is a set of assorted remarks. The thesis gives focus to the whole undertaking, enabling you to show your reader at every moment that you know where you're headed. *Write down that thesis in one clear sentence.* If deadline pressure forces you to skip every step of planning except one, this is the one to be saved.

trial thesis If you have put your topic in question form, you will quickly see that only a limited number of answers to it can be imagined. Treat each of those answers as a *trial thesis*, a possible statement around which to organize the essay. Ask yourself whether the question and answer are (a) interesting enough to engage your reader; (b) plausible enough to be made convincing; and (c) within your reach, in view of the limitations on your time, your access to information, and the expected length of your essay.

What you need is a complete idea—a discovery and its meaning, an experience and the lesson in it, a problem and its solution, a fragment of life and its significance, or a position and your reasons for maintaining that position. Think ahead to the point you expect to make. Is it one that most people already believe? If so, you won't be able to make it interesting. Is it an assertion that will still look questionable after you've run through the available number of pages? Then you should scale down your plans. Your job isn't to revolutionize a reader's whole way of looking at things, but to show why a certain idea makes sense.

Try to gauge how much work you'll need to do in order to be convincing. Would you have to master a whole new field of knowledge? Is research called for, and if so, do you know where to start looking? How reliable are the sources you've already located? Can you frame your essay by contrasting your way of considering the issue with somebody else's? Above all, don't settle on a thesis until you've made sure that some information will be available to support your case. Knowing that you have facts on your side will help you to avoid padding and hedging.

Suppose you've been asked to write an essay within the subject area of sports. You already know that placing "Sports" at the top of a page and beginning to write would be instant trouble. You also know that your topic and thesis should be in effect a question and its answer. But you still may not realize that certain theses would be almost as bad as none at all.

Imagine, for instance, that you chose the trial thesis "I can't get through a weekend without playing a few hard sets of tennis." Without doubt that is a thesis. But is it one that would matter to anyone but you? No: it is simply personal, indifferent information, like yesterday's dinner menu. If you hope to stir interest, you must find a thesis that *bears on general experience or judgment.* Thus, if your thesis were "The shift from grass to artificial surfaces in tournament tennis has revived the art of back-court rallying," you would be asserting something that concerns people beyond yourself, and you could cite recent matches that the reader would have to acknowledge as bolstering your case.

You should also be on guard against *self-evident* theses, which double back on themselves in a meaningless circle:

The growing popularity of sports shows that people are more interested in athletics than ever before.

Contact sports should be banned because they involve the violent impact of one body on another.

Victory after victory produced an unbeaten season for our team.

Each of these statements says in effect that x = x. The popularity shows the popularity; contact is bad because it involves contact; win every game and you'll be undefeated. This is hardly news.

With more thought, though, you could change each of these hollow statements into a meaningful thesis:

With increased leisure time and the influence of television, sporting equipment has become one of the nation's fastest-growing industries.

The violence of contact sports encourages violence in society at large.

Opponents of a championship team are often "psyched" by the idea of that team's unbeatability.

Note that in each case the revised thesis makes a definite assertion that *remains to be established;* that is the business of the essay.

Watch out, too, for the *weaseling* thesis. Tormented by doubts, a writer who is asked to debate a certain topic may cling to the thesis "Topic x is very controversial," or "Some people approve of x, but others don't." Here the appearance of open-mindedness is only indecisiveness in thin disguise. If you want your essay to be engaging, you can't dodge the issue you yourself have raised.

Yet the fact that you have had to wrestle with doubts in the process of arriving at a thesis can be extremely important to the success of your essay. Those same doubts may also occur to your reader, and you will want to show that you have *anticipated objections* (p. 85). That anticipation can be captured in the wording of your thesis statement:

Although *society must protect itself against maniacs*, people should not be forced to live in asylums simply because they strike others as "insane."

While *strip mining may cause local environmental damage*, there can be no escaping America's dependence on coal for at least the next twenty years.

The two-party system has its defects, but it has survived too many critical tests to be lightly cast aside.

The usefulness of theses phrased this way, with the main contrary argument openly named, is that you have that argument before you as you write. Then you *must* come to terms with it, acknowledging its merit while showing that your own thesis still prevails.

Taking Notes

As soon as you have a subject area, you should begin taking notes. Their purpose is to record possibly useful ideas so that you can assemble, compare, and consult them as you plan and write. Anything that might sharpen your thinking or supply evidence for your ideas is worth putting into a note. Your notes can:

quote passages from articles and books:

> Loercher (p. 14) cites Ronsard as saying: "There does not live a man in the world who so greatly hates cats as I with a deep hatred. . . . I hate their eyes, their brow, their gaze."

summarize facts or conclusions from those and other sources:

> Montaigne (Loercher, p. 14) once asked himself whether his cat wasn't more amused with him than he with her.

analyze texts that have to be interpreted:

> Consider Chateaubriand's praise of "the independent, almost ungrateful character of the cat, . . . the indifference with which it moves between salons and the gutters of its origin" (Loercher, p. 14). Relate to Ch's noble origins and adventurous period in America?

draw distinctions between apparently similar things:

> Felix the Cat grows out of Krazy Kat visual tradition — but note the political and countercultural emphasis of the sixties.

launch trial theses that will be approved or rejected later:

> My guess is that the eras that produce sentimentality about cats are the same ones in which the "evil cat" image flourishes. Cf. periods when cats are depicted as just cats. A thesis here?

express doubts and warnings that will have to be met:

> Watch out for exclusively Western emphasis. Loercher, e.g. (p. 14), cites Buddhist, Hindu, and Muslim traditions of esteeming cats.

record random observations that may or may not prove relevant:

> Any chance of tossing in something about T. S. Eliot's *Practical Cats?*

comment on earlier notes, developing a *dialogue of pros and cons:*

> Forget about starting with idea that cats figure prominently in the art of every civilization. According to Loercher, cats have practically no place in Bible and the lit. of ancient Rome (p. 14).[1]

In addition, notes from reading should be accompanied by special *bibliographical notes* (pp. 217–219), giving precise references to the sources consulted.

Once in a while you may find that you've already fully developed

your thesis in one of your notes. More often, though, a thesis emerges from a *clash* of assorted observations. An idea that looked good on
Tuesday may need modifying on Wednesday. Certain insights pull
you toward one conclusion, but certain others make you feel cautious
about it. Your notes amount to a continual record of possible assertions, examples, hints, and objections. The essential fact about ser-
viceable notes is that, taken together, they contain a more complicated, subtle view of the topic than you're likely to have in mind at any
given moment. Even if you formed your thesis at the outset and were
taking notes only to collect evidence for it, you can check the thesis
against the notes to make sure that you still agree with yourself.

notes for analysis   If your task is to analyze a text, reread it as many times as you
can, marking all passages (in your own copy) that look significant for
any reason. Then take notes on the basis of these preliminary indica-
tions. If one part of the text looks thematically connected to another
part, try to define the connection and see whether you haven't begun
to solve certain problems of interpretation. If things *don't* add up, ask
yourself why not. Perhaps you've found a real inconsistency of attitude on the author's part. Your first supposition, though, should be
that you've overlooked some theme or pattern that makes the text
more coherent than you thought it was. Go back and try to see how
the "unexplainable" element might be accounted for after all.

One especially useful exercise, when your task is to analyze a literary work, is to take a passage that seems typical or important and to
write about it at random, allowing your mind to play freely with it.
What you say about this one passage may prove to be true of the
whole work, and you may be able to use some of this close analysis in
your final essay.

notes are only a tool   A large part of good notetaking consists in knowing when
to stop. Some writers, anxious to postpone a first draft as long as
possible, seem to develop an unnatural fondness for the notes themselves. Instead of taking down the selective facts and ideas that they'll
need for the one essay at hand, they copy out whole pages, amassing
an impressive-looking stack of cards or sheets. This stack reassures
them that they possess great knowledge — yet it's never quite enough
for them to begin writing. And indeed it isn't, for they've been
collecting the makings of an almanac, not an essay. If they ever
get around to writing, their concern shifts from acquiring knowledge
to not wasting it: they dump their entire hoard of information on the
reader's head with an unspoken *"That'll* hold you!" They have forgotten that notes are only aids to composition, not documents having
meaning in themselves.

form of notes   Since your notes are for no one's eyes but your own, they can take
any form you please. They can be written on index cards, slips of

paper, or large pages. They can employ all sorts of eccentric abbreviations whose meaning is known only to you. They can, if you like, include obscene snarling at authors who didn't anticipate your views. But the notes must give you all the information you'll need, and do so with accuracy.

If all your notes consist of your own ideas, you don't have to be systematic in the way you handle them. But for some essays, and especially for a research paper (pp. 242–260), you'll be taking notes on books and articles by other writers, and such notes do require certain precautions. You must take care to *quote and summarize accurately* (pp. 82–83, 86–87) and to avoid any possibility of *plagiarism*, or the stealing of other people's words or ideas (pp. 223–225).

Once you have a sizable number of notes, it's a good idea to *index* them, writing one or more topic headings on an upper corner of each note. This will help you rearrange the notes to see where they lead and what your strongest points will be.

Exploratory Writing

Every writer sometimes finds it necessary to *write through* uncertainties, testing whether or how far an idea should be pursued in the essay proper. Notes, after all, can encourage you to choose any number of possible theses, most of which, if adopted, would prove to involve unforeseen difficulties. If you're hesitating between two theses or wondering just where to put your emphasis, exploratory writing can settle the question. Similarly, if you've just had a brainstorm and want to develop your new idea before it slips back into obscurity, by all means put it into a sample paragraph or two.

With luck, some of this prose may survive in your "real" essay. You'll defeat the point of exploratory writing, however, if you polish each sentence as you go. Rather, put aside all worry about correctness and just let the words pour out for as long as they will come. There will be time enough afterward to discard unusable material and find exact phrasing for the ideas you decide to pursue further.

COMPLETING A DRAFT

Organizing and Outlining

The final organizing of an essay, once enough notes have been gathered and a topic and thesis have been chosen, is a vital step that many writers are too impatient to take. Brimming with new-found information, they want to let it out in a nonstop flow. And perhaps they can. An essay, though, isn't a miscellaneous stream of facts but a structure with a purpose: to interest and convince a reader. If all your hard work isn't to be wasted, you must pause and consider the best avenue to those goals.

As you move from taking notes and finding a thesis to organizing and outlining, ask yourself:

1. *Which points will lend strongest support to my thesis?* Given your limited space and the reader's impatience with triviality, it's vital that your paragraphs and paragraph blocks (pp. 184–185) be devoted to major ideas, not passing curiosities. Go through your notes and decide which are the *main* ideas, and weed out points that would only distract a reader from the chief line of reasoning. Put the surviving statements on separate notecards or slips of paper, so that you can test various possible orders of presentation.

2. *Where should I put my thesis statement?* Do you want to state your thesis near the beginning of the essay — say, after one introductory paragraph that sets the stage? If so, you'll have the advantage of showing your reader at an early moment that you do have a clear case, which will then be supported in the rest of the essay. This doesn't mean you should begin with the deadly formula "The purpose of this essay is to show x"; that approach simply reveals discomfort. But putting your thesis fairly near the beginning is one way of making sure that things are under control.

An early thesis does make for one problem: by "giving away" your most challenging point, you may leave your reader feeling that it's all downhill from there. Think, then, about ways of *leading to* the thesis statement, so that readers can have a sense of making up their own minds — and, of course, of arriving at the conclusion you've withheld from them. Saving the thesis for last would be too coy. But once you know how your other main points will *support* or *modify* the thesis, you can consider different strategies until you find one that allows for some dramatic suspense without turning the whole essay into a game of hide-and-seek.

3. *Do I have the pros and cons sorted out?* If your essay is an argument (pp. 15–16), readers will inevitably think of certain objections to your thesis. The most important of those objections — the ones that ought to make even you a little uneasy — should be dealt with in your essay, either by *concession* or *refutation* (p. 85). That is, you should show why a contrary argument is either *true but not very damaging* or simply *untrue*. In either case you should budget a few paragraphs for this work of heading off the reader's doubts.

Where should your treatment of the "cons" be placed? There are several possibilities, but one should be considered first: *raise the doubts as soon as you have announced your thesis.* This is the moment when you are most exposed to the reader's misgivings. The most usual, and perhaps the best, strategy is to disarm readers by voicing the very objections they were about to make—and then by calmly demonstrating that those objections aren't powerful enough to overthrow your thesis. You can also raise one objection, deal with it, and then repeat the process for a second objection. Beware, though, of extending this method too far; every reader is bored by an endless shuttling between negative and positive arguments.

4. *How can I catch the reader's interest?* You can't assume that your reader is already so fascinated by your topic that you need only mention what it is. Adding a sincere-looking declaration that *you* are interested in it won't be very effective, either. What you need is some way of overcoming indifference and arousing curiosity. Though it isn't necessary in every essay to "bait" the reader with an unexplained description or story, it's important to offer some *movement toward* the main issue.

The most common movement is a *narrowing* one: you begin by calling attention to a general problem area and then gradually focus on the matter at hand. Thus, in an essay opposing wiretapping, you might use the first paragraph to give a rapid survey of recent threats to civil liberties—threats your reader may have heard about separately, but without combining them in this unsettling manner. Then you could begin your second paragraph with a sentence like *Of all these threats, none is more ominous than the growing use of wiretapping by police and public agencies.* Having been stirred in a general way, your reader is now ready to settle down with your particular argument.

Forms of opening paragraphs are more fully discussed on pages 185–192.

5. *How should I conclude?* Your reader will feel let down if your essay just stops at the end, without giving any sense of completion. Of course you can always repeat your main points; but such restatements usually sound too routinely dutiful and plodding. The best course is to save some strong observation or quotation for the end—something that *feels* conclusive without your having to say in effect, "Now I've done everything I said I was going to do."

Since good conclusions often "double back" on phrases or insights appearing in the rest of the essay, the precise form of a concluding paragraph needn't concern you until you write it. Just be aware that the task awaits you, and see what material you can set aside for use at that time.

Forms of concluding paragraphs are more fully discussed on pages 193–196.

use and abuse of outlines   Organizing can be a complicated process. It isn't easy to remember that one idea should be included and another excluded, that this piece of evidence should follow that assertion, that this thought should come first and that one should be saved for a conclusion. You need a device to keep all these considerations before you as you begin your first draft. That device is the *outline*, the most resented and misunderstood of all aids to composition.

Students have two usual complaints about the outline requirement. The first is that they don't in fact *use* the outline as they write; they just fake it afterward if they're obliged to hand it in. And the second is that the outline, if they do try to use it, gets radically altered in the process of writing. Students wonder why they bothered with a "guide" that turned out to need revising in view of the essay's actual shape.

The brief answer to these protests is that an imperfect guide is always better than none. As new problems come to light during the writing of drafts, an outline does get altered. This shows, not that the outline wasn't needed, but that planning an essay is a continuing business, one that you can't consider finished until you've arrived at the last paragraph of your final draft. This is all the more reason to start from an outline. The outline systematizes everything you've decided about *emphasis, subordination,* and *order;* and it helps you to check those decisions by conspicuously displaying the *relative importance* and the *sequence* of your ideas. In short, an outline is useful because it forces you to lay out your intended strategy and review it before undertaking a complete first draft.

You should, however, be wary of using a plausible-looking outline as a *substitute* for meeting difficulties as they arise. If your mind is fixed, not on the developing shape of your essay, but on the neatly indented and numbered headings of your outline, you will only get a false sense of control over unmastered problems. And if you follow that outline as if it were some divine command, you may sound less like an essayist than an outline monger—somebody who can't let his readers forget how orderly he is. In a ponderously "well organized" essay the main points protrude like elbows from sleeves. You can almost hear the writer sighing as he finishes section II.C and gathers himself up to tackle section III.A. What's needed is just the reverse, a sense of natural flow from point to point. An outline can't provide that flow; it merely frees you to concentrate on achieving it.

One major reason for having an outline is that you can refer to it at every stage of writing, checking your latest thoughts against its categories and seeing whether you're going astray or finding some unanticipated line of argument that has to be pursued, outline or no outline. In other words, you know you have one skeletal essay already in mind, and your only concern is whether you may discover an even better one as you proceed. Compare this relative security with having to wonder what, if anything, you'll be able to write from one paragraph to the next.

But writers who often feel blocked aren't the only ones who can profit from outlining. Consider also the writers who spin out whole series of paragraphs without pausing—indeed, without really thinking. They have developed the knack of making small transitions, hooking one sentence into the next, picking up a theme from the end of one paragraph and using it to launch the opening of the next paragraph. Yet their elegant prose may arrive nowhere at all. Lacking a total plan, they merely *sound* purposeful for a while, ending by exasperating readers by their inability to make a case.

scratch outline You may find yourself most comfortable with the so-called *scratch outline*—that is, a list of phrases or sentences showing the intended order of your major points. Such a list gives you a bare minimum of guidance; you should use it only if you're sure you can adequately develop each of the named points when you arrive at it. If you do settle for a scratch outline, you may want to combine it with references to your notes, reminding yourself of the right places to include examples and other supporting material.

full outline If your paper is to be long and complex, or if you simply want to guarantee that your main organizational decisions will be carried out, you should develop a full outline. Its advantage is that it shows detail and *subordination*—that is, the need to give contributory ideas less emphasis than the main ones they must support. Look, for instance, at the following outline for a paper attempting to show that rent control is not the answer to off-campus housing problems:

WHY OFF-CAMPUS RENT CONTROL WON'T WORK

Thesis: Although rent control of off-campus housing looks desirable at first, it brings about too many negative long-term effects.

  I. The Problem
   A. Rent Gouging
   B. Students Forced to Live Far from Campus

 II. The Promise: Fixed, Reasonable Rents near Campus

III. The Reality
   A. Expensive, Permanent Rent-Control Bureaucracy
   B. Landlord Neglect of Property
   C. *Worse* Shortage of Units
     1. No incentive to increase number of units
     2. Increased competition for rent-frozen units
   D. No Possible Reduction of Currently Excessive Rents

The first thing to notice here is that the writer's outline establishes three degrees of importance among her ideas and organizational categories. First, with her Roman numerals she sets up the underlying structure of her essay: from *problem* to *promise* to the disappointing *reality* that shows the wisdom of her thesis. Second, with her indented capital letters she subordinates specific ideas to those larger units. *The problem*, she reveals in the first part of her outline, *has two aspects, rent gouging and the forcing of students to seek lower rents far from campus.* By listing those two aspects as A and B, she is announcing that they have approximately the same importance. So do items A, B, C, and D in the final section of her essay. But one of those items, C, is supported by two narrower points; hence she forms a third grouping, the Arabic numerals 1 and 2, further indented to show the added degree of subordination. The three sets of numbering and three degrees of indention clearly display the essay's intended logic, helping the writer to portion out her paragraphs and emphasis accordingly.

This is not to say, though, that each degree of outline subordination can be precisely equated with a certain amount of writing in the essay itself. Once in a while an important idea can be treated in fewer words than a secondary idea that may be harder to get across. But the outline helps to remind you that this is what's happening, and thus to make you look for other ways of showing how significant the major point is.

Note, too, in the rent-control outline, that the writer feels no obligation to strive for a perfect symmetry of categories, like this:

I.	II.	III.
A.	A.	A.
B.	B.	B.
C.	C.	C.

She happens to have very little to say about category II and quite a bit to say about category III. Instead of making her outline into a meaninglessly balanced showpiece, she allows it to reflect the natural shape of her argument.

Observe, however, that a heading or subheading in an outline can never appear alone—no I without II, no A without B. The reason is that headings and subheadings represent *divisions* of a larger unit, either a more general point or the thesis of the entire essay. It is of course impossible to divide something into just one part. If you have a lonesome *A* in a draft outline, work it into the larger category:

ILLOGICAL:
I. Problems
  A. Excessive Noise
II. Cost Factors
  A. Overruns

BETTER:
I. Problem of Excessive Noise
II. Cost Overruns

In addition, you should always check a draft outline to make sure that all the subheadings under a given heading logically contribute to it. Don't try to tuck in irrelevant items just because you want to get them out of the way.

topic outline versus sentence outline If you are required to hand in an outline with your essay, your instructor may ask you for either a *topic outline* or a *sentence outline*. The rent-control example illustrates the *topic* outline, in which each heading and subheading consists of a concise phrase. A *sentence* outline, as the name implies, uses full or nearly full sentences instead of phrases. (The sentences can be shortened in headline style: *Witchcraft craze increases broomstick sales.*) Which kind is better? That depends on what you're seeking. The topic outline has the advantage of brevity, while the sentence outline, with its explicit propositions, ensures that you will actually say something *about* the topic named.

Here is a relatively complex outline in sentence form. It offers its author clear and precise directions for shaping his essay:

HAS THE SUPREME COURT REALLY SOLVED THE PORNOGRAPHY PROBLEM?

Thesis: The Supreme Court's 1973 rulings have spread confusion without seriously reducing the traffic in pornography.

I. How the 1973 Rulings Changed the Law
   A. One national standard of obscenity was replaced by many local standards.
   B. Instead of being defined as "utterly without redeeming social value," an obscene work was now one that "taken as a whole" lacked "serious" value.
   C. States were invited to draw up specific lists of forbidden acts.
   D. The judgment of "the average person" was to prevail.

II. The Apparent Advantage Gained
   A. Power would be returned to states and communities, where it belongs.
   B. Ordinary citizens would have more influence over policy, as they should in a democracy.
   C. Fairness would be served by applying definite tests instead of vague ones.

D. With tighter and clearer standards in effect, pornographers would be driven out of business.

III. Actual Confusion and Unworkability of the New Guidelines
   A. The "average person" is not a trustworthy censor.
      1. The "average person" said for decades that abstract painting "wasn't art."
      2. The "average person" thought that Joyce's classic fiction was obscene.
      3. The "tyranny of the majority" should not settle questions of free speech.
   B. The rulings have been found more complicated and inconsistent than the ones they replaced.
      1. A person can go to jail in one community for doing what another community might welcome.
      2. States and communities have been given overlapping jurisdiction.

IV. The Proof of Failure: Pornographers Are Still Thriving
   A. They have concentrated in "freer" cities.
   B. Mail-order business enables them to reach into "conservative" communities without fear of prosecution.
   C. Convictions have become harder than ever to obtain.
      1. Inconsistent standards have resulted in dismissed cases.
      2. Changes of venue to "free" areas have found "conviction-proof" juries for pornographers.

V. Conclusion: A New Approach Is Needed
   A. Repeated frustration shows that pornography can't be "stamped out" without seriously infringing artistic license and ordinary free speech.
   B. The law should concentrate only on preventing *exposure* of pornography to minors and unwilling adults.

Note that this writer, realizing that his main Roman headings won't correspond to actual paragraphs of his essay, hasn't tried to put all of them into sentence form. All the lesser headings do point toward paragraphs or parts of paragraphs, and consequently they are all stated as full sentences.

The First Draft

Nothing is more normal than a feeling of reluctance and anxiety during the writing of a first draft. Those first few paragraphs are likely to prove especially troublesome. Since the great enemy of the first draft is uncertainty, however, you will find your work much less awesome if you've done a sound job of taking notes, finding a plausible thesis, and outlining. Knowing that you have a clear and interesting point to make, and knowing that the paragraph you're struggling with now will be followed by others whose main ideas are already there in your outline, you can talk back to that little demon who keeps saying, *You're stuck, you're stuck, you're stuck. . . .*

Some people can write only after dark; others, only before breakfast; still others can't sit down, or need to have a radio blaring, or can write for two hours a day and not a minute more. How you manage is your affair. Maybe you should start with a later paragraph if the introductory one looks too forbidding. If you're worried about losing inspiration in the middle of a sentence, you can use a private shorthand, keeping your mind on the continuity of thoughts instead of on the words. Instead of writing, you may find it easier to talk into a tape recorder and then transcribe the better parts. Whether you write or dictate, don't be afraid to include too much, and don't be embarrassed by minor imperfections. What matters is that you get the draft finished — and that you understand how much more work remains to be done afterward.

The work you have put into outlining will obviously be wasted if you set the outline aside while writing. Use the outline to judge, not only what each paragraph ought to be *saying,* but also where it ought to be *leading.* That is, look ahead to the next subheading and try to make each paragraph end in a way that will allow a smooth *transition* (p. 179) to the next one.

Suppose that, despite all precautions, you find yourself lost halfway through the rough draft. Your paragraphs have gradually strayed from an outline whose defects have become all too apparent to you, and suddenly you're without guidance. Have you made some drastic blunder? Not necessarily. You may simply be groping toward a better essay than the one you first conceived. But don't just keep groping; that's inefficient. Go back and make a list of the points you've imperfectly developed so far, and begin a new outline based on your present view of the topic. In this way you can decide what remains to be said and how your emphasis will have to be shifted. Remember, as you work out a new plan, that your aim isn't to save as many paragraphs as possible from the early pages, but to make one strong, consistent whole — no matter how much of your prose ends in the wastebasket.

Choice of Title

As soon as you have a thesis (but not before), you can select a title for your essay. The ideal time for that choice, however, is after you've finished one draft. Reread the draft, looking for especially striking phrases that capture your point; perhaps you can fashion one of them into a title. If not, now is the time to think of a concise and pointed title. If you come up with an attractive but not very informative phrase, you may want to add a subtitle to it:

Uncivil Liberties: American Disregard for Law

Unequal Before the Law: The Economic and Social Injustice of Bail

Medium Burger: The Supreme Court's Middle Way

But don't feel obliged to find catchy titles every time. You can always draw a title directly from your topic or thesis:

topic-title	thesis-title
Should Faculties Unionize?	The Need for Faculty Unions
Can Hollywood Survive?	The Decline and Fall of Hollywood
Are Federal Pollution Standards Too Strict?	Federal Pollution Standards: The Economic Folly of Purism

For the form and placement of titles, see page 50.

REVISION

Why Revise?

Unpracticed writers usually hold both of the following opinions: *I will never be able to say what I mean* and *What I've just written will do, because it's mine.* One of these ideas replaces the other as a first draft limps toward completion. Writers are so relieved to find the page before them no longer empty that they draw a protective curtain across it: *I have suffered enough: here are my precious thoughts, exactly as they flowed from my brain.* And so they insulate themselves from advice about revision. Having discovered that they aren't completely blocked, they prefer not to ask whether people will be likely to accept what they have written.

Another way of characterizing this defensiveness is to say that writers invest *themselves* in their first draft. They don't see it as a collection of sentences and paragraphs, more or less intelligible and convincing, but as an expression of their inner worthiness. What they feel, of course, is a normal dread of rejection, but their way of coping with the feeling is to imagine that the work has already been approved. All writers, no matter how experienced, become temporarily swept up in this false success. A veteran may differ from a novice only in being more willing to descend from the clouds and begin re-reading with a critical eye.

Because the creative demands of the first draft are bound to inter-fere somewhat with your concern for the reader's opinion, revision is indispensable. Without necessarily abandoning any of your first-draft ideas, you've got to develop some skepticism toward them. To revise is to see your essay as public property, a case that has to stand or fall on its merits. Instead of overrating your words and then forget-ting them, you change the nature of your investment; what you final-ly admire is the way you've made the presentation, not the fact that you're the one who made it.

Resistance to revision often takes the form of a faith that one's thoughts are clear, whether or not they've been given adequate expression. The writer can't understand how the reader failed to grasp his point:

"But I *said* that!"
"Where did you say it?"
"Right here! Umm . . . well, I thought I said it. At least I knew what I *meant* to say."

But what good does an unfulfilled intention do? Though the writer may think his difficulty in communicating is technical and minor—a small matter of his not having done full justice to his thoughts—he really hasn't acknowledged that *the only thing that counts is what is there.*

Experienced authors will tell you, furthermore, that revision is of-ten their best means of finding out what they wanted to say. This may seem like a strange remark after all the emphasis I've put on planning, but it's true nonetheless. Composition is a continual strug-gle against a wish to keep your familiar bearings, and originality is possible only when this struggle has been won. In order to challenge a reader you must first suffer a little disorientation yourself. Some-times the habit of thinking in clichés prevails over every contrary effort until a slight change of wording allows a suppressed idea to burst through. As the anthropologist George Devereux has said of his own work:

In correcting the first draft of a scientific manuscript, I deliberately look for ambiguously worded passages, whose obscurity is usually due to the presence of some still latent and pre-conscious supplementary insight. I also realize that my occasional—highly puzzling and some-times quite exasperating—inability to express clearly, on the first try, some seemingly simple idea, is nearly always due to the subliminal stirrings of some additional, still repressed insights. Hence, whenever this happens to me, I stop struggling with syntax and seek to discover instead precisely what suppressed idea is trying to force its way into the "simple" statement I *consciously* seek to make. I stumbled upon some of my best ideas in this manner.[2]

Whether or not you gain new ideas through revision, you will probably catch errors of spelling, punctuation, or usage, and you will be able to make your prose more concise. Choppy or overblown paragraphs will come to your notice; so will redundancies and monotonous sentence patterns. By repairing all such defects before submitting the essay, you can put your reader in an agreeable mood for receiving your ideas.

What to Look for in Revising

Effective revision, it should be clear, isn't a simple matter of error-hunting. You do want to be especially watchful for weaknesses that have been found in your previous work—a tendency, say, to wander from the topic or to misuse commas. But each of your essays will have to meet new and unforeseeable difficulties. It is good, then, to match your drafts against a checklist of the qualities that make for a successful essay. Using the following list, you can recognize problems and, if necessary, turn to the chapters where they are discussed.

A WRITER'S CHECKLIST

1. Is my tone appropriate and consistent? [CHAPTER ONE]
2. Have I followed a well-organized plan and kept to the point? [CHAPTER TWO]
3. Have I included all essential material—and no irrelevant material—from my notes and outline? [CHAPTER TWO]
4. Is my reasoning sound? [CHAPTER THREE]
5. Have I dealt with probable objections to my ideas? [CHAPTER THREE]
6. Have I made my point without exaggeration or oversimplification? [CHAPTER THREE]
7. Have I made fair and acknowledged use of other writers' words and ideas? [CHAPTERS THREE and EIGHT]
8. Is my language appropriate and lively? [CHAPTER FOUR]
9. Do my sentences show enough variety of structure? [CHAPTER FIVE]
10. Are my paragraphs unified, emphatic, and fully developed? [CHAPTER SIX]

11. Have I made smooth and effective transitions from paragraph to paragraph? [CHAPTER SIX]
12. Does my introductory paragraph draw the reader's interest? [CHAPTER SIX]
13. Does my last paragraph give enough sense of completion? [CHAPTER SIX]
14. Have I used available library resources without letting them dominate my essay? [CHAPTER SEVEN]
15. Have I followed an accepted form of citing references? [CHAPTER EIGHT]
16. Have I followed standard grammar and usage? [CHAPTERS TEN and ELEVEN]
17. Does my punctuation help to make my meaning immediately clear? [CHAPTER TWELVE]
18. Is my spelling correct? [CHAPTER THIRTEEN]
19. Are my capitals, italics, abbreviations, and numerals handled correctly? [CHAPTER FOURTEEN]
20. Do all my words mean what I think they mean, and do they belong in an essay? [CHAPTER FIFTEEN]

You may be asked to revise an essay even after you have handed it in. The kinds of rewriting needed will be indicated partly by written comments and partly by *revision symbols* (see inside back cover) which your instructor uses to indicate errors or problems. Of course it's annoying to find your paper defaced with those marks. The only remedy is to become your own severest critic, strengthening the essay in all possible ways *before* letting it out of your hands.

You have, in general, two occasions for revising, and you should take advantage of both. In the normal work of writing, you will be continually rereading the most recent paragraph or two in order to get a feeling for what should be said next. During that process you should notice various small problems and adjust your prose to correct them: monotonous sentence structure, misspellings, faulty punctuation, redundant terms, unwanted rhymes, and so forth. Further, when you've finished a draft and come back to it after some hours or days, you should see larger problems such as faulty organization, lapses of logic, and jarring differences of tone between earlier and later paragraphs. As you repair these defects, of course, you can once again make small, sentence-by-sentence improvements. And in both stages of revising, even when your writing impresses you as passably clear and correct, try to *economize*. Never miss a chance to change a leisurely, roundabout phrase into a compact and pointed one.

Here are two paragraphs from a first draft, with improvements the writer made as he went along:

It isn't easy to an~~aly~~ze a poem as difficult as
Shakespeare's Sonnet~~/~~94.

Shakespeare's difficult Sonnet 94 appears to defy
analysis. ~~One-thing-I-notice-is,~~ The ~~the~~ last line, for example, "Lil~~l~~ies
that fester smell far worse than weeds," ~~gives-an-almost~~
~~revolting-indication-of-a-kind-of-bitterness-on-the-poet's~~
~~part~~ sounds bitter, even physically revolted. However, the
beginning ~~of-the-poem~~ is strikingly different in tone.
~~After-all,-it~~/ It loftily characterizes those ~~people~~ who "rightly
do inherit heaven's graces.) (,) What has brought Shakespeare from /~~From~~ heaven's graces to stinking
flowers,~~X-how-can-we-make-sense-of-it?~~ ?
~~Well,-I-would-like-to-suggest-that~~ But perhaps the reversal i~~e~~sn't
quite so complete as it appears ~~to-be~~. ~~Isn't-there-something~~
~~a-little-fishy,~~ strange ~~about-how-negative-the-first-four-lines-sound?~~
The first four lines, for example, although they seem to ~~be~~
describe ~~describing~~ an ideal person, actually ~~don't-do-anything-of-the~~
~~sort.~~ ~~They~~ give a ~~very~~ negative picture of the person who is
supposed to inherit heaven's graces. This seems to me ~~to-be~~
a very significant point. One ~~You~~ might gather from those lines
that ~~sin-is-just-all-but-unavoidable-unless-you-sort-of-give~~
~~up-all-your-impulses~~ impulse always leads to sin. ~~So-the~~
~~The-only-hope-is-to-make~~ The good person is one who <u>doesn't</u>
hurt others, <u>doesn't</u> exercise power, <u>isn't</u> moved--but what does
he actively and positively <u>do</u>? Shakespeare gives ~~us-nothing~~
~~remotely-approaching-an~~/ no answer. ~~Rereading-the-earlier-lines~~
~~in-the-light-of-the-later-ones,~~ Could we say that the negative
emphasis of the closing lines is ~~already-present-in-an-undevel~~
~~oped-form~~/ latent in the opening/~~lines~~ ones? ~~In-the-following-paragraphs~~
~~I-will-show~~
~~it-will-be-shown-that-this-is-the-case.~~

When he had finished a complete draft and returned to these revised paragraphs, the writer still wasn't satisfied. He saw that his opening statements could be made more dramatic and his sentence structure more varied. Furthermore, he detected a general vagueness in his discussion and realized that he was trying to analyze lines he hadn't quoted; his reader wouldn't have an adequate awareness of the poem. Here are the two paragraphs as finally revised:

"Lilies that fester smell far worse than weeds." The closing line of Shakespeare's difficult Sonnet 94 is memorable for its harshness--even, I would say, for an air of physical revulsion. Yet the poem begins with a strikingly different tone, loftily characterizing those people who "rightly do inherit heaven's graces." The descent from heaven to stinking flowers appears at first to make no sense. How can we explain Shakespeare's reversal of mood?

Perhaps if we begin by looking closely at the first part of the poem, we will see that it is less opposed to the ending than it seems. Whatever is bothering--or, to use Shakespeare's own word, "infecting"--the poem's conclusion may already be latent in the opening lines. Those who "inherit heaven's graces" are identified as

> They that have pow'r to hurt and will do none,
> That do not do the thing they most do show,
> Who, moving others, are themselves as stone,
> Unmoved, cold, and to temptation slow.

What a strangely negative picture of virtue! "Will do none," "do not do": we might gather that it is better to do nothing at all than to act. Again, it is hard to admire people likened to "stone" and described as "unmoved," "cold," and "slow," even if they are <u>not</u> committing crimes. In short, there is something stifling about this poem from the very beginning. We shouldn't be totally surprised, then, by the emphasis on corruption at the end. If goodness requires people to smother their impulses, sooner or later the lilies of such "virtue" will start to fester.

This writer hasn't been magically transformed, between his first and final drafts, into a permanently better critic and more confident essayist. In this one instance, however, his successive efforts to improve communication with his reader have given him a sharper view of the poem and a firmer command of his argument. Like every other writer who cares about results, he will have to resume the work of persistent revision with every new essay he undertakes.

THE FINAL COPY

No matter how many changes you've made between drafts, the essay you eventually submit should look unscarred. It should also meet certain technical requirements of form. The following advice reflects general practice, and should be followed wherever your instructor doesn't specify something different:

1. Type your essay if possible, using standard-sized (8½" × 11") unlined white paper of ordinary weight, not onionskin. If you must write longhand, choose paper with widely spaced lines, or write on every other line.
2. Type with a black ribbon that isn't faded, or write in dark ink. Use only one side of the paper.
3. If you have a separate title page for your essay, follow the form illustrated on page 245, and repeat the essay's title at the top of the first page of text, as on page 247. If you don't have a separate title page, put your name, the course and section numbers, and the instructor's name in an upper corner of page 1.
4. Allow ample margins: about 1½" at the top and left, and 1" at the right and bottom. Your right margin needn't be perfectly even. A handwritten paper should leave as much marginal space as a typewritten one.
5. You may leave the first page of text unnumbered, but all other pages should have Arabic numerals (2, 3, 4) in the upper right-hand corner.
6. Leave at least a triple space, on page 1 of your essay, between the title and the first line.
7. Indent the first line of each paragraph five type-spaces or, in a handwritten paper, about an inch. Do not skip extra lines between paragraphs.
8. If you place your notes at the foot of each page (see pp. 226–227), be sure to allow ample space for them. A line running across

about one-third of the page (as on p. 247) should separate those notes from the text above. You may also choose to place all your notes in order after the main text is completed (see pp. 60–61). Unless you are writing for publication, single-space the notes regardless of where they appear.

9. Except for notes and extracted quotations (p. 445), double-space the whole essay.

10. Revisions should be made before the final copy has been typed or written out. If you must revise on the final copy, put a caret (∧) at the point of insertion and type or write the added word direct-

    like

    ly above it, just ∧ this. Retype any page containing more than a few such changes.

11. Carefully proofread your final copy, looking especially for typing errors. Check all quotations against your notes or, better, against the printed passages.

12. Make sure your pages have been assembled in their proper order. Fasten them with a paper clip—or, if you don't have one, with a staple.

13. Make a carbon copy of your essay or have it duplicated, and retain the copy until you get the original back. Keep the graded original at least until the course is over. These steps will protect you if your instructor mislays a paper or misrecords a grade.

ONE ESSAY FROM START TO FINISH

A freshman student found herself with two weeks in which to write a thousand-word essay on any topic within the subject area of "Energy Sources." She knew, of course, that her topic would have to be narrower than that. Having previously visited a California facility called The Geysers, where power is generated from hot springs, she thought at once of geothermal energy. Although she hadn't been required to do library reading, she realized that some technical knowledge would be essential. By consulting her reference librarian and the *Reader's Guide to Periodical Literature* (pp. 208–209), she was able to locate several pertinent articles and pamphlets, and these in turn led her to others.

Taking notes on her reading, the student became convinced that geothermal power deserves greater recognition and support than it has received. Here are two of her notecards:

Henahan (p. 64) states the key fact: now they can get steam artificially, just by drilling into hot rocks. This means that a surface water supply + drilling in right spot = geothermal power!

Peach (p. 22) says that "recent developments at Los Alamos may make it possible to supply U.S. needs for thousands of years." If this is right, I should revise my estimates (and my emphasis?) upward. Make geothermal power into _the_ alternative?

The student did come to feel that geothermal power was "*the* alternative"; like most people who get engrossed in one line of reasoning, she had begun losing sight of rival possibilities. After studying a few paragraphs of her exploratory writing, however, she saw that she couldn't fully support an extreme view. What if some other technology were even safer and more efficient than the geothermal one? She had better scale down her thesis statement from its first, rather boastful form: *The safe and efficient way to meet America's present and future energy needs is to replace all existing plants with geothermal ones.*

While she was limiting the scope of her claims, the student also became aware of an opportunity for sharper focus. She had intended to deal with geothermal power in relation to the whole energy problem, but her sources pointed toward a special contrast between *geothermal and nuclear* power: the enormous governmental support of one solution, she decided, was driving the other into obscurity. Now she would seize on this fact and develop her argument around it. The much-publicized hazards of nuclear plants ought to make an ideal contrast to the safety and simplicity of nonradioactive geothermal processes. Hence her revised thesis statement: *Intensive development of geothermal energy could prove to be an attractive alternative to relying on expensive and dangerous nuclear plants.*

Working toward an outline, the student next listed the main ideas she expected to cover, and began thinking about how they could be subdivided and rearranged for maximum effect:

1. The energy problem
2. Nuclear power
3. Geothermal power
4. High cost of nuclear power
5. Low cost of geothermal power
6. Risks of nuclear power
7. Safety of geothermal power
8. Abundance versus scarcity
9. Conclusion (yes, but what ? ?)

Her final outline, using subordination to show how some of her main assertions would be supported, gave her a much surer guide for the actual writing of her essay:

I. The Energy Problem

II. Geothermal Power Defined

III. History and Uses of Geothermal Power

IV. Why Geothermal Power *Seems* Insignificant: The Nuclear Preoccupation

V. Objections to Nuclear Plants
    A. Economic
        1. Slow start-up
        2. High cost
    B. Safety
        1. Leaks
        2. Waste storage
        3. Bomb construction
        4. Terrorism

VI. The Geothermal Alternative
    A. Economic Advantages
        1. Fast start-up
        2. Low cost
        3. Huge potential capacity
    B. Safety Advantages
        1. No radioactive wastes
        2. Negligible pollution

VII. From the Nuclear to the Geothermal Age

The student finished a first draft of her essay in time to put it away for a couple of days, in the hope of gaining enough detachment to notice its weaknesses. Meanwhile she tried to decide on a title. Her first choice was "The Power Beneath Our Feet"—a catchy phrase. But on rechecking her sources, she saw that this was an example of unintentional plagiarism (pp. 223–225); she had all but copied another writer's subtitle, "The Power under Our Feet." The title she finally chose, "Steaming into the Eighties: The Case for Geothermal Power," was less memorable, but it was distinctly her own.

In her instructor's comments on earlier papers, this student had been urged to be alert against wordiness, monotonous sentence patterns, and a tendency to overstate her case. These and other problems struck her when she returned to her first draft. Here are a few of the improvements she made:

FIRST DRAFT	**FINAL VERSION**
If we turn our attention from this very depressing picture of all the problems of safety and cost associated with nuclear power, to the prospect for a full development of geothermal energy, here is what we discover the contrast to be.	Compare this glum picture with the prospect for fully developed geothermal energy. [The wordiness is gone, and a dramatic effect is achieved through use of the command "Compare."]
The real problem is safety. The chances for a full-scale "melt-down" of a nuclear plant have been estimated at five billion to one. This is obviously no great worry. But leaks of radioactive water have already occurred within and around several plants. No one knows what to do with the rapidly accumulating nuclear wastes. Those wastes will remain lethal for thousands of years after they are stored.	The real problem, however, is safety. Although the chances for a full-scale "meltdown" of a nuclear plant have been estimated at five billion to one, leaks of radioactive water have already occurred within and around several plants. More seriously, no one knows what to do with the rapidly accumulating nuclear wastes, which will remain lethal for thousands of years after they are stored. [By moving secondary ideas from whole sentences into subordinate clauses (*Although the chances . . . , which will remain . . .*), and by using modifiers (*however, More seriously*) to indicate logical relations, the writer has eliminated the monotony of sentence structure.]
A person would have to be crazy to think that those wastes could be transported safely for long distances by truck or railroad. And only incredibly callous, cynical people would build nuclear plants that could be sabotaged by terrorists.	The idea of transporting those wastes for long distances by truck or railroad is frightening. So, too, is the possibility that terrorists may sabotage nuclear plants. [Now the points are made without offensive slander of those who might disagree with them.]

Since she hadn't been asked to write a research paper, and since her footnotes mentioned all the sources she had consulted, the student didn't add a bibliography (pp. 234–238). But she did double-check all her quotations and citations against the magazines and pamphlets she had consulted, and she eliminated several inaccuracies. Then she was ready to type her final copy:

Cynthia Shieh

English 1A, sec. 8

Ms. Gonzales

STEAMING INTO THE EIGHTIES:

THE CASE FOR GEOTHERMAL POWER

Providing enough energy to meet an ever-increasing
demand is one of the gravest problems now confronting the
United States. Energy is the key to our highly industrialized
economy, which calls for a doubling of electrical output every
eight to ten years.[1] Meanwhile, however, the era of cheap,
abundant, and environmentally acceptable power may be coming
to an end. Coal is plentiful but polluting; natural gas is
scarce; oil puts us at the mercy of foreign exporters; and
nuclear power, which seemed until recently to be the ideal
solution, now appears costly, cumbersome, and nightmarishly
risky. In these circumstances, it is understandable that keen
interest is being shown both in new energy sources and in
older ones that were by-passed in favor of oil and gas. Among
the familiar but largely undeveloped sources, geothermal energy
deserves consideration on several counts.

Geothermal power is essentially heat, in the form of

2

steam or hot water, generated from the earth's core and
captured at the surface. In certain areas hot springs occur
naturally and are exploited on the site. The technology now
exists, however, to tap geothermal energy elsewhere by drilling two holes into deep-lying hot rocks, then pumping water
down one of those holes, and finally collecting the resultant
steam that rises through the other. The energy isn't limited
in use to nearby heating; more promisingly, it can run tur-
bines and thus generate electricity.

To say that geothermal power is familiar would be an
understatement. Various industries have made use of hot
springs from the eighteenth century until now, and electric
power has been derived from natural steam since 1904. One
plant in Italy has been running continuously since that year
with no sign of depleted capacity. In Iceland, about forty
percent of the population lives in geothermally heated housing.
There and in parts of Russia where the growing season is short,
natural emissions have been used to heat enormous greenhouses
for the raising of fruits, vegetables, and flowers. And many
other countries, from Algeria and Ethiopia to New Zealand and
Taiwan, are actively engaged in geothermal exploration.[2]

Yet the impression persists that geothermal power is insignificant in comparison with other sources of energy. Why?
Many people evidently believe that natural hot springs are
the only usable sites and that the one possible application of

3

this power is in local heating. But such misconceptions
certainly don't affect geologists, industrialists, and government officials. The neglect of geothermal resources has re-
sulted, it appears, from a governmentally coordinated policy
to favor nuclear power as <u>the</u> alternative to fossil fuels.
The relatively small federal expenditures on geothermal research have been insufficient to tempt the utility companies
away from their nuclear commitment.[3]

If the earth's heat is still mostly untapped, then, the
reason lies in a concerted push for nuclear power. Yet we
realize this at a moment when the glamour of atomic energy is
being replaced by concern and outright fear. In part the difficulties are economic. Nuclear plants have proved much cost-
lier to install than experts predicted, and their start-up
time of about fifteen years, from the first plans to the actual
delivery of electricity, is disappointingly slow.[4] Few people
today still talk about the "miracle" of cheap nuclear power.

The real problem, however, is safety. Although the chances
for a full-scale "meltdown" of a nuclear plant have been estimated at five billion to one, leaks of radioactive water have
already occurred within and around several plants. More seriously, no one knows what to do with the rapidly accumulating
nuclear wastes, which will remain lethal for thousands of years
after they are stored. The idea of transporting those wastes
for long distances by truck or railroad is frightening. So,

4

too, is the possibility that terrorists may sabotage nuclear plants. The lax safeguards now in effect count on the whole population to behave rationally for centuries. In any case, whether or not nuclear power _is_ safe, the opposition it arouses has recently brought plant construction to a near standstill.[5]

Compare this glum picture with the prospect for fully developed geothermal energy. In cost and efficiency alone, everything points to the superiority of natural steam power. The average start-up time for a geothermal plant is not fifteen but three years. Uranium is expensive; the earth's heat is all but free. And though the supply of uranium from _foreign_ sources will last a long time, geothermal power from our own land is practically inexhaustible. Analysts are now talking about harnessing enough steam and hot water to supply all American electrical needs for hundreds and even thousands of years.[6]

On grounds of safety, too, the geothermal alternative is appealing. There are no radioactive wastes to be disposed of, nor even the less hazardous wastes caused by mining coal and oil. About eighty percent of the used steam can be condensed into water and harmlessly evaporated; the remaining twenty percent, though it does contain boron and ammonia, can be re-injected into the deep wells. Noise pollution on the site can also be readily controlled. And the small quantities of non-condensable gases that do enter the atmosphere in geothermal

5

extraction could be trapped if necessary. As one knowledgeable
observer, surveying the whole area of geothermal safety, has
commented, "So far, none of the obstacles have proved insur-
mountable or even serious."[7]

Like other sources, geothermal power may face unexpected
setbacks that will limit its application. We must continue
to investigate ways of gathering power from the wind, tides,
and sun. None of the newer technologies, however, appears
cost-efficient today, and none has been tested over decades
and found workable. It seems plausible to put our major research effort where success has already been shown. If leaders
of government and industry, finding their nuclear ambitions
thwarted, arrive at this conclusion themselves, we may find
ourselves standing on the threshold of the geothermal age.

NOTES

[1]W. N. Peach, The Energy Outlook for the 1980's. A Study
Prepared for the Use of the Subcommittee on Economic Progress
of the Joint Economic Committee, U.S. Congress (Washington:
Govt. Printing Office, 1973), p. 22.

[2]See Peach, p. 22; "Geothermal Energy: The Power under
Our Feet," Editorial, Science Digest, July 1974, p. 12; and
Geothermal Resources: Foundation for a Potentially Significant
New Industry in California. Senate Permanent Factfinding
Committee on Natural Resources, Fourth Progress Report to the
California Legislature, 1967, p. 9.

6

[3]John F. Henahan, "Energy from the Earth's Core," Saturday Review/World, 23 Mar. 1974, p. 64; and "Geothermal Energy," p. 12.

[4]See Henahan, p. 64.

[5]See Peter Gwynne with James Bishop, Jr., and Stephen G. Michaud, "How Safe Is Nuclear Power?" Newsweek, 12 Apr. 1976, pp. 70-75.

[6]Peach, p. 22.

[7]Both the quotation and the facts cited in this paragraph are drawn from "Geothermal Energy," p. 13.

(For footnote form, see pp. 226-234.)

EXERCISES

I. Some of the following items would be suitable as *topics* for a three-page essay, and others would not (see pp. 29–30). Briefly discuss each item as a possible topic. If you find a given item too broad, propose a more workable topic in the same subject area.

    1. World Peace
    2. Should the United States Sell Arms to Underdeveloped Countries?
    3. The Olympic Games
    4. The War Against Smoking in Public Places
    5. My Life
    6. Air Pollution

II. Within each of the following subject areas (pp. 28–29), write (a) a possible topic for an essay; (b) a thesis statement; and (c) a title for that essay:

    1. Ecology
    2. Drug laws
    3. An important public event that has affected you

III. For items 1 and 2 in the previous exercise, restate your thesis in *a form that includes a major objection* (p. 32).

IV. Briefly discuss the suitability or unsuitability of each of the following statements as a *thesis* (pp. 30–32) for an essay. Where you find an unsuitable thesis, explain what you find defective about it.

    1. Although some people disapprove of welfare reform, others do not.
    2. Vanilla ice cream makes me break out all over.
    3. The United States can no longer afford to have its energy prices dictated by foreign powers.
    4. People who think that Communists should be allowed to teach schoolchildren are completely crazy and should be locked away in asylums.
    5. Hospitals should spend less money on "showcase" equipment and more on clinical services for the poor.

V. Suppose you have been taking notes for an essay *defending the private automobile* against those who regard it as a social menace. Your notes include the following miscellaneous statements:

We could find new fuels and impose limits on horsepower.

Cars waste precious energy.

We don't have to make all-or-nothing choices between private cars and mass transit.

Congestion and smog are real problems.

Cars give people initiative and individualism.

Thousands of people are killed every year in traffic accidents.

Without cars, no one could live outside major population centers.

The government can require stricter safety standards.

Abolish the dangers and inconveniences, not the cars themselves.

Using some or all of these statements — and *a few* more if you like — draw up a well-organized *topic outline* for the essay. (Take pp. 35–42 into consideration.)

VI. Take your topic outline from Exercise V and restate it as a sentence outline.

VII. Review the Writer's Checklist on pages 46–47. Although the Checklist anticipates later chapters, you can already use some of its points to spot difficulties in essay prose, your own or others'. Examine the following ineptly written passage. Then list the *defects* you find in it, along with the *kinds of revision* you would recommend. You needn't rewrite the passage, but do specifically indicate the features or expressions that appear faulty.

Poor nutrition in pregnancy can result in an approximately thirty percent permanent brain neuron development loss. This means that the unborn child may go through life possessing a lack of three billion brain cells. Believe it or not, its true!

The government will obviously have to make sure that all pregnant women get an adequate diet. Another thing newborn children need is "stimulus nutrition. You cant increase the no. of brain cells that way. But you can get them to enlarge by fifteen percent. You can also get them to form new interconnections. Stimulus nutrition is when an infant gets to exercize their senses, which is obviously essential. The government can do that too it can put all newborn children into special nursery schools that will bombard them with stimulations.

Another thing to be considered is reconsideration of the childbirth experience. Because that is a very important experience for both mother and child.

VIII. Write a complete essay of two to three pages on a topic of your choice, beginning from some broad subject area such as "Climate," "Adolescence," "Literature," or "Politics." The essay can be descriptive, narrative, expository, or argumentative, as you choose (pp. 13–16). As a record of the composing process, submit the following items:

1. the subject area;
2. the topic;
3. two or three sample notes that helped you focus on a thesis;
4. the thesis;
5. the final outline;
6. an unrevised first-draft paragraph;
7. the essay itself, following the form of the essay on pages 56–61.

NOTES

[1]The sample quotations are from Diana Loercher, "The Cat: Friend, Villain, Enigma?" *Christian Science Monitor,* 16 Mar. 1976, p. 14.

[2]George Devereux, *From Anxiety to Method in the Behavioral Sciences* (The Hague: Mouton, 1967), p. 207.

3 BEING REASONABLE

No writer feels equally at home with all four modes of the essay (pp. 13–16). Some of us enjoy describing the world or telling a story, but would rather not expound a subject or take a stand; for others it's just the reverse. Whatever your talents and interests are, you can't hope to spread them evenly across the whole range of nonfictional writing. You can, however, learn what readers of each mode expect, and thus check your drafts against common standards. This holds true especially for *argument,* the attempt to win agreement to an idea. A good storyteller's secrets aren't easily learned, but you can build strong arguments by keeping to the spirit of certain well-known principles — the principles, that is, needed for overcoming the natural and healthy skepticism that readers feel toward other people's ideas.

When you want to make a point, you can't say to your reader *Believe it because I told you* or *Believe it or else.* Readers aren't easily frightened, and they rarely take things on faith. You have to appeal to common sense, demonstrating that your thesis rests on sound *reasoning* about established *facts.* Though some readers may resist even the strongest argument, you can ensure that your *logic,* or method of supporting what you believe, is in perfect order.

Logic is our means of making inferences from statements we are willing to accept as facts. If you say to someone, "Rock music is dying; it hasn't developed significantly in the past eight years," you're doing more than putting two remarks together; you're *inferring* or *deducing* one from the other. Or, more precisely, you're drawing your *conclusion* ("Rock music is dying") from two propositions, one stated and one assumed. These are called *premises:*

PREMISE (STATED):
Rock music hasn't developed significantly in the past eight years.

PREMISE (ASSUMED):
A popular art form that doesn't develop significantly in eight years is dying.

CONCLUSION:
Rock music is dying.

Here we have a classic *chain of reasoning,* in which a *valid* (or "logical") conclusion is reached by finding an implication already present in the relation between two premises. Is the conclusion true? Yes, if it was validly drawn from *true* premises. If not, it may be true anyway, but only by chance.

Essayists, like people conversing, rarely spell out all the steps of their reasoning; they usually omit broad, silently understood assumptions such as the second premise above. There is little point in proving or even mentioning points that can confidently be taken for granted between writer and reader. But leaving a premise unstated is one thing and "jumping to conclusions" is quite another. Conscientious writers tend to be wary of certain *fallacies,* or illegitimate shortcuts in deduction, that will be discussed in this chapter:

faulty generalization (pp. 68–69), in which a few instances are incorrectly taken to hold for all cases;

catchall explanation (p. 70), in which one among many possible causes of something is misrepresented as *the* cause;

false analogy (pp. 83–84), or using a resemblance between two things to "prove" that they must be alike in other respects;

evading the question (p. 86), treating a minor or irrelevant point as if it were the central issue;

extension (pp. 86–87), or exaggeration, of an opposing position in order to refute (disprove) it more easily;

either-or reasoning (pp. 87–88), or artificially narrowing alternatives to make the writer's position look like the only plausible one; and

begging the question (pp. 88–92), or treating an unproven conclusion as if it had already been established.

The aim of argument, however, isn't merely to avoid fallacies; technical correctness is of value only when you actively *make a case,* showing the merits of your ideas and inspiring trust in your openness and reliability. Your whole attitude toward facts, guesses, and doubts is on display when you argue. If you *make defensible assertions,* limiting your claims and admitting uncertainties; if you *supply evidence* in a responsible way; and if you *meet objections* candidly, you will have an excellent chance of gaining support for your position. Gaining that support is what argument is all about.

MAKING DEFENSIBLE ASSERTIONS

Limit Your Claims

Reasonableness in argumentation can't help you if you've chosen as a thesis an improbable, indefensible idea. Yet some writers do exactly that, thinking perhaps that a show of total commitment will blow away all opposition. Commitment in itself leaves readers quite unmoved. However sincerely you believe in a dangerously broad proposition, your best course as a writer is to pare it down to something plausible and arguable. In particular, you would do well to steer clear of *faulty generalizations* and *catchall explanations.*

In daily life we have to play the averages and assume that what we already know will enable us to meet and understand new events, and in conversation we're usually unconcerned with exceptions. "It never rains here in summer," we say, or "Nobody ever learned anything from a correspondence course." It's understood that we're speaking in an approximate manner. But an argument in writing should be more responsive to small differences. If you mean *most* or *usually,* don't write *all* or *always. Rarely* and *never* aren't synonyms; neither are *hardly anybody* and *nobody.* Reaching for the absolute term may gratify your wish to have done with the subject once and for all, but it leaves you open to attack as a shallow thinker. If you feel undecided between two degrees of inclusiveness, choose the one that's less assertive and less open to disproof.

The risk of faulty generalization is especially great when a group isn't modified at all: "New Englanders are stingy." Does this mean all or only some New Englanders? The difference becomes critical if the generalization is being used to determine whether a given New Englander is stingy. Prejudice against individuals often takes the form of assigning them a trait that supposedly covers their group. People making the judgment don't ask themselves whether they mean to include every last member, and if pressed they would almost certainly admit that they didn't. Meanwhile, though, they don't really see the individual standing in front of them; all they see is a type.

In argumentation, one usual source of faulty generalizing is over-confidence in the writer's own experience. If the question is whether the human species has an aggressive instinct, you may feel inclined to look in your heart and say either yes or no. To do this, however, would be to rely on guesswork and an inadequate sample of one case. The same lapse occurs when a foreign-born writer asserts, "The idea that immigrants want to become 'Americanized' is contradicted by all experience." Meaning: *I, for one, don't want to be Americanized.* Someone else writes, "Professors actually enjoy making students suffer." Meaning: *I had an ugly experience in History 10.* Personal experience can have a great anecdotal value, but only if you recognize it *as* personal experience and not as a basis for generalization.

Especially in their opening paragraphs, many essays indulge in vague throwaway comments that aren't meant to be demonstrable. They're simply a way of leading into the one problem that will be treated carefully. Used in moderation, these passing remarks are harmless enough; the reader takes them for what they are, a bit of throat-clearing. But they become a serious problem as soon as rhetorical emphasis is laid on them. If the main argument of your essay rests on a proposition like "The West is guided by Christian morals," or "The purpose of evolution is to create a higher form of man," or "The decay of our culture has been accelerating every year," you're being naïve. How is anyone going to confirm or disprove such a gas bubble? Astute readers won't even try; they'll simply conclude that you have a weakness for overstatement.

Beware, too, of the catchall explanation. Consider this paragraph:

> The decline of the Roman Empire has been variously ascribed to libertinism and luxury, to the advent of Christianity, and to an overextension of military commitments. Some scholars have even resorted to misty theories about inevitable cycles of development and senility, as if every civilization followed the same laws. Now, however, we can put aside all such fantasies. Recent analysis of Roman earthenware has shown that highly toxic quantities of lead were being absorbed into the Romans' daily diet. The Roman Empire was literally poisoned to death.

Is this good reasoning? No, because the writer hasn't succeeded in doing away with the explanations that he intends to replace with his new one. For all we know, all five ideas may be partially right. Furthermore, the single fact that Romans were eating lead doesn't entail the intangible "decline of the Roman Empire." This paragraph illustrates a tendency to favor new ideas simply because of their newness; it's a matter, once again, of overrating one's own discoveries without considering that they too could be challenged or assigned a minor place.

Remember that two events or conditions can be associated in time without being related as cause and effect. Perhaps this seems self-evident, but most of us become superstitious when partisan feelings or pet beliefs are involved. Democrats claim that Republican administrations "cause" economic recessions; Republicans call their rivals "the war party" because most wars have erupted when Democrats were in power; and mystics of various kinds support their faith by arguing that their dreams were fulfilled or that some good result followed the performance of a ritual. We all yearn for certainty, and we all relax our skepticism on a few points where the will to believe overrides every other motive. The trouble comes with expecting others to share our superstitions. On the whole they won't do so without being shown a better reason than mere temporal sequence between the supposed cause and effect.

The time to think hardest about limiting your claims is when you're choosing a thesis for your essay. Avoiding vague and grandiose generalities is a start, but even a highly particular thesis may need modifying. Recall the two thesis statements considered by the writer on geothermal power (pp. 51–61):

DRAFT THESIS:
The safe and efficient way to meet America's present and future energy needs is to replace all existing plants with geothermal ones.

FINAL THESIS:
Intensive development of geothermal energy could prove to be an attractive alternative to relying on expensive and dangerous nuclear plants.

This writer, by drawing back to surer ground before attempting a first draft, spared herself a desperate effort to prove the unprovable. Compare:

	draft thesis	final thesis
Geothermal power	*is* *the* safe and efficient way to meet *all* present and future needs; it should replace *all* existing plants.	*could prove to be* *one attractive* alternative to *one* source of power.

Show Your Moderation

It's fine to make limited claims — and still better if your reader understands that this is what you've done. Have other writers, to your knowledge, taken a more extreme stand on the same topic? If so, put them to work for you. By quoting or citing an incautious rival and indicating why you can't go that far yourself, you make your reader grateful that a little sanity remains in the world:

> To some observers, the problem of dealing with Soviet interference in Africa is delightfully simple. Representative Appleman, for example, tells us we should notify Moscow that we "won't permit" the next wave of arms and military advisers. To the voters in his constituency this must sound very courageous. But what exactly does it mean? Are we prepared to risk all-out war over a relatively minor confrontation? And what do we gain by making threats that later turn out to have been empty? I suggest that we try to get along without thoughtless, inflammatory rhetoric, and begin asking instead what our real political options are.

If you find yourself situated between extremists on *both* sides, so much the better. Notice, for example, how a student prepares us for his moderate, objective treatment of Saul Bellow's novels:

> Even by the standards of the sixties, recent critical discussion of Saul Bellow and his work has been extraordinary in its fervor and blunt emotionalism. Maxwell Geismar, who merely expressed reservations about Bellow's stature as a novelist in the fifties, declared him "commercial and corrupt" and a "sellout" after the publication of *Herzog,* which, according to Geismar, showed the "deterioration of Bellow's craft into sheer nihilism, into nastiness, and even a kind of spiritual obscenity." For John Aldridge, *Herzog* is merely a "fatty sigh of middle-class intellectual contentment." On the other side, Bellow's own outspokenness against intellectual fashions — his condemnation of what he has called "the commonplaces of the Wasteland outlook, the cheap mental stimulants of Alienation, the cant and rant of pipsqueaks about Inauthenticity and Forlornness" — has won him some of the reverence inspired by a great national leader. Julian Moynahan, for example, concluded a review of *Herzog* by suggesting that with Bellow on hand, "things are looking up for America and its civilization." Perhaps so; but all this zeal for and against Bellow's allegiances has tended to blur his actual achievement as a novelist.

By this point we've begun to think of the writer as someone who isn't easily carried away, and we're ready to listen sympathetically to his own assessment of Bellow.

Be Open about Uncertainties

Even when you're convinced of your position and are sure you can demonstrate its correctness, you may find that some of your assertions are shakier than you'd like them to be. You lack certain information, or you perceive certain difficulties, or you find that you can't foretell events with perfect confidence. Should you by-pass the doubts, hoping that no one will think of them? Absolutely not. The points of uncertainty offer you a valuable chance to show your fair-mindedness; what you give away on small issues is amply repaid in the reader's good opinion of your trustworthiness. Notice, for instance, how the writer on rival sources of power cheerfully admitted that the geothermal alternative "may face unexpected setbacks that will limit its application" (p. 60). Far from damaging her case, that statement helped to give it a more judicious, impartial air.

Watch to see that the doubtful aspects of your argument don't evaporate in the course of your essay. Conscious of the reader's skepticism, some writers begin by nestling their thesis in words like *perhaps, conceivably,* and *let us imagine;* then, emboldened by their own irresistible prose, they switch to *definitely, obviously,* and *thus we have seen.* An idea that may have been the merest conjecture on one page is treated as Scripture on the next. This saves effort, but it accomplishes nothing. Readers usually notice that the rules of fair reasoning aren't being followed, and at that moment the game is lost.

Control Your Tone

When you have a strong feeling about an idea or a fact, you naturally want to communicate your emotion to readers. In a written argument, however, emotion can't be directly transmitted as if it were an electric charge. Something intervenes: the necessity of offering *reasons* why other people should share your position. The danger of emotionalism in prose is that it tends to short-circuit reasons. Instead of presenting a case, the writer becomes a case—of unthinking enthusiasm or hysteria or snarling anger.

Compare the effects made by two passages on the same topic. The first is full of indignant agitation:

A. The slaughter of whales is butchery pure and simple! Can you imagine anything more grotesque than the hideous, tortured death of a whale, shot with a grenade-tipped harpoon that *explodes* deep inside its body? *And for what?* Why the sadistic murder? Because certain profiteers want to turn the gentlest creature on this planet into *crayons, lipstick, shoe polish, fertilizer, margarine,* and *pet food,* for God's sake! If this doesn't make you sick—well, all I can say is that you must be ripping off some of those obscene profits yourself.

The second passage also shows conviction, but without the emotionalism:

B. The killing of a whale at sea isn't pleasant to witness or even to contemplate. Hunted down through sonar and other highly specialized equipment, the whale has no more chance of escape than a steer in a slaughterhouse. The manner of his death, however, is very different. A grenade-tipped harpoon explodes deep within his body, often causing prolonged suffering before that gentle giant, whose intelligence may be second only to our own, is reduced to a carcass ready for processing into crayons, lipstick, shoe polish, fertilizer, margarine, and pet food.

    The inhumane manner of death, however, is the least part of the scandal known as the whaling industry. Much more important is the fact that the killing is quite unnecessary. Adequate substitutes exist for every single use to which whale carcasses are currently put, and although some 32,000 whales are killed every year, the sum of commodities they provide is insignificant in the world's economy. Indeed, two already wealthy nations, Russia and Japan, account for eighty percent of all the whales "harvested" annually. Though the Japanese claim that whale meat is a vital source of protein for them, less than one percent of the Japanese protein diet actually comes from that source. Yet the slaughter goes on unchecked. The alarming truth is that one of the noblest species on earth is being pressed toward extinction for no justifiable reason.

If you already agree with the author of passage A, you may find yourself aroused by his overemphatic prose. In that case nothing has been gained or lost. If you disagree, you find yourself insulted as a profiteer. And if you're neutral, wondering which side possesses the strongest argument, you may notice how little relevant information is offered here. Should whaling be stopped because of the mere fact that whales are slaughtered and turned into commodities? Don't many other animals endure a similar fate? In his outrage the writer has neglected to supply a reasoned argument that would keep him from being regarded as a sentimentalist.

    The stern calm that pervades passage B is much more effective than the exclamations and italics of passage A. Take the description of a whale's death: we see, not the writer emoting over the fact, but the fact itself, which becomes more impressive without the signs of agitation. Similarly, by not calling special attention to the list of commodities from *crayons* through *pet food*, passage B achieves a powerful quality of *understatement*, whereby the mere reality appears more eloquent than any editorializing about it would be. And above all, note that writer B provides detailed, dispassionate *evidence* for the belief that whale slaughter, whether or not it revolts us, is economically unnecessary. Even if we lean initially toward a pro-whaling stance, we find it hard to dismiss writer B's objectively reported facts about the economic insignificance of whale products. In reading passage A, by contrast, our only options are to share or reject a fit of temper.

Writers who allow themselves to be carried away by a sense of their own rightness often indulge in *sarcasm,* the heaping of abusive ridicule on some person or group or idea. It would be sarcastic, for example, to write *What a wonderful sense of humanity and justice these whale butchers display!* I won't say that sarcasm can never be found in the prose of accomplished writers. A very small amount of it, however, is usually all that an essay can stand without sacrificing its air of reasonableness. The more disgust or ridicule you express, the more doubts you raise about your good faith. Why aren't you going about the business of building your case? By trying to make a fool of someone else, you give the impression of serving up a scapegoat to the reader instead of addressing the issue.

SUPPLYING EVIDENCE

Support Your Most Important Assertions

A writer arguing a point has to back that point with information that readers will accept as true. The old cliché *the facts speak for themselves* describes the ideal rhetorical situation — even though facts really speak only for someone who has unearthed them, put them in the strategically right place, and explained their significance. But after all your labor, the facts you've managed to reveal should have a look of naturalness and inevitability; you chose your thesis (the reader thinks) because the facts compelled you to. In actuality you may have chosen your thesis on a hunch. Yet you would have abandoned it — you *should* have abandoned it — if, sooner or later, you couldn't find enough evidence to convince a reader.

But what *is* "enough" evidence, and where should it be concentrated in your argument? Obviously these questions have to be reconsidered with each new essay you write; you must decide which readers you are addressing and then put yourself in their place, asking what statements you would need to accept before agreeing with the thesis being proposed. Your own commitment should count for nothing. The case should "stand on its merits" — that is, reveal its factual basis at just those points where a reader might be inclined to raise objections.

To illustrate this idea, let's return to the deduction about rock music and its decline:

PREMISE:
Rock music hasn't developed significantly in the past eight years.

PREMISE:
A popular art form that doesn't develop significantly in eight years is dying.

CONCLUSION:
Rock music is dying.

If this conclusion were your thesis, you wouldn't spend pages trying to show that "A popular art form that doesn't develop significantly in eight years is dying"; that would be tiresome hairsplitting. But the other premise, "Rock music hasn't developed significantly in the past eight years," would be disputed by some readers, neutrally received by others, and automatically accepted by relatively few. You would therefore have to support it with facts — that is, with statements that aren't themselves in dispute, or that you can establish to a reader's satisfaction. Consider the following assertions:

No individuals or groups have gone beyond the Beatles' merger of rock idiom with classical and Indian motifs.

The greatest star of the sixties, Bob Dylan, eliminated the rock elements from his music long ago.

Would-be rock idols of the seventies, such as Bruce Springsteen and Peter Frampton, are far from being cultural or even musical innovators.

Sales of rock albums have plummeted; rock concert halls have closed.

In order to keep any following, rock groups have had to become more bizarrely theatrical in their antics.

Eminent critics X and Y have declared that rock music no longer approaches country and western in mass appeal, even within the age group that once overwhelmingly supported rock.

In order to serve as evidence, these statements themselves would have to be either recognized by your typical reader as true or backed in their turn by further evidence. The observation about Bob Dylan, for example, might stand by itself, though a few dates and titles of records would be welcome. The contention about record sales could be buttressed by some figures. But what about the idea that Springsteen and Frampton "are far from being cultural or even musical innovators"? That looks like trouble. Some readers would instantly resent it, and many others would regard it as vague and highly subjective. How many facts — indisputable statements — could you assemble to give it meaning and force? If you couldn't locate such facts, your best course would be to drop the statement altogether. In brief, *don't support opinion with more opinion.*

A final glance at the essay on geothermal power can show another principle of evidence selection: *support those statements, and only those statements, that are needed to make your case.* Toward the end of her essay, you may recall, the writer asserts, *On grounds of safety, too, the geothermal alternative is appealing.* This statement is clearly of central importance to her argument that geothermal power is an attractive alternative to nuclear power. By itself, however, it carries no weight; few readers would already know the safety aspects of geothermal power. Realizing this, the writer spends a paragraph supporting her statement with evidence. She mentions the lack of radioactive and mining wastes; the harmless disposal of steam; the reinjection of boron and ammonia into deep wells; the easy control of noise pollution; and the possibility of trapping noncondensable gases. Together, these observations strongly back the main statement of the paragraph. But if the writer had paused to discuss any one of them at length, she would have strayed too far from the business of her essay.

Think of the logical structure of an argument as a pyramid of sorts with the thesis at the peak:

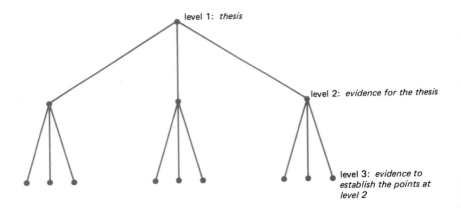

In terms of this scheme, the guidelines for including or excluding evidence can be restated:

a. at level 2, supply statements that, if accepted, would persuade a reader to agree with your thesis;
b. at level 3, provide evidence for all second-level statements that a reader might hesitate to accept; and
c. spend as little space as possible giving evidence for third-level statements. At level 3, that is, try to give only noncontroversial facts. Otherwise you may find yourself arguing at too great a logical distance from your thesis.

Once you have decided, on the basis of "closeness to the thesis" and your sense of your reader's likely views, that a given statement deserves support, be as specific as possible in backing it. The following paragraph, taken from a student essay arguing that Shakespeare uses the character of Laertes to make the strongest possible contrast to Hamlet, sets a good example. A major point in the argument is that Hamlet and Laertes are paired in significant ways:

> We need only abstract Laertes' five brief appearances in order to see that he and Hamlet are meant to be taken as parallel figures. In Act I, scene 2, Laertes asks the King for permission to return to France; in the same scene we learn that Hamlet has asked the King for permission to return to Wittenburg. In Laertes' second appearance he reproaches his sister for her receptivity to Hamlet; Hamlet later gives a comparable lecture to Gertrude. Hamlet's loss of a father through murder is mirrored by Laertes' loss of Polonius to Hamlet's own sword, and in Act IV, scene 1, Laertes reappears with the Hamlet-like idea of killing his father's murderer. Again, Laertes' cries of grief at Ophelia's funeral are travestied by Hamlet, who leaps after him into the grave. And in Laertes' fifth appearance, in Act V, he and Hamlet square off for a duel of offended sons — and the result of the scene is that both of them die and both are avenged. Laertes, we might say, scarcely exists apart from Hamlet. Superficially, at least, they harbor the same desires and grievances, love the same woman, behave alike, and are drawn into a single fate at the end.

This is a useful factual paragraph, setting up an opportunity for the writer to show how Hamlet's character stands out from Laertes'. That point too will require ample evidence, but we already know that the writer has a firm grasp of his materials and a respect for precise detail. In terms of our pyramid of evidence, he has assembled seven facts of "third level" significance to back an essential "second level" assertion:

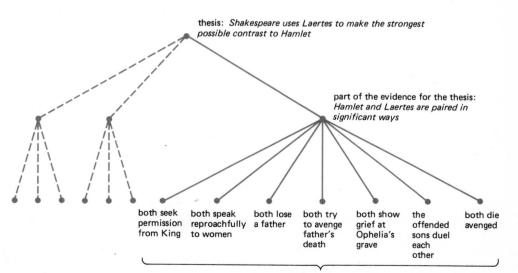

thesis: *Shakespeare uses Laertes to make the strongest possible contrast to Hamlet*

part of the evidence for the thesis: *Hamlet and Laertes are paired in significant ways*

both seek permission from King

both speak reproachfully to women

both lose a father

both try to avenge father's death

both show grief at Ophelia's grave

the offended sons duel each other

both die avenged

facts to support that statement

When you're building an argument on a disagreement with some other writer or position, your evidence should usually be concentrated at the points of dispute. If you overcome resistance there, the rest of your case shouldn't be hard to secure. Look at the following paragraphs from an essay called "The Dangers of Early Schooling." The joint authors begin by noting that most people take for granted the desirability of getting children into school as early as possible. They remark, however, that no real evidence has ever been produced to show the advantages of early schooling, and they refer to "an impressive body of research indicating that the late starter generally does better through school than the child who starts early."[1] Then they zero in on the received ideas opposing their thesis:

Advocates of early schooling usually start from two well-proved points: the fact of incredibly rapid growth in the child's intelligence between birth and age five, and the need for the child's social development to keep pace with his intellectual maturity. But then they go on to make unfortunate twin assumptions: that a child's intelligence can be nurtured by organizing it, and that brightness means readiness for the world of schooling. In short, their happy vision is that early schooling offers the best garden for a child's budding intelligence and developing social awareness.

These assumptions, however comforting or promising, are contradicted by clear-cut experimental evidence. A wealth of research has established that one of a child's primary needs in these formative years is for an environment free of tasks that will tax his brain, and an equally important need is for a setting that provides warmth, continuity, and security. That normal school experience does not successfully meet these needs has been established by three different kinds of studies: those that compare early and later school entrants; those that explore important but little understood changes in the young child's brain; and those that compare the effectiveness of parents and teachers in the development of young children. All three lines of investigation point to a common conclusion: early schooling, far from being the garden of delights its advocates claim, may actually be a damaging experience.[2]

We can see from these paragraphs just what the authors will do next, and why: they will survey those "three different kinds of studies" that refute the advocates of early schooling, so that the "impressive body of research" on their side of the quarrel will have maximum rhetorical impact. Clearly, the pyramid of evidence in this essay is going to have a strong base:

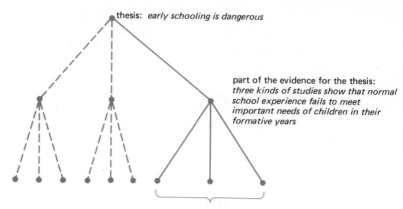

thesis: *early schooling is dangerous*

part of the evidence for the thesis: *three kinds of studies show that normal school experience fails to meet important needs of children in their formative years*

facts to support that statement: *specific findings of the three kinds of studies*

Use Facts and Figures Appropriately

While detailed facts and figures are more vital to some arguments than others, they are almost always useful. Apart from their role in supporting a thesis, they work to reduce a reader's suspicion that the writer is expressing "mere opinion." Even an argument about right and wrong can borrow some authority from statistics. Here, for instance, is the opening paragraph of an essay condemning "grade inflation," the trend toward easier grading in college:

> College transcripts are becoming so crowded with A's and B's that chapters of Phi Beta Kappa are reported to be raising the minimum grade average required, to safeguard the honor society's traditional exclusivity. A case study of grades in one community college found that the proportion of the school's students receiving an A in the first semester rose from 9.7 percent in 1963–1964 to 12 percent in 1968–1969 and 21 percent in 1971–1972. A 1974 study of recent grading procedures in 544 colleges across the country found that a student receiving a poor grade can often take the course over. This held for any grade in 303 colleges, for D or F in 442, and for F alone in 295 out of the 544 schools. In 325 of the institutions studied, when a course was repeated, only the last grade was taken into account in computing the grade point average.[3]

By proving that the phenomenon of grade inflation actually exists, these facts whet our interest in the writer's still unstated attitude.

They show, as well, that he has taken the trouble to do some research; we begin thinking of him as someone who attends to reality.

The adjectives most commonly used to modify the word *facts*— terms like *hard, cold,* and *dry*—suggest that facts are rather stony. One doesn't negotiate with a fact; it is what it is, whether we like it or not. This impression can be useful to you as a writer seeking to build your argument on firm ground. Yet facts needn't always make a *hard, cold,* and *dry* effect; they can also appeal to the imagination. Here, for example, is a paragraph from another student essay on the subject of energy sources. This writer, having shown that most of the earth's fossil fuels are either depleted or polluting or both, has just asked a pivotal question: *Is there a satisfactory power source which is neither scarce nor poisonous?*

> Yes! Every second, the sun fuses four million tons of hydrogen into helium, producing 380 billion trillion kilowatts of power. Of this power, 173 trillion kilowatts reach the earth's atmosphere; 85 trillion kilowatts reach the surface of the earth. On the average, the earth receives 1.395 kilowatts of power per square meter. If we could capture the solar energy dissipated on earth in forty days, we would have enough electricity to last a century. The energy shed on the earth in three days is greater than the total amount of energy contained in the world's fossil fuel supply.

Of course this paragraph doesn't begin to wrestle with the problem of how, and how efficiently, solar energy can be harnessed; that comes later in the essay. But by giving us a sense of the awesome solar power that bombards us at every second, it stirs our hopes that the sun can extricate us from our energy crisis.

Statistics, however, aren't always what they seem. You should know that figures dealing with even the most seemingly neutral matters—the crime rate, the price of an airplane, the increase or decrease of smog over a city—are subject to manipulation and error. Some imposing studies, especially those financed by lobbies, are biased from the start. A news report in a liberal paper may differ remarkably from a conservative paper's coverage of the same event. And experts can honestly disagree without having any self-interested motives. Even when the facts are indisputable—a movement of troops, a change in climate—their interpretation can introduce new openings for debate. Was the movement "offensive" or "precautionary"? Is pollution to blame for the rise in temperature? As an evaluator and presenter of evidence you've got to be skeptical. Where have the so-called facts come from? Are they up to date? Can the source be precisely cited? Could contrary "facts" be located elsewhere? Choose your emphasis prudently, making allowance for reasonable doubts and putting weight only on the facts that seem unassailable.

Someone who can show the difference between figures and reality is in a good position to win a reader's confidence. Thus one writer, in an essay asserting the importance of small-town life in the 1920's, questions the meaning of a famous statistic:

> Those employed by the Bureau of the Census for the decennial count-ing of the American people discovered that in 1920, for the first time in the Republic's history, more than 50 percent of the American popula-tion was definably urban.
>
> Half-truths in history probably outnumber the outright whoppers. This particular statistic has been interpreted ever since as marking a great watershed in American history, as the moment when the long opposition between the country bumpkin and the city slicker entered its final phase. Thomas Jefferson's agrarian faith that those who labor in the earth are the chosen people of God had apparently lost out to Alexander Hamilton's vision of the rich, the well born, and the able presiding over an industrial America. The "roar" of the Roaring Twen-ties seemed to be the roar of urban traffic and industry. According to a music critic writing in 1929, even the preindustrial human rhythms of jazz had become "caught up in the incessant movement of the ma-chine, pounding not only in our ears but also continuously in our con-sciousness . . . with its unrelieved tension." Except for a few nostal-gic rallyings—the Scopes trial in Dayton, Tennessee, or the defeat of Al Smith—the rural America of the founding fathers is supposed to have lost its hold on the American imagination after 1920.
>
> The half-truth in the 1920 statistic lay in the census-takers' defini-tions of "rural" and "urban" populations as those inhabiting towns of less than 2,500 people and those inhabiting towns of more. By an act of mathematical magic resembling Whitehead's fallacy of misplaced con-creteness, a community of only 2,499 souls became a benighted village, while 2,501 residents made a cosmopolis. Such figures make the urban hegemony look less convincing. And in fact, gazing away from Man-hattan's Great White Way any night during the decade following 1920, one could have seen wide, dark stretches of the continent where the roar of the Twenties was muted indeed; where life was lived by a rhythm in which there was no faintest echo of jazz.[4]

This writer isn't content to accept the arbitrary statistical means of distinguishing between "rural" and "urban." A town is still a town, he is saying, whether or not some mindless survey counts it as a city. He is right, of course, and his refusal to be awed by the census takers' misleading inference makes a strong impression of independence and clear thinking.

Again, a student writer chose to question a Defense Department study purporting to show that the Soviet Union was spending fifty percent more on military preparedness than the United States. The student became suspicious when she reflected that the Defense Department, year after year in peacetime and wartime, invariably favors increased American arms appropriations. Having given "the facts" a second look, and having read some doubting articles, she assembled a rebuttal:

> The United States and the Soviet Union are not of course facing each other like boxers in a ring. Each of them is the dominant member of an alliance; it is the two alliances, not the two nations, that ought to be compared. Suppose for the moment that the Russians do outspend us by fifty percent. Using the same figures, we discover that NATO outspends the Warsaw Pact alliance by fifteen percent. Although our military superiority may be slipping, the Pentagon figures present an unnecessarily gloomy picture.
>
> But do the Soviets outspend us at all? How does the Pentagon arrive at its dollar estimates of foreign costs? A congressional report informs us that "Soviet spending" is calculated by determining how many dollars it would cost *this* country, under its private contracting system, to pay for the total amount of the other country's manpower and armaments. But apples aren't lemons, and rubles aren't dollars. Though the Soviets do commit a large proportion of their wealth to weapons, it makes little sense to report that last year they put "$114 billion" into defense. Quite simply, they did nothing of the sort.

Note, by the way, that this writer hasn't lost sight of the first principle discussed in this chapter, *limit your claims*. She doesn't argue that America is becoming stronger or that the Soviets put less of their national wealth into arms than we do; those would be risky statements indeed. Simply, she has launched an effective counterattack on an apparently misleading set of figures. As is usual with factual counterarguments, the exposing of somebody else's "stretching" of statistics gives the writer a definite rhetorical advantage.

Quote Accurately and Succinctly

Direct quotation, accurately transcribed and acknowledged, is one of the standard means of presenting evidence. Quotations give readers a sense of being in the very presence of the source; the words have a ring of authenticity that's never quite matched by summary or restatement, however precise. And when the source is an authority whose opinions are known to be backed by years of experience and reflection, quoting can be an especially effective way of supporting an idea.

Remember, though, that excessively lengthy quotations can sap the vitality of your essay. Quote only passages whose exact wording is useful for your purposes, and don't allow quoted material to crowd your own argument. If you're quoting a work of literature, be aware that quotation is no substitute for analysis; an unexplained passage may strike two readers in entirely different ways. And if you're quoting some authority with whom you agree, note that agreeing with an already formulated idea doesn't carry you especially far. The dominant voice in your essay must be your own. Cite the points of agreement in as few words as possible and go on to develop *your* separate thesis.

The rule that all quotations should be checked against the original is doubly important for material that you're using as a contrast to your own ideas. Nothing is more embarrassing than to be caught misquoting a passage that you've triumphantly declared to be inadequate. Get in the habit of assuming that your quotations will need correction; they usually will. If you've deliberately omitted an unnecessary part of a quoted passage, make sure you've signaled the omission with *ellipses* (pp. 347–348) and that you haven't made the passage say something unintended. It's all too easy, for example, to leave out an author's modifying phrases and then accuse him of having taken a wild position.

Keep in mind that all of your quotations need to be correctly acknowledged, to avoid any possibility of *plagiarism* (pp. 223–225) on your part.

Use Analogies with Care

One useful way of making a point is to say that the matter at hand is much like some other matter, and that the principle at work in that other case also applies in this one. Here, for example, is a university president trying to persuade his alumni to be generous in spite of their disapproval of certain professors' ideas:

> When someone is asked to support a university he is not asked to agree with all that is spoken or written or taught there. No more is the supporter of the open market asked to approve of all policies, practices or products in the financial, commercial or industrial market place. Certainly supporters of democracy are not expected to approve of all parties, platforms and candidates. In all three instances — academic freedom, economic freedom, and political freedom — it is a *process*, not all its products, which commands our faith.[5]

The writer has drawn a pointed *analogy*, or likeness based on a relevant similarity, between the sensitive, perhaps negatively charged area of academic freedom and two other kinds of freedom, economic and political, that he knows his alumni cherish. His strategy in simplest form is to make them see resemblance where they were inclined to see only difference; *all three* kinds of freedom deserve their support.

The essential mechanism of an analogy is that if A resembles B, and if certain consequences follow from A, then comparable consequences also follow from B. This can be a vivid and often effective form of argument. You should realize, though, that it isn't "logical" in the strict sense of the term. A and B are of course *un*like in certain respects, and they may be unlike in just the way that matters in this instance. Readers feel no obligation to accept analogies as proofs.

Suppose, for example, that you wanted to argue against democratic reforms in the leadership of a political party. The party, you might say, is just like an army: it's vast and complex, it has battles to wage, and it will be held responsible for the outcome. Would a wise general share his command, allowing himself to be overruled at every point? An army led in this fashion would be easily defeated. Just so, you conclude, the party must preserve its central leadership and chain of command. What have you really proved by this analogy? Nothing. At best you've made your point in a vivid way, and this is all to the good. A shrewd opponent, however, could make you suffer for your "militaristic" conception of a nonmilitary organization whose strength lies in popular sentiment. Every analogy, even the most telling one, provides such openings for rebuttal.

Analogies can serve you well if you bear in mind that they only illustrate, never prove. They are simply extended metaphors (pp. 117–121). Perceiving the point at which the metaphor ceases to be effective, you can sometimes turn dissimilarities to your advantage. Here, for example, is a radical who doubts whether the Keynesian idea of "fine tuning" the economy can solve the chronic problems of capitalism:

> Fine tuning doesn't do much good when the tubes are weak; but economists these days are much like the TV audience in that they don't understand how the set works. Where that analogy breaks down, and uncomfortably, is that TV-watchers can call in a repairman; but the economist *is* the repairman.[6]

By pointing out the limits of his own analogy, the author underlines his main point, that liberal economists are less wise and competent than you might have thought.

MEETING OBJECTIONS

Anticipate Contrary Points

Writers who are unsure of their positions will usually want to erase contrary arguments from their minds. The thought of a strong objection rattles them. If the objection turned out to be right, all their labor would have been wasted. And so they forge ahead with their affirmative case, perhaps with an added hint that there's no room for dissent on such self-evident points as these. But readers are an inquisitive and skeptical lot. If you try to suppress doubts, you risk making them appear weightier than they really are. Finding no discussion of the censored, nagging question, readers may assume that you couldn't have answered it if you'd tried.

Your best course is to raise the doubts yourself and meet them actively through *refutation* or *concession* or a combination of the two. If a contrary argument strikes you as superficially attractive but valueless, you should *refute* it — that is, give your reader sufficient reason to reject it. If the argument is sound but not especially damaging, you should *concede* it — that is, admit its rightness — and show why your thesis still holds true.

Thus Jacques Barzun, in an essay advocating capital punishment, meets one of his opponents' chief arguments by granting it and trying to show that it doesn't address the real issue:

> I readily concede at the outset that present ways of dealing out capital punishment are as revolting as Mr. Koestler says in his harrowing volume, *Hanged by the Neck.* Like many of our prisons, our modes of execution should change. But this objection to barbarity does not mean that capital punishment — or rather, judicial homicide — should not go on. The illicit jump we find here, on the threshold of the inquiry, is characteristic of the abolitionist and must be disallowed at every point. Let us bear in mind the possibility of devising a painless, sudden, and dignified death, and see whether its administration is justifiable.[7]

By recognizing the counterargument Barzun reduces its force, and by setting it to one side he deprives the abolitionists of a major point and implies that his own case is less "emotional" than theirs.

Think carefully, though, before building a whole argument on a series of refutations. The essay can turn out to be excessively defensive, dry, and "overorganized," with a hypnotic swinging from negative to positive and a tone of superiority: "Watch me knock over the opposition!" Try to meet objections without becoming preoccupied with scorekeeping.

Address Issues Without Evasion

Faced with a difficult case to make, some writers simply change the subject, hoping that the reader's agreement with an obvious or emotionally charged irrelevancy will somehow cover the original point. Arguing against a specific tax reform, for example, a writer might contend, *This proposal strikes at the very heart of our free-enterprise system. Yet no one has invented a better system. Is socialism preferable? Clearly not. . . .* The writer's plan would be to blend the definite and difficult issue of tax reform with the large and easy one of free enterprise. Then some readers, not noticing that the specific merits and faults of the tax proposal hadn't been discussed, would feel that it had been exposed as un-American. Others, however, would catch the sleight of hand, and the writer would be discredited in their eyes. Keeping to the immediate issue is the best policy if you have facts on your side. If you don't, find a more defensible thesis.

Most frequently, question-evading takes the form of *ad hominem* (Latin 'to the man') argument. That is, the writer dismisses a position or proposal on the grounds that the wrong person is in favor of it:

> Comrade A claims that the Soviet government should abolish the censorship of literature. In order to decide this matter, let us recall that Comrade A has long been an apologist for American imperialism and bourgeois revisionism.

> Should we extend medical insurance to every citizen? I find it interesting that subversives have been trying for many years to get this legislation enacted.

> The oil and highway lobbies are doing everything in their power to defeat this anti-pollution initiative. If you believe in ecology, that should be all you need to know in order to decide how you're going to vote.

You can see that an argument needn't smear one individual in order to be *ad hominem*. All that's necessary, alas, is a channeling of interest from the idea itself to a prejudice about the people or faction supporting it.

Summarize Opposing Positions Fairly

Perhaps the strongest temptation in any dispute is that of distorting an opponent's argument while restating it. Without quite realizing the trick you're playing, you put your emphasis on the weakest part of the case or rephrase it to make it appear self-evidently absurd. After this act of *extension* or exaggeration of the idea opposing your own, everything suddenly looks delightfully simple. Instead of having to deal with serious objections, you have manufactured what's known as a *straw man*—a harmless manikin of an opponent that will topple with the slightest push.

This, needless to say, is poor ethics—and it's also poor rhetoric. Your sarcasm and mock outrage will almost certainly show a perceptive reader that you've been tampering with the facts. And suppose no one does notice the deception. In the act of making things easy for yourself, you've made them boring for others. If the holder of a contrary view is *this* stupid, they think, why has anyone bothered to refute him? The more lopsided your victory over the straw man, the weaker its effect.

When readers decide that they're being presented with a straw man, they're apt to turn stubborn and resist the writer's whole case, even if it's a sound one. Examine your own response to this passage, which introduces a sensible and incisive essay about ecology:

> Man's occupance of the earth is everywhere under attack by environmentalists and conservationists. Man is harassed for using nature's resources, for building dams, for exterminating bothersome species, for disposing of his refuse, for using the waters, for cultivating the topsoil, and for just being present. One gets the impression from this cacophony that nature has been contrived for all species of life except man.[8]

If we had no other source of information than this author, we would gather that environmentalists bully ("harass") other people, not only for abusing nature, but "for just being present" on the earth. The environmentalist position appears to be that the human species should move to another planet or execute itself as a collective criminal. *Is* this what environmentalism is about? Do environmentalists object to "cultivating the topsoil"? To whose ears are their statements a "cacophony" or meaningless mixture of discordant sounds? Such inflammatory language can appeal to no one who doesn't already despise the people being slandered. Others may be stung into drawing up a *rebuttal*, or contrary case. The writer's strategy has backfired, and the rest of his argument—keen, challenging, and well worth considering—may go unread. If, by contrast, he had taken pains to state the environmentalists' case fairly, his own argument would have benefited from the essay's general atmosphere of objectivity.

Avoid Either-Or Reasoning

Still another means of unfairly silencing objections is to depict one's own argument as the best of an artificially limited and "loaded" set of alternatives. This gives the writer a chance to force his position on readers as the only sane choice—provided, of course, that those readers aren't very alert. Thus a writer favoring legal abortion might claim, *We must legalize abortion or the world will become disastrously overpopulated*, and a writer on the opposite side might reply, *We must prevent legal abortion or the family will cease to exist*. Both writers would be delivering an ultimatum. *Which do you choose, overpopulation or legal abortion? What'll it be, legal abortion or the survival of the family?* The choice, as always in fallacious reasoning, is supposed to be automatic. All a reader must do, however, to escape the bind is to think of one other possibility. Is there no means to control population except through abortion? Might legal abortion have some lesser consequence than destruction of family life?

People who have to justify unpopular decisions are especially fond of either-or rhetoric:

> In this crisis the President could, as he told the people, have done nothing at all, thus allowing the enemy to enslave our allies. Or he could have retaliated with our whole nuclear arsenal, endangering the planet. That would have been shamefully reckless. Fortunately for the cause of civilization and peace, a middle course was found. By bombing only carefully selected targets and using conventional weapons, the President demonstrated once again that he is a man of forethought and moderation.

In order to represent this as valid reasoning, you would have to begin by stating, "Only one of the following three alternatives was open to the President." This proposition would appear very unlikely. The writer hopes that you'll pick up the emotional force of his rhetoric and count yourself thankful to be still alive, without thinking too precisely about his logic.

Avoid Prejudgments

You're *begging the question* or indulging in *circular reasoning* if you treat a debatable idea as if it had already been proved or disproved. Sometimes this happens in the very wording of the problem. Consider these two questions:

A. Is it a wise policy to let hardened criminals out of prison prematurely so that they can renew their war on society?

B. Does society have the right to take the victims of poverty and inequality and lock them up indefinitely, brutalizing them in the name of "rehabilitation"?

Writers A and B are addressing the same issue, but each of them has settled it in advance. The word *prematurely* already contains the idea that many convicts are released too soon, and other terms— *hardened criminals, renew their war*—reinforce the point. For writer B there's no such thing as a criminal in the first place. When "victims" have been "brutalized," it isn't hard to decide whether the brutalization should be prolonged. The trouble is that both A and B, in their eagerness to sweep away objections, have shown at the outset that their "investigations" will be phony. If you want to engage your reader's mind, you have to pose a genuine question, not a question with a built-in answer.

Be especially watchful for question-begging in the main statements justifying your thesis. Precisely because those "second level" ideas are close to the thesis, they sometimes wrongly *build on* it instead of *demonstrating* it. Suppose, for example, that the familiar theses below were "supported" by the ideas in the right column:

THESIS	SUPPORTING STATEMENT
The slaughter of whales should be stopped because it is inhumane and without economic justification.	The lack of a good economic justification for hunting whales shows that governments must intervene against the short-sighted whaling companies.
Rock music is dying.	Another style will come along soon to fill the place vacated by rock music.
Hamlet and Laertes are paired in significant ways.	The pairing of Hamlet and Laertes illustrates Shakespeare's keen interest in dramatic parallelism.
Early schooling is dangerous.	The risks of early schooling oblige us to look for a better alternative.

In each instance the "supporting" statement is really a new structure *using the thesis as a base.* The economic indefensibility of whaling, not yet established, is said to prove something else; the prediction about musical style assumes that rock music, whose vitality or lack of it is at issue, has already died; the unproven pairing of Hamlet and Laertes yields a further insight; and so do the risks of early schooling, which the whole essay was supposed to identify. All four of the right-hand statements would be question-begging unless they appeared in concluding paragraphs, after the thesis had in fact been properly argued.

As a final exercise in alertness to prejudgment, consider a long passage dealing with "free schools" within public school systems. The author, Jonathan Kozol, is himself a leading advocate of unstructured teaching, but in this article he asks whether real freedom is compatible with the nature and purpose of the public schools:

In an unjust nation, the children of the ruling-classes are not free in any way that matters if they are not free to know the price of pain and exploitation that their lives are built upon. This is a freedom that no public school in the United States can willingly give children. Businessmen are not in business to lose customers; public schools do not exist to free their clients from the agencies of mass-persuasion. "Innovative schools" with "open-structured" classrooms speak often about "relevant learning-processes" and "urban-oriented studies," but the first free action of such a class of honest children in an unmanipulated, genuinely open classroom in a segregated school within an all-white suburb, would be to walk out of class, blockade the doors and shut down the school building. School serves the state; the interest of the state is identified, for reasons of survival, with the interests of industrial dominion. The school exists to turn out manageable workers, obedient consumers, manipulable voters and, if need be, willing killers. It does not require the attribution of sinister motives, but only of the bare survival instincts, to know that a monolithic complex of industrial, political and academic interests of this kind does not intend to build the kinds of schools which will empower pint-sized zealots to expropriate their interests. It is in the light of considerations such as these that all innovations, all liberal reforms, all so-called "modern" methods and all new technologies ought to be scrutinized: Do they exist to free consumers, to liberate citizens, to inspire disagreement, inquiry, dissent? Or do they exist instead to quiet controversy, to contain rebellion and to channel inquiry into accepted avenues of discreet moderation? Is it conceivable that public schools can serve at once the function of indoctrinating agent and the function of invigorating counterfoil? I find this quite improbable and view with reservations of the deepest kind such genteel changes as may appear to offer broader liberties to captive children.[9]

This is an impassioned piece of writing, and to some people it might seem persuasive and even eloquent. Before the first sentence is over, though, Kozol has begun prejudging. The United States is casually described as "an unjust nation"—as compared to what others? The "price of pain and exploitation" is mentioned but not explained. All freedoms but one are judged valueless—in whose eyes? And is it true that the children of the unspecified "ruling-classes" generally go to public schools? Kozol has jammed a series of questionable, if perhaps defensible, ideas into the crannies of his prose, as if to forbid us an opportunity to disagree about any of them.

Instances of question-begging occur throughout the paragraph:

> . . . public schools do not exist to free their clients from the agencies of mass-persuasion.

(To call students "clients" is to dispose in advance of the possibility that their freedom will be respected.)

> "Innovative schools" with "open-structured" classrooms speak often about "relevant learning-processes" and "urban-oriented studies". . .

(The sarcastic quotation marks are a giveaway.)

> The school exists to turn out manageable workers, obedient consumers, manipulable voters and, if need be, willing killers.

(Other, more benign purposes are excluded without discussion. If Kozol's description is accurate, the main question of his essay — whether the schools can be truly free — lacks real content. Should we strive for "innovative" ways to produce "willing killers"?)

> Is it conceivable that public schools can serve at once the function of indoctrinating agent and the function of invigorating counterfoil?

(To impart one ideology is "indoctrinating"; to impart the author's is "invigorating.")

> I . . . view with reservations of the deepest kind such genteel changes as may appear to offer broader liberties to captive children.

(When children are defined as captives, anyone would harbor "reservations" about their liberties. Once again the author's triumph is too easily earned.)

In a certain limited sense Kozol's paragraph is "logical." His core argument could be stated in two interlocked chains of reasoning:

PREMISE:
• Public schools exist either to free people or to enslave them.

PREMISE:
• Public schools can't possibly exist to free people.

CONCLUSION:
- Public schools exist to enslave people.

PREMISE:
- All reform of the public schools serves the fundamental purpose of those schools.

PREMISE:
- The fundamental purpose of the public schools is to enslave people.

CONCLUSION:
- All reform of the public schools serves to enslave people.

These deductions are valid but they are also absurd, for they rest on wildly dogmatic premises that seem to settle in advance *all* questions about the reform of our institutions. The more "logical" Kozol becomes, the more his radicalism sounds like a snobbish refusal to concern himself with public education.

The lesson here, and the point of this chapter, is that reasonableness in prose can't be simply a matter of going through certain motions. However many times you prove that captives aren't free, you're still not thinking. *Being reasonable means showing concern for what you don't yet know.* It means aiming for a level of complexity where the choice between one idea and another is really open, not fixed by a gross contrast between right and wrong. Reaching for certainty, you should also show an awareness of uncertainty, adjusting your tone as you find yourself on stronger or weaker ground.

EXERCISES

I. The following passages typify the way essayists often *omit a premise* that the reader is expected to take for granted (p. 67). In each instance, (a) *identify the conclusion,* and (b) *supply the missing premise* that would make the reasoning valid. Example: If the passage said *The hydrogen bomb is a monstrous weapon; it goes on slowly killing its victims for decades after the explosion,* you would (a) identify the first statement as the conclusion, and (b) supply the missing premise: *Any weapon that goes on slowly killing its victims for decades after the explosion is monstrous.*

1. It is essential that Congress solve the problem of water pollution as soon as possible. Congress *must* pass the current sewage-control bill.

2. The price of digital watches is bound to decrease. Prices always fall when a new technology becomes available to many competing companies.
3. Soccer is much better for conditioning than football, because the game isn't continually interrupted by huddles, penalties, and time-outs.

II. **Check through the sections of this chapter called "Making Defensible Asser-tions" and "Supplying Evidence" (pp. 68–84). Then closely examine the fol-lowing passage by Adolf Hitler, and write a paragraph or two evaluating the ade-quacy or inadequacy of Hitler's reasoning. Don't just apply labels to the passage as a whole; isolate parts of it and *explain why* they do or don't meet common standards of reasonableness.**

No more than Nature desires the mating of weaker with stronger individuals, even less does she desire the blending of a higher with a lower race, since, if she did, her whole work of higher breeding, over perhaps hundreds of thousands of years, might be ruined with one blow.

Historical experience offers countless proofs of this. It shows with terrifying clarity that in every mingling of Aryan blood with that of lower peoples the result was the end of the cultured people. North America, whose population consists in by far the largest part of Ger-manic elements who mixed but little with the lower colored peoples, shows a different humanity and culture from Central and South America, where the predominantly Latin immigrants often mixed with the aborigines on a large scale. By this one example, we can clearly and distinctly recognize the effect of racial mixture. The Ger-manic inhabitant of the American continent, who has remained ra-cially pure and unmixed, rose to be master of the continent; he will remain the master as long as he does not fall a victim to defilement of the blood.[10]

III. **Here are five thesis statements that an essayist might find hard to defend (pp. 68–70). Revise each statement to make it more defensible, and briefly explain the advantage gained through each revision.**

1. The financial problems of major American cities doom them to certain de-struction.
2. The former European colonies in Africa, now that they control their own destinies, have shown themselves completely incapable of any semblance of self-government.
3. The high suicide rate in socialist Sweden proves that socialism opposes every normal instinct of human nature.
4. The absence of insane asylums in the Middle Ages proves that mental ill-ness is entirely a result of modern capitalism.
5. If the murderous thugs who enslaved the helpless Chinese people in 1949

are still in power today, the explanation must lie in their total suppression of dissent.

IV. Think of some question on which many people take too extreme a position (pp. 68–71). Write an introductory paragraph to an essay about that question, contrasting the extreme view with your own moderate one. Note: you don't have to *present* your view; just prepare your reader for it as an alternative to the extreme one.

V. Write another paragraph of the essay begun in Exercise IV, this time *openly allowing for uncertainties* in your position (p. 72). The paragraph needn't immediately follow the introductory one.

VI. The following paragraph by George Orwell illustrates how a writer who feels strongly about something can nevertheless manage to exercise control over tone (pp. 72–74). Rewrite one of Orwell's sentences to make it more obviously — *too* obviously — "emotional." Then write a paragraph analyzing Orwell's tone here. In your paragraph, compare the effects produced by the two versions of Orwell's sentence:

> In our time, political speech and writing are largely the defence of the indefensible. Things like the continuance of British rule in India, the Russian purges and deportations, the dropping of the atom bombs on Japan can indeed be defended, but only by arguments which are too brutal for most people to face, and which do not square with the professed aims of political parties. Thus political language has to consist largely of euphemism, question-begging, and sheer cloudy vagueness. Defenceless villages are bombarded from the air, the inhabitants driven out into the countryside, the cattle machine-gunned, the huts set on fire with incendiary bullets: this is called *pacification*. Millions of peasants are robbed of their farms and sent trudging along the roads with no more than they can carry: this is called *transfer of population* or *rectification of frontiers*. People are imprisoned for years without trial, or shot in the back of the neck or sent to die of scurvy in Arctic lumber camps: this is called *elimination of unreliable elements*. Such phraseology is needed if one wants to name things without calling up mental pictures of them.[11]

VII. Suppose you were going to write an essay with the thesis *The honor system of unsupervised testing cannot survive*. Which of the following items would you *exclude* from your *main evidence* in writing the essay (pp. 74–79)? Briefly explain why each omitted item strikes you as inappropriate. (Assume that all the statements are true.)

1. Only military academies and a few private colleges have continued to find the honor system workable.

2. The honor system requires each student to sign a pledge that he or she "will neither give nor receive aid on this examination."

3. Enforcing the honor system today involves a university in extensive legal battles.

4. In 1974, after fifty-one years, Johns Hopkins University voted to do away with the honor system.

5. Cheaters are going to cheat under any system.

6. Getting into law school or medical school is harder than ever today.

7. A faculty committee at Princeton University recently observed that "The present status of the honor spirit has been variously characterized as a 'joke,' as 'shaky,' as 'a farce,' or as 'dead.' "

8. The colleges that still retain the honor system tend to be those that were founded a long time ago.

9. Most students remain honest in spite of all the pressure for high grades.

VIII. **To get a feeling for the way detailed evidence can strengthen an argument (pp. 74–82), find a magazine article containing abundant facts and figures, and use some of those facts and figures in a paragraph arguing a point of your own. (Submit a precise reference to the original article, and be sure not to copy the author's wording.)**

IX. **Facts and figures, even when accurate, can often be misleading (pp. 79–82). Picture yourself as a reader of the following statements. What questions would you want to raise, and what further information would you want to have, before accepting the writer's position?**

1. The Department of Agriculture has discovered that America has 500,000 fewer farms than was previously thought.

2. Firemen are grossly overpaid; they make twenty to thirty dollars an hour for the work they do.

3. Students have an easy time of it these days; some fellowships are actually larger than a college teacher's starting salary twenty years ago.

4. "Elbows" Lodgepole is the greatest basketball player in the country; nobody else matched his average of 45 points a game.

5. The sexist Sanskrit Department didn't hire a single woman last year.

X. **Each of the following items deals with material appearing earlier in this book. Check each item against the passage being quoted or cited, and comment on the fairness or unfairness of quotation or summary in each instance (pp. 82–83 and 86–87).**

1. Abigail Zuger (pp. 10–12) reveals herself to be a typically mixed-up member of the present generation. "What shall I be?" she asks. "What shall I do? Will I succeed?"

2. Kenneth Stampp (pp. 17–18) believes that it was Lincoln's "innate generosity, his inner tenderness, and nothing else, that impelled him to extend to the South his generous terms. . . ."
3. Jacques Barzun (p. 85) could never have called capital punishment "painless, sudden, and dignified" if he had witnessed an actual execution.
4. Cynthia Shieh (pp. 56–61) would like us to believe that there are no serious obstacles to the safe and efficient production of geothermal power.
5. Jonathan Kozol (p. 90) is quite a mischief-maker; he urges all "honest children . . . to walk out of class, blockade the doors and shut down the school building."

XI. Examine and comment on the following use of *analogy* in reasoning (pp. 83–84). Does this analogy "work"? Is it open to attack by someone who rejects the writer's main point?

> People who make up school regulations never seem to realize that you can't force children to benefit from an activity they despise. Trying to make students healthy through required physical education classes is like sending them to concentration camps to learn how to concentrate.

XII. Consider the thesis *Every American President should travel around the country and meet his people at first hand, to discover what they're thinking.* List two *objections* that the writer of an essay with this thesis ought to deal with (p. 85).

XIII. Write one paragraph of the essay described in Exercise XII, raising one of your listed objections and *refuting* or *conceding* it (p. 85).

XIV. The following passage was written by a member of a cooperatively owned grocery store who believes that the store's board of directors should take stands on political issues. Write a paragraph showing *what kind of reasoning* is illustrated by this passage, and naming *possible objections* an opponent might raise.

> Some people will tell you that the Co-op has no business siding with one political faction against another, since its only business is to provide food at bargain prices. But where can we draw the line between "political" and "nonpolitical" today? To breathe is now a political act, since political decisions determine whether or not the air we breathe is going to make us sick. Or consider the fact that lettuce these days can be highly toxic because of poisonous sprays. To eat a salad has become a totally *political* act, an act of solidarity with the growers against the farm workers and ecologists. Isn't it ridiculous, then, to

complain about "politicization" of the Co-op? The only serious question to be answered is whether the Co-op's politics should be progressive or reactionary.

XV. In order to sharpen your alertness to the *evasion* and *begging* of questions (pp. 86–92), choose an issue about which you hold a strong conviction, and write five passages in defense of it. The first four, which can be very brief, should *illegitimately* defend your belief by (a) indulging in *ad hominem* argument (p. 86); (b) *extension* of an opposing argument (pp. 86–87); (c) use of arbitrary *either-or logic* (pp. 87–88); and *prejudgment* (pp. 88–92). For the fifth passage, write a full paragraph supporting your belief in a way you consider generally acceptable.

NOTES

[1]Raymond S. Moore and Dennis R. Moore, "The Dangers of Early Schooling," *Harper's*, July 1972, p. 58.

[2]Moore and Moore, pp. 58–59.

[3]Amitai Etzioni, "Grade Inflation," *Science*, 190 (10 Oct. 1975), 101.

[4]Paul A. Carter, "Of Towns and Roads, Three Novelists, and George McGovern," *Columbia Forum*, Spring 1973, pp. 10–11.

[5]Kingman Brewster, *The Report of the President*, Yale Univ., 1974–75 (New Haven: Yale Univ. Printing Service, 1975), p. 16.

[6]Doug Dowd, "Watch Out: Prosperity Is Just Around the Corner (Again)," *Ramparts*, Mar. 1971, p. 36.

[7]Jacques Barzun, "In Favor of Capital Punishment," *The American Scholar*, 31 (Spring 1962), 182.

[8]Amos H. Hawley, "Ecology and Population," *Science*, 179 (23 Mar. 1973), 1196.

[9]Jonathan Kozol, "The Open Schoolroom: New Words for Old Deceptions," *Ramparts*, July 1972, p. 41.

[10]Adolf Hitler, *Mein Kampf*, trans. Ralph Manheim (Boston: Houghton Mifflin, 1943), I, 286.

[11]George Orwell, "Politics and the English Language," in *A Collection of Essays* (Garden City, N.Y.: Anchor, 1954), pp. 172–73.

PART II
STYLE

4 WORDS

Diction, or the choice of words, is obviously a central element in every writer's style. Although good diction is partly a matter of trial and error, of tinkering with sentences until they sound right, it's also a matter of following certain general preferences that careful readers and writers tend to share. Those preferences underlie the following suggestions for using diction effectively in your own writing.

MAKE USE OF YOUR DICTIONARY

The first principle of diction is that you have to know the exact meanings of the words you choose. To this end you should own and make continual use of a dictionary. It will give you the definitions of unfamiliar words, and it can settle most questions of spelling, alternate forms, pronunciation, capitalization, and syllable division. These, of course, are matters of correctness, not style, but to some extent the dictionary can also help you to make subtler judgments. Above all, you can use the dictionary to increase your working vocabulary: the more words you know, the more precisely and confidently you can write. When you come across a new word, or an old word that's being used in an unfamiliar way, don't scurry past it with a sense of discomfort, but routinely look it up.

Your dictionary ought to be small enough to be easily handled and large enough to answer nearly all your questions about *denotation* (the primary meanings of words) and at least some of your questions about *connotation* (overtones and associations). For these purposes you should have a recent edition of a "college" dictionary such as *The Random House College Dictionary, Funk and Wagnalls Standard College Dictionary, Webster's New World Dictionary of the American Language,* or *The American Heritage Dictionary of the English Language.* Although such dictionaries are three to four times shorter than their parent *unabridged* dictionaries such as *Webster's Third New International Dictionary* or *The Random House Dictionary of the English Language,* they are handy source books, not only for words, but also for abbreviations, symbols, biographical and given names, places and population figures, weights and measures, names and locations of colleges, and basic principles of usage. And to a limited extent, varying from one dictionary to the next, they will tell you which words belong to standard English and which ones are regarded as colloquial, nonstandard dialect, or slang.

To see what a college dictionary can and can't do, look at Random House's entry under *fabulous:*

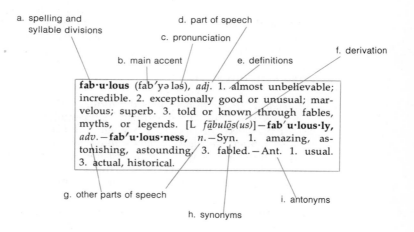

The entry shows, in the following order:

a. how the word is spelled and the points where syllable divisions occur (*fab-u-lous*);

   Comment: The lower-case *f* shows that *fabulous* isn't normally capitalized.

If this word could be spelled correctly in different ways, the less common form would appear in a separate entry with a cross reference to the more common form; thus the entry for *reenforce* merely sends you to *reinforce*. In your writing, use the spelling under which a full definition has been given.

Syllable division isn't completely uniform from one dictionary to another, but you can't go wrong by following your dictionary's practice in every case. (You can also spare yourself trouble by not breaking up words at all; a little unevenness in right-hand margins is normal.)

b. where the main accent falls (*fab′*);

> *Comment:* If the word has another strongly stressed syllable, like *hand* in *beforehand*, you would find it marked with a secondary accent: bi • for′hand′.

c. how the word is pronounced;

> *Comment:* The pronunciation key at the bottom of every pair of pages reveals, among other things, that ə = *a* as in *alone*. (One dictionary's key will differ from another's.) College dictionaries make no attempt to capture regional or nonstandard pronunciations, like $\overline{noo}$′*cul* • ər for $\overline{noo}$′*klē* • ər (nuclear).

d. the part of speech (*adj.* for *adjective*);

> *Comment:* Some words, like *can* and *wait*, occupy more than one part of speech, depending on the context. Definitions are grouped according to those parts of speech. Transitive verbs (those that take an object — p. 268) are usually listed separately from intransitive verbs (those that take no object — p. 269). Thus Random House gives all the intransitive senses of *wait* (*v.i.*) before the transitive senses (*v.t.*), as in *Wait your turn!*

e. three definitions;

> *Comment:* No dictionary lists definitions in the order of their acceptability. The dictionary illustrated here begins with the most common part of speech occupied by a given word and, within each part of speech, offers the *most frequently encountered meaning* first. Some other dictionaries begin with the *earliest* meaning and proceed toward the present. The system used in your dictionary is clearly set forth in the prefatory material, which you should read through at least once.

f. the word's derivation from the first three syllables of the Latin word *fabulosus*;

> *Comment:* The derivation or *etymology* of a word is given only if its component parts aren't obviously familiar — as they are, for example, in *freeze-dry* and *nearsighted*. Many symbols are used in stating etymologies; look for their explanation in the prefatory material of your dictionary.

g. an adverb and a noun stemming from the main word;

Comment: Fabulously and *fabulousness* are "run-on entries," words formed by adding a suffix (p. 361) to the main entry.

h. synonyms (words with nearly the same meaning) of definitions 1 and 3;

Comment: In most dictionaries a word with many apparent synonyms is accompanied by a "synonym study" explaining fine differences. Thus, this dictionary's entry for *strength* concludes:

> —**Syn. 4.** STRENGTH, POWER, FORCE, MIGHT suggest capacity to do something. STRENGTH is inherent capacity to manifest energy, to endure, and to resist. POWER is capacity to do work and to act. FORCE is the exercise of power: *One has the power to do something. He exerts force when he does it. He has sufficient strength to complete it.* MIGHT is power or strength in a great degree: *the might of an army.*

This would be useful information if you were wondering which of the four similar words to use in a sentence. If you looked up *power, force,* or *might,* you would find a cross reference to the synonym study under *strength.*

i. antonyms (words with nearly the opposite meaning) of definitions 1 and 3.

Comment: If you're searching for a word to convey the opposite of a certain term, check its listed antonyms. But if you still aren't satisfied, *look up the entries* for the most promising antonyms and *check their synonyms.* This will greatly expand your range of choice.

In addition, two typical features of dictionary entries are not illustrated here. If the word has uncommon or dubious *inflected forms —* that is, changes expressing different syntactic functions — the entry will supply them. Such forms include unusual *plurals (louse, lice);* unusual *principal parts of verbs (run, ran, run —* see p. 270); *pronoun forms (I, my, mine,* etc.); and *comparative and superlative degrees of adjectives (good, better, best —* see pp. 281–282). Also, every dictionary offers *restrictive labels* where necessary. Those labels, often abbreviated, indicate the *region* where a word is used in a given sense (*Southern U.S., Austral., Chiefly Brit.*); a *rare or obsolete* term or meaning (*Archaic, Obs., Poetic.*); the *subject or discipline* within which a certain meaning is understood (*Bot., Anat., Law*); and, most important for the writer, the *level of usage* for words not clearly within standard American English (*Nonstandard, Informal, Slang*).

Beyond its usage labels, your dictionary may offer especially valuable *usage studies* for certain controversial words or meanings, such as *ain't, different from/than,* or *hardly* with negative forms:

—**Usage.** HARDLY, BARELY, and SCARCELY all have a negative connotation, and the use of any of them with a supplementary negative is considered nonstandard, as in *I can't hardly wait* for *I can hardly wait.*

Unfortunately, however, you can't regard one such study, or even several of them in competing dictionaries, as reporting the final verdict on a given form. College dictionaries are mainly concerned with telling how a word is actually used by contemporary *speakers*, not writers. You as a writer of serious essays may want to own, in addition to your college dictionary, a specialized *guide to usage* such as Wilson Follett's *Modern American Usage* or Roy H. Copperud's *American Usage: The Consensus.* Some guides, like Follett's, express the preferences of their authors; others, like Copperud's, summarize what other authorities have said; but all of them tend to be more discriminating about usage than a college dictionary. As a case in point, you can see by the absence of restrictive labels that Random House considers *fabulous* to be standard American English in all three of the given senses. This, however, is what Copperud has to say about *fabulous:*

> Criticized by Bernstein, Evans, and Fowler as a vogue word for *incredible, astounding, astonishing,* and the like. The original sense, it is pointed out, was *mythical, legendary;* that is to say, relating to a fable. The faddish use of the word is found mostly in advertisements, where it may be applied to anything from girls to typewriters. This sense is recognized as standard, however, by American Heritage, Random House, and Webster.[1]

Where the specialists in usage disagree with "the dictionary," as they do here, you would do well to follow their advice.

There are, of course, many other things a college dictionary won't tell you about a word. For example, the entry we have anatomized says nothing about the pronunciation of *fabulous* in various nonstandard dialects. Though it gives one source in the Latin *fabulosus,* it doesn't report that *fabulosus* is itself derived from *fabula* 'story' and that *fabulous* is related in origin to *affable, fib,* and *ineffable.* Nor does it show how *fabulous* came down to modern English by way of Old French; nor does it quote the earliest known sentence in which *fabulous* appeared in English. Nor, finally, does it provide several meanings of *fabulous* that were once standard and are still available to precise writers: "fond of relating fables or legends," "celebrated in fable or myth," "unhistorical," "absurd, ridiculous." For any of this information you would have to consult an unabridged or specialized dictionary (p. 216).

Writers are sometimes advised to use a *thesaurus* (a dictionary of synonyms and antonyms) as a way of avoiding repetitiousness in their prose. But there is a danger here. Synonyms are rarely exact, and the thesaurus won't indicate fine differences of meaning. The risk of inaccuracy or faulty tone is great when you borrow unfamiliar terms. It's important not only to build your vocabulary, but also to keep new words out of your writing until you've seen how other writers use them.

SEEK A MIDDLE LEVEL OF DICTION

Most successful essays occupy what I have called a *middle tone* (p. 10), one that avoids the extremes of slanginess and pompous formality. Such a tone serves especially well for the typical college essay, whose topic tends to be a serious issue and whose reader hopes to find language that is lively but not flashy, precise but not fussy, humane but not theatrically emotional.

Choosing a *middle level of diction* is the single most effective means of striking a middle tone. As you saw in the examples given in Chapter One (pp. 8–10), slang produces "low" effects while fancy words tend to make an essay stiff and ceremonious. What you want, for most purposes, is the thoughtful yet unpretentious effect that goes naturally with middle diction—the characteristic language of a clear but nontechnical lecture, a newspaper editorial, a general-circulation magazine (*Harper's, The Atlantic, The National Review, The Nation,* etc.), or, for that matter, the paragraphs you have been reading here.

Thus, for example, in choosing between *mug, face,* and *visage,* you should usually prefer *face;* it is the ordinary term that will convey your meaning without giving your reader a jolt. So, too, you should reject both *croak* and *expire* when what you mean is *die.* And don't write *I dug where the dude was at* or *The coincidence of our perspectives gave occasion for not inconsiderable gratification;* write *I agreed with what he said.*

This isn't to rule out all "low" and "high" diction, but to say that it should be used only for limited, controlled effects—for example, effects of irony (p. 447). Thus the boxing reports of the late A. J. Liebling had a formal elegance that was purposefully "above" the fight game, and they juxtaposed literary references and colloquialisms:

> I do not know what took place in Mr. Moore's breast when he saw him
> get up. He may have felt, for the moment, like Don Giovanni when the
> Commendatore's statue grabbed at him—startled because he thought
> he had killed the guy already—or like Ahab when he saw the Whale
> take down Fedallah, harpoons and all.[2]

And James Herndon's style in his books about education is pitched deliberately "below" the administrative jargon of the school officials who see achievers, nonachievers, and intolerables, but never human "kids":

> There had always been kids in school who were smart—that is, the school said they were smart, they could be shown to have been smart at some time in their lives on the school's own tests—but who did not do well in school, who got bad grades and who were a pain in the ass. Naturally they annoyed the school. Smart kids who got good grades were O.K., and dumb kids who got bad grades were O.K., but smart kids who got bad grades weren't O.K., since the implication was that they were deliberately rejecting advantage, the whole notion of winning, the very virtue of the school.[3]

Both Liebling and Herndon effectively use *mixed diction* to detach themselves from what they're describing. This is altogether different from stumbling into mixed diction through carelessness about tone: *Hamlet withdraws from Ophelia's chamber like a regular dodo.* You would do well to avoid even intentional mixed diction until you're quite sure you can find the middle level and stay with it.

CALL THINGS BY THEIR NAMES

If you aim for middle diction you will already be somewhat on guard against *euphemism*, the substituting of vague or "nice" expressions for more direct ones. This work of prettification often has commercial or political motives behind it—a wish to sell a product, appease a faction, or make a harsh policy appear mild. Thus cemeteries become *memory gardens;* unemployment becomes *human resources development;* concentration camps are *relocation centers;* statements discovered to be false are called *inoperative* now that they have been *clarified* (retracted); and unprovoked bombing is packaged as *limited duration protective reaction retaliatory strikes.* The user of deliberate euphemism fears vividness above all. "Continued driving with a failed bearing," said a letter recalling certain defective cars, "could result in a disengagement of the axle shaft and adversely affect vehicle control." Just *how* inconvenienced a driver would be when his rear axle dropped onto the road the concocters of the letter preferred not to say.

You, however, do want your prose to be concrete and informative; you can't afford to leave the impression that you have something to hide. Don't give in to the advertiser's lingo and write *discomfort* when you mean *pain*, or *wetness* when you mean *sweat*. An old man is an *old man*, not a *senior citizen*. When you mean *teacher*, write *teacher*, not *educator*. And call a rape a *rape*, not an *assault*; don't write *The victim's skull was fractured, but tests proved she had not been assaulted*. The seeming dignity and delicacy implied by euphemisms often comes across as squeamishness or insincerity. Without going to the opposite extreme and dealing in blunt obscenities, you should generally prefer a forthright term to its euphemism.

Note, however, that many people have found racist or sexist implications in some apparent "names for things." It is best to use accepted alternatives to such terms (pp. 112–113).

AVOID REDUNDANCY AND CIRCUMLOCUTION

The fewer words you use to convey your meaning unmistakably, the fresher your reader's attention will be. This doesn't mean that you must fanatically squeeze every phrase into the smallest possible space, or that you can't repeat certain words for emphasis. It does mean that you should be watchful for redundancies and circumlocutions, and eliminate them wherever you can.

A *redundancy* is an expression that conveys the same meaning more than once. Thus *circle around* is redundant because the idea of *around* is already contained in *circle*; *new innovation* says nothing not already apparent in *innovation*; *shuttle back and forth* is a redundancy for *shuttle*; and a *personal friend* is simply a *friend* accompanied by an irrelevant adjective.

Your first drafts, like those of any writer, will almost certainly contain redundancies that you can expose by constantly applying the test *Is this word necessary?* Finding *advance planning* in one of your sentences, you should ask whether *advance* says anything not contained in *planning*. No; so out it goes. *Share in common* fails the same test and should be reduced to *share*; *deliberate lie* becomes *lie*, *set of twins* becomes *twins*, *adequate enough* becomes either *adequate* or *enough*, and so on. The revision makes for a cleaner, more purposeful effect.

All redundancies fall into the broader category of *circumlocutions* — that is, roundabout forms of expression. But some circumlocutions, instead of saying the same thing twice, say next to nothing in a ponderous phrase. Formulas like *in a manner of speaking* and *to make a long story short* are simply ways of sounding deliberate, or perhaps of making a short story long.

Some circumlocutions are so brief that they might almost be mistaken for concise phrasing. Yet even the most inconspicuous use of wordiness saps a reader's attention. If you have written *He was of a kindly nature*, pare it to *He was kind*, and your prose will be slightly more energetic. Instead of writing *It was of an unusual character*, try *It was unusual.* Don't surrender at once to cumbersome verbs like *give rise to, make contact with,* and *render inoperative;* prefer *arouse, meet,* and *destroy.* And if you mean *because,* don't settle for *due to the fact that.* When five words do the work of one, all five sound anemic.

In order to develop an aversion to circumlocutions, you might try to use as much padding as you can in one gruesome paragraph. For example:

> As far as the wolf was concerned, Little Red Riding Hood was basically a person who was acting, rightly or wrongly, on the hypothesis that by dint of exhibiting a tendency to girlish charm, so to speak, she might play a leading role in militating against being devoured. The contributing factors, by and large, that entered the area of concern that indicated a less sanguine conclusion had the effect, frankly speaking, of rendering inconsequential whatever ambitions the diminutive lass might have possessed in terms of establishing truly positive relations with a beast who was one of such a disputatious and unpredictable nature. It stood to reason that with respect to a simple-type female along the lines of herself, and with a viewpoint toward clarifying for a certainty the premises that might take effect should the wolf succeed in giving grounds for apprehension, Little Red Riding Hood felt strongly impelled toward the posing of a query serving the purpose of allowing the wolf to give expression to his intentions in a forthright manner and to the fullest extent. In this instance, however, things soon came to the point that further speculation either pro or con, as the case may have been, was reduced to zero — as, to make a long story short, was our heroine herself.

See also the discussion of conciseness in sentence structure, pages 141 – 142.

AVOID CLICHÉS

A cliché is an expression so overworked that it has become an automatic way of getting around the main business of writing, which is to suit each word to the meaning at hand. We all use clichés when speaking, and few of our listeners seem to mind. But writers who habitually resort to clichés — who describe money as *filthy lucre,* whose indifference to language comes *from the bottom of their hearts,* and whose meaning is lost *like a needle in a haystack* — end by sounding careless and lazy. And they don't improve matters by bracing their clichés with quotation marks or by inserting *so to speak* or *as the saying goes,* as if to assure us that they too know a cliché when they spot one.

One reason to shun clichés is that cliché-ridden prose lacks all vividness, except where it becomes absurdly vivid through an unintended clashing of images (*mixed metaphor,* p. 120). Certain sentences ascribed to the late movie producer Sam Goldwyn illustrate this revenge of the language on cliché-mongers:

x This atom bomb is really dynamite.
x An oral agreement isn't worth the paper it's written on.
x A man who goes to a psychiatrist should have his head examined.

Clichés in speech may sound casual or even sprightly, but in writing they have a numbing effect. When the reader sees *nuclear,* he knows that *holocaust* will follow; what is *foreseeable* must of course be the *future;* a *mixture* is *heady, praise* is *unstinted,* and so on. The resultant prose—*to be brutally frank*—is a *far cry* from being a *sure winner* in the *minds and hearts* of readers *from every walk of life.*

It's fairly easy, in the process of revision, to catch gross clichés such as *bring home the bacon, conspicuous by its absence, eat one's cake and have it too,* and *a miss is as good as a mile.* More insidious are harmless-looking pairs of "inseparable" adjectives and nouns (*supreme moment, vicious circle, vital role*) and the pat phrases that lend pseudo-importance to one's rhetoric (*it stands to reason, far be it from me, in a very real sense, in the last analysis*). Such handy expressions are *a snare and a delusion,* for they are *part and parcel* of recognizably weak prose.

It isn't necessary to memorize a list of all clichés or to purge them totally from your prose. Both tasks would be impossible. Just check your drafts for suspiciously dead-looking language, and watch especially for those clichés that your instructor or others have found in your earlier work. Since clichés are by nature habit-forming, you can be sure that old favorites will reappear.

AVOID JARGON

Technical terms have technical uses, and there's no need to apologize for them if the technical meaning is the one you must have. There are important differences between *liquidity* and *cash, ego* and *self, kinship structure* and *family, bankrupt* and *poor, metabolic* and *digestive.* The first term in each pair would be considered jargon only if the second, more common, term would have conveyed all that's really meant. If you write *ecosystem* when all you had in mind was *area,* or *goal-direct-*

ed instead of *purposeful,* or *reinforcement schedule* for *inducements,* you've indulged in jargon.

Popular academic fields such as sociology and psychology have contributed much to contemporary jargon, for their subject matter is close to everyday affairs. Thus the user of *sociologese,* hoping to sound scientific without taking pains over exactitude, not only writes *sociological* when he means *social,* he also uses *upwardly mobile* for *ambitious* and *parameters* for *borders.* If two things resemble each other, he sees them *on a continuum,* draws a *correlation* between them, and describes one as *a function of* the other. In his world people don't do things, they indulge in *behavior,* taking *orientation* from their *peer groups.*

As for the user of *psychologese,* he thinks that every pattern is a *syndrome,* that vanity shows *a big ego,* that hostility means *getting rid of aggressions,* and that a strong interest in anything amounts to an *obsession* or *fixation.* In sad people he detects a *death wish;* in happy ones, *manic* tendencies. But he himself, luckily, is *adjusted,* although he does face the *trauma* of paying income tax or waking up in the morning.

Advertising, journalism, business, and bureaucracy also exert warping effects on diction. If you find yourself writing about *pay hikes* and *Russ subs;* if your writing is full of *probes, vows, tolls, blazes, slates,* and *boosts;* if you feel possessed by the urge to say *inks the contract, gets the nod,* and *OK's the pact,* then you have a desperate case of *journalese.* Bureaucratese, in contrast, shows up in *breakthroughs, dialogue, decision-making process, brainstorm, viable, massive* (meaning "not small"), *maximize, finalize, potential* as a noun, *air* as a verb, *priorities, profiles,* and so on. Journalese is breezy, concrete, and cryptic; bureaucratese is self-important and abstract.

For a choice sample of bureaucratese, look at these paragraphs about graduate education:

It is reasonable to assume that graduate education in the United States developed on undergraduate college campuses because its presence was somehow synergistic with respect to the higher education enterprise. The most important factor was probably the presence of a cadre of scholars engaged in the learning pursuit, both with neophytes and on their own. In addition, libraries, laboratories, and skilled artisans were available.

For half a century or more, the whole clearly exceeded the sum of the parts, whether considered from the viewpoint of quality, cost effectiveness, or a combination of both. Now, however, the proliferation of graduate programs on the individual campus, the increase in the number of campuses providing graduate education, the current oversupply of these graduates, and the seeming inflexibility of many peo-

ple with advanced degrees calls into question the synergism argument
in favor of graduate education on the country's campuses.[4]

Note the redundancy in this passage (*campus* and *campuses* occur
three times in one sentence), the abstractions, the unnecessarily fancy words (*synergistic, cadre, neophytes*), the use of nouns in place of
adjectives (*the higher education enterprise, the learning pursuit, the synergism argument*), and the impersonal tone. Nothing is *happening*
here; no one is doing anything to anybody. Instead we have ghost-
ly states: a factor was a presence, libraries were available, the whole
exceeded the sum, the proliferation calls into question the synergism. . . . The ratio of rhetorical noise to information is so high
that you probably had some difficulty concentrating on the argument.

Politics, too, has its expanding store of jargon. A generalissimo
may be called either *a running dog of the imperialist oppressors* or *a
staunch friend of the American way of life*, depending on the writer's
affiliation. The labels are opposite in meaning, but they both express
the same contemptuous attitude toward language. Whether the jargon sets off a stink bomb or a perfumed mist, the idea isn't really to
describe, but to manipulate and deceive.

Less obviously, you may notice that the difference between *propaganda* and *consciousness-raising*, or between *mobilization* and *incite-
ment*, is entirely political. An army invades a neighboring country;
this is *liberation* if it's your army, *conquest* if it's your country. You
may, of course, strongly believe that one of these nouns is accurate.
When habitual users of political jargon say something true, however,
they are right only by accident; they would have used the same flag-
waving terms in any case.

USE WORDS IN THEIR ESTABLISHED SENSES

English has always been indulgent toward coinages, extensions of
meaning, and *back formation* of verbs (as in *drowse* formed from *drow-
sy, diagnose* from *diagnosis*). But most new terms disappear after a
short while, and a weakness for them may imply that you're too sus-
ceptible to fads. It's better to draw your main vocabulary from words
that have a history; the evocativeness of good prose comes in part
from readers' long acquaintance with familiar terms.

Many faddish-sounding words have a common feature: they belong to one part of speech but are being used as another. Sometimes
a suffix such as *-wise* or *-type* has been hastily added to turn a noun
into an adverb or adjective: *Preferencewise, she was looking for a com-
muter-type car*. More often a noun is appropriated as a verb (to *author*

a book), a noun becomes an adjective (a *fun* party), an adjective becomes a noun (the *feline*) or adverb (she did it *first-rate*), a verb becomes a noun (a long *quote*, an effective *rewrite*), and so forth.

The use of nouns as adjectives deserves special mention in the age of bureaucratese. Standard English allows some latitude for such attributive nouns, as they're called, but officials have a way of jamming them together in a confusing heap. A frugal governor, for example, once proposed what he called a *community work experience program demonstration project*. This row of attributive nouns was meant to describe, or perhaps to conceal, a policy of getting welfare mothers to pick up highway litter without receiving any wages.

AVOID OFFENSIVE LANGUAGE

Since you are writing in order to convince, not to insult, nothing can be gained from using terms that shock and offend people. Some readers, of course, wouldn't mind obscene words; but neither would they mind the generally acceptable alternatives that you ought to prefer. Extensive use of "dirty language" proves only that you're more interested in sounding tough than in winning agreement to your ideas. Racial slurs like *nigger*, *honky*, and *wop*, and demeaning stereotypes like *pushy Jew* and *dumb Swede*, are inexcusable. And sexually biased phrases such as *lady driver*, *schoolgirl gush*, *female logic*, and *typical male brutality* mark their user as a prisoner of condescending stereotypes.

Sexism in language has become an especially sensitive topic in recent years. You would be foolish as well as obtuse to include depersonalizing terms like *chick*, *tomato*, and *broad* in your serious essays; and "humorous" use of such words is rarely funny. Less obviously, you should realize that the word equivalent to *man* is *woman*, not *lady* or *girl* or *gal*. If William Shakespeare is *Shakespeare* in your prose, then Emily Dickinson should be *Dickinson*, not *Miss Dickinson* or *Emily*. And designations such as *authoress* and *lady lawyer* should be avoided for their objectionable hint that genuine, normal authors and lawyers are always men. Even *coed* should be dropped on these grounds; it insinuates that the higher education of women is an afterthought to the real (male) thing.

Yet because the idea of sexism is relatively new, and because different groups have reached different stages of resentment against sex-weighted language, it isn't easy to say how far you should go toward purging English of its longstanding favoritism to the male. The title *Ms.*, which doesn't indicate marital status, is becoming well established as the female counterpart to *Mr.*, and you can't go wrong by changing *stewardess* to *flight attendant* and *cleaning lady* to *house-*

keeper. Actress and *waitress*, on the other hand, have so far resisted all pressure to step aside for genderless words; if you used *actor* and *waiter* to indicate women, readers would be misled or taken aback. Are *mankind, man-made*, and *chairman* offensive? As of now, most educated users of the language, male and female, would say *no;* but opinion is shifting. You can substitute *humanity* for *mankind*, and *artificial* for *man-made*, without attracting notice; but *chairperson*, though it is rapidly becoming common, will still bother some readers. Many people find *person*-suffixed words clumsy and self-conscious. Before using one, see if you can't find a truly neutral alternative: not *chairperson* but *head*, not *congressperson* but *representative*, not *policeperson* but *officer*, not *weatherperson* but *meteorologist*.

The sorest of all issues in contemporary usage is that of the so-called *common gender*. Which pronouns should be used when an indefinite person, a "one," is being discussed? Traditionally, that indefinite person has been "male": *he, his, him*, as in *A taxpayer must check his return carefully*. For the centuries in which this practice went unchallenged, the masculine pronouns in such sentences were understood to designate, not actual men, but people of either sex. Today, however, many readers find those words an offensive reminder of second-class citizenship for women. Remedies that have been proposed range from using *he or she* (or *she or he*) for the common gender, to treating singular common words as plural (*A taxpayer must check their return*), to combining masculine and feminine pronouns in forms like *s/he*, to adopting radically new common forms such as *tey, tem*, and *ter*.

Unfortunately, none of these solutions can be recommended with much enthusiasm. Continual repetition of *he or she* is cumbersome and monotonous; most readers would regard *A taxpayer must check their return* as a blunder, not a blow for liberation; and they would find new pronoun forms disconcerting. What can be done, then? I have four suggestions:

1. Use *she* wherever the indefinite person is more likely to be female than male.
2. Use an occasional *he or she* to indicate your awareness that the common-gender *he* has unfair implications.
3. Avoid the singular wherever your meaning isn't affected: *Taxpayers must check their returns*.
4. Omit the pronoun altogether when it isn't essential: not *Everyone needs his vacation* but *Everyone needs a vacation*.

This is a cautious, imperfect strategy, a holding action until some new consensus about common gender is reached. My view is that it's a bad bargain to be forever proving your advanced attitude at the expense of your reader's concentration and ease. Your instructor, however, may see the matter differently.

SAY NO MORE THAN YOU MEAN

In conversation most of us use words like *basically, certainly, definitely, incredibly, intensely, just, of course, perfectly, positively, quite, really, simply,* and *very* without pausing to worry about their meaning, if any. These terms bolster our morale as we pick our way through a maze of half-formed ideas; their actual sense is *maybe* or *I hope.* Our friends have to forgive us for talking this way, so that they in turn can be forgiven. But written prose is expected to convey fully developed thoughts, and readers are impatient with authors who include intensifiers just for their reassuring sound. If you mean *very* you can write it without apology, but first make sure you do mean it; most of the intensifiers in a typical first draft deserve to be pruned away.

While we're talking, we don't hunt for adjectives to express the exact degree of our enthusiasm or dismay. We veer toward the extremes of *fantastic, terrific, sensational, fabulous,* and *awful, horrible, terrible, dreadful.* In print these words are often doubly inaccurate: they misrepresent the writer's true mood and they violate their own proper meaning. Something *fantastic* should have to do with fantasy; *dreadful* means "inspiring dread." Don't, in a formal essay, write *I am awfully glad* or *It was terribly thoughtful of him to come* — unless the one who came was Dracula.

BE AS CONCRETE AS YOUR MEANING ALLOWS

You have already been introduced to the difference between *concrete* and *abstract* language (pp. 9, 13). Concrete words convey observable things or properties like *classroom* and *smoky,* whereas abstract words convey intangible ideas like *education* and *pollution.* Of course there are gradations between the extremes: a *university* is more concrete than *education* but less so than a *classroom,* which is a distinct physical place. The more concrete the term, the more vivid it will be to a reader. Thus it's a sound idea to strive for concreteness wherever possible. Since first-draft prose tends to be weighted down with abstractions, the advice might be posed this way: *revise in the direction of concreteness.*

Accomplished writers don't hesitate to write abstractly, however, when they want to get from the mere fact of a thing to its significance. Look, for example, at the way this paragraph of Frank Conroy's gracefully moves between exact description and general principles:

> The greatest pleasure in yo-yoing was an abstract pleasure — watching
> the dramatization of simple physical laws, and realizing they would

never fail if a trick was done correctly. The geometric purity of it! The
string wasn't just a string, it was a tool in the enactment of theorems. It
was a line, an idea. And the top was an entirely different sort of idea, a
gyroscope, capable of storing energy and of interacting with the line. I
remember the first time I did a particularly lovely trick, one in which
the sleeping yo-yo is swung from right to left while the string is interrupted by an extended index finger. Momentum carries the yo-yo in a
circular path around the finger, but instead of completing the arc the
yo-yo falls on the taut string between the performer's hands, where it
continues to spin in an upright position. My pleasure at that moment
was as much from the beauty of the experiment as from pride. Snap-
ping apart my hands, I sent the yo-yo into the air above my head,
bouncing it off nothing, back into my palm.[5]

Should we criticize this author for relying on the abstract terms
*pleasure, dramatization, laws, geometric purity, enactment of theorems,
idea, energy, momentum,* and *nothing?* Frank Conroy's paragraph succeeds because he has been able to show precisely how his intellect
was engaged by the abstract properties of a childhood toy. The effect
he achieves is very different from that of a writer who typically *hides*
his meaning behind abstractions. Such a writer, given Conroy's
theme, might have foggily invoked *the illustration of various physical
laws by the component elements of toys, the discipline of mastery of di-
verse techniques, and combined intellectual and esthetic satisfactions,*
without describing the activity itself as Conroy does.

Here is what can happen when abstract language is unrelieved:

> On the positive functional side, a high incidence of certain types of
> patterns is essential to our occupational system and to the institutional
> complex in such fields as property and exchange which more immedi-
> ately surround this system. In relatively common-sense terms it re-
> quires scope for the valuation of personal achievement, for equality of
> opportunity, for mobility in response to technical requirements, for
> devotion to occupational goals and interests relatively unhampered by
> "personal" considerations. In more technical terms it requires a high
> incidence of technical competence, of rationality, of universalistic
> norms, and of functional specificity. All these are drastically different
> from the patterns which are dominant in the area of kinship relations,
> where ascription of status by birth plays a prominent part, and where
> roles are defined primarily in particularistic and functionally diffuse
> terms.[6]

Talcott Parsons, to be sure, does know what he's talking about, and
he has good reason not to pause over concrete examples: the whole
purpose of his essay is to isolate general laws. But was it necessary

for him to lull his readers with those strings of prepositional phrases, those monotonous adjective-noun pairs, and those uniformly colorless terms? Excessively abstract prose is always noun- and preposition-ridden. Only eight of Parsons' 133 words are verbs, and they're all forms of the inert *be*, *surround*, *require*, and *play*. No action is visualized; no energy flows from subject to object; all we can discern are cloudy relationships. An incidence is essential to a and b, it requires scope for the valuation of c, for d of e, for f in response to g, for h to i and j relatively unhampered by k. It also requires a high incidence of l, of m, of n, and of p. . . . *What* did the man say?

If your prose is needlessly abstract, you may also get caught in unintended metaphors (pp. 117–121) and in misplaced agency. *This area of concern*, you may write, *plays a role in the formation of the high mortality of cancer*. But can an area play a role, and can an area of concern be in any sense a cause of disease? For that matter, how are we to understand the formation of a mortality? The abstract nouns, looped together by prepositions, blur the causal relations they're supposed to explain. Worst of all, once you've written such a sentence you may imagine that you've actually said something, and thus lose contact with your reader.

USE LOGICAL TERMS PRECISELY

Words like *proof*, *refutation*, *validity*, *premise*, and *conclusion* have technical meanings that ought to be respected. It's true that good writers often use *valid* to mean *legitimate* or *correct*, as in *This is a valid proposal*. But when you mean *rebut* or *challenge*, you shouldn't write *refute*; a refutation is a disproof, not a mere disagreement. Similarly, a *premise* is meaningful only in relation to a conclusion it will yield when it's combined with another premise. If you use it as a synonym of *idea*, you're displaying, not logic, but only a wish to sound logical. The abuse of logic also extends to more common words like *because*, *since*, *therefore*, *then*, and *thus*. These terms assert that one thing is the cause of, or reason for, another, and you shouldn't use them to mean anything less.

KEEP NEGATIVES TO A MINIMUM

Negative *statements* are, of course, just as legitimate as positive ones; it's often necessary to point out that something didn't happen or that an idea leaves you unconvinced. But the negative *modifiers*, *no* and *not*, can become a nuisance when overused. A sentence in which they are bunched together may prove hard to follow. *There is no rea-*

son not to suppose, for example, leaves the reader dizzy, yet all the writer really meant was *I think.* And sometimes the writer as well as the reader gets tripped up by negatives: *The fact that psychologists did not themselves find the key to such symbols until the twentieth century does not rule out the possibility that a great novelist might not have intuited their meaning on his own.* If you have the patience to untangle this sentence, you'll find that it says the opposite of what the writer intended.

On a finer level of style, observe that negatively worded sentences tend to be slightly less emphatic than positive ones. Compare:

NEGATIVE:
• We are not in agreement on that point.

POSITIVE:
• We disagree on that point.

NEGATIVE:
• She did not do well on the test.

POSITIVE:
• She did poorly on the test.

The sentences containing *not* are correctly formed, but the others have a more assertive ring. If you are searching for ways to lend more force to your writing, look for opportunities to change *negated* terms *(not early, don't believe)* to terms that contain the full intended meaning *(late, disbelieve).*

MAKE YOUR METAPHORS VIVID AND APPROPRIATE

A *metaphor,* strictly defined, is an implied comparison, and a *simile* is an explicit one:

METAPHOR:
• George's hedgeclipper mind gives a suburban sameness to everything it touches.

George's mind is compared to hedgeclippers, but without a term of comparison such as *like* or *as.*

SIMILE:
• Like a patio rotisserie, George's mind always keeps turning at the same slow rate, no matter what is impaled on it.

George's mind is explicitly likened to a rotisserie.

In practice, you can see, the difference between metaphor and simile isn't very important. One kind of image isn't necessarily more poetical or risky than the other. What does matter is whether the figures of speech you use (I'll call them all "metaphors" for convenience) are clear and pertinent and helpful.

Although metaphors usually find their way into the driest paragraph, some writers prefer to use them sparingly. Ernest Hemingway's descriptions, for example, are intentionally flat and literal:

> Then there was the bad weather. It would come in one day when the fall was over. We would have to shut the windows in the night against the rain and the cold wind would strip the leaves from the trees in the Place Contrescarpe. The leaves lay sodden in the rain and the wind drove the rain against the big green autobus at the terminal and the Café des Amateurs was crowded and the windows misted over from the heat and the smoke inside. It was a sad, evilly run café where the drunkards of the quarter crowded together and I kept away from it because of the smell of dirty bodies and the sour smell of drunkenness.[7]

Hemingway writes vividly, but he wants his scene to appear as stark reality, and so he tries to do without metaphor.

At the other extreme is the style of Norman Mailer, who recklessly piles one figurative image onto another. Here, for instance, is Mailer describing Miami Beach:

> Over hundreds, then thousands of acres, white sidewalks, streets and white buildings covered the earth where the jungle had been. Is it so dissimilar from covering your poor pubic hair with adhesive tape for fifty years? The vegetal memories of that excised jungle haunted Miami Beach in a steam-pot of miasmas. Ghosts of expunged flora, the never-born groaning in vegetative chancery beneath the asphalt came up with a tropical curse, an equatorial leaden wet sweat of air which rose from the earth itself, rose right up through the baked asphalt and into the heated air which entered the lungs like a hand slipping into a rubber glove.[8]

Some readers might object to this passage as lush and imprecise. Hauntings and a curse, vegetal memories, and ghosts of unborn flora seem a bit melodramatic when the literal subject is the history and climate of Miami Beach. What exactly is a *leaden sweat?* Isn't there something wrong with saying that *ghosts* came up with a *curse*, which was in fact a *sweat of air*, which once again *rose*, and rose into still more *heated air*, which now resembled a hand? Yet for many readers the daring of Mailer's total idea and the vividness of images like the adhesive tape on pubic hair and the hand slipping into the rubber glove override all such objections.

You should think of metaphors, not as arty flights of imagination, but as means of being both clear and lively. Some successful metaphors are in fact quite simple. I recall, for example, a famous runner saying that his conditioning program was like shoveling a little more snow each day with great strain, and by this means gradually enlarging the space (meaning the speed and distance) in which his running would be effortless on the following day. The words he used were ordinary, but they became memorable through their truth to the experience described. So, too, a student once impressed me with this simple but carefully worked-out figure of speech:

> For me, the idea of going on for an advanced degree is like that of rowing across the ocean. Perhaps I could do it and perhaps I couldn't. But what, I wonder, is waiting for me on the other side, and isn't there some faster and safer way of getting there? Until I know the answers to these questions, I intend to keep my feet planted on familiar soil.

And thus the novelist Saul Bellow, speaking through a fictional hero, once characterized his contemporaries' attitude toward death:

> This generation thinks—and this is its thought of thoughts—that nothing faithful, vulnerable, fragile can be durable or have any true power. Death waits for these things as a cement floor waits for a dropping light bulb. The brittle shell of glass loses its tiny vacuum with a burst, and that is that.[9]

A weak metaphor typically fogs up like a windshield, obscuring our view of the main idea. Compare these two figures from the same magazine:

> Technology has given Goliath a club so heavy he cannot lift it. And it has given every David a sling: mass communications.[10]

> The American landscape is littered with the hulks of federal social programs—launched amid noisy trumpetry from on high—which have subsequently been dismembered, truncated for lack of funds, or strangled by the problems they set out to conquer.[11]

The first of these images concisely embodies the author's whole argument, namely that technology has enhanced human freedom instead of constricting it. Warfare, his article maintains, is becoming obsolete because the destructive power of weapons is now too large for them to be used effectively for political ends; and mass communications have meanwhile given ordinary people access to information and power they never possessed before. The image of David and

Goliath epitomizes this case in two brief, unpretentious, but emphatic sentences.

What about the second example? Here is a labored metaphor of a landscape covered with junk. It begins with an air of authority, but then new and inconsistent elements are rushed in to keep the sentence from sagging. Federal social programs, first likened to ships that were *launched* and are now *hulks*, are littering the whole *American landscape*. Ships in Kansas? And is a ship *dismembered*, much less *strangled?* The author seems to have forgotten that the image in view is an inanimate object. Does a ship, furthermore, *set out to conquer problems?* The whole sentence has an air of empty, confused grandeur.

The technical term to describe such a clash of figures is *mixed metaphor*. A mixed metaphor isn't a succession of distinct images, but an awkward inconsistency within an image that's still being developed. If one image is unmistakably finished, you're free to take up a new one; a truly mixed metaphor is one that can't be visualized without absurdity. President Eisenhower once created a classic mixed metaphor when he remarked that *The Japanese have a tough row to hoe to keep their economic heads above water.* Thinking in clichés rather than in concrete images, the President called up a picture of farmers hoeing their rice paddies while neck-deep in water.

More mixed metaphors result from clichés, in fact, than from deliberate efforts at figurative expression. Most ordinary terms, and nearly all clichés, are *dead metaphors*—that is, they contain latent implications of an image but aren't usually intended to evoke it. When clichés are used in close succession, they revive each other and become mischievously vivid:

✗ The community should vomit up this moral question mark.
✗ Climbing to the heights of oratory, the candidate tackled the issue.
✗ Either we get a handle on these problems or we are all going down the drain.

And sometimes a cliché-metaphor isn't exactly mixed, but just lamely abandoned:

✗ I would like to rattle all the skeletons in the current outlook.
✗ He had no intention of providing grist for this debate.

If you're going to *rattle skeletons* at all, they have to be in a *closet;* and *grist for the mill*, uninspired in itself, is made still more unacceptable by being left incomplete.

Test your sense of metaphor, finally, against these sentences written by two political analysts:

The wave of political reaction which has threatened to engulf the left since 1968 has certainly not been broken, and, although it only hovers in the wings of this study, the immediate concerns it generates occupy a stage front position in the minds of the authors. However, only a larger historical and theoretical context can begin to light the way beyond the impasse we face.[12]

Here the metaphors are themselves mostly clichés: *wave of reaction, hover in the wings, stage front position, light the way.* Reaching always for the nearest phrase, the authors create an image of a giant wave quivering at the side of a stage while *the immediate concerns it generates* (everything is suddenly abstract) *occupy a stage front position* (we're back in the aquatic theater after all). And what will *light the way?* Not a lamp, but a *context.* To light the way beyond an impasse, incidentally, makes as much sense as to turn left at a dead end. If you can get beyond it at all, it isn't an impasse. The authors simply aren't listening to the sense of the words they've chosen.

Metaphors, then, are as treacherous as they are useful. When you intend an abstract meaning, you have to make sure that your dead metaphors stay good and dead. And when you do wish to be figurative, see whether you're getting the necessary vividness and consistency. If not, go back to literal statement; it's better to make plain assertions than to litter your verbal landscape with those strangled hulks.

EXERCISES

I. After consulting your dictionary (see pp. 100–105 of this chapter), briefly define in your own words both terms in each of the following pairs:

1. accent, accentuate *(verbs)*
2. accused, suspected *(adjectives)*
3. adverse, averse
4. alternate, alternative *(adjectives)*
5. barbaric, barbarous
6. childish, childlike
7. elemental, elementary
8. healthful, healthy
9. infect, infest
10. possible, feasible

II. Using your dictionary, explain the chief differences of meaning between the following paired words:

1. ample, excessive
2. policeman, cop
3. cunning, politic
4. overhear, spy
5. ecstatic, happy
6. bold, brash
7. erotic, lustful
8. impartial, indifferent
9. simulate, fake
10. opponent, enemy

III. Use your dictionary, if necessary, to help you decide which level of diction (formal, middle, or informal) is illustrated by each of the following words. Wherever you label a word as formal or informal, provide a middle-level equivalent (pp. 105–106):

1. irritate
2. hyperbole
3. birdbrain
4. groovy
5. fluoridate
6. refractory *(adjective)*
7. indemnify
8. gal
9. oafish
10. resist

IV. For each of the following middle-level words, give one formal and one informal equivalent:

1. friend
2. understand
3. smell *(noun)*
4. clothes
5. rob
6. see
7. idea
8. change *(verb)*
9. leave *(verb)*
10. good

V. Rewrite the following sentences to eliminate any needlessly formal diction, euphemisms, redundancies, circumlocutions, jargon, or clichés (pp. 105–111):

1. Welcome to the Heavenly Lift-Off Funeral Home; in the adjacent chamber you may visit with the departed one.
2. Biff paid handsome tribute to his coach for instructing him in the desirability of being physical with competitors sporting rival colors.
3. It is certain and beyond question that Dr. Dollar will take every conceivable advantage of the Internal Revenue provisions that pertain to his medical and authorial vocation.
4. The company announced today that certain facilities, along with their attendant personnel, would henceforth be granted an indefinite respite from utilization in view of demand slackness throughout the consumer sector.
5. Crazy Hoarse made no bones about his dissatisfaction; he put his foot down and said, straight from the shoulder, that a little million-dollar contract dispute with Acne Records shouldn't nip in the bud his hopes of having "Should I Hug Ya or Mug Ya?" played in every home from sea to shining sea.

VI. Here is a fictitious letter making fun of a certain "official" style. Pick out several examples of jargon (pp. 109–111) in the letter, and comment on the way they convey or disguise meaning:

Dear Miss Dodds:

Thank you for your letter deploring the 14,000 fish deaths apparently related to thermal outflow into Long Island Sound from our nuclear power facility at Squaw Point. While the blame for this regrettable incident might most properly be ascribed to the fish, which swam closer to the Connecticut shore than is their normal habit, we believe that the ultimate solution must be found in terms of "the human element." Specifically, it is a task of public education in this era when customer demand for power markedly exceeds the deliverability capability of the electrical segment of the energy usage industry.

Do you ever stop to think, Miss Dodds, where the power comes from when you flick on your air-conditioner, your hair dryer, your cake mixer, your vacuum cleaner, and the myriad other appliances that enable you to live in "the lap of luxury" vs. the meager subsistence standard enjoyed by most of the peoples of the world? Until the American housewife is willing to go back to the egg beater and the broom, the utilities industry cannot be made the scapegoat for occasional episodes of ecological incompatibility.

Many consumers today advocate "zero growth" and a turning back of the clock to a simpler agrarian past. Quite frankly, if the rural

American of 1900 had been as counter-oriented to the ongoing thrust of technology as certain romantic elements are in 1973, the outhouse would never have been supplanted by the flush toilet.

Very truly yours,

NORMAN R. HOWELL
Vice President for Consumer Relations
AFFILIATED UTILITIES COMPANY[13]

VII. Rewrite the following sentences to avoid words used in awkward or offensive constructions (pp. 111–113):

1. Betsy was enthused to discover that her relating to men problems, along with all other problems, were covered in Dr. Dollar's new book.
2. He gifted her with an autographed copy of the work he had authored.
3. Any reasonable person and his wife or girlfriend could learn something from Dr. Dollar.
4. Betsy was unsure how literally to interpret the publisher's complete-satisfaction-guaranteed assurance.
5. She didn't know whether to believe Dr. Dollar's assertion that the universe was already pulsating with all the love a chick could wish, but she knew that *Three Easy Steps to Perfection* was a start-to-finish good read.

VIII. Rewrite these sentences to make them more vivid and concrete (pp. 114–116):

1. He attended scheduled sessions at the institution of higher learning with unfailing regularity.
2. Daytime serial dramatic programs had her undivided concentration.
3. The smaller rodents are of lasting interest to cats, who would never willingly forgo an opportunity for the pursuit and seizure of same.
4. In northern regions, conspicuous display of emotions on the part of members of the populace is rather the exception than the rule.
5. Loss of control of one's sense of reality has come to be recognized by courts of law as a factor tending to favor the acquittal of a defendant who was afflicted in that manner.

IX. Professor X describes himself as follows in a classified advertisement:

Sophisticated, debonair college prof., 35, recently divorced, with liberal values and classical tastes, seeks broadminded female companion for travel and cultural pursuits. Knowledge of vintage wines and modern verse desirable. Send photo. Box 307, NYR.

What do you think Professor X is really like? Write a paragraph describing him *vividly*, and then underline all the concrete diction you have used.

X. Without reversing the meaning of these negatively framed sentences, make them more emphatic by replacing *not* constructions with stronger words (pp. 116–117):

    1. It is not unlikely that Biff will try to return his own kickoff.
    2. A person who does not go into cities when it is not necessary will not experience some fine pleasures.
    3. The Easter Bunny didn't like hearing himself described as a basket case.
    4. He did not agree with the mental-health experts who did not approve of hiding painted eggs in gardens.
    5. Few of his critics, he suspected, weren't subject to little quirks of their own that didn't harm anyone.

XI. List all the metaphors you find in the following passage, and briefly discuss the relation of each metaphor to the one preceding it. Do you find any problems of effectiveness here? If so, explain (pp. 117–121):

> Academics, it has been said before, are very much like people who drive their cars by looking through their rear-view mirrors. Looking backward does offer certain satisfactions and provides splendid intellectual vistas, but it hardly brings into focus the best view of the road ahead. Academics may seem to bemoan the fact that the federals now hold the cards, and that they must do their bidding, however reluctantly. But the facts would appear to be otherwise: it is the federals who are at least trying to game-plan an extremely delicate future, while most academics remain on the sidelines, seized by fits of moral indignation about the felt deprivation of their intellectual autonomy. It would rarely occur to them that the federal planners would like nothing better than a showing of academia's own imaginative initiatives and social vision, if only they would gird themselves for that sort of resolve.[14]

XII. Using what you have learned about types of diction, write an essay of 500–750 words analyzing the diction of a columnist in a local paper. Don't run through a set list of subjects borrowed from this chapter. Rather, clip and study the author's columns for several days and plan your emphasis around the traits you find most noteworthy in his or her work.

NOTES

[1]Roy H. Copperud, *American Usage: The Consensus* (New York: Van Nostrand Reinhold, 1970), p. 97.

[2]A. J. Liebling, *The Sweet Science* (New York: Viking, 1956), pp. 299–300.

[3]James Herndon, *How to Survive in Your Native Land* (New York: Simon and Schuster, 1971), p. 122.

[4]Norman Hackerman, "The Future of Graduate Education, If Any," *Science*, 175 (4 Feb. 1972), 475.

[5]Frank Conroy, *Stop-time* (New York: Viking, 1967), pp. 114–15.

[6]Talcott Parsons, "The Kinship System of the Contemporary United States," in *Essays in Sociological Theory*, rev. ed. (1949, 1954; rpt. New York: Free Press, 1964), p. 191.

[7]Ernest Hemingway, *A Moveable Feast* (1964; rpt. New York: Bantam, 1965), p. 3.

[8]Norman Mailer, *Miami and the Siege of Chicago: An Informal History of the Republican and Democratic Conventions of 1968* (New York: Signet, 1968), pp. 11–12.

[9]Saul Bellow, *Herzog* (1964; rpt. New York: Viking, 1967), p. 290.

[10]Lewis M. Branscomb, "Taming Technology," *Science*, 171 (12 Mar. 1971), 973.

[11]Constance Holden, "Community Mental Health Centers: Storefront Therapy and More," *Science*, 174 (17 Dec. 1971), 1221.

[12]Greg Calvert and Carol Neiman, *A Disrupted History: The New Left and the New Capitalism* (New York: Random House, 1971), p. 8.

[13]William Zinsser, "Frankly, Miss Dodds," *Atlantic*, Apr. 1973, p. 94.

[14]G[eorge] W. B[onham], "The Decline of Initiative," *Change*, Apr. 1973, p. 16.

SENTENCES

"A sentence," wrote Henry Thoreau, "should read as if its author, had he held a plow instead of a pen, could have drawn a furrow deep and straight to the end." The image is memorable but not easily translated into practice, as Thoreau's own work reveals. *A Week on the Concord and Merrimack Rivers*, where this statement appears, is a peculiar example of verbal plowing, with more zigzags and arabesques than straight furrows. Thoreau's advice was probably directed at himself: he was trying to reform the bookish manner he had acquired at Harvard in the 1830's, and as yet he wasn't having much success. If he later became a master stylist, it wasn't simply by continual writing, but by progressively simplifying his prose — indulging in fewer quotations and reveries, exercising greater concreteness and sharper wit. Thoreau's sentences began approaching his ideal when he spoke directly to his countrymen instead of daydreaming in their presence.

If, like the young Thoreau, you tend to write somewhat windy sentences, you too should work toward a plainer style. But if your sentences are too brief, with little subordination and a monotonous sameness of pattern, you must revise in the direction of complexity and flexibility. Following one master plan for sentence construction won't do. The point is to take the skills you already have and develop them, gradually eliminating weaknesses that you or others have noticed in your prose.

This chapter assumes that you know what a sentence is and what its essential elements are (pp. 264–266). Many things that can go wrong with sentences—blunders of usage, spelling, and punctuation, inappropriate word choices, illogic—are treated elsewhere. If, for example, your main problems are with faulty agreement or predication, fragmentary sentences, misrelated modifiers, and the like, you should concentrate on Chapter Eleven before going further.

Sooner or later, though, you will have the elements of formal correctness under control and will want to find the best ways of *making sentences convey your meaning effectively*. This is our concern here. The points of advice below indicate how you can phrase your statements definitely; place coordinate thoughts in coordinate structures; subordinate to sharpen the relation between main assertions and modifying elements; eliminate unnecessary words; vary your sentence structure; maintain consistency of tone; and smooth the general flow of your words. Work especially on those points that correspond to recognized difficulties in your writing. You will find that seemingly minor improvements—the moving of a clause from one position to another, a shift from the passive to the active voice, even a slight change in rhythm—can make the difference between drab sentences and pointed ones.

DEFINITE STATEMENT

Avoid Irrelevancy

A sentence is typically a single unified statement. Even if it consists of several independent parts linked by commas or semicolons, those parts ought to be logically related. Don't allow incompatible elements to weaken the whole:

x Computers, *whose memory capacity has been increasing rapidly in recent years*, would have had a major influence on the conduct of World War II if they had existed sooner.

The italicized clause has nothing to do with the point of the sentence; instead of simply registering that point, we have to juggle conflicting references to the 1940's and the 1970's. The sentence should be shortened and rearranged to bring out its "if-then" logic: *If computers had been available in time, they would have had a major influence on the conduct of World War II.*

Make Real Assertions

Try to avoid sentences that simply mark time between other statements, or that assert vague or self-evident truths:

x There are, of course, two sides to every question.
x It is interesting to consider this problem more closely.
x Let us remember that the full story won't be known until all the facts have been assembled.
x As inflation continues unchecked, prices are steadily rising.

Make every sentence count. "Filler" sentences naturally occur in first drafts as you feel your way toward meaning, but you should eliminate them after they've served their purpose.

Rely on the Active Voice

An *active* verb, as in *Max ate the chili dog,* shows that the grammatical subject (*Max*) is doing the acting. A passive verb, as in *Max was taken to the emergency room,* shows that the grammatical subject is being acted upon (see pp. 271–272). The great majority of sentences deserve to be cast in the active form, which highlights both the agent (*Max*) and the act performed (*ate the chili dog*). But a passive construction is sometimes called for, too. In *Max was taken to the emergency room,* the agent of the action—perhaps some anonymous hospital orderly—is properly de-emphasized in favor of poor Max, who is the center of concern. The writer needn't feel guilty, for the sentence says just what it should.

But habitual use of the passive is another matter. It makes for a colorless, evasive, and sometimes ambiguous impression, and it disguises the relation between the doer and the thing done. Compare these sets of active and passive statements:

passive	active
It is believed by the candidate that a ceiling must be placed on the budget by Congress.	The candidate believes that Congress must place a ceiling on the budget.
The consequences of a thermonuclear war could not be escaped by any country in the world.	No country in the world could escape the consequences of a thermonuclear war.
Their motives were applauded by us, but their wisdom was doubted.	We applauded their motives but doubted their wisdom.

In each instance the active construction is more vivid and succinct. Note especially that, in the passive versions, prepositional phrases using *by* occupy more or less clumsy positions: *by the candidate, by any country*, etc. This is bound to happen when the agent of action differs from the grammatical subject.

Look through your drafts to locate passive constructions, and ask yourself in each case whether the passive form conveys some special emphasis that you want to retain. Wherever it doesn't, switch to active verbs.

COORDINATION

The devices that link elements within a sentence fall into two general groups, those that *coordinate* and those that *subordinate*. In coordination, the elements are given equal value: *a or b; a and b; a, b, and c; of a, of b, and of c;* etc. In subordination, one element serves to limit or support or explain the other: *although a, nevertheless b; since a, therefore b; seeing a, she did b; if not for a, b would win;* etc. The one controlling rule is that coordination and subordination should reflect your meaning. Coordinate when, and only when, you want to give the same weight to all the items being linked. Subordinate when, and only when, you want to place limitations or conditions on a main idea (pp. 135–141).

Coordinate to Show That Ideas Belong Together

Compare the following passages:

A. Animals think, but they think *of* and *at* things; men think primarily *about* things. Words, pictures, and memory images are symbols that may be combined and varied in a thousand ways.[1]

B. Animals think *of* things. They also think *at* things. Men think primarily *about* things. Words are symbols that may be combined in a thousand ways. They can also be varied in the same number of ways. This can be said of pictures as well. The same holds true for memory images.

Passage B is an attempt to convey the meaning of passage A without recourse to coordination. Two sentences have become seven, thirty-one words have become fifty-one, yet the longer passage is much harder to understand than the shorter one. The reason is that B lacks A's signals of coordinate structure—signals that immediately show us which ideas belong together.

In A we have:

1. coordinate clauses:

Animals think,
       but
they think *of* and *at* things

2. coordinate halves of a sentence:

Animals think, but they think *of* and *at* things;
men think primarily *about* things

3. coordinate prepositions:

of
       and
at

4. coordinate nouns in a series:

words,
pictures,
       and
memory images

5. coordinate past participles:

combined
       and
varied

6. a repeated word:

think
think
think

Each of these instances of coordination serves the author's meaning by putting related thoughts into sentence positions that make the relation immediately clear. Those thoughts are now structurally *parallel* (pp. 319–321).

Elements joined by a coordinating device should be comparable in meaning, but they needn't be strictly symmetrical in form. When they are, the special effect of *balance* occurs. Compare:

COORDINATE BUT NOT BALANCED:
x Love of country is admirable, but I think that it is more important today to love the human species as a whole.

COORDINATE AND BALANCED:
- Love of country is a virtue; love of the human species, a necessity.

Balanced structures are especially noticeable in *aphorisms* — that is, in memorable sentences conveying a very general assertion:

- What is *written without effort* is in general *read without pleasure*. (Samuel Johnson)
- We must indeed *all hang together,* or, most assuredly, we shall *all hang separately.* (Benjamin Franklin)
- Democracy substitutes *election by the incompetent many* for *appointment by the corrupt few*. (George Bernard Shaw)

Obviously you don't want to write whole essays in this highly formal manner. But when not overused, balanced structures can be an excellent means of gaining emphasis.

Repeat Words, Phrases, and Clauses for Emphasis

A repeated sentence element always draws attention. If the repetition is rhetorically meaningless, it constitutes *redundancy*, a distracting failure to get ahead with the essay's business. But there are many opportunities in a typical essay for effectively pointed repetition. Thus in the following sentences, which abound with coordinating devices, the name *Ottawa* (italicized here for emphasis) is artfully plucked out from other names:

> Perhaps a visitor cannot truly understand the country until he has traveled from the genteel poverty of the Atlantic coast with its picturesque fishing villages and stiff towns through the Frenchness of sophisticated Quebec cities and rural landscapes, past the vigorous bustling Ontario municipalities and industrial vistas, over mile after mile of wheat fields between prairie settlements into the lush and spacious beauty of British Columbia; but he must also visit *Ottawa* and the House of Commons. *Ottawa* the stuffy, with its dull-looking houses, its blistering summer heat, its gray rainy afternoons; *Ottawa* the beautiful, on a snowy day when the government buildings stand tall and protective, warmly solid above the white landscape; on a sunny spring afternoon with the cool river winding below, and people moving easily through the clean streets, purposeful but not pushed. Even during the morning and evening traffic rushes, *Ottawa* seems to remain sane.[2]

In the first sentence *Ottawa* belatedly emerges as the key name among several; it gains importance by being weighted singly against all the "travelogue" references before the semicolon. In the second sentence (or independent sentence fragment) the name is used insistently and fondly. And the author exploits this effect in her final sentence, using the name yet again to reinforce her idea that Ottawa stands apart from the rest of Canada. This, clearly, isn't redundancy but calculated and successful rhetoric.

In the following passage the rhetoric is that of a debater, not a scene-painter. But here too repetition is effective:

> Are we returning to more rigid controls because our recent experience demonstrates that they are an effective method of stopping inflation? Hardly. Consumer prices rose. . . .
>
> Are we returning to more rigid controls because other experience demonstrates that controls are an effective method of stopping inflation? Hardly. The standard life-history of controls — documented time and again — is initial apparent success. . . .
>
> Are we returning to more rigid controls because economic reasoning demonstrates that they are an effective method of stopping inflation? Hardly. A few economists — John Kenneth Galbraith is the most prominent — argue that they are. But for two centuries and more, most economists have regarded controls as an attack on symptoms, not causes. . . .[3]

Here the author's repetitions are like the authoritative pounding of a fist on a table. His insistence may seem excessive, but in context, with full paragraphs between the question-answer pairs, the passage conveys a balance between indignation and logic, challenge and hard evidence.

Make Your Series Consistent and Climactic

A series of coordinated items, whether they be single words, phrases, or clauses, is often an effective means of making a concise, logical, and crisply energetic effect. Of course, you must be careful to keep your syntax and punctuation in order, or the series will become a mere jumble (see pp. 319–320, 334). In addition, you should be sure that the items really belong together and that they occur in the most emphatic order.

You don't want to write, for example, *She gathers pears, apples, and assorted fruits;* the third category, *fruits,* overlaps with the first two. Nor should you toss in items of markedly different importance:

x Travelers in this part of the country fall in love with *the fields of waving grain, the infinite sky,* and *the deluxe jumboburgers.*

Such effects of anticlimax are good for a laugh, but embarrassing if the laugh is unexpected.

Although the parts of a series must be parallel in form, they may have different degrees of importance or impact. Since the final position is by far the most emphatic one, that's where the climactic item should go:

- He was prepared to risk everything—*his comfort, his livelihood,* even *his life.*

Put *his life* in either of the other positions in the series and you'll see how vital a climactic order is.

SUBORDINATION

Subordination, the placing of certain elements in modifying roles, is a fundamental principle of writing. Adjectives and adverbs, phrases of all types, and subordinate clauses all serve to specify or qualify words that convey primary meaning. There are, to be sure, ways of making a technically subordinate element more prominent than anything else in its sentence, but in general, subordination is the main device for indicating the difference between core statements and elements of support or elaboration.

Subordinate to Show Which Is the Main Statement

In a set of consecutive sentences, some remarks will inevitably be dependent in meaning on others. They should be made dependent in structure as well. It would be imprecise, for example, to write:

x The government collects billions of dollars in taxes, *and* it must meet its own obligations.

To be sure, the coordinating conjunction *for* in place of *and* would sharpen the sentence. But devices of subordination would be even more appropriate:

- *Because* the government must meet its own obligations, it collects billions of dollars in taxes.
- The government collects billions of dollars in taxes *so that* it can meet its own obligations.
- *By* collecting billions of dollars in taxes, the government manages to meet its obligations.

Words like *because, so that,* and *by* allow us to see at once that a limitation is to be placed on an otherwise independent assertion.

The following pairs of sentences illustrate some of the details and relations that typically (though not always) belong in subordinate constructions. The sentences in the right column are more precisely focused, sparing us the trouble of deciding which idea is the main one.

	without subordination	with subordination
Time	The earthquake struck, and then everyone panicked.	Everyone panicked *when* the earthquake struck.
Place	William Penn founded a city of brotherly love. He chose the juncture of the Delaware and Schuylkill rivers.	*Where* the Schuylkill River joins the Delaware, William Penn founded a city of brotherly love.
Cause	She was terrified of large groups, and debating was not for her.	*Because* she was terrified of large groups, she decided against being a debater.
Concession	He claimed to despise Vermont. He went there every summer.	*Although* he claimed to despise Vermont, he went there every summer.
Condition	She probably won't be able to afford a waterbed. The marked retail prices are just too high.	*Unless* she can get a discount, she probably won't be able to afford a waterbed.
Exception	The grass is dangerously dry this year. Of course I'm not referring to watered lawns.	*Except for* watered lawns, the grass is dangerously dry this year.
Purpose	The Senators moved to Texas. They hoped to find more enthusiastic supporters there.	The Senators moved to Texas *in search of* more enthusiastic supporters.
Description	The late Edward Steichen showed his reverence for life in arranging the famous exhibit "The Family of Man," and he was a pioneer photographer himself.	The late Edward Steichen, *himself a pioneer photographer*, showed his reverence for life in arranging the famous exhibit "The Family of Man."

The spelling out of logical relationships in each right-hand example makes for greater clarity and control.

Subordinate to Avoid Monotony

Although it's impossible to write without using some degree of sub-ordination, some people rely excessively on independent clauses (p. 264) to carry their meaning. The near-absence of modifying clauses and phrases gives their prose a clumsy, staccato effect, as if they were grudgingly answering questions instead of pursuing their thoughts. Compare these passages:

A. The AFL under George Meany has been accused of favoring an aggressive foreign policy. The accusation is entirely justified. But critics may not realize that there is nothing new about this. The first president of the AFL, Samuel Gompers, advocated American expansionism. Labor has tended to suffer under peacetime administrations and to prosper under wartime ones. Leaders of the AFL don't like to point this out in so many words. But they have consistently advocated a pugnacious American stand toward rival nations. They have probably been motivated by self-interest.

B. Although the AFL under George Meany has been justly accused of favoring an aggressive foreign policy, this is no break with the past; the union has advocated expansionism since the days of its first president, Samuel Gompers. Labor has tended to suffer under peacetime administrations and to prosper under wartime ones. While AFL leaders don't like to point this out in so many words, it is clear that self-interest underlies their pugnacity toward America's rivals.

Passage A, containing one subordinate clause (*that there is nothing new about this*), takes seven rigid sentences to say what passage B says in three varied ones. The entire second sentence of A has been condensed in B into one subordinate word, *justly*. Where passage A leaves the reader to decide which statements have prime importance, passage B saves its independent clauses for the major ideas. And note, above all, that the choppiness of A is remedied in B, where one brief and straightforward sentence stands between two complicated ones.

Subordinate to Break up Lengthy Compound Sentences

Some writers, anxious to avoid a string of brief, abrupt sentences, loop independent clauses together with coordinating conjunctions. But the resulting *compound sentences* aren't much of an improvement:

x The right to secede is very dubious, *and* perhaps it shouldn't be considered a right at all, *for* it threatens the existing order, *and* that order denies the right in the first place.

Subordinate clauses or phrases can tighten the loose joints:

- Perhaps the right to secede, *dubious at best*, shouldn't be considered a right at all. Can the existing order grant a right *that threatens its own existence?*

One difficult sentence has become two clear ones, thanks largely to the use of subordination.

Choose an Appropriate Means of Subordination

Depending on the degree of attention you want a subordinate element to receive, you can decide to allot it a word, a phrase, or a clause. Other things being equal,

1. clauses tend to be most emphatic;
2. phrases tend to be less emphatic;
3. words tend to be least emphatic.

Thus:

- George listened *politely* as Susan's lawyer explained why she should have custody of their goldfish and parakeet.

  The single adverb *politely* is unemphatic.

- George listened *with determined politeness* as Susan's lawyer etc.

  Emphasis is gained through use of a prepositional phrase containing a modifier.

- George, *whose politeness never wavered*, listened as Susan's lawyer etc.

  The subordinate clause is still more emphatic.

- Although he had to listen in silence as Susan's lawyer explained why she should have custody . . ., *George never allowed his politeness to waver.*

  The writer has decided to make the formerly subordinate element into the main statement; it has now become an independent clause.

Place Subordinate Elements Where They Will Convey Your Exact Meaning

Native speakers usually have a good intuitive sense of where to place adjectives and most adverbs. But because adverbs are more flexible in position than adjectives, they sometimes cause problems of awkwardness and ambiguity. Shadings of meaning are controlled by the position of an adverb:

- *Only* I can understand your argument. [No one else can.]
- I can *only* understand your argument. [I can't agree with it.]
- I can understand *only* your argument. [But not your motives; *or* The arguments of others mystify me.]

Although most adverbs belong immediately before the words they modify, emphasis and sentence rhythm may sometimes dictate other positions if there's no danger of ambiguity. The placement of *sentence adverbs*—conjunctive adverbs like *therefore* and *however*—is especially flexible. Unlike other adverbs, sentence adverbs place a stress on the words that immediately precede them:

- I, *however*, refuse to comply. [I contrast myself with others.]
- I refuse, *however*, to comply. [My refusal is emphatic.]

In the initial and final positions, sentence adverbs are less emphatic and more diffuse in effect:

- *However*, I refuse to comply.
- I refuse to comply, *however*.

The final position is the least emphatic of all.

Some authorities recommend that sentence adverbs never be used in the initial position, but most people ignore this supposed rule. What you must avoid is a monotonous, automatic choice. Put your adverbs where they'll convey the particular modifying effect and the degree of stress you intend.

The same advice applies to larger subordinate elements as well. It isn't enough to avoid the outright blunders of misrelated and dangling modifiers (pp. 315–317) that can destroy whole sentences. You also have to consider which of two "correct" positions most clearly expresses your meaning. The following sentences make quite different assertions:

- He knew that he had been a coward throughout the great battle.
- Throughout the great battle he knew that he had been a coward.

The first sentence describes a *later* thought about cowardice *in* the battle. In the second sentence the soldier realizes, *during* the battle, that he has *formerly* been a coward. The position you assign your subordinate elements won't usually make such a fundamental change of meaning as this, but it will always contribute something to the way the sentence is understood.

You can usually discover which positions are emphatic by reading a sentence over, trying each alternative in turn. When in doubt, remember that:

1. Subordinate elements tend to gain emphasis whenever they appear in unexpected (but not awkward) positions:

* *With heroic determination* he continued to stay afloat.

2. Main elements are usually most emphatic at the end of a sentence:

* In spite of the apparent hopelessness of his situation, *he somehow knew he would be rescued.*

3. Main elements are least emphatic when they appear neither at the beginning nor at the end:

* In spite of the apparent hopelessness of his situation, *he knew he would be rescued,* without being able to say how he knew it.

The position you assign a subordinate element can make for a subtle difference of connotation. Compare these sentences:

* *Although Patsy still loves Paul,* she has finally asked him to choose between her and his set of electric trains.
* Patsy has finally asked Paul to choose between her and his set of electric trains, *although she still loves him.*

In the first sentence, the subordinate clause occupies a subordinate position; it opposes a main statement that literally has the last word. In the second sentence, the main statement is weakened by being placed first and then chipped away by the *although* clause. Instead of feeling that Patsy has made her decision once and for all, we wonder whether she hasn't already begun to change her mind.

Subordinate in One Direction per Sentence

A sentence can contain several subordinate elements if each of them has a clear and useful function. But even if your modifying elements aren't technically misrelated (pp. 315–316), they can end in a tangle. Look at this sentence:

x Although he was reluctant to accuse Patsy of sabotage, Paul wondered why his toy freight train had exploded, because he hadn't been playing "munitions shipment" at the time, although he did have some gunpowder in the basement.

Here there is one main clause, *Paul wondered why his freight train had exploded.* If the sentence ended after *exploded* there would be no problem; the structure would be *Although a, b.* What we actually have is *Although a, b, because c, although d.* This is too much twisting and turning for a reader to bear without discomfort. Once you have launched a subordinate clause in the direction of an *although*, a *because*, an *unless*, etc., you have committed the whole sentence to a basic movement of thought: *although a, b; because a, b; unless a, b*. When you then begin qualifying *b* (the main clause), you are hacking away at the effectiveness of your own statement. Take care of the extra qualifications in a new sentence:

• Although he was reluctant to accuse Patsy of sabotage, Paul wondered why his toy freight train had exploded. It is true that he had some gunpowder in the basement, but he hadn't been playing "munitions shipment" at the time.

CONCISENESS

The fewer words you can use without sacrificing essential meaning or falling into a choppy style (pp. 142–145), the better chance you stand of being attentively read. This is partly a matter of avoiding redundancy and circumlocutions (pp. 107–108), but there are other means of economizing as well. Look, in your early drafts, for cluttered heaps of words, and try to recast each whole thought succinctly:

wordy	concise
in the event that he finds it possible to get away and make the trip	if he can come
There aren't many things that cause a person to feel worse than he does when the time comes for him to pack up his bags and say farewell to his parents' home.	Leaving home is always difficult.
He wondered how in the world a woman like her could summon up the sheer nerve to cause him so much pain when there had been no reason to expect anything of the sort from her.	How could she do this to him?

No doubt some scrap of information is lost in trading the wordy examples for the concise ones, but the gain in sharpness is far more important. It does no good to lavish details on a reader who has fallen asleep.

Often the most effective way to be concise is to reduce a clause to a phrase, or a phrase to a word:

CLAUSE:
• although she was in a hurry

PHRASE:
• feeling hurried

WORD:
• hurriedly

Take the following sentence and see how it can be improved:

• At the present time, the realities of nuclear terror are such that countries that possess equal power find, when they oppose each other, that the weapons that carry the most force are precisely the weapons they cannot use.

There are no errors of usage here, but neither is there any snap. The conspicuousness of *that* reveals the problem: elements that might have been put into single words and phrases have been allowed to bloat into full clauses. Compare:

• In this age of nuclear terror, equal adversaries are equally powerless to use their strongest weapons.

Here thirty-eight words have been compressed into sixteen; clauses have dissolved into phrases and words; and a slack, cud-chewing sentence has become tight and balanced (*equal adversaries are equally powerless*). Notice, too, how the grammatical core of the sentence is no longer empty of meaning: not *realities are such* but *adversaries are powerless*. Strong, message-bearing elements of thought have been moved into naturally prominent positions, where they belong.

VARIETY

No one sentence pattern is right for all occasions, and one sentence creates the expectations against which the next sentence will be heard. If, for example, you follow one complex construction with another one, you're probably subtracting emphasis from both of them; your reader needs a little breathing space before granting you another extraordinary effort of attention. You have to pace yourself, either by reading your prose and listening for the spots where more variety is needed, or, second best, by systematically checking to see that one sentence pattern isn't crowding out all others.

Break the Monopoly of Declarative Sentences

Nearly all the sentences in a typical essay will be declarative—that is, they will make statements—but an occasional question or, less frequently, an exclamation can vary the pattern. One standard way of organizing a paragraph is to open with a question and then to supply a detailed answer. Thus Rachel Carson asks, "Why does the spider mite appear to thrive on insecticides?"[4] There are, she says, three likely reasons, and she proceeds to spell them out. Here the question is simply a blunt way of letting the reader know what issue the paragraph will address. But precisely because the question is a standard opening device, you should be careful not to overuse it.

You can also resort to an occasional *rhetorical question*, one that requires no answer. Once again you should be wary of overuse, for rhetorical questions can sound melodramatic. But observe the sensitive use to which Jason Epstein puts such a question as he considers his involvement with New York City:

> In desperate fantasy one thinks, at times, of escaping. From childhood there remains a faint memory, nearly lost, of a stream in a Northern forest: a stone dam, a trickling sluice, a hut of some sort where the dam-keeper lives. The loon cries over a lake, the pines stretch endlessly, black against the sky. And then one thinks of *The New York Times* on Sunday, five pounds of newsprint, a million-and-a-half copies a week. How many miles of forest, birds flung from their nests, the work of honey bees wasted, does our Sunday paper, thrown aside between breakfast and lunch, consume?[5]

This passage starts to undermine its own "desperate fantasy" after the third sentence, and the question completes that process by linking the two previous thoughts—the fantasy of a forest escape and the reality of the Sunday *Times*—in a dawning realization that New York is devouring nature itself. The paragraph might well have ended with an exclamation point instead of a question mark, but that would have expressed outrage rather than ironic reflection.

If you do use exclamations in your own writing, use them seldom and only at moments of climactic emphasis. You may want to show that a certain idea is exciting, but you don't want to sound constantly upset.

Vary the Order and Complexity of Sentence Elements

We have seen that a lack of subordination is one of the most common weaknesses of style. Otherwise stated, *simple* and *compound* sentences — those containing no subordinate clauses — too often prevail over *complex* and *compound-complex* sentences, which do contain at least one subordinate clause apiece (see p. 441). Although a relentless use of any one sentence type is monotonous, the inherent flatness of simple and compound sentences makes them especially tedious when placed in a row. The remedy is to revise toward complexity of structure wherever your meaning allows it.

Here are two passages conveying exactly the same information:

x The high snow in the Wasatch Mountains is light and dry. You can't make a snowball out of it. This is Utah powder. It makes for some of the West's greatest skiing. The numerous slopes are regularly groomed. The snow crunches under your skis. It forgives your rusty technique. It gives gently under your fall. There is deep, new powder in the back bowls. You float up and over the ground. Plumes of white mist curl around your waist like smoke.

• The snow that falls high in the Wasatch Mountains is so light and dry that you can't make a snowball out of it. This is Utah powder, and it makes for some of the West's greatest skiing. On the numerous slopes that are regularly groomed, the snow crunches under your skis, forgiving if your technique is rusty, giving gently if you fall. On the deep new powder of the back bowls, you float up and over the ground, plumes of white mist curling around your waist like smoke.[6]

The second passage, with its pleasant mixture of simple, compound, and complex sentences, "feels like" the easy, exhilarating skiing that it describes. The first passage, consisting entirely of simple sentences, goes almost nowhere in little jerks, like a stalled snowmobile being nudged by its starter motor.

This example also shows that subordinate clauses are by no means the only remedy for flatness. Any sentence element that delays or interrupts the ordinary sequence of subject-verb-object/complement can be a useful instrument of variety. Thus the final sentence of the improved passage, though technically simple (it has just one brief clause, *you float*), has been richly complicated by prepositional and participial phrases that "float" that clause on either side. Note, too, the subtle *a a b b* pattern of development among the four sentences of the passage. The first two sentences begin with their grammatical subjects, matter-of-factly setting the scene; the two intimate, descriptive sentences that follow begin with vivid prepositional phrases.

So, too, though Jason Epstein's sentences on page 143 contain only one subordinate clause, *where the dam-keeper lives*, they make an impression of great flexibility. That feeling comes chiefly from three things: variation in sentence length (from nine to thirty-one words), many pauses for modifying phrases and elements in series, and delay of the grammatical subject:

MODIFYING PHRASE	SUBJECT	VERB	
• In desperate fantasy	one	thinks	

MODIFYING PHRASE		VERB	SUBJECT
• From childhood	there	remains	a faint memory

The most extreme and difficult form of delay occurs in a *suspended* (sometimes called *periodic*) sentence, in which an essential grammatical element is withheld until the end. Suspended sentences generally require greater concentration to be understood; the reader has to keep the unfinished core of meaning in mind while taking in secondary elements:

• How many miles of forest, birds flung from their nests, the work of honey bees wasted, does our Sunday paper, thrown aside between breakfast and lunch, consume?

Until we get that final verb, the whole sentence remains in limbo. Again, look at this suspended sentence by Virginia Woolf:

And, what was even more exciting, she felt, too, as she saw Mr. Ramsay bearing down and retreating, and Mrs. Ramsay sitting with James in the window and the cloud moving and the tree bending, how life, from being made up of little separate incidents which one lived one by one, became curled and whole like a wave which bore one up and threw one down with it, there, with a dash on the beach.[7]

Here the suspended construction is intimately related to the author's meaning. As perceptions come together for Woolf's artist-heroine, the sentence that describes them picks up one leisurely phrase after another, gathers momentum, and becomes itself a wave that crashes in its final words.

Elaborately suspended sentences are usually ambitious, cumulative, conclusive flights of rhetoric. Obviously, then, you shouldn't write several of them in a row. Intricate sentences in general, whether or not they employ suspension, deserve to be relieved by relatively brief and straightforward ones. Woolf's sentence, for example, follows this one: *The sky stuck to them: the birds sang through them.* What you want is never complication for its own sake, but an effortless-looking balance between brisk and fully developed statements.

CONSISTENCY

Sentence-by-sentence variety should occur within a general consistency of style. Because this consistency necessarily differs for every writer, no rules for developing it can be stated. In studying the following examples, however, you may get a feeling for the way good essayists, no matter how many sentence patterns they use, always remain themselves.

Look first at the coldly bitter prose of Imamu Amiri Baraka (LeRoi Jones):

> Being a writer does not necessarily mean that a man will be singular. There are more bad writers than bad atomic scientists. Being sensitive means primarily that you do not like to see lynchings. But the vacuum behind such a circumstance can be, and usually is, immense. Men like Baldwin and Abrahams want to live free from such "ugly" things because (they imply) they simply cannot stand what it does to men.
>
> FACT: There is a racial struggle.
>
> FACT: Any man had better realize what it means. Why there is one. It is the result of *more* than "misunderstanding." Money is not simply something one gets for publishing novels or selling paintings.
>
> FACT: "People should love each other" sounds like Riis Park at sundown. It has very little meaning to the world at large.[8]

This passage is full of apparent defects: the emphatic capitals, the belittling quotation marks, the sentence fragment (*Why there is one*), and the succession of brief, harsh, disconnected sentences. But is Baraka trying to write gracefully and not succeeding? On the contrary, he is insisting on plainness as an ideological matter, a repudiation of "sensitive" people like James Baldwin who, in his opinion, have no stomach for "FACTS." The ugliness of this prose is pointed: the sentences stand apart from one another like those unpleasant truths that novelists and painters had better start facing.

For a more relaxed style, examine these sentences by Pauline Kael:

> What those who believe in the perennial greatness of the Western may not have caught on to is that the new big Western is, likely as not, a studio-set job. What makes it a "Western" is no longer the wide open spaces but the presence of men like John Wayne, James Stewart, Henry Fonda, Robert Mitchum, Kirk Douglas, and Burt Lancaster, grinning with their big new choppers, sucking their guts up into their chests, and hauling themselves onto horses. They are the heroes of a new Western mythology: stars who have aged in the business, who have

survived and who go on dragging their world-famous, expensive car-
casses through the same old motions. That is the essence of their hero-
ism and their legend. The new Western is a joke and the stars play it
for laughs, and the young film enthusiasts react to the heroes not because they represent the mythological heroes of the Old West but because they are mythological movie stars. . . .

. . . Wayne has a beautiful horse in this one — but when he's hoisted
onto it and you hear the thud, you don't know whether to feel sorrier
for man or beast.[9]

Kael writes with the mildly slangy air of an insider who can set us
straight about Hollywood; she holds out an implicit promise of trans-
forming us from naïve "film enthusiasts" into hardened sophisti-
cates who can see "the business" for what it is. Accordingly, her sentences are distinguished by a crisp, purposeful air. Although some of
them are rather long, they have none of the suspended reflectiveness
of Epstein's and Woolf's constructions. A phrase like *a studio-set job*
deliberately breaks the mood of *the perennial greatness of the Western*,
and the active participles *grinning, sucking, hauling*, and *dragging* keep
reminding us of the meaty figures behind the screen images. There is
plenty of variety to Kael's sentence patterns, but note the scarcity of
qualifying phrases; except for *likely as not*, the author never interrupts herself to make small adjustments of meaning. The gross truth
about the movies, she seems to say, requires no embellishment: take
it or leave it.

Finally, this passage from Willie Morris's *Yazoo* can illustrate a
more intricate style:

The most terrible burden of the writer, the common burden that makes
writers a fraternity in blood despite their seasonal expressions of malice, jealousy, antagonism, suspicion, rage, venom, perfidy, competition over the size of publishers' advances — that common burden is the
burden of memory. It is an awesome weight, and if one isn't careful it
can sometimes drive you quite mad. It comes during moments when
one is half asleep, or after a reverie in the middle of the day, or in the
stark waking hours: a remembrance of everything in the most acute
detail from one's past, together with a fine sense of the nuances of old
happenings and the most painful reconsideration of old mistakes, cru-
elties, embarrassments, and sufferings, and all this embroidered and
buttressed by one of the deepest of urges, the urge to dramatize to
yourself about yourself, which is the beginning of at least part of the
urge to create.[10]

If we pause to study this passage we can find some questionable features. Words like *rage, venom, perfidy, awesome*, and *mad* border on

the overdramatic, and the repetitions—four *burdens* in one sentence and three *urges* in another—might be considered excessive. Putting items in series comes so naturally to Morris that it almost seems like a tic instead of a useful device. His syntax, again, is persistently complicated, with only a minor relief in the middle sentence. Yet these features do make a consistent, purposeful effect. The author's sentences are "burdened" as if to match his idea about the burden of memory, and if they just barely survive the load, that too seems to be part of the point. The passage is written confidently, even daringly, and its assurance is contagious.

As you can gather from comparing Baraka, Kael, and Morris, no rule adequately covers the practice of all good writers. An essayist uses sentence patterns not only to make a point, but to make it in a certain manner that amounts to a personal signature. How can you get such effects yourself? Simply by writing often enough, and carefully enough, to acquire your own way of presenting reality.

SOUND

Avoid Distracting Repetitions of Sound

Unless you're after some special effect, don't make your reader conscious of rhymes (*the side of the hide*) or alliteration (*pursuing particular purposes*) or repeated syllables (*apart from the apartment*). These snatches of poetry usually result from an unconscious attraction that words already chosen exert on subsequent choices. Having written *the degradation,* you automatically write *of the nation* because the *-ation* sound is in your head. You may have to read your first draft aloud, attending to its sound and not its sense, in order to find where you've lapsed into jingling.

Abstract Latinate words—the ones that usually end in *-al, -ity, -ation,* or *-otion*—are especially apt to make for redundancy of sound. In Talcott Parsons' sentences on page 115, for example, *functional, essential, occupational,* and *institutional* are too alike, and so are *equality, opportunity,* and *mobility.*

Knowing that repeated sounds draw attention, you can sometimes use them deliberately, as Mark Twain did in referring to

• the *c*alm *c*onfidence of a *C*hristian with four a*c*es,

or as Thomas Paine did in writing

• These are the *times* that *try* men's souls,

or as Theodore Roosevelt did in advising his countrymen to

- Speak softly and carry a big stick.

In these examples the "poetic" quality goes along with a studied attempt to be aphoristic, to "make a phrase." What you must avoid is repetition that makes your words stand out for no apparent reason.

Listen for Sentence Rhythm

Without consciously realizing it, readers will be listening to your prose with what Robert Frost called the audial imagination. There is, as Frost perceived, a "sentence sound," or rather many sentence sounds, whose patterns are deeply fixed in our minds. "You may string words together without a sentence sound to string them on," Frost remarked, "just as you may tie clothes together by the sleeve and stretch them without a clothesline between two trees, but — it is bad for the clothes."[11]

The words in a "sleeve-tied" sentence pull against each other discordantly and oppressively. For instance:

x The subject of rhythm in speech or writing is one of those subjects which deal with complex sets of interrelationships between multiple but not altogether specifiable variables such as rise-fall patterns and the like, which makes it a sea-to-wave and wave-to-wave kind of thing.

There is a near-absence of significant pauses here; we have to plod ahead two or three words at a time, trying not to become dizzy. All the nouns, furthermore, have about the same degree of stress on their accented syllables, and there is no alternation between brief, emphatic phrases and longer ones. Read the sentence aloud and you'll hear its monotony.

Now compare this with the actual words of H. W. Fowler:

Rhythmic speech or writing is like waves of the sea, moving onward with alternating rise and fall, connected yet separate, like but different, suggestive of some law, too complex for analysis or statement, controlling the relations between wave and wave, waves and sea, phrase and phrase, phrases and speech.[12]

Although this sentence is elaborate in structure, we grasp it without much difficulty as it proceeds. Fowler's commas are like architectural supports that spare us the necessity of trying to bear the weight of the whole sentence at once. We see that one main clause is going to govern a sequence of phrases that will carry us along *like waves of the sea,* and our voice pauses naturally on accented syllables: *like wáves of the séa, móving ónward.* These long, heavily stressed vowels make a pleasing contrast with harsher, more staccato phrases like *Rhýthmic spéech or wríting.* Fowler has illustrated his principle of complex relationship in the act of naming it—as, for example, in his "like but different" sets of three-word phrases:

• connected yet separate, like but different
• waves and sea, phrase and phrase, phrases and speech.

To return from Fowler's example to the first one is like going from navigation to seasickness.

For a quite different use of "sentence sounds," listen to this paragraph of Peter Matthiessen's about the Kilimanjaro area of east Africa. Matthiessen, in search of "the tree where man was born," comes across Maasai herdsmen at a pool:

> By the water's edge man squatted, worn rags pulled low over his brow against the sun. Manure smell, flies, the stamp and lowing of the herds, the heat. In the shallows a naked dancing boy darted and splashed. Then cloud shadow dimmed the water shine on his round head, and he turned black. In foreboding he paused; the water stilled, and clouds gathered in the water. He picked at his thin body, one-legged in the evanescent pool that will vanish in summer like the haze of green on this burning land.[13]

This prose gains some of its force from a bunching of strongly accented syllables:

• wáter's édge mán squátted, wórn rágs púlled lów
• Manúre sméll, flíes, the stámp and lówing of the hérds, the héat
• a náked dáncing bóy dárted and spláshed
• Thén clóud shádow dímmed the wáter shíne on his roúnd heád, and he túrned bláck
• the wáter stílled, and cloúds gáthered in the wáter
• He pícked at his thín bódy, óne-légged in the evánéscent póol . . .

The jolting rhythm, accentuated by the shackled nouns *Manure smell, cloud shadow,* and *water shine,* is subtly loosened in the final clause, which comes closer to regular meter—that is, to an alternation of accented and unaccented syllables:

• that will vánish in súmmer like the háze of gréen on this búrning lánd.

Thus the paragraph as a whole accumulates tension and releases it like rain after thunder. The controlled uneasiness of Matthiessen's prose matches the vague ominousness of the scene: human life is precarious in this setting, and any change of weather seems to bear a threat of extinction.

The lesson here is that in reading and writing you should use your ears as well as your brain. The principles that go to make up a pleasing rhythm are too obscure even to formulate, much less to turn into advice; but by reading good stylists you can pick up a general feeling for graceful and emphatic cadences.

EXERCISES

I. Each sentence below illustrates *one* **of the following defects: inclusion of irrelevant detail, self-evidence, or empty generality (pp. 129–130). Name the defect in each instance. Where irrelevant detail is the problem, remove it by rewriting the sentence.**

1. The speaker, who wore a conservative blue suit, never did get around to saying what he meant by his title.
2. The lateness of the train required the engineer to pull into the station behind schedule.
3. Researchers have made little progress in isolating the causes of malignant tumors, whose medical name is *carcinoma*.
4. All things being equal, life turns out to be very much a matter of just *living*.
5. She has earned her promotion through hard work, and she graduated from Briarcliff in 1972.

II. All of the following sentences are built around passive verbs. Study each instance to see if you think the passive voice is justified (pp. 130–131). Wherever it isn't, recast the sentence in an active form.

1. The defendant was brought to trial after a delay of eleven months.
2. The ball was kicked out of bounds by Biff on his own four yard line.
3. Novosibirsk has been called the most important city in Siberia.
4. Pollution of lakes and rivers is deeply resented by the typical Minnesotan.
5. The Declaration of Independence was called by Thomas Jefferson "the holy bond of our union."

III. Make each of the following pairs of sentences into a single sentence, using an appropriate coordinating or subordinating conjunction (pp. 131–141). You needn't keep exactly the same wording.

1. He is going to apply for the job. He doesn't have a chance.
2. She can spend her vacation in Nova Scotia. She can also spend it in South Carolina.
3. The price of corn may rise this year. Many farmers will otherwise be driven out of business.

4. There has been very little snow this year. Most of the ski resorts are closed.
5. Most species of American animals have recently been declining in population. The sea otter is one exception to the rule.

IV. What are the main devices of coordination used in the paragraph by George Orwell on page 94? Isolate at least three types of coordination and supply examples.

V. For each item, compose a sentence that places the three terms in a parallel series. Be sure that you choose the most emphatic, climactic order of arrangement for those terms (pp. 135–136).

1. courage   cheerfulness   patience
2. the neighborhood   the county   the city
3. grade school   college   high school
4. terrors   worries   fears
5. an inconvenience   an outrage   a disturbance

VI. Combine each pair of sentences to form two new sentences using subordination. First subordinate element *a* to element *b*, and then vice versa. Briefly explain the difference in emphasis between your new sentences.

1. a. Fraternities and sororities made a strong comeback after the Vietnam War.
   b. Political activism on campus isn't necessarily dead.
2. a. Postage rates are discouragingly high.
   b. There are few real alternatives to using the mails.
3. a. Hang-gliding is growing in popularity.
   b. It will never catch on in Kansas.
4. a. I am an avid sports fan.
   b. I don't intend to watch next Sunday's underwater tug of war between the Miami Dolphins and a team of alligators.
5. a. The alligators will do all they can to win the prize.
   b. It is hard to imagine what the alligators would do with $500,000.

VII. The following passage lacks adequate subordination. Rewrite it, subordinating minor elements for emphasis and variety. You may combine sentences if necessary (pp. 135–141).

Hippocrates used garlic as a pharmaceutical. He used it to treat different diseases, and so did other early doctors. They believed that a plant or herb had a very penetrating odor so it must have a lot of therapeutic value. Tuberculosis and leprosy are not at all alike but garlic was used to treat both of them. There was a Roman naturalist named Pliny. He listed sixty-one diseases; garlic was supposed to cure them all. And he added the information that garlic has very powerful properties and you can tell this because serpents and scorpions are driven away by the very smell of it.[14]

VIII. Rewrite the following sentences concisely (pp. 141–142). Don't worry about losing minor elements of meaning.

1. At this point in time I think it would be useful to pause, stand back, and reflect that every problem has, as it were, two sides, and that, having examined one side of the problem under review, we might do well now to turn our attention to the other side of the problem.
2. It is her sense of the situation that the total picture would not be very different, in terms of her willingness to take the job, if an extra thousand dollars were added to her salary.
3. He found it extremely difficult to walk in a manner that he considered sufficiently comfortable when he was wearing his very recently purchased boots, which were made of vinyl chloride and which had cost him quite a large amount of money.
4. One thing that alarms many people in these recent times is the fact that control of those sources that emit pollution seems to go directly against the interest that the whole country ought to have in making sure that the productivity of industry continues to increase.
5. No one should have any reason to doubt that, when it comes to being able to enjoy eating spaghetti on cold toast, the British take second place to no other people on the face of this earth.

IX. The following passage, taken from an essay about the pleasures of woodcutting, has been deliberately altered to minimize variety of sentence structure. It is meant to sound monotonous. Rewrite the passage, supplying the missing variety (pp. 142–145). You may combine sentences if necessary.

You can do a considerable amount of creative resting in the woods. You can sit on a log and absently rub tired muscles. You can study the intricate topography of bark. Also, you can read the now-ended calendar of tree rings. You can smell the fresh woody fragrances. Or you can watch the chipmunk or bluejay come closer to scout the meaning of your silence. Woodcutting is not like most other outdoor pursuits. It is unaffected by weather. It can be engaged in at all times, except for drenching cold rain or driving sleet. It is quite magical during a snowstorm. You automatically work at a tempo attuned to the temperature. You work easily enough to keep from steaming on a golden day in Indian summer. You work briskly enough to keep comfortable when north winds icily rake the woods.[15]

NOTES

[1]Susanne K. Langer, "The Lord of Creation," *Fortune*, Jan. 1944, p. 140.

[2]Edith Iglauer, "The Strangers Next Door," *Atlantic*, July 1973, p. 90.

[3]Milton Friedman, "Monumental Folly," *Newsweek,* 25 June 1973, p. 64.

[4]Rachel Carson, *Silent Spring* (1962; rpt. Greenwich, Conn.: Fawcett, n.d.), p. 224.

[5]Jason Epstein, "Living in New York," *New York Review of Books*, 6 Jan. 1966, p. 15.

[6]"Skiing Utah Powder," *Sunset*, Jan. 1976, p. 39.

[7]Virginia Woolf, *To the Lighthouse* (1927; rpt. New York: Harvest, 1955), p. 73.

[8]LeRoi Jones, *Home: Social Essays* (New York: Apollo, 1966), pp. 118–19.

[9]Pauline Kael, *Kiss Kiss Bang Bang* (1968; rpt. New York: Bantam, 1969), pp. 53, 57.

[10]Willie Morris, *Yazoo: Integration in a Deep-Southern Town* (1971; rpt. New York: Ballantine, 1972), p. 9.

[11]Quoted by Lawrance Thompson, *Robert Frost: The Early Years 1874–1915* (New York: Holt, 1966), p. 434.

[12]H. W. Fowler, *A Dictionary of Modern English Usage* (1926; rpt. n.p.: Oxford Univ. Press, 1937), p. 504.

[13]Peter Matthiessen, *The Tree Where Man Was Born* (New York: Dutton, 1972), p. 193.

[14]Adapted from Michael Field, *All Manner of Food* (New York: Knopf, 1970), pp. 4–5.

[15]Adapted from Frank Rowsome, Jr., "Apple & Beech, Birch & Oak," *Atlantic*, Oct. 1975, p. 98.

6
PARAGRAPHS

The most important unit of meaning in every essay is the paragraph. Although each sentence conveys a thought, an essay isn't a sequence of, say, eighty thoughts; it's rather a development of one central thesis through certain steps. Those steps are paragraphs. Within an effective paragraph you'll find that the sentences support and extend one another in various ways, making a single, usually complex, unfolding idea.

A writer who works from an outline will generally allot one paragraph to each subheading (pp. 35–42). But this isn't an iron rule. A paragraph is a unit of attention as well as a unit of meaning; a reader should be able to read and digest it comfortably with one continuous effort. Instead of mechanically dividing the essay into paragraphs corresponding to outline categories, a conscientious writer forms new units wherever major pauses seem called for. One paragraph may cover several subheadings, or, conversely, a subheading may require such intricate development that it spills into a second paragraph. Nor is there a single "right" size or structure for all paragraphs. Like the sentences that compose them, paragraphs should be flexible in size, in complexity, and in the degree of emphasis they carry.

You don't have to feel, however, that paragraph construction is a completely subjective, hit-or-miss affair. Paragraphs serve a limited number of purposes, and they can be successfully formed according to certain classic strategies of development. By familiarizing yourself with typical functions, patterns, and standards of effectiveness, and by testing your own draft paragraphs against those norms, you can learn how to launch and sustain paragraphs of every type.

UNITY, COHERENCE, EMPHASIS

Pursue One Main Idea

A paragraph can, and usually should, contain sentences that *limit* its central idea, but it should have no sentences that *stand apart* from that idea. Examine this well-organized (if notably dated) paragraph:

> (1) Harry Robbins Haldeman is, as he once cheerfully put it, Richard Nixon's son of a bitch. (2) He sits 100 gold-carpeted feet down the hall from the Oval Office, glowering out at the world from under a crew cut that would flatter a drill instructor, with a gaze that would freeze Medusa. (3) He is neither quite so forbidding as he looks nor quite so fierce as his reputation as the keystone of a Berlin wall around Mr. Nixon; he even has a sense of humor, about subjects other than the boss. (4) But he is the man who says No for the President of the United States, a mission he executes with a singleness of purpose and an authority that are respected — and feared — throughout official Washington. (5) "Bob Haldeman is probably the most powerful man in the country next to the President," says one ex-colleague — and he got that way because he spends more time next to the President than anybody else in government.[1]

Here the opening sentence clearly states the paragraph's main idea, which is that Haldeman is tough on behalf of the President. The other four sentences all bear directly on this assertion either positively or negatively:

1. Haldeman is	tough	on behalf of the President
2. He is		close to the President
He is	fierce in aspect	
3. He is	not as fierce as he looks	
He even has	a sense of humor about subjects	other than the President
4. But he	says no	for the President
And he	does this with a respected purpose and authority	
5. He has	power	second only to the President's
And he got it by		being closer to the President than anyone else

(Suppose the paragraph had contained a further sentence: *Like another of the President's close advisers, Haldeman has a degree from UCLA.* This would have constituted a violation of paragraph unity.)

Be ruthless about keeping irrelevant material out of your paragraphs. No matter how interesting a statement may be, it will damage the whole paragraph if it doesn't advance or modify the one central point.

The traditional way of ensuring unity is to see that each paragraph contains a *topic sentence* (sometimes called *thesis sentence*). Like the opening sentence of the sample paragraph above, the topic sentence plainly states the leading idea, showing both the reader and the writer what the whole paragraph ought to be about. The test for unity then becomes whether each subordinate sentence is adequately related to this main one. In a tightly organized, logical argument, the topic sentences of all the paragraphs sum up the writer's case, and a reader who scans those sentences can see at once where the essay is headed.

But you needn't become a fanatic about the topic sentence. In narrative and descriptive essays, where the logical subordination of elements isn't always apparent, topic sentences tend to be inconspicuous and sometimes completely missing. Some paragraphs, like this description by Albert Goldman of a rock dance, gain their unity from presenting one continuous experience and the reflections that follow from it:

> Magnetized by the crowd, impelled by the relentless pounding beat of the music, one is then drawn out on the floor. Here there is a feeling of total immersion: one is inside the mob, inside the skull, inside the music, which comes from all sides, buffeting the dancers like a powerful surf. Strangest of all, in the midst of this frantic activity, one soon feels supremely alone; and this aloneness produces a giddy sense of freedom, even of exultation. At last one is free to move and act and mime the secret motions of his mind. Everywhere about him are people focused deep within themselves, working to bring to the surfaces of their bodies their deep-seated erotic fantasies. Their faces are drugged, their heads thrown back, their limbs extended, their bodies dissolving into the arcs of the dance. The erotic intensity becomes so great that one wonders what sustains the frail partition of reserve that prevents the final spilling of this endlessly incited energy.[2]

This paragraph subjects us to the author's "total immersion" while we feel what he wants us to. It would have been much less engaging if he had thought his job was to present a thesis and defend it with arguments and examples. A paragraph must first of all be interesting, and any formal order gained at the expense of liveliness is a bad bargain.

If lack of unity were the only problem a writer of paragraphs had to watch out for, it could always be handled in revision. But real first-draft paragraphs usually call for so much sentence-by-sentence re-writing that a disunity of idea can pass unnoticed. Here, for instance, is a first-draft paragraph that you can recognize as faulty in various ways:

> I don't believe that Christian civilization has succeeded because of all the wars we still have. This is my conclusion, and I think it is justi-fied by a lot of evidence, but some people might disagree with it any-way. Since I want to convince everybody, I am going to set forth my reasons in detail, because otherwise some people might still disagree. This is why this paper is going to emphasize the mass murders, the witch trials, and the intolerance that completely and totally dominate the record of a religion of this type. In his book *The Pursuit of the Mil-lennium* the author, Norman Cohn, gives many examples of the sort of behavior to which I am referring, but this tome unfortunately didn't discuss the wars alluded to in the first sentence of this paragraph.

In order to strengthen his individual sentences, this writer would have to work on such problems as faulty subordination, redundancy, circumlocution, and confusion of tenses. Yet if all those problems were solved the paragraph would still be flawed. In the first place, the writer hasn't made up his mind why he rejects Christian civiliza-tion. Is it because of "all the *wars* we *still* have" or is it because of "the mass murders, the witch trials, and the intolerance" of the *past?* The two reasons are compatible, of course, but the writer hasn't yet recognized that they *are* two reasons, and so he sends his paragraph off in opposite directions. And second, the paragraph trails away in its final sentence. The writer probably meant to say that *The Pur-suit of the Millennium,* even though it doesn't discuss the present age, corroborates his own idea about Christian barbarity. Instead, however, he seems to be adding an irrelevant criticism of the book, and we feel a loss of what little coherence the paragraph had mus-tered. The moral here is that incoherence is the *first* problem to look for, before you waste any time improving sentences that don't be-long in the paragraph at all.

Let's assume that a paragraph of yours has passed the minimum test for coherence. Is that enough? Consider the following example:

> (1) It seems impossible for television programs to give anything but a falsely romantic account of doctors' lives. (2) Currently there are four medical dramas on prime-time TV. (3) These programs are immensely

popular, but only a fool would mistake their heroes for typical real-life physicians. (4) It serves no purpose — except possibly the purposes of greedy sponsors — to indulge in this distortion. (5) A doctor on the screen is always well-meaning, handsome, and self-sacrificing. (6) He (never she) also has plenty of free time to solve other people's intimate nonmedical problems. (7) Real doctors must wince with envy — that is, if they aren't too exhausted to watch the program at all. (8) Perhaps the most unrealistic point is that the television doctor always happens to have only one patient to care for during each episode of the show.

Here are the makings of a fine paragraph, developing one general point through a set of definite observations. Everything marches briskly along in the first three sentences. If you reread sentences 3, 4, and 5, however, you'll see that number 4 constitutes an interruption; the writer was about to detail the ways in which TV doctors are unrealistic, but first he threw in an extra remark about the purposes of greedy sponsors. Sentence 7, too, interrupts a logical sequence running from 3 through 8. Once these elements of disunity were pointed out, the writer chose to discard sentence 4 and to move sentence 7 to the end. Try reading the paragraph this way and you'll sense the value of continuous and logical development.

Place the Main Idea Emphatically

Most paragraphs do contain topic sentences, and most of these come right at the beginning, plainly governing everything that follows:

> There is a paradox about the South Seas that every visitor immediately discovers. Tropical shores symbolize man's harmony with a kind and bountiful nature. Natives escape the common vexations of modern life by simply relaxing. They reach into palms for coconuts, into the sea for fish, and into calabashes for poi. But when the tranquilized tourist reaches Hawaii, the paradise of the Pacific, he finds the most expensive resort in the world and a tourist industry that will relieve him of his traveler's checks with a speed and ease that would bring a smile to the lips of King Kamehameha.[3]

Here the topic sentence announces a *paradox* — that is, a seeming contradiction — and the rest of the paragraph sets forth the two halves of that paradox. The result is extreme clarity: the structure of the paragraph fulfills the promise given in the topic sentence, and the reader feels securely guided by that structure at each moment. Even when the relation between an initial topic sentence and its sequel isn't this tight, the conspicuousness of that main statement will help to keep things focused and purposeful. If you've ever had to skim an essay in a hurry, you've probably given most of your attention to those "big" first sentences, which typically outline the general shape of the argument.

In some paragraphs, however, the topic sentence comes second, after a transitional, "tugboat" sentence that maneuvers the previous paragraph into a new alignment:

> The statistics, then, paint a depressing picture. *Yet if we set aside the government reports and take the trouble to interview farm workers one by one, we find an astounding degree of confidence in the future . . .*

This is still an emphatic position. Indeed, any position can become emphatic if you make a sharp, conspicuous turn as you begin the topic sentence; you can even build a paragraph inductively, taking the reader through a set of particulars and then presenting the conclusion that follows from them. In paragraphs of narrative, in fact, the "punch line" is quite often saved for the end:

> (1) Manuel (Manolo) Orantes is a modest, engaging gentleman in a sport dominated by temperamental individualists; he applauds his opponents' best shots and smiles broadly in apparent wonderment at his own successes. (2) But beneath his friendly gestures, the 26-year-old Spaniard has the instincts of a superb matador. (3) When charging, churning Jimmy Connors consented to play the role of the bull last week, Orantes coolly displayed all his guile and finesse and captured the U.S. Open at Forest Hills.[4]

The three sentences in this example (1) create a disarming impression of Orantes' mildness, (2) overrule that impression and introduce the key metaphor of the bullfighter, and (3) use that metaphor to convey the surprising news that Orantes defeated Connors. This form of paragraph structure, like that of the suspended sentence (p. 145), calls for exceptional forethought, and (when it works) yields an exceptional degree of satisfaction at the end.

PRINCIPLES OF DEVELOPMENT

The ways of successfully developing a paragraph are necessarily tied to the modes of whole essays: description, narration, exposition, and argument. As we saw in examining those modes (pp. 13–22), few essays simply describe or narrate or expound or argue from start to finish. An essay typically combines two or more of those functions — narrating an event, for example, in order to lay the basis for an argument about its historical meaning. If you study an essay paragraph by paragraph, you will usually discover that many distinct functions are being served. Each paragraph has its own job to do and its own means of accomplishing that job. Within an essay of any sort, a given paragraph can:

announce the topic
anticipate misunderstandings and objections
define a term
isolate a problem
solve a problem
launch a generalization
test a hypothesis
explain a cause
compare and contrast
raise an objection
concede a limitation
supply evidence
analyze a passage
give an illustration
tell a story
draw an analogy
describe something
announce a key transition
call for action
recapitulate and emphasize

How can these purposes be effectively served? I believe that the following ten principles of paragraph development, some covering the *function performed* and some the *order of presentation*, can equip you for any conceivable situation:

1. State a thesis and support or illustrate it

You have already seen that the most common way of organizing a paragraph is to propose a topic sentence and then spell out its implications. If the topic sentence is one that needs to be backed by evidence, that evidence characteristically occupies the rest of the paragraph. Sometimes, as in the paragraphs on pages 71, 78, and 79, items of evidence are assembled in a spirit of debate; the facts and figures defend an initial statement against all disbelievers. But this point-scoring approach, if carried unremittingly through a whole essay, can make for a rigid and hostile impression. More usually, a paragraph shows a relaxed relation between main and secondary assertions, all of which are put forward with an air of confidence:

It is far easier (and perhaps more rewarding, given current priorities) to develop a reputation for quality research than for excellent teaching.

A spectacular discovery by one faculty member can draw nationwide attention to him and his department. Groups producing and publishing excellent research in a specific area can rise to prominence rapidly, attract colleagues of high caliber, sponsor conferences, and begin to establish their reputations. Institutions at which a number of departments attract such attention are recognized as being "up-and-coming" in the academic community. The signs of research activity are tangible and quantifiable, in the number of papers published in reputable journals. In contrast, the rewards of good teaching are less tangible, are more localized, and do not materialize as rapidly. As a consequence, the temptation can be great for some departments to take advantage of the tight job market and hire new faculty members primarily on the grounds of research promise.[5]

Here, once again, we have an initial topic sentence stating a general proposition. The sentences that follow, taken together, buttress that topic sentence, but they don't actually prove it. Rather, they fill out its meaning, indicating how the collegiate reward system works. Instead of feeling defeated by the author's logic, we go along readily with a string of reasonable and plausible statements.

So, too, a distinguished novelist-critic, writing about the makings of her art, follows a strong topic sentence with statements that illustrate it in a confident, nonbelligerent manner:

The novelist—it is his distinction and his danger—is terribly exposed to life. Other artists, partially at least, withdraw; they shut themselves up for weeks alone with a dish of apples and a paint-box, or a roll of music paper and a piano. When they emerge it is to forget and distract themselves. But the novelist never forgets and is seldom distracted. He fills his glass and lights his cigarette, he enjoys presumably all the pleasures of talk and table, but always with a sense that he is being stimulated and played upon by the subject-matter of his art. Taste, sound, movement, a few words here, a gesture there, a man coming in, a woman going out, even the motor that passes in the street or the beggar who shuffles along the pavement, and all the reds and blues and lights and shades of the scene claim his attention and rouse his curiosity. He can no more cease to receive impressions than a fish in mid-ocean can cease to let the water rush through his gills.[6]

Observe, incidentally, how this fine paragraph saves a vivid, powerful metaphor (pp. 117–121) for the end. Even with her topic sentence in the customary first position, the writer senses that the potentially emphatic final position deserves a flourish.

2. Build toward a conclusion or question

Instead of revealing your thesis at the outset of a paragraph, you can, as we've already remarked (p. 161), save it for last. Such paragraph organization is usually called *inductive*, since a conclusion is arrived at through the accumulation of single observations that justify it. This student paragraph is typical:

> Tests show that joggers have significantly lower resting heart rates than nonjoggers, and that their recovery time after exertion is much briefer. Heart attacks, which some people still wrongly associate with the enlarged "athlete's heart," are more common in the general population than among joggers. Then, too, every jogger experiences an exhilarating sense of well-being and vitality, not just while running but throughout the day. A daily half-hour of jogging is time invested at the highest rate of return.

Here the topic sentence comes last, having been made plausible by all the points that lead up to it.

In fact, however, not many paragraphs of exposition or argument are strictly inductive in form. In the first place, the flow of thought in a lively paragraph tends to be somewhat looser than a lock-step parading of instances that demonstrate a final point. As in Albert Goldman's paragraph about the rock dance (p. 158), it's less a matter of proof than of expanding toward a more general assertion or reflection at the end. And second, the inductive pattern is often violated—but *usefully* violated—by a strong and informative opening statement that might easily be mistaken for the paragraph's topic sentence:

> Women candidates, to win entire approval, have to be both chic and brilliant, and so the woman who is plain-looking, a spinster-scholar type, evokes a negative response, for she is not a complete woman; she lacks sociability, and will not flatter the egos of male department members. Dossier after dossier divulges irrelevant, negative commentary: "—— is a large broad-boned somewhat awkward young woman who must be close to six feet in height"; her mousiness belies a sharp mind; "—— is . . . tall and proportioned like an Olympic swimmer"; she is a steady woman who will never marry. And within a single paragraph from a male at an elite graduate school, she has a "comfortably upholstered" person and personality, she performed "athletically" in a particular course, she would be the "wheel-horse" of any committee on which she served. And of an older woman, "if she has any faults, they are those that usually accompany the ambitious woman of her age." In other words, the rare comment on a male's

appearance is simply a footnote, the frequent comment on a female's, a thesis statement.[7]

Here a fairly strong sentence at the beginning and an even stronger, more general one at the end give the paragraph a maximum of emphasis and effect.

Some paragraphs, while avoiding the cramped aspect of a logical demonstration, gradually "open up" from particular statements to more sweeping ones, ending with a broad assertion or—as in the next example—a question that has been brought into focus by the rest of the paragraph:

> Four years ago, when I was 21 and newly school-sprung, many of the women I knew—myself included—were agonizing about whether to marry. Most of us finally did. Now a lot of my friends and other women of my generation are agonizing about whether to get pregnant. Many of us haven't so far. And the troubling thought has crept into our souls or our wombs (presuming they are separate places, and sometimes I'm not so sure they are) that we just might never make babies, that we might enter middle age alone—perhaps divorced or widowed—childless, womb-tight and woebegone. Why, if women face this almost certain aloneness later on, are so many of us so strangely steeled against pregnancy?[8]

The first four sentences of this paragraph bring the writer from her own situation of four years ago to that of herself and "other women of my generation" today, and from doubts about marriage to doubts about motherhood. The fifth sentence (*And the troubling thought . . .*) projects all those women into a childless middle age, giving a broader and still more disturbing picture than those that have gone before. And from this general perspective the writer launches her question at the end—a question that forcefully introduces the rest of her essay. Without consciously noting this widening movement, a reader is likely to feel its structural rightness.

3. Develop an explanation

Another alternative to stating your main idea right away is to begin with a problem or question to which that idea is the answer. If the explanation consists of several items, those items can form the backbone of the paragraph:

> Many factors were responsible for the success of psychoanalysis in America. Certain well-known American character traits—optimism and the belief in individualism, for example—must have contributed

to the acceptance of a therapy founded on the hope that it is possible for people to change themselves by their own efforts. A child-centered culture responded enthusiastically to the notion that infantile patterns affect adult behavior and to the tendency to idealize childlike spontaneity in the face of civilization's restraints. America's affluence and leisure, and lack of a coherent national culture, must also have helped psychoanalysis; a poorer society, or one with more rigidly institutionalized centers of learning, would have been less receptive to a new influence such as Freud's. And to the extent that America is a nation of immigrants, cut off from foreign roots, each American must construct an individual history to make up for the uncertainty of his collective past. Finally, Americans, unlike the French or the Swiss, lacked a thriving psychiatric tradition of their own. And it should go without saying that the genuine abilities of these students of Freud also helped ensure their immense success.[9]

But this itemizing approach may produce too mechanical an effect. Instead of rigidly listing what the "many factors" are, it's usually better to *develop* an explanation less formally, as this student writer does:

Why do people feel so moved, in the late 1970's, by a seemingly old-time musical such as *A Chorus Line?* Some observers probably take this phenomenon as a mere exercise in nostalgia, a return to the Broadway and Hollywood thirties and forties. But there are telling differences between *A Chorus Line* and its ancestors of forty years ago. The typical old musical was a celebration of the magical opportunities that America held out to the poor-but-resourceful-and-talented. (Just think of all those predictable backstage success stories featuring Judy Garland and Mickey Rooney.) *A Chorus Line* provides almost exactly the opposite: an instance of the fact that hardly anybody succeeds on Broadway and that stardom is mostly an illusion. To be blunt about it, most people no longer believe in the American dream. They flock to *A Chorus Line* because it confirms their feeling that hard work *isn't* rewarded, that good luck strikes only a few, and that a job—even one on Broadway—is just a job after all.

Notice how the writer *unfolds* her explanation instead of just blurting it out. The strong final sentence completes an extended chain of reasoning that began at the third sentence: *But there are telling differences . . .*

4. Replace one view with another

Apart from outright incoherence, choppiness, or long-windedness, perhaps the most common flaw in paragraph construction is rigidity of presentation. Having something to say, the writer merely says it — and goes on to do just the same in the following paragraph. As a result, the reader feels, not like a participant in the writer's thought, but like someone receiving instructions or being shown a rapid succession of slides.

An adept writer will frequently give the reader a chance, if not to think things over, then at least to see that opposite possibilities haven't been neglected. He or she starts the paragraph on a certain tack, evoking one expectation or opinion or set of facts, and then takes a sharp turn in the preferred direction. Seeing perfectly well that a contrast is in the making, the reader nevertheless feels involved in its development. The gains are a heightened dramatic quality and a stronger sense of the writer's fairness, assurance, and control.

This principle is so common that it could be illustrated almost at random. Look, for example, at the paragraph about Manuel Orantes (p. 161), which conjures up a picture of the modest gentleman before revealing the guileful matador who won the tournament. The authors haven't changed their minds about Orantes in mid-paragraph; they've just chosen to create a little suspense and to sharpen our pleasure in Orantes' upset victory. Again, consider the student paragraph about *A Chorus Line*. The author has a definite position to maintain, but she puts some flexibility into her paragraph by using her second sentence to report what other people may think. When she then goes on to present her case, we feel a pleasing interaction of ideas.

Further examples:

In Randall Jarrell's *Pictures From an Institution,* the wittiest novel about academia, a foreign visitor exclaims, "You Americans do not rear children, you *incite* them; you give them food and shelter and applause." One recent form of applause for America's college youth has been "grade inflation," the bestowing of high honors on almost everyone. But now there are small portents of significant change. Yale has reinstituted the F grade, and Stanford has reinstituted the D. These and similar developments elsewhere, quiet as snow, may be the first stirrings of a counterrevolution against the strange egalitarianism that had helped produce "grade inflation."[10]

Since its invention, the camera has been used primarily (at least consciously) as a recording device, a playback machine, an instrument for making instant sketches of whatever the apparent physical reality is "out there." The mainstream of photography has been, and still is, from the outside in. But also there has been, at least from the lifetime of Hippolyte Bayard (flourished circa 1839), a minority of photographers concerned with doing things the other way around, of using the camera as a means of objectifying inner emotional and psychological states, of going from the inside out. . . .[11]

Both of these paragraphs hinge on the "tip-off" word *But*, which allows us to see that the first-mentioned idea is now to be trumped by the main one.

Of course the reversal needn't be simply a rhetorical trick; you can make a genuine concession (p. 85) to one attitude before insisting that another attitude should prevail:

> I view radicalism as a great reservoir of energy which moves the establishment to pay attention to the most serious and urgent problems, and tells it when it has failed. To a more limited degree, it is also a reservoir of potential creativity — a reaching for new solutions and new approaches. What radicalism is not, and what it can no longer be, is the great sword of vengeance and correction which goes to the source of the distress and cuts it out. There is no longer a single source, and no longer a single sword.[12]

Notice how this writer helps to disarm criticism by the very structure of his paragraph. That paragraph "bends" toward a rival notion in a display of real sympathy; but then, like most good paragraphs making a concession, it saves the emphatic final position for the writer's own idea.

5. Develop a comparison or contrast

This principle overlaps with the previous one: to "replace one view with another" is of course to contrast the two of them. But special attention deserves to be focused on the paragraph in which term *a* doesn't fade out when term *b* has been introduced. Rather, both terms are kept before us, each of them serving to highlight certain aspects of the other. Thus two fundamental principles of thought — aligning items by resemblance and distinguishing them by difference — find orderly rhetorical expression.

A paragraph of comparison typically works by creating a sequence of parallel observations establishing likeness:

> Both Seaver and Palmer have been World Series heroes. Both are handsome, intelligent and articulate men who are team leaders and spokesmen. They share a scholar's curiosity about their game and probably are the two best all-round pitchers in baseball today. Certainly many of the men who bat against them think so. "Seaver's the best pitcher around," says the Cards' hard-hitting Ted Simmons. "Palmer's

top in the American League in my book," says Lee Stanton, even though one of his Angel teammates is the reigning fastballer, Nolan Ryan. But last year Seaver had an 11–11 record and Palmer was 7–12. They were at the abyss.[13]

In this paragraph Seaver and Palmer, the rival pitchers, have equal roles. From start to finish they are *compared*— that is, the same traits (handsomeness, curiosity, talent, etc.) are ascribed to both of them. Such a paragraph hangs together by the simple device of running through the qualities that terms *a* and *b* have in common.

Paragraphs of sheer comparison are less usual than paragraphs of *contrast*, in which the *differences* between *a* and *b* are detailed. This student example is characteristic:

> That Hawthorne and Melville couldn't be friends for long is hardly amazing. What is surprising is that they ever got along at all. Melville, if I can believe what I have read by and about him, was outgoing and expansive; Hawthorne was retiring and quiet. Hawthorne worked in an established, genteel mode of fiction, but Melville longed to create extravagant new forms. And Melville, unlike his companion, had daring ideas about the ultimate purpose of the universe and the nature of good and evil. If Hawthorne had anything of the religious seeker in him, he did a good job of keeping it to himself.

You should bear in mind that a special danger of monotony accompanies paragraphs of comparison or contrast (or both). The parallelism between *a* and *b* can degenerate into a mindless symmetry: *a* does this but *b* does that; *a* is like this but *b* is like that. . . . The remedy, as in both of the examples above, is variety of sentence structure (pp. 142–145). Such variety is always welcome, but here it spares the paragraph from resembling an electronic ping-pong machine, hypnotically bouncing the reader from one side to the other.

6. Establish the basis for a contrast

You have already seen the value of prefacing one idea with a quite different one that makes for a suitable point of departure. But the shift between the two ideas needn't always be made *within* a given paragraph. Sometimes you may want to devote a whole paragraph to the "misleading" impression in order to set up the strongest possible contrast:

> A visitor's first impression of Brigham Young University is likely to be that BYU is out of synchronization with most of American higher education. It is partly the striking setting on a plateau at the foot of the

Wasatch Range and the pristine look of the campus. No litter. No graffiti. The buildings all seem to be new, with few of the signs of the wear and tear many university buildings are showing in these days of budget paring. But it's also the look of the students. Seemingly all of them are neatly dressed and shorn and shod, the result of a dress and grooming code which, for example, specifies that men shall not wear beards nor their hair below the collar. And to heighten the contrast with other campuses in the 1970's, every morning and evening ROTC details come out to raise and lower the flag and an amplified "Star-Spangled Banner" echoes across the campus. Even parking seems to be under control.[14]

We know, reading this paragraph, that the impression of conformity established here is going to be torpedoed. The very next sentence does the job: *Therefore, when in mid-October BYU announced that it would not comply with some of the new federal regulations prohibiting sex discrimination in educational institutions, the challenge seemed to come from an unlikely quarter.* Incidentally, the first paragraph doesn't just brace us for this reversal; its concrete detail about the physical look of BYU keeps us from having to plunge straight into the cold and abstract legal argument that follows.

7. Put a definition to work

Especially near the beginning of an essay, you may want to devote at least one paragraph to defining rare or tricky terms that are central to your thesis. It would of course be a boring waste of space to define ordinary, familiar terms instead of addressing the topic:

x The poem I have been asked to analyze is about lying. What is lying? According to *Webster's Eighth New Collegiate Dictionary*, to lie is "1: to make an untrue statement with intent to deceive; 2: to create a false or misleading impression."

But if a key word is unusual, or if you intend to use it in some specially limited sense, you would do well to define it before any confusion can arise.

As the following student paragraph shows, a definition can itself become a strong element of support for a thesis:

We often hear today that police should be concentrating on violent offenses instead of wasting so much time, effort, and taxpayers' money on so-called victimless crime. This seems like a fine idea; nobody, after all, would want an officer to make a possession-of-marijuana arrest while a rape or murder was occurring across the street. But what exactly *is* a "victimless" crime? Are there no victims when pimps, prostitutes, and drug pushers take over the streets of a residential neighborhood, confining the fearful citizens to their homes at night? I too am against the prosecution of truly victimless "crimes"; I don't regard them as crimes at all. But let's be clear about our terms. For me, *victimless* means that the act in question produces *neither direct nor indirect* victims. If this meaning of the term is understood, the whole issue of victimless crime loses its air of simplicity and righteousness.

Notice, by the way, that this writer doesn't just announce her definition; she prepares for it with careful reasoning. First she shows us why a definition is necessary: without it, only a superficial and distorted view of the problem would be possible. Her paragraph amounts to a further illustration of point 4 above, "Replace one view with another."

8. Classify or divide a subject

In some essays an early paragraph is usefully devoted to *classifying* the topic—that is, showing what general kind of issue it falls under— or, more commonly, to *dividing* it into its logical parts. Division in particular can bring a needed sense of order into a subject that looks confusing or unmanageable. Here a student writer addresses the problem of population control:

> In order to have any hope of holding down the population in countries that already lack food, shelter, and employment for many of their present citizens, we must first recognize the components of the problem. To begin with, population growth is not simply a matter of more births; it is also a matter of fewer deaths, thanks largely to advances in health care and emergency relief. Needless to say, we can hardly propose to aid these countries by restoring the old death rate! But recognizing that birth control is only part of the dilemma can spare us from becoming too easily discouraged when a campaign of birth control fails to stabilize a certain population completely.
> Secondly, we ought to realize that the problem we *can* deal with, namely the birth rate, has several distinct aspects. First, there are the society's cultural or religious beliefs about birth control. It is obvious that foreigners can and should exercise only a limited influence in that area. Then there are the circumstances, mostly economic, that favor or discourage the practice of having large families. Here again it is clear that outsiders cannot do much. Even if we could dictate another country's economy, it is not at all apparent whether a higher standard of living would make for larger or smaller families. It is the third aspect of the problem—the available means of contraception—that provides an

opportunity for constructive help. When members of another society do decide to control births, they face better and worse ways of doing so, and we can cheaply supply them with the knowledge and assistance that will ensure the most effective program.

This writer has spent two paragraphs subdividing his subject, perhaps at some risk of losing the reader's attention. Now, however, he has earned the right to focus on the specific issue, contraception, that he has patiently isolated as the important one.

9. Analyze a statement or passage to bring out its meaning

One strong way of making a point is to devote a paragraph or two to a specific quotation that tends to illustrate or prove that point. You can start with the quotation and then show what is significant about it, or you can bring in the quotation to show that the earlier part of your paragraph is justified.

In its most usual form, analysis consists of the "close reading" of a presented text, revealing its thematic unity or its structure or its implications. My own analysis of the paragraph about childless women (p. 165) may serve as a simple example. Often, though, a writer concentrates on a single phrase or sentence typifying the intended meaning:

The stock phrase most used during the Watergate hearings was "at this point in time" and its variations, e.g. "at that point in time." At first these expressions sound merely like pretentious, elaborate ways of saying, "then," "now," "at that time," "at this time," etc. But the stock phrases are much more useful. "At that point in time" serves to isolate the event being discussed, to detach it, bracket it and set it apart from all other events and people. It becomes a moment existing by itself. Questionable conduct is thereby voided by being reduced to a mathematical point, a fiction having no dimensions, connections, history or relation to the present. Surgeons prefer to operate in a "clean field" established by isolation of the area of incision through elaborate operating room techniques. Only a swatch of flesh is presented to the surgeon's eyes instead of a whole patient. The surgeon is thus spared the unnerving sight of the patient's face, posture, and general human appearance at the critical time of surgery. "At that point in time" accomplishes an analogous effect. The difference of course is that the surgical procedure serves a legitimate medical purpose, while the Watergate linguistic procedure obscures personal political and moral responsibility. Two of the axiomatic requirements of personal responsibility are motives before the deed and awareness of consequences after the deed. "At that point in time" foils both.[15]

And sometimes the quoted material, instead of being examined in detail, is merely integrated into the writer's chain of reasoning, as in these connected paragraphs from a student essay:

> Anyone who doubts that Charlotte Brontë's novels have a certain violence and vindictiveness behind their Victorian good manners would do well to reread the closing pages of *Jane Eyre*. There we find the predictable "happy ending," with the heroine's expected total submission to her hero-husband. But look what has become of the hero before a reconciliation is brought about: "He was taken out from under the ruins, alive, but sadly hurt; . . . one eye was knocked out, and one hand so crushed that Mr. Carter, the surgeon, had to amputate it directly. The other eye inflamed: he lost the sight of that also. He is now helpless indeed — blind and a cripple."
>
> No doubt Jane sincerely loves what is left of Rochester — but listen to her own words. "I love you better now, when I can really be useful to you, than I did in your state of proud independence, when you disdained every part but that of the giver and protector." Isn't it apparent that Jane, the former humiliated servant, is now herself "the giver and protector"? Fate, in the form of a terrible fire, has paid back Rochester for his lordly ways. A conventional reading might be that Jane now loves him *despite* his handicaps, but this is belied by what she says. It is the reversal of roles that makes him acceptable to her now. And though Jane herself certainly feels no vengeful satisfaction, the case may be very different for Charlotte Brontë, who created and then totally humbled a proud, dominating hero.

(For the use of quotations to support an argument, see pp. 82–83.)

10. Move climactically through time or space

Most of the principles we have reviewed apply chiefly to paragraphs of exposition or argument (pp. 14–16), but description and narration deserve interest as well. To be brief, exactly the same guidelines that hold for a descriptive or narrative *essay* (pp. 13–14) can be used for the descriptive or narrative *paragraph*. That is, such a paragraph should be vivid, precise, and climactic, so that the details add up to something more than random observations.

Look back, for example, at Albert Goldman's paragraph about a rock dance (p. 158). The reader is led through time as the paragraph develops: *one is then drawn out on the floor . . ., Here there is a feeling . . ., one soon feels supremely alone . . . , At last one is free to move . . .* This progression has a purposeful, even necessary, feeling about it. And as the paragraph picks up momentum, it also shifts artfully from a cramped and passive feeling (*impelled . . . , one is then drawn, one is inside the mob*) to a sense of increased control and autonomy (*At last one is free to move and act and mime the secret motions of his mind*), and finally to an ample, willed reflection: *one wonders what sustains the frail partition of reserve that prevents the final spilling of this endlessly incited energy.* In other words, the writer's mind "recovers" from the narrated experience in the course of the paragraph, emerging with a relatively philosophical, if still troubled, relation to the sensory overload of the rock dance. This isn't, of course, what you yourself should attempt in every descriptive paragraph. But you do need some ordering principle—whatever you decide it should be—that will keep your paragraph moving in one direction.

Consider the paragraph about Brigham Young University (pp. 169–170). Though it looks casually descriptive, here again the fundamentals of purposeful organization are at work. The paragraph begins with a classic topic sentence: BYU appears *out of synchronization with most of American higher education.* Then follow several progressively narrower observations, from the situation of the campus *on a plateau at the foot of the Wasatch Range* to the new-looking *buildings* to the neatly dressed *students.* If you stop for a moment and imagine these three elements in any other sequence, you will appreciate the writer's command of ordered detail. Finally the paragraph arrives at a highly specific scene, the daily raising and lowering of the flag by the ROTC—and an ironic little aside about parking, a trivial but usually sensitive issue. We have been taken from the very general—geographically and intellectually—to the very specific, establishing an all-too-perfect image of tranquillity that is ready to be overturned in the paragraph that follows.

Here again is a paragraph with a narrowing movement—in this case an ominous one:

It is a beautiful spring day in San Francisco, a welcome relief from the incessant winter rains. Crowds stroll aimlessly around Union Square, inspecting the craftwork of sidewalk peddlers. Department stores are jammed with shoppers in search of seasonal bargains. Restaurant workers gird themselves for the dinnertime crush. In the subway, BART commuters stand shoulder to shoulder, cursing the laggard Fremont trains. The freeways are hopelessly clogged with weekenders eager to get away as early as possible on this lovely Friday afternoon. The time is 4:32 P.M.[16]

You may not know what the author is pointing toward here—he is about to describe a possible earthquake—but the funnel-like movement from the "beautiful spring day" to the precise minute surely leaves you uneasy. It is almost as if the fateful time had been shown on a smashed watch lying in the rubble. Once again, a paragraph of storytelling or description has drawn the reader artfully toward a point that can be made pivotal.

CONTINUITY

Link Your Sentences Within Each Paragraph

A paragraph, for all its possible complexity, should make a single impression of developing thought. Its sentences should not only *be* related; they should also *sound* related. Most of those sentences ought to contain signals of *identity* or *transition* or both, so that a reader can easily see the kind of relation that's implied between one statement and the next one. The terms of *identity* assert that *something already treated is still under discussion;* the *transitional* words assert that *the previous statement will be expanded or qualified in some way.*

The signals of *identity* are chiefly *pronouns, demonstrative adjectives, repeated words and phrases,* and *omissions* that are understandable in the light of a previous sentence.

PRONOUNS:

• In the third round Miller sustained his precarious one-stroke lead. *He* teed off on Sunday knowing that eleven endorsement contracts hung in the balance.

DEMONSTRATIVE ADJECTIVES:

• The whole football team showed a significant improvement in reading and arithmetic scores. *This* result came as a surprise to everyone but the coach, who had volunteered to do the grading.

REPEATED WORDS AND PHRASES:

• Mayor Bradley's foremost concern is with rapid transit. It is a *concern* that is bound to be shared by those citizens who are not already asphyxiated.

OMISSIONS:

• The treaty placing a limited ban on nuclear tests has now been signed by 119 nations. More than a hundred [*nations*], including Togo and Burundi, have also subscribed to a nonproliferation treaty.

(For other examples of rhetorical identity, review the examples on pp. 133 and 134.)

The signals of *transition* consist of all the words and phrases that show *how* a statement will build on the previous one. The types of transition, with a few examples of each type, are:

CONSEQUENCE:
* therefore, then, thus, hence, accordingly, as a result

LIKENESS:
* likewise, similarly

CONTRAST:
* but, however, nevertheless, on the contrary, on the other hand, yet

AMPLIFICATION:
* and, again, in addition, further, furthermore, moreover, also, too

EXAMPLE:
* for instance, for example

CONCESSION:
* to be sure, granted, of course, it is true

INSISTENCE:
* anyway, indeed, in fact, yes, no

SEQUENCE:
* first, second, finally

RESTATEMENT:
* that is, in other words, in simpler terms, to put it differently

RECAPITULATION:
* in conclusion, all in all, to summarize, altogether

TIME OR PLACE:
* afterward, later, earlier, formerly, elsewhere, here, there, hitherto, subsequently, at the same time, simultaneously, above, below, farther on, this time, so far, until now

Such signals needn't appear in every sentence, but they become useful wherever the relation between two sentences wouldn't be immediately clear without them. The following paragraph, which isn't difficult to follow, "coasts" between its four (capitalized) marks of transition:

I have little hope that my plea for patriotism will succeed, and much anxiety that it will be heard by many as fatuous or wrong-headed. Citizens would not need the argument, and noncitizens probably cannot hear it. STILL, I shall make the argument. I do so partly out of block-headedness, partly out of a wish to repay a welcome debt to patriotic predecessors and contemporaries, and partly for two reasons that might carry more weight. The FIRST REASON stems from my affection and respect for fellow-citizens, and from my wish to see them even more respectable than they are. We have lost patriotism. Although many count the loss small, and many others do not know it has occurred, I believe that the loss is great. The SECOND REASON stems from my wish to see a revitalized radical politics in this country, and from my conviction that Susan Sontag is correct when she says that "probably no serious radical movement has any future in America unless it can revalidate the tarnished idea of patriotism." The radicals of the 1960s did not persuade their fellow-Americans, high or low, that they genuinely cared for and shared a country with them. AND no one who has contempt for others can hope to teach those others. A revived radicalism must be a patriotic radicalism. It must share and care for the common things, even while it has a "lover's quarrel" with fellow-citizens.[17]

In a well-constructed paragraph, marks of continuity tend to appear without any conscious design on the writer's part. If you keep a feeling for what your reader knows and needs to learn, the connective signals will usually fall where they belong. In rereading, however, you may find that you've neglected to reveal the linkage between certain pivotal sentences. Ask yourself what step has been taken without sufficient notice, and supply the word or phrase that will keep your sentences flowing.

Of course you would gain nothing by just peppering your writing with *marks* of continuity; your ideas themselves have to be placed in an order that makes for natural connections. Thus:

(1) Robert Nisbet's *Twilight of Authority* is the most recent illustration of the perplexities of conservatism in America. (2) The difficulty for theoretically minded conservatives is to find the appropriate categories for identifying continuities in a society so passionately dedicated to change that the only consistent conservatives may be the conservationists. (3) The difficulties are compounded for the conservative when, like Nisbet, he perceives the society as radically corrupted in its culture and values, deranged in its institutions. (4) Then the conservative is apt to find his conservatism an embarrassment. (5) For, as Nisbet argues, nothing less than "a fundamental change" can reverse the forces of decay.[18]

Here the repetition of *conservative* or *conservatism* in nearly every sentence, and the key signals of transition *Then* and *For* in the two last sentences, only make apparent a continuity that is more deeply embedded in the logic of the paragraph. You can see this by trying to follow each sentence with an imaginary question to which the next sentence would be the answer:

1. Robert Nisbet's *Twilight of Authority* is the most recent illustration of the perplexities of conservatism in America.

    What's so perplexing about it?

2. The difficulty for theoretically minded conservatives is to find the appropriate categories for identifying continuities in a society so passionately dedicated to change that the only consistent conservatives may be the conservationists.

    Would some conservatives be more bothered by this than others?

3. The difficulties are compounded for the conservative when, like Nisbet, he perceives the society as radically corrupted in its culture and values, deranged in its institutions.

    What happens to such a conservative?

4. Then the conservative is apt to find his conservatism an embarrassment.

    Why?

5. For, as Nisbet argues, nothing less than "a fundamental change" can reverse the forces of decay.

Try this test on some of your own paragraphs. Beginning with the second sentence in each case, write out a question to which that sentence seems to reply, and then see if your question appears to flow directly from the preceding sentence in your paragraph. If it doesn't, you've pinpointed a lapse in continuity.

Sentence patterns, too, can make for continuity within a paragraph. Oddly enough, both sameness and variety of pattern can serve this end. If certain ideas are parallel in meaning, a parallelism of structure can bring out the fact that they belong together. Thus, for example, a series of questions, or a row of sentences beginning with the same sentence element, highlights connections of meaning:

QUESTIONS:

Do single-parent households always produce children as disturbed as these? Let's hope not. But if they do, *what can we expect* from the generation that will come of age fifteen years from now? And *shouldn't we begin thinking,* before time runs out on us, about ways of revitalizing the traditional family?

PARALLEL SYNTAX:

If the family is to survive, laws about divorce and taxes will have to favor the married state. *If this in turn is to occur,* legislators who are sympathetic to the family will have to be elected. And *if we grasp this simple fact,* we will do all we can to put those legislators into office at the next election.

When your ideas aren't parallel in meaning, however, you ought to vary your structure from one sentence to the next. Mixing the patterns will link sentences in a continuous, easy flow.

Link One Paragraph to the Next

Most of your paragraphs ought to begin with sentences containing at least one indication of continuity with the foregoing paragraph. Exactly the same devices that make for internal paragraph unity can be called upon to hook one paragraph into the next one. In an essay by Lewis Mumford, for example, some paragraphs begin as follows:

- But at present these happy prospects are heavily overcast . . . [*But* and *these* show transition and identity].
- I shall not end on this negative note; but it is necessary . . . [*this* and *but* show identity and transition].
- But we are in the midst of other explosions . . . that will be just as fatal as long as they go in the present fashion . . . [*But* and *other* show transition; *the present* shows identity].
- Closer comparisons make our own achievements seem even more destitute . . . [*Closer* and *even more* show transition].
- Some of this attitude is doubtless left over from pioneer days . . . [*this* shows identity].
- I have of course intentionally, and doubtless grossly, caricatured the life of the representative American today . . . [the whole statement announces a transition].[19]

VARIETY

Vary the Length of Your Paragraphs

Paragraph length is partly a matter of convention and partly a matter of style. In newspaper reporting, where the main purpose is to com-

municate bits of information with a minimum of analysis, paragraphs consist of one, two, or three sentences at the most. Paragraphs
of dialogue also tend to be short; most writers indent for every change
of speaker. Some essayists—for example, Imamu Amiri Baraka (p.
146)—employ quite brief paragraphs to emphasize that certain plain
facts can't be overlooked. At the other extreme lie the immense fic-
tive paragraphs of, say, James Joyce and William Faulkner—passages
that disregard our sense of form so as to follow the unending stream
of a character's thoughts.

Most essayists, however, write paragraphs averaging 100–200
words in length, with two or three paragraphs to the typewritten,
double-spaced page. If your own paragraphs regularly take up a
whole page or more, they need to be scaled down to meet a reader's
normal attention span. If they rarely contain more than three brief
sentences, they're lacking in development and are probably making a
simple-minded impression. Consider this passage:

> Yesterday I saw my little brother watching a horror movie on televi-
> sion. This made me think of how much television influences children.
>
> What can we do about this social disorder? My little brother was
> certainly not being improved by this experience. This is a serious
> problem.
>
> In other countries there is state control of television. This is a bad
> thing, yes. But it is also a good thing, because it prevents the above-
> mentioned damage to little minds that may not grow up to be as so-
> phisticated as you and me.

Paragraph construction is only one of this writer's problems, but
the mere size of his paragraphs is a handicap. He won't be able to
fashion a thoughtful argument if he short-circuits his prose before it
gets properly started. Each break sets him back to zero again, forcing
him to raise a new topic without adequate preparation for it. He has,
for example, forgotten to justify his belief that horror movies cause
"damage to little minds," and he implies that the unspecified influence of television is itself a "social disorder." These paragraphs read
like sketchy notes that haven't yet been sorted, much less developed
for the eyes of a reader.

If the paragraphs in your first drafts go to the other extreme and
seem to ramble endlessly, don't be alarmed. It's easier in revision to
cut paragraphs down to size than to puff them out with new material.
Often you'll find that an unwieldy paragraph has shifted its topic
somewhere near the middle, and that you need only mark a new paragraph there in order to retain most of your sentences. If you do this,
however, make sure that both of the new paragraphs are tightly organized.

Establishing a middle-sized paragraph as your norm, you can depart from that norm with good effect. A reader who comes across a somewhat longer paragraph will know that a particularly complex point is being developed. Occasionally you can insert a very short paragraph—a sentence or two, or even a purposeful sentence fragment—to make a major transition, a challenge, an emphatic statement, or a summary. The emphasis comes precisely from the contrast between such a paragraph and the more developed ones surrounding it.

Move Between Generality and Detail

Paragraphs, like whole essays, should back up their main assertions with detail. Although there's nothing wrong with an occasional paragraph consisting entirely of general statements or entirely of particulars, in most paragraphs these elements should be mingled. It isn't simply that the reader deserves to see the basis for your broadest remarks; it's also a question of avoiding monotony. A series of paragraphs like the following, excessively abstract one would make a suffocating effect:

> Fate, which can be defined as the destiny of a human being, can turn out to be either good or bad. There are probably two general interpretations of fate as this idea occurs in literature. One interpretation is that a person's fate is a direct consequence of the rightness or wrongness of his actions, while the other interpretation is that nothing can alter the pattern that was established at birth or even earlier.

Does the writer have any sense of fate, or is he just reciting what he's been told? By not getting down to examples he makes a vacant impression.

The author of the following paragraph has one assertion to make about the amount of coastline in the United States. The assertion, though important to his argument, is obvious and potentially dull, but he enlivens it by combining precise statistics with a vivid and witty image:

> On the map, the simple fact is that we have plenty of seashore to go around. We are no landlocked Switzerland, but a nation of coasts. Even if all 210 million of us went to the beach in a legion, we could get wet together. To be precise, there would be 2.102 feet of ocean frontage for each of us—enough to wade in abreast, arm-in-arm, in a continental chorus line.[20]

Since topic sentences typically appear at the beginning of a paragraph, the transition from generality to detail often occurs after the opening sentence. Note the wealth of supporting material that follows a broad statement in this paragraph by Sonya Rudikoff:

> Although more marriages nowadays seem to be performed by clergymen, often hip ministers or "modern" rabbis, or, alternatively, very old-fashioned ones, their doctrine may not be part of anyone's daily life or conduct. The clergyman seems indistinguishable from the guests, and nothing prepares us for the moment when he steps forward in the garden and begins, all of a sudden, "Dearly Beloved . . .," or something of the sort. The Navajo or Hopi ceremonies, the dawn or midnight, garden or woodland nuptials, the Our Relationship sermons by the bridal pair, all borrow sanction and dignity from a sacramental tradition which is probably dropped as unceremoniously as possible after the ceremony. The couple married in the woods do not live by the law of the woods, the Hopi vows do not make a Hopi marriage in a modern California setting, the girl who circles seven times around the groom or the groom who stamps on a glass may ignore the imperatives of their actions, and their conduct after the marriage may bear no relation to the ceremony that made it; indeed, no rules of conduct for the future can be deduced from the ceremony. The couple is unlikely to say, as Thomas and Mary Ellwood did of their Quaker marriage in 1669: "We sensibly felt the Lord with us and joining us, the sense whereof remained with us all our lifetime, and was of very good service and very comfortable to us on all occasions."[21]

But an opposite movement, from the particular to the general, is also possible. Examine the following paragraph by Paul Goodman:

> During the hearings on Vietnam before the Senate Foreign Relations Committee, Senator Thomas Dodd of Connecticut—who had been mentioned as Lyndon Johnson's choice for Vice President in 1964—was asked what he thought of the sharp criticism of the government. "It is the price that we pay," he said, "for living in a free country." This answer was routine and nobody questioned it. Yet what an astonishing evaluation of the democratic process it is, that free discussion is a weakness we must put up with in order to avoid the evils of another system! To Milton, Spinoza or Jefferson, free discussion was the strength of a society. Their theory was that truth had power, often weak at first but steady and cumulative, and in free debate the right course would emerge and prevail. Nor was there any other method to arrive at truth, since there was no other authority to pronounce it than

all the people. Thus, to arrive at wise policy, it was essential that everybody say his say, and the more disparate the views and searching the criticism, the better.[22]

Goodman wants to make an abstract point about free discussion in a democracy, but he begins by telling a story and then draws us into examining its meaning. Our anger is stirred: the prominent senator, the would-be vice-president, has casually downgraded a precious right. By beginning with the anecdote about Senator Dodd, Goodman makes us more inclined to accept his own point of view.

ADVANCING THE ARGUMENT

Keep Things Moving

A writer, while composing and revising, is bound to feel occupied by problems of organization. A reader, though, has no interest whatever in sharing the writer's worries. Paragraphs that merely communicate those worries are self-defeating:

x We have now seen that the first part of the question posed at the beginning of this essay cannot be easily answered, and that, specifically, two serious considerations stand in our way. The first of those considerations has now been dealt with, though not perhaps as fully as some readers might prefer. It is time now to go on to the second point, after which we can return to our original question with a better sense of our true options.

What this really says is: *Please bear with me as I try to get through that cumbersome outline of mine.*

As a rule, then, don't devote whole paragraphs to maneuvering yourself from one part of your essay to the next. To do so would make you about as popular as a bus driver who required his passengers to get out after every few blocks and admire the wheels and steering column. Yet every now and then you may find an essay of yours taking such a major shift of direction that it deserves to be announced with fanfare. All right: do it briefly, with a crispness that bespeaks your eagerness to get on with the substantive points to follow. Thus:

• And now what has all this to do with the Dickens we already know? Why should he have occupied the last years of his life in concocting this sinister detective story?[23]

These two clipped sentences, instead of interrupting and obscuring the writer's case, simply whet our curiosity about it. The paragraph passes by so quickly that we suffer no loss in concentration.

Write in Paragraph Blocks

A well-organized essay typically develops, not simply paragraph by paragraph, but in groups of paragraphs that address major points. Just as each paragraph usually has one primary sentence and an array of supporting ones, so the paragraph block has a "thesis" paragraph and one or more contributory ones. Subordination, in short, is just as important in the succession of paragraphs as it is in sentence structure (pp. 135–141). The following excerpt from a graduate student's paper about the English novelist E. M. Forster gives an indication of the way paragraphs of general assertion can be played off against paragraphs of evidence:

(1) Despite his general liberalism and tolerance, and despite his explicit support of women's rights, E. M. Forster allows a deep resentment of the female sex to pervade his novels. Most of his women are not the benign creatures that the critics speak of, but outright troublemakers who injure the major characters—usually men. Nearly every novel contains what I call a "crisis of chivalry," a situation in which the men are required to protect or defend women, and this crisis triggers the downfall of the male protagonist. One could say, of course, that the code of chivalry rather than womankind is to blame, but this doesn't work out in practice. The truth is that Forster was rarely capable of portraying a sympathetic female character, and that he regarded the chivalric code as rooted in female weakness and malice.

(2) Perhaps the best-known of Forster's "crises of chivalry" is the scene in *A Passage to India* in which Fielding rescues Adela from the angry crowd that awaits her after Aziz's trial. Fielding must stay beside Adela because of the chivalric demand that men protect women from violence, but in so doing he loses his friend Aziz and misses their victory celebration. Aziz is offended by Fielding's absence, and from that point on their friendship (the most valued relationship in the novel) is spoiled by resentment and suspicion. Adela is regarded as the cause of all this; both Fielding and the narrator talk as if she were to blame for needing Fielding's protection in the first place.

(3) This note of blame directed at women is struck by comparable episodes in the other novels. In *Where Angels Fear to Tread*, the hero, Philip Herriton, is thwarted in his attempt to enjoy Italy and the comradeship of the engaging Italian, Gino, by his obligations to women. Here the "crisis of chivalry" is Philip's effort to rescue his sister-in-law, Lilia, from the hands of Gino, who is suspected of wanting to marry her for her money. Philip would like to befriend Gino, but his artificial role as Lilia's "protector" forces him to act as Gino's antagonist,

and indeed as the antagonist of all that is human and appealing in Italy.

(4) Lucy Honeychurch is the young lady who needs protection in *A Room With a View,* and the necessity of her being kept away from George Emerson, who has been cast in the role of "seducer" by Lucy's puritanical female chaperone, prevents the friendship of George and Lucy's brother, Freddy. In *Howards End* the consequences of chivalrous behavior are disastrous in the extreme. Helen is the wronged maiden whose seduction by Leonard Bast must be avenged, and the crisis occurs when Charles Wilcox confronts Leonard and strikes him down with a sword. The consequences are that Leonard dies, Charles is imprisoned, and Henry Wilcox collapses—bringing the whole Wilcox family down with him. What this shows is that female mischief causes male disaster.

(5) Thus there is a contradiction, and a deep one, in Forster's treatment of women. In simple terms it is the contradiction between his advocating greater freedom for women and his "demonstration" that women aren't deserving of such freedom. In a more sophisticated sense, it is the incompatibility of Forster's *asserting,* in his theoretical passages, that the chivalrous mentality should be eliminated for the sake of the women whom it oppresses, and his *showing,* through the operation of his plots, that it should be eliminated for the sake of men, who are its real victims.

Here paragraph 1 states a thesis, paragraphs 2–4 support it with evidence, and paragraph 5 recapitulates, bringing the whole issue into sharper focus. Whether or not we agree with the argument, we appreciate the author's sense of proportion and her command of facts. If each paragraph had asserted a new general idea and tried to defend it, the effect would have been weaker.

BEGINNINGS AND ENDINGS

Make Your First Paragraph Count

The most important paragraph in an essay, though it is also likely to be the one containing the least information, is the opener. An experienced reader can usually tell after two or three sentences whether the writer has command of the material at hand and is capable of making it interesting. Little can be expected from essays whose opening paragraphs begin with obviously unneeded dictionary definitions (p. 170) or with self-evident platitudes:

x Conservation is a very important topic now that everyone is so interested in ecology.

x One of man's greatest enemies is disease.

or with restatements of an assigned topic:

x It is interesting to inquire into the reasons for the emergence of fascist ideology after World War I.

or with laments over the difficulty of it all:

x A person like me, situated far from the scene in both space and time, faces an almost impossible task in trying to assess the meaning of the Counter-Reformation. However, ...

A good opening paragraph customarily accomplishes three things. It catches the reader's interest, it establishes the tone of the essay, and—usually but not always—it reveals the one central problem that's going to be addressed. In its simplest form the first paragraph just states the writer's thesis:

> After a short but severe recession, economic growth is beginning again in the United States and, more slowly, in other countries. But the economy will not be restored to the precise conditions existing in 1973. The reasons can be found in a new set of realities affecting energy and raw materials. That supplies of these basic commodities will remain adequate in the future can no longer be taken for granted. Indeed, the prospects for economic prosperity and perhaps for peace in coming decades will depend on how the world adjusts to new constraints and new expectations regarding these key ingredients of human endeavor.[24]

But more often—and this is usually preferable—the opener makes a forceful, perhaps somewhat surprising assertion that demands a response of some sort:

> The revival of the forties and fifties is upon us. The Middle-American time of my youth is gaining its place in our historical imagination. Movies, essays, stories, novels, and the sheer passage of time have already begun transforming that era from banal to exotic. The record is being filled not only with nostalgia but with critical insight, as writing men of wit try to pin down those days. Nevertheless, something crucial is missing, for the reality being recorded about that era is essentially a male reality, the experience male experience. And until the

female side is acknowledged and recorded, the era cannot even begin
to emerge in perspective.[25]

This paragraph certainly could be strengthened: the first five sentences are constructed alike, the diction is somewhat repetitive, and
little progress is made from the first sentence through the fourth. Yet
the author does what needs doing. Her opening sentence gives us
orientation and a promise of interesting details to follow; we can tell
from the tone that this will be a no-nonsense essay, factual and critical in its emphasis; and the paragraph ends with a thesis sentence for
the whole essay, thus concluding one movement of thought and
opening up a more ambitious one. Not very much has been said, but
we have settled back and prepared ourselves for the rest.

Another opening succeeds in a quite different way:

> Old men, old women, almost 20 million of them. They constitute 10
> percent of the total population, and the percentage is steadily growing.
> Some of them, like conspirators, walk all bent over, as if hiding some
> precious secret, filled with self-protection. The body seems to gather
> itself around those vital parts, folding shoulders, arms, pelvis like a
> fading rose. Watch and you see how fragile old people come to think
> they are.[26]

This essay, like the previous one, tries to tell the truth about a poorly
understood aspect of American life, but its approach is descriptive
rather than argumentative. Though the author has managed to slip
two statistics into her first two sentences, her paragraph emphasizes
feelings that will dominate the rest of her essay. Her deliberately fragmentary opening sentence, her early use of physical detail, and her
bold figurative language (pp. 117–121) give her paragraph a more
intimate, subjective air than the one above.

Like most opening paragraphs, the three examples given so far allow the reader to see what the topic of the whole essay will be. None
of them, however, relies on the handiest and most frequently used
device for introducing the topic, namely the so-called *funnel paragraph*. The funnel-shaped opener begins with an assertion *covering a
broader area than the topic will;* this gives the reader a wide perspective and a context for understanding the actual topic when it is stated.
Then, in perhaps two or three subsequent sentences, the funnel paragraph *narrows to the topic*, which is usually revealed just as the paragraph ends. The following example is typical:

> Only a few politicians have taken a craftsman's pride in self-expres-
> sion, and fewer still—Caesar, Lord Clarendon, Winston Churchill, De
> Gaulle—have been equally successful in politics and authorship. Of

these, Churchill may be the most interesting, for he was not only among the most voluminous of writers, but also commented freely on the art of writing. He was, in fact, a writer before becoming a politician.[27]

By the end of this paragraph we know that the topic will be Churchill's writing, but we arrive at that knowledge by sliding down the funnel:

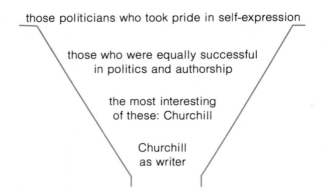

those politicians who took pride in self-expression

those who were equally successful
in politics and authorship

the most interesting
of these: Churchill

Churchill
as writer

You should certainly try your hand at some funnel paragraphs and keep this structure in your repertoire. Instead of waiting tensely for some thunderclap of inspiration, you can call on the funnel opener to get you easily moving toward the substance of your essay.

Observe two points, though: many fine essays *don't* begin with a narrowing pattern, and those that do, like the one just quoted, put precise and meaningful statements into the opening sentences. What you want to avoid is funneling for the sheer funnel of it, as here:

The subject of psychotherapy is definitely one of the major issues of our time. In this democratic, post-Freudian age, we all have an interest in learning which kinds of therapy are more likely to work than other kinds. It is therefore very interesting to all of us when new books are published on this important subject. In this essay we shall examine two such books, respectively entitled *The Love Treatment* and *The Radical Therapist*. The thesis of the former is that sexual intimacy between therapists and patients may be beneficial, and the thesis of the latter is that therapy is all too often a reflection of social injustice. These are certainly challenging ideas. Six points in particular deserve to be made about them.

This paragraph, to be sure, is superficially "well organized," with a single line of development from the general area of psychotherapy to the points that will be made about two particular books. But the first

three sentences, by saying almost nothing, foreclose a reader's interest in the rest of the paragraph — indeed, in the whole essay.

Compare the fictitious example just given to Ellen Willis's actual
opening paragraph on the same topic:

> I am a sucker for psychology books, so when the paperback edition of
> *The Love Treatment* appeared on the rack at Woolworth's, I picked it
> up and leafed through it. Its premise, I discovered, was that the taboo
> on sexual intimacy between psychotherapists and their patients should
> be re-examined, not only because it was being broken all the time any-
> way but because in the right circumstances such intimacy might have
> therapeutic value. My immediate hostility to this idea — I'd heard any
> number of horror stories from friends who had slept with or been
> propositioned by their therapists — did not keep me from admiring
> its brilliance. Psychotherapy, as conventionally practiced, had proved
> a useful tool for exploiting women, and so had the ideology of sexual
> revolution — why not combine them? It didn't take much imagination
> — or excessive cynicism — to foresee the practical result of giving (most-
> ly male) therapists a professional rationale for going to bed with their
> (mostly female) clients. After all, the argument that sex is therapeutic
> had been a favorite of amateur psychiatrists for years.[28]

Now, this might be considered too breezy a beginning for the purposes of most student papers. The author is deliberately slangy in her
first sentence, and she makes no effort to get both of the assigned
books within her sights. Her offhand, autobiographical manner is
that of a typical piece in *The New Yorker* or *The Village Voice*. Yet
her paragraph accomplishes a good deal without seeming to labor
over the obvious requirements of a book review. Note, for example,
that instead of dutifully announcing the thesis of *The Love Treatment*,
she manages to integrate it into a little story about herself. We've
been told what we somehow had to learn, but the information has
been put in an active setting. More important, the author has shown
us that she's not in fact a "sucker" but a skeptic who can be counted
on to resist the self-interested arguments of male therapists. We want
to read further because we see that she cares about her subject and is
determined to deal with it fairly.

One common way of drawing a reader into an essay is to use the
first paragraph as "bait," without disclosing the exact topic. A very
general reflection, an alarming fact, a story, an opinion that flies in
the face of received views — whatever the item, it teases the reader by
its very refusal to say what the argument will be. We suspect that a
writer who can start at the periphery of the topic in this way must
have an unusual control over the total conception of the essay. Of

course we could also suspect that the writer is simply being evasive or sloppy; much depends on the paragraph that follows this one. When used responsibly, though, the baited opener has the merit of stirring our thoughts and emotions before we have a chance to draw back and say, "Oh, is that the topic? I'm not interested in reading about *that*."

Thus Terence Des Pres, beginning a book about death-camp survivors, gets close to his real thesis — that those survivors are the characteristic heroes of our modern world — but doesn't quite reveal it. Instead, he offers us a sweeping overview of the age:

> Men have always been ready to die for beliefs, sacrificing life for higher goals. That made sense once, perhaps; but no cause moves without live men to move it, and our predicament today — as governments know — is that ideas and ideologies are stopped by killing those who hold them. The "final solution" has become a usual solution, and the world is not what it was. Within a landscape of disaster, places like Auschwitz, Hiroshima or the obliterated earth of Indo-China, where people die in thousands, where machines reduce courage to stupidity and dying to complicity with aggression, it makes no sense to speak of death's dignity or of its communal blessing. We require a heroism commensurate with the sweep of ruin in our time: action equal to situations in which it becomes less self-indulgent and more useful to live, to be there. History moves, times change, men find themselves caught up in unexpected circumstance. The grandeur of death is lost in a world of mass murder, and except for special cases the martyr and his tragic counterpart are types of the hero unfit for the darkness ahead. When men and women must live against terrible odds, when mere existence becomes miraculous, to die is in no way a triumph.[29]

In the following opener, J. Bronowski, writing about the uses of technology, doesn't even hint at his topic in the first paragraph, but arouses our curiosity in a way that he can exploit immediately afterward:

> We all know the story of the sorcerer's apprentice; or *Frankenstein* which Mary Shelley wrote in competition with her husband and Byron; or some other story of the same kind out of the macabre invention of the nineteenth century. In these stories, someone who has special powers over nature conjures or creates a stick or a machine to do his work for him; and then finds that he cannot take back the life he has given it. The mindless monster overwhelms him; and what began as an invention to do the housework ends by destroying the master with the house.

These stories have become the epitome of our own fears. . . .[30]

The novelist Ralph Ellison, in disputing an article by a literary critic, Irving Howe, startles us by beginning with angry challenges:

> First, three questions: Why is it so often true that when critics confront the American *as Negro* they suddenly drop their advanced critical armament and revert with an air of confident superiority to quite primitive modes of analysis? Why is it that sociology-oriented critics seem to rate literature so far below politics and ideology that they would rather kill a novel than modify their presumptions concerning a given reality which it seeks in its own terms to project? Finally, why is it that so many of those who would tell us the meaning of Negro life never bother to learn how varied it really is?[31]

And Gay Talese opens his book on the Mafia by putting us inside the shoes, not of a main character, but of a doorman who wants no trouble:

> Knowing that it is possible to see too much, most doormen in New York have developed an extraordinary sense of selective vision: they know what to see and what to ignore, when to be curious and when to be indolent; they are most often standing indoors, unaware, when there are accidents or arguments in front of their buildings; and they are usually in the street seeking taxicabs when burglars are escaping through the lobby. Although a doorman may disapprove of bribery and adultery, his back is invariably turned when the superintendent is handing money to the fire inspector or when a tenant whose wife is away escorts a young woman into the elevator — which is not to accuse the doorman of hypocrisy or cowardice but merely to suggest that his instinct for uninvolvement is very strong, and to speculate that doormen have perhaps learned through experience that nothing is to be gained by serving as a material witness to life's unseemly sights or to the madness of the city. This being so, it was not surprising that on the night when the Mafia chief, Joseph Bonanno, was grabbed by two gunmen in front of a luxury apartment house on Park Avenue near Thirty-sixth Street, shortly after midnight on a rainy Tuesday in October, the doorman was standing in the lobby talking to the elevator man and saw nothing.[32]

The ingenuity of this paragraph consists in its subtle way of conferring a privilege on us. As real people in the path of the Mafia we would have to suppress our curiosity, see no evil; but in fact we are only reading a book, and now we can leave the doorman behind and learn what he would swear he hadn't witnessed.

It isn't necessary, then, to get right down to the point, either in your opening sentence or in your whole opening paragraph. Remember, though, that introductory material shouldn't take up a disproportionate amount of space. The briefer your whole essay, the less room you have to play games with the reader's curiosity.

I have said that the most important paragraph in an essay is the opening one. Similarly, among the sentences in that paragraph the first one is of paramount interest. If it is vague and slack, the prospects for arousing the reader's sympathy immediately plummet. If it is crisp and tight and energetic, its momentum can carry through the next few sentences at least. This is why some writers take pains to make that first sentence *epigrammatic* — pointed and memorable. Thus Theodore Solotaroff begins a review of a book about Jewish immigrants by declaring:

* The first generation tries to retain as much as possible, the second to forget, the third to remember.[33]

Sonya O'Sullivan wittily begins an essay on divorce:

* There was a time when a woman customarily had a baby after one year of marriage; now she has a book after one year of divorce.[34]

And a student writer advocating gun control begins:

* Thousands of people in this country could make an overwhelming case for the banning of handguns, except for one inconvenient fact: they aren't so much *in* the country as *under* it, abruptly sent to their graves with no chance to protest or dissuade. Arguing with a gun nut may be futile, but have you ever tried arguing with a gun?

As this last example shows, the epigrammatic sentence needn't be the very first one; the point is to get a decisive start.

How, you may ask, are you to come up with attention-drawing openers like these? The answer is that you shouldn't even try when writing your first draft. A decisive introductory sentence can only be written after most of the other problems with the essay have been solved. When you're quite sure where your main emphasis will fall, what tone you will take, and how much of your case you want to reveal at the outset, *then* you can hone and polish that opening sentence. And this advice applies to the entire first paragraph as well. You can save time in composing by writing a deliberately sketchy or mechanical introduction in the first draft, and then starting anew when the rest of the essay has been blocked out.

End with a Strong Paragraph

Nobody knows why, but human beings have a persistent need for a sense of completion. They want to feel that a piece of writing, at its end, is truly *finished* and not just stopped like some toy soldier that needs rewinding. What's more, they like to anticipate, through a revealing change in tone or intensity or generality of reference, when the end is about to occur.

Yet many student writers refuse to consider this desire. Why? I believe it is usually because they think of the concluding paragraph, as they have previously been taught to write it, as unbearably phony. The common, but groundless, idea of a last paragraph is that it should restate the essay's point with as much pomp and ceremony as possible:

x Thus we have seen that leash laws violate all three of the cardinal principles of canine liberation. It will be a far, far better world for both man and beast when these outrages have been halted once and for all.

Well, that *isn't* what it means to conclude an essay. There has to be some middle course between saying nothing and trying to knock the planets from their orbits.

Let's assume you want to conclude your essay in some way or other. Now what? The only general rules for the final paragraph are, unfortunately, negative ones:

1. Don't merely repeat your thesis.
2. Don't embark on a completely new topic.
3. Don't pretend to have proven more than you have.
4. Don't apologize or bring your thesis into doubt.

The reason for these cautions is that readers come away from an essay with the last paragraph ringing in their ears. If you end by sounding bored or distracted or untrustworthy or hesitant, you're encouraging readers to discount everything you've worked so hard to establish. Of course you want to give the impression that things are falling in place. Do so without compromising your position, but also without making preposterous claims for its significance.

The rules against embarking on a new topic and exaggerating what you have proved shouldn't stop you from *taking a wider view* at the end of an essay. Up till now you have carefully limited your focus to a chosen problem or situation; now, without claiming supernatural insight, you can look beyond that immediate subject to its possible significance or its future development. Thus, for example, an article about financial irresponsibility in the governing of New York City concludes:

There are signs today that some political leaders, in New York and elsewhere, have discovered a "new realism." If, by this term, its proponents mean realism in the Burkean sense of restraint, caution, and reliance on practical experience, rather than in the conventional sense of what is politically palatable at the moment, we may witness an improvement in our political condition. Let us hope that this great city's difficulties will indeed bring a *genuine* sense of realism into our political life.[35]

And here is the last paragraph of a student essay analyzing a recent play, *Rosencrantz and Guildenstern Are Dead*, whose "heroes" are two minor characters taken from *Hamlet:*

What Stoppard has done with Rosencrantz and Guildenstern isn't just ingenious and amusing; it is also characteristically modern. In Shakespeare's tragedy, Hamlet's old schoolmates perform their minor service to the plot and disappear before we have learned which of them is which. We leave them without regret or further curiosity, for the play must get on with the fates of its "real" characters, the figures that we and Shakespeare agree to regard as significant. But it is precisely the "nonpersons" who catch the modern playwright's interest. Is Hamlet any more substantial than Rosencrantz? Though Shakespeare knew as well as Stoppard that all art rests on convention, he never thought of turning convention itself into a dramatic issue. The modern author is more single-mindedly theoretical, devoting his whole play to a comic discourse on the real and the unreal. And if the joke continually threatens to become tedious — well, that too is typical of our age, when playwrights would rather make a skeptical point than allow larger-than-life characters to "strut and fret their hour upon the stage."

Both of these writers have achieved a conclusive effect by presenting their freest, most general reflections in the last paragraph.

Since essayists generally reveal their theses near the outset, closing paragraphs rarely "conclude" in the sense of uncovering the main idea as a logical inference from premises (p. 67). Sometimes, however, they review the ground that has been covered, bringing out some noteworthy point that doesn't coincide exactly with the thesis. If you do use a last paragraph to summarize, try to avoid the lifeless *Thus we have seen* effect. Mix your summary with some fresh element that keeps your reader's mind engaged through the final sentence. That element can be a vivid image, a witty reflection, a challenge, a reminder of yet-unsettled questions, or an evocative return to some idea, episode, or figure of speech that occurred near the beginning.

One especially sound policy is to put aside a striking quotation, fact, or story that you might have used earlier, and to present it at the end *in light of* the thesis that you've now demonstrated. This last unexpected detail should memorably capture or illustrate or corroborate your point. Thus one writer uses a famous scientist's own words to praise his career:

> Heisenberg once likened the role of the scientist to that of Columbus, "who had the courage to leave behind him all inhabited land, in the almost insane hope of finding land again on the other side of the sea." Heisenberg's journey was a long one, and the land he discovered one of the richest in all of science.[36]

Another writer, taking a more hostile view of his subject, turns a quotation against its source:

> Robert M. Hutchins has described the editors of *Britannica 3* as pioneers. After they had established their design "the question became one of execution . . . there were no models to imitate and no horrible examples to shun." One of these deficiencies has been made good by *Britannica 3* itself: they have their horrible example now.[37]

The wide-ranging uses of a concluding anecdote may be shown by three final examples. First, a writer who explored the supposed route that the Israelites took in escaping their bondage in Egypt ends by narrating a special moment in his adventure:

> Picking my way to the other side of the valley, I came to a lovely little cave, hidden from above. The waters of Ayn Musa drop right over the cave's mouth so that, ducking inside, I could look out through the bright prismatic colors of the falling water to Mount Nebo and to the hills of the Promised Land. If the presence of Moses rests anywhere outside the hearts of his descendants, I think it must be here.
>
> Looking out, I saw a shepherd boy leading his goats into the valley to feed on vegetation watered, in a sense, by the rod of Moses himself. Putting down his shepherd's rod, the lad knelt on a spur of rock and performed the evening prayer, his figure silhouetted starkly against the reddening sky. I was moved beyond words. No sight could have been more fitting. My search for Moses had reached its end, and a new beginning.[38]

In the next example a lighter-hearted story makes the writer's point incisively:

Somehow, as I think of all the faculty members who are getting leaves from the classroom these days to work out solutions to restlessness among students, it seems to me that the best commentary is contained in an old, now famous, Herblock cartoon. It was drawn when the late John Foster Dulles was incessantly engaged in missions outside Washington, D.C. It showed President Eisenhower sitting at the telephone saying: "Foster, don't just *do* something; *stand* there."[39]

And here are the two final paragraphs of an autobiography:

One day in the spring of 1945, when the war against Hitler was almost won, I sat in a newsreel theater in Piccadilly looking at the first films of newly liberated Belsen. On the screen, sticks in black-and-white prison garb leaned on a wire, staring dreamily at the camera; other sticks shuffled about, or sat vaguely on the ground, next to an enormous pile of bodies, piled up like cordwood, from which protruded legs, arms, heads. A few guards were collected sullenly in a corner, and for a moment a British Army bulldozer was shown digging an enormous hole in the ground. Then the sticks would come back on the screen, hanging on the wire, looking at us.

It was unbearable. People coughed in embarrassment, and in embarrassment many laughed.[40]

Here the story is so powerful that it requires no commentary; the writer leaves us with his own unfinished task of trying to comprehend the Nazi death camps.

What matters most about a final paragraph is simply whether it works — whether readers are borne along with it and satisfied at the very end. If their parting thought is *So that's what it all means* or *There's nothing more to say*, you've done your job. If, somewhere before the last sentence, they tell themselves with a smirk, *Ah, yes, the customary ringing summary*, you've laid on the rhetoric of conclusiveness too thickly. Try to keep readers engaged until the last line, so that they never feel they can stop reading wherever they please.

EXERCISES

I. Find the irrelevant sentence that was inserted into the following paragraph, and explain why it doesn't belong there (pp. 157–158):

In 1886 Grinnell suggested in the pages of *Forest and Stream* that concerned men and women create an organization for the protection of wild birds and their eggs, its administration to be undertaken by the magazine's staff. Grinnell did not have to grope to name this organization. He had grown up near the home that the great bird painter, John James Audubon, had left to his wife and children at his death. As a boy Grinnell had played in an old loft cluttered with stacks of the red muslin-bound copies of the *Ornithological Biography* and boxes of bird skins brought back by Audubon from his expeditions. He had attended a school for small boys conducted by Lucy Audubon nearby. All his life he would remain an avid reader. Grinnell quite naturally called the new organization the Audubon Society.[41]

II. **The following five sentences, presented out of order, belong to a paragraph by Wilson Follett. Rearrange them in what you take to be the best order, and briefly explain why you placed each sentence where you did (pp. 159–160).**

1. The right way is believed to be clearer, simpler, more logical, and hence more likely to prevent error and confusion.
2. Despite the modern desire to be easy and casual, Americans from time to time give thought to the language they use — to grammar, vocabulary, and gobbledygook.
3. And as on other issues they divide into two parties.
4. Good writing is easier to read; it offers a pleasant combination of sound and sense.
5. The larger, which includes everybody from the proverbial plain man to the professional writer, takes it for granted that there is a right way to use words and construct sentences, and many wrong ways.[42]

III. **Here is the topic sentence for a paragraph. Write two alternative paragraphs that include it. In the first, put the topic sentence at the very beginning; in the second, at the very end (pp. 160–161).**

If we don't revoke the licenses of drunken drivers, we are leaving them with a license to kill.

IV. **Here is a paragraph from which a needed topic sentence is missing. Supply that sentence. Make it assertive, and place it in the most emphatic position you can find for it (pp. 160–161).**

There must be something dreadfully wrong with a system that turns millions of more or less honest Americans into guilt-ridden sneaks and cheaters every spring. Of course the damage isn't confined to the feelings and morals of taxpayers; the public treasury suffers as well. For the complexity of federal tax laws — a complexity having nothing to do with justice and everything to do with special-interest pressures on Congress — guarantees that the rich, and *only* the rich, will be able to play the game to their advantage.

V. Write a paragraph in which you first pose a problem or question and then supply the answer (pp. 165–166). The topic of the paragraph is up to you.

VI. Take the main idea of the paragraph you have written for Exercise V and write a new paragraph *proposing that idea after first considering an alternative to it* (pp. 166–168).

VII. Consider two college courses, or major programs, or careers, that are similar enough to be worth comparing. Jot down some of the resemblances and differences you find. Then compose a paragraph, *bringing out some of the resemblances but emphasizing the points of contrast* between the two items (pp. 168–169).

VIII. Think of something dramatic or important that has recently happened to you or others. Then compose a paragraph effectively *leading up to that event and revealing it at the end* (pp. 163, 173–175). Note that the "leading up" should be, not a list of things that happened earlier, but a series of remarks that will lend the event a maximum dramatic impact.

IX. Study the following paragraph by Joseph Wood Krutch. Taking the sentences one by one, discuss their elements of *continuity* (pp. 175–179).

(1) This is an appalling demonstration of the cruelty of nature, not much worse, perhaps, than many others, but seeming so just because of the huge size of the victim. (2) Perhaps the commercial slaughters of the whale are less cruel; but one curious fact does remain and illustrates a general law: killer whales do not exterminate the race of gray whales. (3) In fact, I doubt that there is a single known case in historical times where any large animal living in its native environment has been responsible for the extermination of any other. (4) Presumably during the great crises of evolution something of the sort did take place — when, for example, the advanced mammals all but exterminated the marsupials over almost the whole surface of the earth. (5) Something of the sort also happens when goats, dogs, and cats are established by man on islands where nature had worked out no balance taking them into account. (6) But in general, live and let live is the motto — even of predators.[43]

X. Each of the following three sentences should be imagined as *ending* a paragraph. For each one, write a sentence that might serve as the *beginning* of the *next* paragraph. The point is to create a sense of continuity from one paragraph to the following one (p. 179).

1. It seems unlikely that colleges will ever devote equal funds to men's and women's athletic programs.
2. Without local control of programming, public television loses much of its reason for existence.
3. Most people today have no clear idea why the liberal arts deserve to be studied at all.

XI. Using a "funnel opener" (pp. 187–188), write the first paragraph of an essay on any topic you can make interesting.

XII. Write an alternative opening paragraph for the essay proposed in Exercise XI, this time using a "baited opener" (pp. 189–192).

XIII. Write an emphatic and conclusive *last* paragraph for the same essay (pp. 193–196).

XIV. Turn back to the essay by Abigail Zuger on pages 10–12, and write a paragraph describing and judging the relationship between the *opening* and *closing* paragraphs of that essay.

NOTES

[1]"The President's Palace Guard," *Newsweek*, 19 Mar. 1973, p. 24.

[2]Albert Goldman, "The Emergence of Rock," *New American Review*, No. 3 (1968), p. 119.

[3]Timothy E. Head, *Going Native in Hawaii: A Poor Man's Guide to Paradise* (Rutland, Vt.: Charles E. Tuttle, 1965), p. 7.

[4]Pete Axthelm with Patricia J. Sethi, "The Matador," *Newsweek*, 22 Sept. 1975, p. 61.

[5]Alan H. Schoenfeld, "Exploiting the Job Market," *Chronicle of Higher Education*, 26 Jan. 1976, p. 24.

[6]Virginia Woolf, "Life and the Novelist," in *Granite and Rainbow* (New York: Harvest, 1975), p. 41.

[7]Nancy Jo Hoffman, "Sexism in Letters of Recommendation," *MLA Newsletter*, Sept. 1972, p. 5.

[8]Anne Taylor Fleming, "Making Babies," *Newsweek*, 11 Aug. 1975, p. 13.

[9]Paul Roazen, *Freud and His Followers* (New York: Knopf, 1975), p. 4.

[10]George F. Will, "D Is for Dodo," *Newsweek*, 9 Feb. 1976, p. 84.

[11]Arthur Goldsmith, "Ralph Gibson Quadrants," *Popular Photography*, Mar. 1976, p. 100.

[12]Nathan Glazer, "The New Left and Its Limits," *Commentary*, July 1968, p. 39.

[13]Ron Fimrite, "Kings of the Hill Again," *Sports Illustrated*, 21 July 1975, p. 15.

[14]John Walsh, "Brigham Young University: Challenging the Federal Patron," *Science*, 191 (16 Jan. 1976), 160.

[15]Richard Gambino, "Watergate Lingo: A Language of Non-Responsibility," *Freedom at Issue*, Nov.–Dec. 1973, pp. 15–16.

[16]Marshall Koughan, "Goodbye, San Francisco," *Harper's*, Sept. 1975, p. 30.

[17]John H. Schaar, "The Case for Patriotism," *American Review*, No. 17 (May 1973), pp. 61–62.

[18]Sheldon S. Wolin, "The New Conservatives," *New York Review of Books*, 5 Feb. 1976, p. 6.

[19]Lewis Mumford, "California and the Human Horizon," *The Urban Prospect* (New York: Harcourt Brace, 1968), pp. 3, 4, 6, 8, 11.

[20]Anthony Wolff, "We Shall Fight Them on the Beaches . . . ," *Harper's*, Aug. 1973, p. 55.

[21]Sonya Rudikoff, "Marriage and Household," *Commentary*, June 1973, p. 59.

[22]Paul Goodman, "The Psychology of Being Powerless," in *People or Personnel* and *Like a Conquered Province* (New York: Vintage, 1967), p. 344.

[23]Edmund Wilson, "Dickens: The Two Scrooges," in *Eight Essays* (Garden City, N.Y.: Anchor, 1954), p. 84.

[24]Philip H. Abelson and Allen L. Hammond, "The New World of Materials," *Science*, 191 (20 Feb. 1976), 633.

[25]Alix Kates Shulman, "The War in the Back Seat," *Atlantic*, July 1972, p. 50.

[26]Sharon Curtin, "Aging in the Land of the Young," *Atlantic*, July 1972, p. 68.

[27]Manfred Weidhorn, "Blood, Toil, Tears, and 8,000,000 Words: Churchill Writing," *Columbia Forum*, Spring 1975, p. 19.

[28]Ellen Willis, "The Fantasy of the Perfect Lover," *New York Review of Books*, 31 Aug. 1972, p. 7.

[29]Terence Des Pres, *The Survivor: An Anatomy of Life in the Death Camps* (New York: Oxford Univ. Press, 1976), p. 6.

[30]J. Bronowski, "Science, the Destroyer or Creator," in *The Common Sense of Science* (1955; rpt. New York: Vintage, n.d.), p. 136.

[31]Ralph Ellison, "The World and the Jug," in *Shadow and Act* (1964; rpt. New York: Signet, 1966), pp. 115–16.

[32]Gay Talese, *Honor Thy Father* (1971; rpt. Greenwich, Conn.: Fawcett-Crest, 1972), p. 16.

[33]Theodore Solotaroff, rev. of *World of Our Fathers*, by Irving Howe, *New York Times Book Review*, 1 Feb. 1976, p. 1.

[34]Sonya O'Sullivan, "Single Life in a Double Bed," *Harper's*, Nov. 1975, p. 45.

[35]Joseph F. Johnston, Jr., "The Leader as Mass Man," *National Review*, 28 (19 Mar. 1976), 272.

[36]Peter Gwynne with Anthony Collins, "The Quantum Mechanic," *Newsweek*, 16 Feb. 1976, p. 90.

[37]Samuel McCracken, "The Scandal of 'Britannica 3,' " *Commentary*, Feb. 1976, p. 68.

[38]Harvey Arden, "In Search of Moses," *National Geographic*, Jan. 1976, p. 36.

[39]Robert A. Nisbet, "Crisis in the University?" *The Public Interest*, Winter 1968, p. 64.

[40]Alfred Kazin, *Starting Out in the Thirties* (Boston: Little, Brown, 1965), p. 166.

[41]Carl W. Buchheister and Frank Graham, Jr., "From the Swamps and Back: A Concise and Candid History of the Audubon Movement," *Audubon*, Jan. 1973, p. 7; one sentence added.

[42]Rearranged from Wilson Follett, *Modern American Usage: A Guide* (New York: Hill & Wang, 1966), p. 3.

[43]Joseph Wood Krutch, *The Forgotten Peninsula: A Naturalist in Baja California* (1961; rpt. New York: Apollo, 1970), p. 177.

PART III
SOURCES

USING THE
7 LIBRARY

Few people feel altogether at home in a library, with its several systems of classification, its various catalogs and special rooms, its rules and privileges, its imposing tiers of stacks and their busy-looking habitués. It's hard to believe that this labyrinth is there for your convenience and enlightenment. Beyond the worry that you won't be able to track down what others have written about your topic lies another worry that the sources *will* turn up and anticipate or demolish what you were going to say. Half-deliberately, then, many people imagine that the library is impenetrable. Rather than risk unpleasant surprises, they stay home and rely heavily on the few sources that happen to come to their notice.

This attitude is self-defeating. Although there's such a thing as irrational perfectionism (p. 34), there's no such thing as being too well-informed to write. The more you read, the more developed your thoughts will be; and the reading will provide you with opportunities to support your case or to contrast it with others. The embarrassment of having to revise one of your ideas is very slight compared to the embarrassment of learning, too late, that you've written an ambitious paper in ignorance of important, easily accessible sources.

There's no need to master the whole library at once. Most libraries offer free tours and explanatory pamphlets, and there are people on hand at any time—most notably the reference librarian—whose business is to make knowledge available to you. (In fact, a reference librarian will often locate, not only a book or journal, but the one fact you're looking for.) By involving yourself in a specific research project and asking for help whenever you're confused, you can become familiar with certain aspects of the library while leaving others for later.

In essence the library is a vast information-retrieval system. As with a computer, the knack of using it successfully consists in knowing the right questions to present it with. Rummaging through the stacks without any questions at all would be as senseless as fishing blindly in the computer's memory bank. You have to know at least some of the overlapping ways in which sources can be found, and you have to keep narrowing your search as you get a clearer and clearer idea of the way your project is developing.

As you do more research, you'll gradually develop a better sense of the difference between a promising lead and a blind alley. The majority of available books on any topic, you'll find, have already been superseded by others; the more recent the work, the more eager you should be to lay hands on it. This is doubly true because an up-to-date work may contain a selective *bibliography*—a list of key books and articles for further reference—that can save you many hours of scrounging and many mistakes of judgment. An experienced researcher doesn't have to run through *all* the types of information-seeking described in the following pages; he or she finds a few key works as early as possible and then allows those works to suggest further moves. The writer of the sample paper on pages 245–259, for example, consulted his library's card catalog and then an index of book reviews to discover four recent and important studies of W. C. Fields, which led him to his thesis.

LIBRARY RESOURCES

These are the main tools for acquiring information and learning which works on a given subject are important:

The Card Catalog

The card catalog is an alphabetical index of the library's printed holdings, usually including books, periodicals, pamphlets, and items on microfilm (but excluding manuscripts, phonograph records, and tapes). Most libraries use the dictionary form of catalog, in which items are cross-indexed (that is, listed under more than one heading) by author, subject, and title. Thus, one way of beginning to find the relevant materials for your project is to go directly to the subject heading in the card catalog: Flood Control, Magic, etc. In many libraries the author and title cards are kept in one catalog and the subject cards in another.

The most important piece of information on a card is the *call number* in the upper left corner, for this is the key to the book's location in the stacks. Whether you enter the stacks yourself or merely submit a call slip, this number is your way of obtaining the book. Small libraries sometimes have their own systems of numbering, but large ones follow either the *Dewey Decimal System* or the *Library of Congress System* of classification. In the Dewey Decimal System, the first three digits of the call number will be a figure from 1 to 999, grouped as follows:

000 General Works	400 Language	700 The Arts
100 Philosophy	500 Pure Sciences	800 Literature
200 Religion	600 Technology	900 History
300 Social Sciences		

In the Library of Congress System, the call number begins with a key letter:

A	General Works
B	Philosophy — Religion
C	Auxiliary Sciences of History
D	History and Topography (except America)
E – F	American History
G	Geography — Anthropology
H	Social Sciences
J	Political Science
K	Law
L	Education
M	Music
N	Fine Arts
P	Language and Literature
Q	Science
R	Medicine
S	Agriculture – Plant and Animal Industry
T	Technology
U	Military Science
V	Naval Science
Z	Bibliography and Library Science

If you have "stack privileges" and are familiar with your library's code of classification, you can go directly to the shelves and quickly check a large number of volumes. Examine their indexes and introductions to see if they deal with the problem you have in mind. Remember, though, that the more important books are likely to be in circulation, and that you won't even learn of their existence if browsing is your only method of research.

The card catalog itself provides several kinds of useful information. Here, for example, is a representative card from a library using the Library of Congress System:

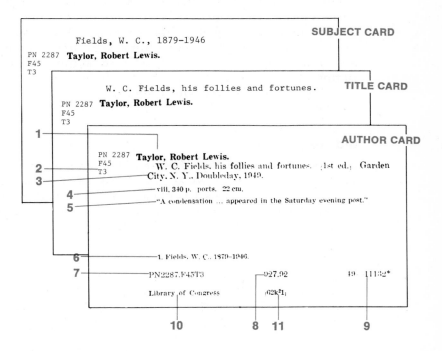

1. Author's name.
2. Call number indicating where in the library this book is shelved.
3. Title of book, number of edition, place of publication, publisher's name, and year of publication.
4. Format of book: "viii, 340 p." means that there are eight preliminary pages which are numbered in Roman numerals and are followed by 340 pages numbered in Arabic numerals; "ports." indicates that the book contains portraits; "22 cm." reveals the size of the book in centimeters.
5. Cataloger's note supplying information unique to the contents of this book.
6. Lists the subject heading under which the book is classified (see subject card above].
7. Library of Congress call number for the book.
8. Dewey Decimal System call number for the book.
9. Order number used by libraries when ordering the catalog card for this book.
10. Signifies that a copy of this book can be found in the Library of Congress.
11. Printer's key for this card.

Note that by glancing at the card you can learn which publishing house issued the book, which edition your library possesses, how recent it is, its length, and whether it contains special materials such as a bibliography. All these facts could help you decide whether you want to look at the book itself.

Once in a while you may come across a reference to an apparently indispensable book that isn't listed in your library's catalog. As there are some sixty thousand new volumes published each year in English alone, no library but the Library of Congress itself could acquire more than a minority of them. You can get essential information about the book's author, title, publisher, and date from the *National Union Catalog,* which reproduces the Library of Congress Catalog and includes titles from other libraries as well. If you can't visit a library that has the book, you can probably borrow it through *interlibrary loan* arrangement. The same holds for journals as well. By consulting the *Union List of Serials in Libraries of the United States and Canada* you can discover which libraries own sets of hard-to-find journals.

Indexes

Indexes, in the bibliographic sense of the term, are periodically issued lists of publications (usually articles). Of all indexes, the most useful for general purposes is the *Reader's Guide to Periodical Literature,* which gives references for articles in about 135 magazines. A typical column of the *Reader's Guide* looks like this:

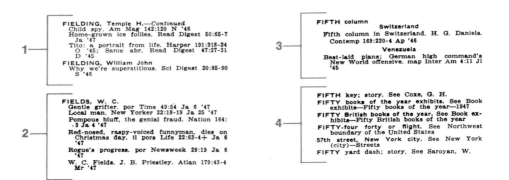

Here you see:

1. *Entries by authors.* The first entry under *Fielding, Temple,* for instance, is an article called "Child Spy" published in *The American Magazine,* volume 142, November 1946, page 120.
2. *Entries about a person.*

3. *Entries about subjects.*
4. *Cross-indexing* (references to entries elsewhere in the index) *by subject and title.*

You may well find that references in the *Reader's Guide* lack the scholarly authority you were hoping to lend your essay. In that case, turn to several indexes that are really one undertaking in different stages of its history:

International Index, Vols. 1–18 (1907–65)
Social Sciences and Humanities Index, Vols. 19–61 (1965–74)
Humanities Index, Vols. 1–   (1974–date)
Social Sciences Index, Vols. 1–   (1974–date)

These four indexes are shelved together in your library's reference room; as you can see, they cover an unbroken period from 1907 to the present. The new *Humanities Index* should be your choice for post-1973 articles in archaeology, area studies, classics, folklore, history, language and literature, literary and political criticism, performing arts, philosophy, religion, and theology. Use the new *Social Sciences Index* for post-1973 articles in anthropology, economics, environmental science, geography, law and criminology, medicine, political science, psychology, public administration, and sociology.

Another central resource is *Book Review Digest,* which locates reviews of current books and summarizes the consensus, if any, about each book's merit. You can use the *Digest* to discover which books, among several you might want to study, are considered most reliable, and if you want to read a full review you can look it up. Here is a typical entry:

TAYLOR, ROBERT LEWIS. W. C. Fields; his follies and fortunes. 340p pl $3.50 Doubleday

B or 92 Fields, William Claude
A life of W. C. Fields which shows that his private life was as eccentric as that of any comic character he portrayed on stage and screen.

Atlantic 184:86 O '49 240w
Booklist 46:81 N 1 '49
Reviewed by Herman Kogan
Chicago Sun O 18 '49 600w
Reviewed by Horace Reynolds
Christian Science Monitor p15 N 10 '49 420w

Cleveland Open Shelf p22 D '49
"Taylor doesn't soft-pedal but neither does he mud-sling, and his account of his subject's life has a distinct love and understanding of such a difficult figure, and makes the most of the wry, biting humor that was part of Fields' life. Not as well written, perhaps, as the Gene Fowler books, but of a definite interest to all theater and moving picture fans."
+ — Kirkus 17:417 Ag 1 '49 160w

"Highly recommended."   George Freedley
+ Library J 74:1605 O 15 '49 70w

"Mr. Robert Lewis Taylor has done a fine job. His book is more than a biography, more than a character study: it is also a cross-section of the entertainment world during the last half-century. Evidently, there is here a work of loving devotion: it abounds in reminiscences, in details, in anecdotes which could only have been garnered by patient inquiry and research. What is perhaps even rarer, it succeeds in giving a really vital impression of the exceptional personality which it commemorates." Iris Barry

+ N Y Herald Tribune Wkly Bk R p1 O 2 '49 1250w
"Robert Lewis Taylor has written a hilarious history of the fabulous comedian, written it with understanding, sympathy and a gay respect for the scandalous facts involved." Richard Maney
+ N Y Times p4 O 2 '49 900w

"Mr. Taylor has tried to keep his account coherent while never neglecting the laughs, and he has undoubtedly done as good a job as can be done."
+ New Yorker 25:107 O 8 '49 200w

"His memory is so beloved of his fans that they would no more brook an author who treats him clumsily than Tiffany's would entrust its diamond-cutting to a blacksmith. Taylor, fortunately, is a skilled literary lapidary. The gems of Fields' comical exploits are neatly cut and polished in his hands. There are flaws, nontheless. One is inherent in the original material. That is to say, in Fields' own exaggerations of fact and in the misty memories of his friends, enemies and relatives. . . If the book lacks accuracy, however, it never lacks entertainment, and we heartily commend it to anyone the least bit interested in reading of one of the most fabulous figures who ever lived." Luther Nichols
+ San Francisco Chronicle p26 O 16 '49 1400w

"Mr. Taylor has written a careful, detailed and exhaustive chronicle of the great man and his work, leaving little out and going about his task with zeal and determination. In addition, he had the valuable aid of the notes and advice of Gene Fowler, an old and understanding friend of the eminent comic." Richard Watts
+ Sat R of Lit 32:26 O 22 '49 800w
Time 54:108 O 17 '49 600w

If your project deals with recent public events or issues, the first place to look for facts is in the *New York Times Index,* which can lead you to news items and articles of commentary in that newspaper.

When a research problem takes you into a narrow area, you may need an index geared to that specialty. The index in turn will lead you to journals devoted entirely to the field you're working in, and some of these journals contain annual bibliographies. Thus an index, even if it doesn't contain exactly the items you want, will usually put you on their trail.

Here are some commonly used indexes and the periods they cover:

Applied Science and Technology Index (1913 – date)
Art Index (1929 – date)
Biography Index (1947 – date)
Book Review Digest (1905 – date)
Book Review Index (1965 – date)
Dramatic Index (1909 – 49)
Education Index (1929 – date)
Index to the Times [London] (1906 – date)
Monthly Catalog of United States Government Publications (1895 – date)
Music Index (1949 – date)
New York Times Index (1913 – date)
Poole's Index to Periodical Literature (1802 – 1907)
Public Affairs Information Service (1915 – date)
Reader's Guide to Periodical Literature (1900 – date)
RILA Abstracts (International Repertory of Art Literature) (1975 – date)
RILM Abstracts (International Repertory of Music Literature) (1967 – date)
Social Sciences and Humanities Index (see p. 209)

Booksellers' Bibliographies

If you know an author's name but not the title of the book; if you have the title but don't know the author; if you want to see whether new books on a certain topic appeared in a certain year; if you want to know whether a book is still in print, or has appeared in a paperback edition; then you should consult one of the following:

Books in Print (1948 – date)
Cumulative Book Index (1898 – date)
Paperbound Books in Print (1955 – date)
Subject Guide to Books in Print (1957 – date)

Guides to Reference Works

Reference works — that is, books that survey a field and tell you how to find materials within that field — are now so numerous that you may need to consult an even more general book that lists reference works and explains their scope:

Mary Neill Barton and Marion V. Bell, *Reference Books: A Brief Guide*, 7th ed. (1970)
Bibliographic Index (1933 – date)
Saul Galin and Peter Spielberg, *Reference Books: How to Select and Use Them* (1969)
Jean Kay Gates, *Guide to the Use of Books and Libraries*, 3rd ed. (1973)
Louis Shores, *Basic Reference Sources: An Introduction to Materials and Methods* (1954)
Raymond H. Shove et al., *The Use of Books and Libraries*, 10th ed. (1963)
Constance M. Winchell, *Guide to Reference Books*, 8th ed. (1967)
A World Bibliography of Bibliographies, 4th ed., 5 vols. (1965 – 66)

Of these works, the most widely used is Constance Winchell's *Guide to Reference Books*. By going to this volume and looking up your field of interest, you can quickly see which are the important reference works and what their scope is. This is also an excellent way of finding indexes and bibliographies that are even more specialized than the ones listed in the present chapter.

General Encyclopedias

An up-to-date edition of a general encyclopedia can provide initial orientation to a field or problem and a limited amount of bibliographic guidance. See especially:

Chambers's Encyclopaedia, 4th ed., 15 vols. (1968)
Collier's Encyclopedia, 24 vols. (1965)
Encyclopaedia Britannica, 15th ed., 30 vols. (1974)
Encyclopedia Americana, 30 vols. (revised annually)
New Columbia Encyclopedia, 1 vol. (1975)

Special Encyclopedias, Reference Works, Handbooks, and General Histories

If you want to locate more facts about a field than you could find in a general encyclopedia article, you can consult a work that surveys the field or a significant portion of it. Such books are helpful both for locating a technical or historical fact and for acquiring a sense of the whole field before working on narrow problems.

The following titles are arranged by field:

art   *Britannica Encyclopedia of American Art* (1973)
Mary W. Chamberlain, *Guide to Art Reference Books* (1959)
Encyclopedia of World Art, 15 vols. (1959 – 1968)
Larousse Encyclopedia of Byzantine and Medieval Art (1963)
Larousse Encyclopedia of Modern Art (1965)
Larousse Encyclopedia of Prehistoric and Ancient Art, rev. ed. (1966)
Bernard S. Myers, ed., *Encyclopedia of Painting*, 3rd ed. (1970)

Bernard S. Myers and Shirley D. Myers, *The McGraw-Hill Dictionary of Art* (1969)

The Praeger Encyclopedia of Art, 5 vols. (1971)

business and economics
Donald T. Clark and Bert A. Gottfried, *University Dictionary of Business and Finance* (1974)

Edwin T. Coman, Jr., *Sources of Business Information,* 2nd ed. (1964)

Douglas Greenwald, *The McGraw-Hill Dictionary of Modern Economics,* 2nd ed. (1973)

Carl Heyel, ed., *The Encyclopedia of Management,* 2nd ed. (1973)

Harold Lazarus, *American Business Dictionary* (1957)

Glen G. Munn, *Encyclopedia of Banking and Finance,* 7th ed. (1973)

Harold S. Sloan and Arnold J. Zurcher, *A Dictionary of Economics,* 5th ed. (1970)

drama
Blanch M. Baker, *Theatre and Allied Arts: A Guide to Books Dealing with the History, Criticism, and Technic of the Drama and Theatre and Related Arts and Crafts* (1952)

Estelle A. Fidell and D. M. Peake, eds., *Play Index* (1949–73)

Alfred Harbage, *Annals of English Drama, 975–1700,* rev. S. Schoenbaum (1964)

Phyllis Hartnoll, *The Oxford Companion to the Theatre,* 3rd ed. (1967)

Myron Matlaw, *Modern World Drama: An Encyclopedia* (1972)

education
Carter Alexander and A. J. Burke, *How to Locate Educational Information and Data,* 4th ed. (1958)

Encyclopedia of Education, 10 vols. (1971)

Encyclopedia of Educational Research, 4th ed. (1969)

International Yearbook of Education (1948–date)

folklore and mythology
Sir James G. Frazer, *The Golden Bough: A Study in Magic and Religion,* 12 vols. (1907–1915; suppl. 1936, 1955)

Funk and Wagnalls Standard Dictionary of Folklore, Mythology and Legend, 2 vols. (1949–50)

Louis H. Gray, ed., *The Mythology of All Races* (1916–32; rpt. 1964)

Larousse World Mythology (1968)

Stith Thompson, *Motif-Index of Folk Literature,* rev. ed., 6 vols. (1955–1958)

history
James Truslow Adams, ed., *Dictionary of American History,* 2nd ed., 6 vols. (1942–63)

Britannica Book of the Year (annual)

The Cambridge Ancient History, 3rd ed., 12 vols. (1970–75)

The Cambridge Medieval History, 8 vols. (1911–36)

The Cambridge Modern History, 14 vols. (1902–26)

Frank Freidel and Richard K. Showman, eds.,*Harvard Guide to American History,* rev. ed., 2 vols. (1974)

William L. Langer, *An Encyclopedia of World History,* 5th ed. (1972)

Richard B. Morris, *Encyclopedia of American History,* rev. ed. (1970)

Richard B. Morris and Graham W. Irwin, eds., *Harper Encyclopedia of the Modern World* (1970)

Helen J. Poulton and Marguerite S. Howland, *The Historian's Handbook* (1972)

literature Albert C. Baugh, *A Literary History of England,* 2nd ed. (1967)

Donald F. Bond, *A Reference Guide to English Studies,* 2nd ed. (1971)

John Buchanan-Brown, ed., *Cassell's Encyclopedia of World Literature,* rev. ed. (1973)

James D. Hart, *The Oxford Companion to American Literature,* 4th ed. (1965)

Paul Harvey, *The Oxford Companion to English Literature,* 4th ed. (1967)

Paul Harvey and J. E. Heseltine, *The Oxford Companion to Classical Literature* (1937)

Lillian H. Hornstein, ed., *The Reader's Companion to World Literature,* rev. ed. (1973)

Howard Mumford Jones and Richard M. Ludwig, *Guide to American Literature and Its Backgrounds since 1890,* 4th ed. (1972)

Stanley J. Kunitz and Howard Haycraft, eds., *American Authors, 1600–1900* (1938)

————, *British Authors Before 1800* (1952)

————, *British Authors of the Nineteenth Century* (1936)

Lewis Leary, *Articles on American Literature, 1900–1950* (1954)

————, *Articles on American Literature, 1950–1967* (1970)

Masterplots (1954–)

Horatio Smith, ed., *Columbia Dictionary of Modern European Literature* (1947)

Robert E. Spiller et al., *Literary History of the United States,* 4th ed., 2 vols. (1974)

Joseph T. Stipley, ed., *Dictionary of World Literature,* rev. ed. (1968)

Roger Whitlow, *Black American Literature* (1973)

Percy Wilson and Bonamy Dobrée, *The Oxford History of English Literature,* 12 vols. (1945–1963)

James Woodress, ed., *American Fiction 1900–50: A Guide to Information Sources* (1974)

music Willi Apel, *Harvard Dictionary of Music,* 2nd ed. (1969)

Theodore Baker, *Biographical Dictionary of Musicians,* 5th ed., rev. Nicolas Slonimsky (1958)

Sir George Grove, *Dictionary of Music and Musicians,* ed. Eric Blom, 5th ed., 10 vols. (1955; suppl. 1961)

The New Oxford History of Music, 10 vols. (1954–)

Percy A. Scholes, *The Oxford Companion to Music,* 10th ed. (1970)

Oscar Thompson, *International Cyclopedia of Music and Musicians,* 10th ed., rev. Bruce Bohle (1975)

Jack A. Westrup and F. Ll. Harrison, *The New College Encyclopedia of Music* (1960)

philosophy James M. Baldwin, *Dictionary of Philosophy and Psychology,* 3 vols. (1901–05; rev. ed. 1925; rpt. 1960)

Frederick C. Copleston, *A History of Philosophy,* 8 vols. (1947–66)

Paul Edwards, ed., *The Encyclopedia of Philosophy,* 4 vols. (1973)

Bertrand Russell, *A History of Western Philosophy* (1945)

J. O. Urmson, ed., *The Concise Encyclopedia of Western Philosophy and Philosophers* (1960)

psychology   Arthur J. Bachrach, *Psychological Research: An Introduction*, 3rd ed. (1974)

Hugo G. Beigel, *Dictionary of Psychology and Related Fields* (1974)

James E. Bell, *Guide to Library Research in Psychology* (1971)

Horace B. English and Ava C. English, *A Comprehensive Dictionary of Psychological and Psychoanalytical Terms* (1958)

H. J. Eysenck et al., *Encyclopedia of Psychology*, 3 vols. (1972)

Robert M. Goldenson, *The Encyclopedia of Human Behavior*, 2 vols. (1970)

Alexander Grinstein, *Index of Psychoanalytic Writings* (1956 – date)

religion   F. L. Cross and Elizabeth A. Livingstone, *The Oxford Dictionary of the Christian Church* (1974)

John W. Ellison, comp., *Nelson's Complete Concordance of the Revised Standard Version Bible* (1957)

James Hastings, *Dictionary of the Bible*, rev. Frederick C. Grant and H. H. Rowley (1963)

John Hick, ed., *Philosophy of Religion*, 2nd ed. (1973)

Isaac Landman et al., eds., *The Universal Jewish Encyclopedia*, 10 vols. (1939 – 48)

Frank Spencer Mead, *Handbook of Denominations in the United States*, 6th ed. (1975)

The New Catholic Encyclopedia, 15 vols. (1967)

Geoffrey Parrinder, *A Dictionary of Non-Christian Religions* (1973)

——, *Faiths of Mankind* (1965)

Cecil Roth, ed., *The Standard Jewish Encyclopedia*, rev. ed. (1962)

Robert C. Zaehner, ed., *The Concise Encyclopedia of Living Faiths* (1959)

science and   Cyril C. Baker, *Dictionary of Mathematics* (1970)
technology   Robert M. Besancon, ed., *Encyclopedia of Physics*, 2nd ed. (1974)

Theodore Besterman, *Technology*, 2 vols. (1971)

Harley Carter, *Dictionary of Electronics* (1972)

John Challinor, *A Dictionary of Geology* (1974)

Peter Gray, ed., *The Encyclopedia of the Biological Sciences*, 2nd ed. (1970)

International Encyclopedia of Chemical Science (1964)

Frances B. Jenkins, *Science Reference Sources*, 5th ed. (1969)

Earl J. Lasworth, *Reference Sources in Science and Technology* (1972)

McGraw-Hill Encyclopedia of Science and Technology, 3rd ed., 15 vols. (1971)

Walter C. Michels, ed., *The International Dictionary of Physics and Electronics*, 2nd ed. (1961)

George E. Speck and Bernard Jaffe, eds., *A Dictionary of Science Terms* (1965)

C. F. Tweney and L. E. C. Hughes, eds., *Chambers's Technical Dictionary*, 3rd ed. (1958)

Universal Encyclopedia of Mathematics (1964)

Van Nostrand's Scientific Encyclopedia, 4th ed. (1968)

social and
political
science

Jack A. Clarke, *Research Materials in the Social Sciences,* 2nd ed. (1967)

John P. Davis, ed., *The American Negro Reference Book* (1966)

Henry Pratt Fairchild, *Dictionary of Sociology and Related Sciences* (1970)

Thelma K. Freides, *Literature and Bibliography of the Social Sciences* (1973)

Bert F. Hoselitz, ed., *A Reader's Guide to the Social Sciences,* rev. ed. (1972)

Barry T. Klein, ed., *Reference Encyclopedia of the American Indian,* 2nd ed. (1973–74)

W. J. Kolb and Julius Gold, *UNESCO Dictionary of the Social Sciences* (1964)

Jack C. Plano, *Dictionary of Political Analysis* (1972)

Jack C. Plano and Milton Greenberg, *The American Political Dictionary,* 2nd ed. (1967)

Political Handbook and Atlas of the World (annual)

Moshe Y. Sachs and Louis Barron, eds., *Worldmark Encyclopedia of the Nations,* 2nd ed. (1971)

E. R. A. Seligman and Alvin Johnson, eds., *Encyclopaedia of the Social Sciences,* 15 vols. (1930–34)

David L. Sills, ed., *International Encyclopedia of the Social Sciences,* 17 vols. (1968)

Edward C. Smith and Arnold J. Zurcher, eds., *Dictionary of American Politics,* 2nd ed. (1968)

Carl M. White et al., *Sources of Information in the Social Sciences,* 2nd ed. (1973)

Almanacs, Yearbooks, and Compilations of Facts

These volumes can be consulted for miscellaneous facts and statistics:

The Americana Annual (1923–date)
Britannica Book of the Year (1938–date)
CBS News Almanac (1976–date)
Collier's Yearbook (1939–date)
Facts on File (1940–date)
Information Please Almanac (1947–date)
The Negro Almanac (1967–date)
The Statesman's Year-Book (1864–date)
Statistical Abstract of the United States (1878–date)
The World Almanac and Book of Facts (1868–date)
Year Book of World Affairs (1947–date)

Atlases and Gazetteers (Geographical Dictionaries)

Geographical knowledge can be located in:

Britannica Atlas: Geography Edition (1974)
Herbert G. May and G. H. Hunt, *The Oxford Bible Atlas,* 2nd ed. (1974)
The National Atlas of the United States of America (1970)
National Geographic Atlas of the World, 4th ed. (1975)

The New York Times Atlas of the World (1972)
R. R. Palmer, ed., *Atlas of World History* (1957)
William R. Shepherd, ed., *Historical Atlas*, 9th ed. (1964)
The Times Atlas of the World, comprehensive ed. (1975)
Webster's New Geographical Dictionary, rev. ed. (1972)

Dictionaries

Dictionaries for everyday reference are discussed on pages 100–105. For research into the origins and changing meanings of words, see:

Sir William A. Craigie and James R. Hulbert, eds., *A Dictionary of American English,* 4 vols. (1938–44)
S. I. Hayakawa, *Modern Guide to Synonyms and Related Words* (1969)
Ernest Klein, *A Comprehensive Etymological Dictionary of the English Language,* 2 vols. (1966–71)
A New English Dictionary on Historical Principles (also called *The Oxford English Dictionary*), 12 vols. and suppl. (1888–1933)
C. T. Onions, ed., *The Oxford Dictionary of English Etymology* (1966)
Eric Partridge, *A Dictionary of Slang and Unconventional English,* 7th ed., 2 vols. (1970)
——, *Origins: A Short Etymological Dictionary of Modern English,* 4th ed. (1966)
Mario Pei and Salvatore Romondio, *Dictionary of Foreign Terms* (1975)
Webster's New Dictionary of Synonyms (1973)
Harold Wentworth and Stuart B. Flexner, *Dictionary of American Slang* (1967)

Biography

Names can be identified and lives studied in the following:

Chambers's Biographical Dictionary, ed. J. O. Thorne, rev. ed. (1969)
Current Biography (1940–date)
Dictionary of American Biography, 22 vols. (1928–58)
Albert M. Hyamson, *A Dictionary of Universal Biography of All Ages and of All Peoples,* 2nd ed. (1951)
International Who's Who (1935–date)
The National Cyclopaedia of American Biography (1893–date)
Leslie Stephen and Sidney Lee, eds., *Dictionary of National Biography* [British], 63 vols. (1885–1901); reissued 22 vols. (1908–1909; suppl. to 1963)
Webster's Biographical Dictionary (1971)
Who's Who [British] (1849–date)
Who's Who in America (1899–date)
Who's Who in the World, rev. ed. (1973)

Quotations

Your best hope of tracking down an unattributed quotation lies with one of these sourcebooks:

John Bartlett and E. M. Beck, *Familiar Quotations,* 14th ed. (1968)
Bruce Bohle, *The Apollo Book of American Quotations* (1970)
Bergen Evans, *Dictionary of Quotations* (1968)
H. L. Mencken, *A New Dictionary of Quotations* (1942)
The Oxford Dictionary of Quotations, 2nd ed. (1953)
William G. Smith and F. P. Wilson, *The Oxford Dictionary of English Proverbs,*
    3rd ed. (1970)
Burton E. Stevenson, ed., *The Home Book of Quotations, Classical and Modern,*
    10th ed. (1967)

TAKING NOTES FROM READING

A typical library book or journal will be available to you for a few hours or days or weeks, depending on its importance to other borrowers. When you try to get it again you may find that it's on loan to someone else, or sent to the bindery, or even misplaced or stolen. Thus you have to be sure to get everything you need from the work on your first try, and your notes must be clear and full enough to be your direct source when you write. Although it's always a good idea to keep the work before you and recheck it for accurate quotation and fair summary, you should assume that this won't be possible. Your notes should contain all the information necessary for full references in your footnotes (pp. 226–234) and bibliography (pp. 234–238), and you should be quite certain that the notes are error-free before you let the book or article out of your hands. (For advice about finding a topic and thesis, organizing an essay, writing a first draft, and revising, see Chapter Two.)

The notes you take from reading will serve two distinct purposes: to keep an accurate list of the works you have consulted and to record key information that you've found in them. Sooner or later, most researchers understand that these purposes demand different kinds of notecards. To compile a *bibliography,* one card per entry is ideal; but *informational notes* may run through many cards, only one of which will contain the needed bibliographical facts. To avoid confusion, use 3″ × 5″ *bibliography cards* to identify the works you've consulted, and larger (usually 4″ × 6″) *content cards* for quotations, summaries, and miscellaneous comments.

Thus a typical bibliography card might look like this:

library call number

identifying name

all information needed for footnotes or bibliography

reminder of the book's scope or interest for your project

> N 8375
> H 34F6
>
> Fowler
>
> Fowler, Gene
> Minutes of the Last Meeting
> New York: the Viking Press, 1954
> (plentiful reminiscences of W.C.
> Fields, John Barrymore, and others.)

And a brief content note might look like this:

page reference

context of quotation

quotation

personal comment

indexing key

> Fowler, p. 103   Cynical Realism
>
> Remark after someone complained that
> an aspect of his will would make him
> "misunderstood and much disliked":
> " ' I've always been misunderstood,' he
> rasped. 'Besides, did you ever hear of a
> corpse complaining of unpopularity?' "
> (Not bad for illustrating Fields' morbid,
> sardonic quality. Cf. p. 223 - ref. to
> coffin vaults as "hope chests.")

Observe that, once a separate bibliography card has been prepared, the researcher can give the briefest of references on a content card: *Fowler, p. 103.*

The more systematic you are about notetaking, the less likely you will be to misquote, summarize unfairly, and supply inaccurate references. Here are some tips about form:

---

1. Use cards of one uniform size for all your bibliography notes, and cards or sheets of another uniform size for all your content notes. This will make for easy filing and reshuffling.

2. Write in ink. Penciled notes smudge when pressed against other notes.

3. Never put entries from different sources on one card or page, and never write on the reverse side. Otherwise you will probably lose track of some of your work.

4. Include the call number of any book or magazine you've found in the library. You never know when you may want to retrieve it for another look.

5. Quote exactly, including the punctuation marks in the original, and check each quotation as soon as you've copied it.

6. Use quotation marks only when you're actually quoting verbatim, and check to see that the marks begin and end exactly where they should. Use the dots known as ellipses (pp. 347–348) to indicate where you have skipped some material within a quotation.

7. Be attentive to oddities of spelling and punctuation in quoted material. If, for instance, the original text omits a comma that you would have included, you can place a bracketed [*sic*], meaning *this is the way I found it*, at the questionable point in your notes; this will remind you not to improve the quotation illegitimately when reproducing it in your essay. But don't retain the [*sic*] unless it refers to an obvious blunder.

8. Supply page references for all quotations, paraphrases, and summaries.

9. Don't allow any ambiguities in your system of abbreviations. If two of your symbols mean the same thing, change one of them.

10. Distinguish between your own comments and those of the text you're summarizing. Slashes, brackets, or your initials can be used as signals that the following remarks are yours, not those of the author.

11. When copying a passage that runs from one page to another, mark where the first page ends: *"The district attorney is a vigilant enemy of crime in the/sheets" (pp. 34–35).* If you finally quote only a portion of the excerpt in your paper, you'll want to know where it ended in the original.

12. Use a portion of the card or page to evaluate the material and to

remind yourself of possibilities for further study. You might say, for example, *This looks useless — but reconsider chapter 13 if discussing astrology.*

13. Leave some space in the margin or at the top for an indexing symbol.

EXERCISES

I. For each of the following proposed topics, list two or three sources (a certain dictionary, a bibliography, the card catalog, etc.) that you would *begin* by consulting (pp. 205–217):

1. The reception of Gore Vidal's novel *1876.*
2. Should abortions be automatically granted on demand?
3. Pickett's Charge.
4. How the Alaska Pipeline was approved.
5. Recent advances in semiconductor memory systems for computers.
6. The development of logical positivism.
7. Beethoven's reputation today.
8. Beethoven's childhood.
9. The origin and evolving meaning of the word *wit* in English.
10. Who wrote the line "The proper study of mankind is man"?

II. Begin working on project 2 above. Copy out references to four *articles* you would read if you were to continue the project. Make your references full enough (including call numbers) so that the articles could be precisely located in the library.

III. Compile a bibliography (pp. 234–238) consisting of three recent *books* and three recent *articles* about the presidency of Franklin D. Roosevelt. Briefly state how you located the items.

IV. Acquire one of the items in Exercise III from your library, and make a sample *bibliography card* (pp. 217–218) for it. Then write two *content notes* (pp. 217–218) about one passage. In the first note, *quote* the passage; in the second one, *summarize* it.

DOCUMENTATION

ACKNOWLEDGING YOUR SOURCES

The Obligation to Document

Writers who are struggling to express themselves without hindrance often feel annoyed by the requirement that borrowed words and ideas be *documented* — that is, acknowledged in *footnotes* and *bibliographies* providing references to consulted sources. Footnotes in particular have a bad name: they seem so dry and fussy and needlessly complex. If you're harassed or pressed for time, you may be tempted to skip the footnotes, even though some of your thoughts are second-hand.

That would be a bad mistake, for two reasons. One is that notes can actually strengthen the effect of your presentation. If you have taken the trouble to do some research for your essay, that fact will work in your favor — provided it comes to light. Any reader will be more impressed by a reference to a standard work than by a claim that might have been invented for the purpose of getting you out of a tight spot.

The second reason for providing documentation is to avoid *plagiarism* — the serious ethical violation of taking others' words and ideas without acknowledgment. In theory a reader should be able to use your notes to track down all your borrowings and see whether you've handled them scrupulously, quoting and summarizing accurately and showing exactly where your own ideas end and someone else's ideas begin. In practice, of course, hardly anyone would be interested in checking your work so thoroughly. But the point of avoiding plagiarism isn't to escape being caught at it, but to refrain from being dishonest.

Yet systematic dishonesty is only part of the problem. For every student who buys a term paper or copies a whole article without acknowledgment, there are dozens who indulge in "little" ethical lapses through thoughtlessness, haste, or a momentary sense of opportunity. Though perhaps ninety percent of their work is original, they too are plagiarists—just as someone who robs a bank of $2.39 is a bank robber.

Unlike the robber, however, some plagiarists fail to realize what they've done wrong. Students whose schoolteachers asked them to copy encyclopedia articles may never have learned the necessity of using quotation marks and citing sources. Others may think that by *paraphrasing* a quotation or *summarizing* an idea—that is, by putting it into their own words—they have turned it into public property. Others acknowledge the source of their idea but fail to indicate that they've borrowed the author's words as well as his idea. Still others plagiarize through sloppy notetaking (pp. 32–35). Since their notes don't adequately distinguish between personal observations and the content of a consulted book, their essays don't do so, either. And finally, some students blunder into plagiarism through misconceiving the difference between fact and opinion. They may think, for example, that a famous critic's opinion about a piece of literature is so authoritative that it belongs to the realm of common facts—and so they paraphrase it without acknowledgment. All these errors are understandable, but none of them constitutes a good excuse for plagiarism.

Consider the following source and three ways that a student might be tempted to make use of it:

SOURCE:

The joker in the European pack was Italy. For a time hopes were entertained of her as a force against Germany, but these disappeared under Mussolini. In 1935 Italy made a belated attempt to participate in the scramble for Africa by invading Ethiopia. It was clearly a breach of the

covenant of the League of Nations for one of its members to attack another. France and Great Britain, as great powers, Mediterranean powers, and African colonial powers, were bound to take the lead against
Italy at the league. But they did so feebly and half-heartedly because
they did not want to alienate a possible ally against Germany. The result was the worst possible: the league failed to check aggression,
Ethiopia lost her independence, and Italy was alienated after all.[1]

VERSION A:

Italy, one might say, was the joker in the European deck. When she
invaded Ethiopia, it was clearly a breach of the covenant of the League
of Nations; yet the efforts of England and France to take the lead
against her were feeble and half-hearted. It appears that those great
powers had no wish to alienate a possible ally against Hitler's rearmed
Germany.

Comment: Clearly plagiarism. Though the facts cited are public knowledge, the stolen phrases aren't. Note that the writer's interweaving
of his own words with the source's does *not* render him innocent of
plagiarism.

VERSION B:

Italy was the joker in the European pack. Under Mussolini in 1935, she
made a belated attempt to participate in the scramble for Africa by invading Ethiopia. As J. M. Roberts points out, this violated the covenant of the League of Nations.[1] But France and Britain, not wanting to
alienate a possible ally against Germany, put up only feeble and half-
hearted opposition to the Ethiopian adventure. The outcome, as Roberts
observes, was "the worst possible: the league failed to check aggression, Ethiopia lost her independence, and Italy was alienated after
all."[2]

---

[1] J. M. Roberts, *History of the World* (New York: Knopf, 1976), p. 845.
[2] Roberts, p. 845.

Comment: Still plagiarism. The two correct citations of Roberts serve as
a kind of alibi for the appropriating of other, unacknowledged phrases.
But the alibi has no force: some of Roberts' words are again being presented as the writer's.

VERSION C:

Much has been written about German rearmament and militarism in
the period 1933–1939. But Germany's dominance in Europe was by no
means a foregone conclusion. The fact is that the balance of power
might have been tipped against Hitler if one or two things had turned
out differently. Take Italy's gravitation toward an alliance with Ger-

many, for example. That alliance seemed so very far from inevitable that Britain and France actually muted their criticism of the Ethiopian invasion in the hope of remaining friends with Italy. They opposed the Italians in the League of Nations, as J. M. Roberts observes, "feebly and half-heartedly because they did not want to alienate a possible ally against Germany."[1] Suppose Italy, France, and Britain had retained a certain common interest. Would Hitler have been able to get away with his remarkable bluffing and bullying in the later thirties?

---

[1]J. M. Roberts,.*History of the World* (New York: Knopf, 1976), p. 845.

Comment: No plagiarism. The writer has been influenced by the public facts mentioned by Roberts, but he hasn't tried to pass off Roberts' conclusions as his own. The one clear borrowing is properly acknowledged.

What to Acknowledge

There *is* room for a small measure of disagreement about what to acknowledge; but precisely because this is so, you ought to make your documentation relatively ample. In addition to citing all direct quotations and paraphrases, you should give the sources of all borrowed ideas and facts that don't belong to general knowledge. That is, give a citation if you think that a serious person might disagree with your second-hand point or inquire whether it came from the most reliable source. You can casually mention how many people live in China, for example, and you can give your opinion that ecology is the most important issue in the contemporary world; but if you write about the way pig manure is recycled in Chinese communes, and if you haven't seen those communes in person, a reference is in order.

How to Document

A note, although it's the most common means of documentation, isn't always the most convenient or considerate one. A reader who has to keep skipping to your notes after every few lines of text will have difficulty concentrating on your essay itself. When most of your references are to one source, you can mention that fact in a brief statement or note, announcing that page references will be inserted parenthetically into the text (p. 233). But you'll find that running away from notes can sometimes be clumsier than using them. It's better to refer your reader to a note than to stuff a sentence full of trivial data. Otherwise you will get clumsy effects like this:

x Mao Tse-tung, as J. M. Roberts remarks on page 823 of his *History of the World* (New York: Knopf, 1976), turned his attention from the cities to the countryside in the 1920's.

All this reference information is necessary, but here it interrupts a substantive remark. The writer should get the merely technical data into a note, freeing the main text to dwell on essentials:

- As J. M. Roberts remarks, Mao Tse-tung's attention turned from the cities to the countryside in the 1920's.[3] Furthermore, . . .

Substantive Notes

The purpose of most notes is simply to provide citations for quoted material and borrowed ideas. Occasionally, though, you can use a note to expand or qualify your main discussion. A point may strike you as worth making, yet as obstructive to the flow of your essay. By placing it in a note, you give the reader a choice between reading it, skimming it, or ignoring it. If he wants to come to grips with your position in a critical spirit, the note is there to remind him that this idea hasn't been overlooked. And if his interest is more superficial, no great claim has been made on his attention.

Most often, a substantive note develops *from* a citation. The book or article being cited raises further issues that bear on your thesis in a challenging way. After giving the reference, you add a sentence or even a whole paragraph dealing with this challenge.

Bear in mind, however, that notes are supposed to remain subordinate elements. The time a reader spends poring over your notes amounts to a loss of concentration on your ideas. If you find, in rereading a draft, that you've given disproportionate weight to commentary in the notes, try to condense the material as much as possible. Inessential chitchat should be deleted, and statements of key significance should be incorporated into the main essay. Your notes, when you've finished with them, should be clear and concise for readers who want to follow them, and unobtrusive for readers who don't. And there are ways (pp. 233–234) of offering all necessary citations while significantly cutting back on the total number of notes.

FOOTNOTE FORM

If you intend to write for publication, you should own a widely accepted guide to all aspects of typescript form such as *A Manual of Style*[2] or *The MLA Style Sheet*.[3] Of course if you know that one magazine or press is going to print your work, you should present it in the style of that house. And you should note that scientific and technical writing follows other conventions than the ones described below.

Placement and Numbering

The word *footnote* is loosely used to cover both a footnote proper, which is given at the bottom of the page on which the reference occurs, and an *endnote*, which is given in a consecutive series with all other notes at the end of the essay or article. Endnotes are preferred if you are submitting material for publication. In classroom work, depending on the preference of your instructor and the number of notes involved, you can choose either system or a combination of them:

footnotes proper   For these, you must make sure to leave enough space at the bottom of each page to accommodate the references occurring on that page. (Sometimes you will have to continue a note on the bottom of the following page.) Five spaces below the text, and two spaces above the first footnote of each page, insert a ruled line one-third the length of a line of type. If you have no more than two or three references per page, you can identify them with asterisks: * for the first note, ** or † for the second, *** or ‡ for the third. But numbering by Arabic numerals is preferable: [1,2,3]. You can use consecutive numbers throughout the essay or begin each page's notes from number 1.

endnotes   If you have many notes, or if some of them are quite lengthy, or if you are writing for publication, endnotes will serve you better than footnotes. Use one set of Arabic numerals and present all your notes in order after the main text, but before a bibliography if you supply one.

For sample endnotes, see pages 60–61.

combined form   In some collegiate essays you may find that you have both substantive notes (p. 226) and page citations, and you may want to make sure that your reader sees the substantive notes at the point where each reference to them occurs in the text. You can accomplish this by using footnotes proper for the substantive notes while putting the page citations into endnotes. Thus your substantive notes are marked by asterisks and given *on* the relevant pages, and the page citations are marked by consecutive Arabic numerals and given *at the end*. The ideal, here and in all aspects of form, is clarity and simplicity of effect without any sacrifice of needed information.

When writing for publication, you should double-space all notes and leave ample space between one note and the next. For academic work you can single-space the notes and put double spaces between them.

Footnote numbers in your main text should look like this:

- George Leonard describes the Wellness Inventory, a $75 true-or-false test offered by the Wellness Resource Center of Mill Valley, California, as "the boldest leap yet past the boundaries of the Old Medicine."[4]

Observe that the Arabic numeral is slightly elevated from the line, and that it isn't accompanied by any other punctuation such as a period or parentheses. It immediately follows all other marks except a dash that falls outside the quotation, as here:

· The Wellness Inventory, designed to reveal how close you may be to falling ill, includes such diagnostic items as "I recycle paper, cans, glass, clothing, books, and organic waste" and "I use low-phosphate detergent"[5] — sure signs of the necessary inner vitality.

In general, footnote numbers should come after, not before, the material to be identified in the note.

Footnote form isn't an earthshaking matter, but as a courtesy to your reader you should adopt a widely recognized set of conventions and use them consistently. The following conventions are those recommended by the second edition of *The MLA Style Sheet:*

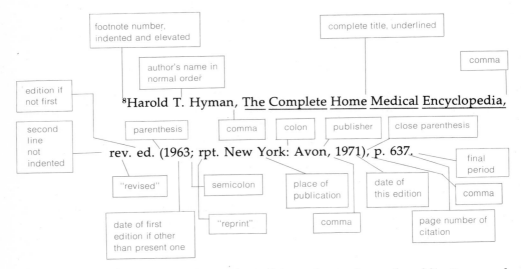

Information about the edition, date, place of publication, and publisher can be found on the back of the title page of the book you are citing. Note that several copyright dates may be given there, even if the book is still in its first edition. This means that some of the material in the book was copyrighted in earlier form. Locate the date of *this* edition, and look for an explicit statement of the first-edition date if this is a later edition.

Both the note diagramed above and the sample notes below illustrate *full citation*, with a maximum of identifying details. If you supply a *bibliography* (pp. 234–238), or if your instructor indicates that a simpler footnote form will do, you can omit certain details — a subtitle, reprint information, and the publisher's name:

[8]Harold T. Hyman, The Complete Home Medical Encyclopedia (New York, 1971), p. 637.

Sample First Notes

books   Your first reference to a book should be fuller in bibliographical detail than all the subsequent ones (pp. 233–234). The following notes indicate some of the typical aspects of book citation in first references:

A FIRST EDITION:
   [1]Robert Langbaum, The Modern Spirit: Essays on the Continuity of Nineteenth- and Twentieth-Century Literature (New York: Oxford Univ. Press, 1970), p. 107.

   If the same work appeared in your bibliography, you could shorten the footnote by dropping the book's subtitle.

AN EDITED BOOK:
   [2]George Abbott White and Charles Newman, eds., Literature in Revolution (New York: Holt, 1972), p. 14.

   The publisher's full name is Holt, Rinehart and Winston, but *Holt* is sufficient.

A BOOK EDITED BY MORE THAN THREE PEOPLE:
   [3]Frank Kermode et al., eds., The Oxford Anthology of English Literature, 2 vols. (New York: Oxford Univ. Press, 1973).

   The title page says that New York, London, and Toronto are the places of publication. When more than one place is listed, you need only supply the first.

A PAGE REFERENCE TO THE SAME BOOK:
   [4]William Hazlitt, "My First Acquaintance with Poets," in The Oxford Anthology of English Literature, ed. Frank Kermode et al. (New York: Oxford Univ. Press, 1973), II, 705.

   Instead of giving the number of volumes as in note 3, you provide the volume number of the passage being cited. With a Roman numeral for the volume number and an Arabic numeral for the page number, there's no need to write *p.* before *705*.

A TRANSLATION:
   [5]Marcel Proust, Swann's Way, trans. C. K. Scott Moncrieff (New York: Random House, 1928).

A LATER EDITION OF A BOOK WITH CORPORATE AUTHORSHIP:
   [6]Sunset Western Garden Book, 3rd ed. (n.d.; rpt. Menlo Park, Calif.: Lane, 1967), p. 79.

   The date of the first edition should come first in the parentheses, but this book gives no indication of when the first edition appeared; *n.d.* means "no date." If the place of publication isn't given, replace it with *n.p.* for "no place." Note that both the city and state—or in some cases the city and country—should be given if the city isn't widely familiar.

A BOOK THAT FORMS PART OF A SERIES:
⁷Thomas S. Kuhn, <u>The Structure of Scientific Revolutions</u>, International Encyclopedia of Unified Science, 2nd series, No. 2, 2nd ed. (1962; rpt. Chicago: Univ. of Chicago Press, 1970), pp. vii–viii.

Kuhn's book is the second item in the second series issued by the editors of the International Encyclopedia. The lower-case Roman page numbers indicate prefatory pages.

A BOOK REVISED BY SOMEONE OTHER THAN THE AUTHOR(S):
⁸Edward F. Ricketts and Jack Calvin, <u>Between Pacific Tides</u>, rev. Joel W. Hedgpeth, 4th ed. (1939; rpt. Stanford: Stanford Univ. Press, 1968), p. 295n.

The cited passage appears in a footnote on page 295.

A BOOK WHOSE VOLUMES WERE PUBLISHED IN DIFFERENT YEARS:
⁹All quoted poems are based on the <u>Poetical Works of William Wordsworth</u>, ed. E. de Selincourt and H. Darbishire, 2nd ed., 5 vols. (Oxford: Oxford Univ. Press, 1952–59).

The dates of the earliest- and last-published volumes are given.

A PAGE REFERENCE TO THE SAME WORK:
¹⁰<u>Poetical Works of William Wordsworth</u>, ed. E. de Selincourt and H. Darbishire, 2nd ed., I (Oxford: Oxford Univ. Press, 1952), 217.

The one volume being cited is indicated along with its date of publication.

AN ESSAY PUBLISHED IN A BOOK:
¹¹Joan Riviere, "A Character Trait of Freud's," in <u>Psychoanalysis and Contemporary Thought</u>, ed. John D. Sutherland (1958; rpt. New York: Grove Press, 1959), pp. 145–49.

The title of the essay or chapter belongs within quotation marks.

A NOTE CITING MORE THAN ONE BOOK:
¹²See Susan Isaacs, <u>The Nursery Years: The Mind of the Child from Birth to Six Years</u> (1929; rpt. New York: Schocken, 1968); Géza Róheim, <u>Magic and Schizophrenia</u> (1955; rpt. Bloomington: Indiana Univ. Press, 1962), and R. D. Laing, <u>Self and Others</u>, 2nd ed. (1961; rpt. New York: Pantheon, 1969).

articles in magazines, journals, and newspapers   Footnote form is slightly different for periodical publications, as these samples indicate:

AN ARTICLE IN A JOURNAL WITH CONTINUOUS
PAGINATION THROUGH EACH YEAR'S VOLUME:
[13]George H. Pollack, "On Time, Death, and Immortality," Psychoanalytic Quarterly, 40 (July 1971), 435–46.

Both the volume number and the page numbers can be given in Arabic numerals, since they are clearly separated by the date of the issue. Because the volume number is provided, *pp.* is unnecessary before *435–46*.

AN ARTICLE IN A MAGAZINE WITH SEPARATE PAGINATION FOR EACH ISSUE:
[14]Fred M. Hechinger, "Who's in Charge Here?" Change, Winter 1971–72, pp. 26–29.

If the paging starts anew with each issue, the volume number can be omitted. This eliminates the parentheses around the date, but it also means that *p.* or *pp.* should be supplied.

AN ARTICLE IN A JOURNAL THAT DOES
NOT IDENTIFY THE EXACT DATE OF EACH ISSUE:
[15]Richard P. Wheeler, "Poetry and Fantasy in Shakespeare's Sonnets 88–96," Literature and Psychology, 22, No. 3 (1972), 151–62.

The number of the issue in the yearly series is given after the volume and/or issue number.

A BOOK REVIEW:
[16]S. K. Oberbeck, rev. of Reminiscing with Sissle and Blake, by Robert Kimball and William Bolcom, Newsweek, 30 Apr. 1973, p. 81.

Note the preferred form for giving the date.

AN UNSIGNED MAGAZINE ARTICLE:
[17]"Drugs That Don't Work," New Republic, 29 Jan. 1972, pp. 12–13.

A SIGNED NEWSPAPER ARTICLE:
[18]Peter Weisser, "Governor Reagan on Grass," San Francisco Chronicle, 29 Jan. 1972, Final Ed., p. 6, cols. 1–5.

It isn't essential to give either the edition or the columns, but both can be helpful. Occasionally a story will appear in one edition of a day's paper and not in others. Note that the city where the paper is published isn't usually underlined.

AN UNSIGNED NEWSPAPER ARTICLE OR EDITORIAL:
[19]"Safety in the Mines," Christian Science Monitor, 16 Mar. 1976, p. 28.

The writer of this note has chosen to omit the edition and column numbers.

encyclopedia entries   [20]L[awrence] K. L[ustig], "Alluvial Fans," Encyclopaedia Britannica, 1974, Macropaedia.

The author's initials appear at the end of the entry; they are identified elsewhere. Note that volume and page numbers are unnecessary when items appear in alphabetical order. But since the *Britannica* from 1974 onward has three sets of contents, the note should indicate which one is intended — in this case the "Macropaedia."

pamphlets SIGNED:

[21]H. H. Koepf, <u>Compost: What It Is/How It Is Made/What It Does</u>, rpt. from <u>Bio-Dynamics</u>, No. 77 (Stroudsburg, Pa.: Bio-Dynamic Farming and Gardening Assn., 1956).

Because pamphlets are hard to locate in libraries, any extra information about their origin should be supplied. The reader of this note could track down the magazine from which the pamphlet was taken or write to Stroudsburg for a copy.

UNSIGNED:

[22]<u>Dye Plants and Dyeing — A Handbook</u>, rpt. from <u>Plants and Gardens</u>, 20, No. 3 (Baltimore: Brooklyn Botanic Garden, 1964).

dissertations [23]Henry Morton Boudin, "The Ripple Effect in Classroom Management," Diss. Univ. of Michigan, 1970, p. 89.

public documents [24]U.S. <u>Constitution</u>, Art. I, sec. 2.

[25]Environmental Quality Committee of the Governor's Science Advisory Council, <u>Some Technology Considerations for Environmental Quality in Maryland</u> (Jan. 1971).

[26]"Shipments and Unloads of Certain Fruits and Vegetables, 1918–1923," U.S. Dept. of Agriculture <u>Statistical Bulletin</u>, No. 7 (Apr. 1925).

[27]"Actual Revenues from Taxes and Monopolies in Taiwan District," <u>Monthly Statistics of the Republic of China</u>, No. 96 (Dec. 1973), Table 27.

mimeographed materials [28]Willie Sutton, "Writing Effective Letters of Recommendation," mimeographed (Ossining, N.Y., 1936), p. 8.

recordings [29]Desmond Dekker, "Shanty Town," on Jimmy Cliff, <u>The Harder They Come</u>, Mango Records, MLPS–9202.

films [30]<u>Metrics for Measure</u> (Santa Monica, Calif.: BFA Educational Media, 1975), 16 mm., 12 1/4 min., color.

radio or television programs [31]KPFA Strike Committee, "Bourgeois Anti-Free Speech KPFA Management Is Ripping Off the World" (Berkeley, Calif., 14 July 1977), KPFA.

[32]Tom Brokaw, "'Mary Hartman, Mary Hartman': Should Stella Dallas Get Equal Time?" CBS Special (New York: CBS-TV, 28 Feb. 1978).

public ³³William H. Peterson, "Freelance or Shaft: Tax Law for the Self-Em-
addresses ployed," address presented at Captain Cartoon Convention, Disney World,
Fla., Oct. 1977.

interviews ³⁴"Grasshoppers Are People, Too," interview with Bernhard Ulrich
Grenzer, president, Insect Protection League, Entomology Today, 6 (Sept.
1977), 351–58.

Parenthetical References and Subsequent Footnotes

If you have many references to one book, your first and only footnote
to it can look like this:

> ¹Alex Comfort, The Nature of Human Nature (New York: Avon, 1968),
> p. 76. Hereafter cited parenthetically as Nature.

Then your next mention of the work in your main text, and similar
references to it afterward, can take the place of footnotes:

• Human longevity has more than doubled since Neanderthal times (see
Nature, p. 150).

If only one work by a frequently cited author is mentioned in your
text, you can simply use his or her last name and the page numbers
to identify your parenthetical references:

• (see Comfort, p. 150)

But don't test your reader's memory or patience; a fuller reference
should be used if the work hasn't been mentioned in recent paragraphs.

A first footnote has to be detailed because a good deal of information is needed to distinguish one source from all others. Subsequent
references can take most of this information for granted; they should
be brief and simple.

Until recently, subsequent footnotes tended to be cluttered with
Latin abbreviations, chiefly:

abbreviation	meaning
ibid.	the same title as the one mentioned in the previous note
loc. cit.	in the same passage as the one cited in a recent note
op. cit.	in the work cited in a recent note; but the page number of this passage is different (op. cit., p. 321)

For other abbreviations, see pages 394–396.

These terms are increasingly being abandoned in favor of shortened references to the author and/or the title of the work, plus the

page number. Now a reader, instead of having to guess which previous reference *loc. cit.* or *op. cit.* alludes to, can see at once what's intended:

> ¹¹Hechinger, p. 27.
> ¹²Cf. Riviere, pp. 148–49.

A slightly fuller reference is useful if the reader isn't likely to recall at once what "Hechinger" and "Riviere" actually wrote, or if more than one item by the same person has been mentioned:

> ¹¹Hechinger, "Who's in Charge?" p. 27.
> ¹²Cf. Riviere, "Character Trait," pp. 148–49.

Once you have established the author and title of a long poem or play, and have specified the edition you're using, you can cite lines by using a combination of Roman and Arabic numerals. The same form can be used in both footnotes and parenthetical references:

citation	meaning
Lear I.ii. 56–59	Shakespeare's King Lear, Act One, scene two, lines 56–59
Aen. III. 201	Vergil's Aeneid, Book Three, line 201
P.L. IV. 32–33	Milton's Paradise Lost, Book Four, lines 32–33
II Kings iv. 6	The Bible, Second Book of Kings, Chapter Four, verse 6

Note that the Bible and its books aren't customarily italicized.

BIBLIOGRAPHIES

A bibliography is a list of works that you've consulted, or that you recommend to your readers for further reference. Research papers, dissertations, and scholarly books typically contain bibliographies at the end, but in shorter or more informal writing they're less commonly seen. Apart from your instructor's preference, you can decide whether or not to include a bibliography by asking yourself whether your footnotes have given a sufficient idea of your sources. If you want to show that you've taken account of unmentioned works, the extra effort of compiling a bibliography may be worthwhile.

Bibliography entries are always full, with complete specification of all information contained in the *first footnotes* above. The presence of a bibliography, in fact, gives you the option of shortening your first footnote references to the same works. In scientific and technical papers, which usually include bibliographies numbered by item, the main text refers parenthetically to those numbers, thus eliminating most footnotes:

> The work being done at Duke University on high-resolution proton beams (12) shows the extremely coherent and detailed nature of analogue resonances. In addition, the findings of Anderson (3) and Wigner (13) deserve comment.

Things aren't so efficient in the humanities, but if you do include a bibliography you can at least drop subtitles, reprint information, and publishers' names from your footnotes.

Most bibliographies follow the alphabetical order of the authors' last names, with anonymous items inserted in the alphabetical order of the first significant word in each title. Bibliography entries are customarily unnumbered in nonscientific writing. When several entries by one author are listed, they are usually given in order of their dates of publication. A long dash replaces the author's name after the first entry. Some bibliographies are divided by categories — for example, into *Primary Sources* indicating works *by* an author being studied and *Secondary Sources* indicating works *about* that author. Most useful of all are *annotated bibliographies*, including brief comments on the content and value of the separate items.

Like footnotes, bibliography entries should be double-spaced if you are writing for publication. Otherwise they can be single-spaced, with double spaces between the entries. The first line of a bibliography entry is not indented, while the second and all succeeding lines are indented five spaces.

The following comparison of a typical footnote and a bibliography entry spells out the differences in form.

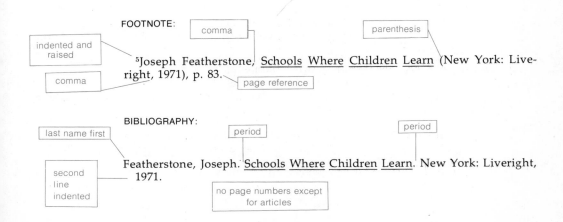

FOOTNOTE:

indented and raised | comma | parenthesis

comma

[5]Joseph Featherstone, Schools Where Children Learn (New York: Liveright, 1971), p. 83.

page reference

BIBLIOGRAPHY:

last name first | period | period

second line indented

Featherstone, Joseph. Schools Where Children Learn. New York: Liveright, 1971.

no page numbers except for articles

Sample Bibliography Entries

A FIRST EDITION:

Langbaum, Robert. The Poetry of Experience: The Dramatic Monologue in
Modern Literary Tradition. New York: Norton, 1963.

————. The Modern Spirit: Essays on the Continuity of Nineteenth- and
Twentieth-Century Literature. New York: Oxford Univ. Press, 1970.

The long dash replaces the author's name after the first entry.

AN EDITED BOOK:

White, George Abbott, and Charles Newman, eds. Literature in Revolution.
New York: Holt, 1972.

Only the first author's name is given last-name-first.

A BOOK EDITED BY MORE THAN THREE PEOPLE:

Kermode, Frank, et al., eds. The Oxford Anthology of English Literature.
2 vols. New York: Oxford Univ. Press, 1973.

A TRANSLATION:

Proust, Marcel. Swann's Way. Trans. C. K. Scott Moncrieff. New York:
Random House, 1928.

A LATER EDITION OF A BOOK WITH CORPORATE AUTHORSHIP:

Sunset Western Garden Book. 3rd ed., n.d.; rpt. Menlo Park, Calif.: Lane,
1967.

A BOOK THAT FORMS PART OF A SERIES:

Kuhn, Thomas S. The Structure of Scientific Revolutions. International
Encyclopedia of Unified Science. 2nd series, No. 2. 2nd ed., 1962; rpt.
Chicago: Univ. of Chicago Press, 1970.

A BOOK REVISED BY SOMEONE OTHER THAN THE AUTHOR(S):

Ricketts, Edward F., and Jack Calvin. Between Pacific Tides. Rev. Joel W.
Hedgpeth. 4th ed., 1939; rpt. Stanford: Stanford Univ. Press, 1968.

A BOOK WHOSE VOLUMES WERE PUBLISHED IN DIFFERENT YEARS:

Poetical Works of William Wordsworth. Ed. E. de Selincourt and H. Darbishire. 2nd ed. 5 vols. Oxford: Oxford Univ. Press, 1952–59.

AN ESSAY PUBLISHED IN A BOOK:

Riviere, Joan. "A Character Trait of Freud's." In Psychoanalysis and Contemporary Thought. Ed. John D. Sutherland. 1958; rpt. New York:
Grove Press, 1959, pp. 145–49.

*articles
in magazines,
journals,
and
newspapers*

AN ARTICLE IN A JOURNAL WITH CONTINUOUS
PAGINATION THROUGH EACH YEAR'S VOLUME:

Pollack, George H. "On Time, Death, and Immortality." Psychoanalytic
Quarterly, 40 (July 1971), 435–46.

AN ARTICLE IN A MAGAZINE WITH SEPARATE PAGINATION FOR EACH ISSUE:

Hechinger, Fred M. "Who's in Charge Here?" Change, Winter 1971–72,
pp. 26–29.

AN ARTICLE IN A JOURNAL THAT DOES
NOT IDENTIFY THE EXACT DATE OF EACH ISSUE:
Wheeler, Richard P. "Poetry and Fantasy in Shakespeare's Sonnets 88–96."
Literature and Psychology, 22, No. 3 (1972), 151–62.

A BOOK REVIEW:
Oberbeck, S. K. Review of Robert Kimball and William Bolcom, Reminiscing
with Sissle and Blake. Newsweek, 30 Apr. 1973, p. 81.

AN UNSIGNED MAGAZINE ARTICLE:
"Drugs That Don't Work." New Republic, 29 Jan. 1972, pp. 12–13.

A SIGNED NEWSPAPER ARTICLE:
Weisser, Peter. "Governor Reagan on Grass." San Francisco Chronicle,
29 Jan. 1972, Final Ed., p. 6, cols. 1–5.

AN UNSIGNED NEWSPAPER ARTICLE OR EDITORIAL:
"Safety in the Mines." Christian Science Monitor, 16 Mar. 1976, p. 28.

encyclopedia L[ustig], L[awrence] K. "Alluvial Fans." Encyclopaedia Britannica, 1974,
entries Macropaedia.

pamphlets SIGNED:
Koepf, H. H. Compost: What It Is/How It Is Made/What It Does. Rpt. from
Bio-Dynamics, No. 77. Stroudsburg, Pa.: Bio-Dynamic Farming and
Gardening Assn., 1956.

UNSIGNED:
Dye Plants and Dyeing—A Handbook. Rpt. from Plants and Gardens, 20,
No. 3. Baltimore: Brooklyn Botanic Garden, 1964.

dissertations Boudin, Henry Morton. "The Ripple Effect in Classroom Management."
Diss. Univ. of Michigan, 1970.

public Environmental Quality Committee of the Governor's Science Advisory
documents Council. Some Technology Considerations for Environmental Quality
in Maryland. Jan. 1971.

"Shipments and Unloads of Certain Fruits and Vegetables, 1918–1923."
U.S. Dept. of Agriculture Statistical Bulletin, No. 7, Apr. 1925.

"Actual Revenues from Taxes and Monopolies in Taiwan District." Monthly
Statistics of the Republic of China, No. 96, Dec. 1973.

mimeographed Sutton, Willie. "Writing Effective Letters of Recommendation." Mimeo-
materials graphed. Ossining, N.Y., 1936.

recordings Dekker, Desmond. "Shanty Town." On Jimmy Cliff, The Harder They Come.
Mango Records, MLPS-9202.

films Metrics for Measure. Santa Monica, Calif.: BFA Educational Media, 1975.
16 mm., 12 1/4 min., color.

radio or   KPFA Strike Committee. "Bourgeois Anti-Free Speech KPFA Management
television   Is Ripping Off the World." Berkeley, Calif., 14 July 1977, KPFA.
programs   Brokaw, Tom. " 'Mary Hartman, Mary Hartman': Should Stella Dallas Get
              Equal Time?" CBS Special, New York: CBS-TV, 28 Feb. 1978.

public   Peterson, William H. "Freelance or Shaft: Tax Law for the Self-Employed."
addresses   Address presented at Captain Cartoon Convention, Disney World,
              Fla., Oct. 1977.

interviews   "Grasshoppers Are People, Too." Interview with Bernhard Ulrich Grenzer,
              president, Insect Protection League. <u>Entomology</u> <u>Today</u>, 6 (Sept. 1977),
              351 – 58.

annotated   Leonard, George. "The Holistic Health Revolution." <u>New</u> <u>West</u>, 10 May
bibliography   1976, pp. 40 – 49.
entry   Argues that traditional medicine, still useful for curing illness, is start-
              ing to give way before a "New Medicine" of ensuring that we stay well
              and cultivate "the tingling feeling of being totally alive and aware and
              at home in the world." Mill Valley, Calif., is the headquarters of the
              revolution.

EXERCISES

**I. If you made the following statements in essays, which ones would require
documentation? What kind of documentation would be appropriate? Briefly defend your answer (pp. 223–225).**

1. The "black hole" hypothesis, once generally dismissed, has been steadily
   gaining favor among astronomers in recent years.
2. To be or not to be: that is indeed the central question for anyone who expe-
   riences suicidal feelings.
3. There can be no denying the fact that industrialization and lung disease
   are inseparable twins; where you find the first, you are bound to find his
   grim brother.
4. The oppressed people of the world must often feel like those who cried out,
   "How long, O Lord, holy and true, dost thou not judge and avenge our
   blood . . .?"
5. The first direct act of atomic warfare occurred at Hiroshima in August 1945.

**II. Write sample notes giving the usual amount of information about these
sources (pp. 229–233):**

1. A quotation from page 428 of this present book.

2. A book by Herman Ermolaev called *Soviet Literary Theories 1917–1934: The Genesis of Socialist Realism.* The book was published in 1963 by the University of California Press, whose offices are in Berkeley and Los Angeles, California.

3. A 1940 pamphlet issued by the United States Department of the Interior, Bureau of Indian Affairs, called *Navajo Native Dyes: Their Preparation and Use.* The pamphlet was published by the Government Printing Office in Washington, D.C.

4. A story by Philip Roth called "On the Air," published in Number 10 of *New American Review,* on pages 7 through 49. This magazine does not carry dates, and its pagination begins anew with each issue.

5. A two-volume book called *American Literary Masters,* edited by Charles R. Anderson and seven other people. The work was published in 1965 by Holt, Rinehart and Winston, whose places of publication are listed on the back of the title page as New York, Chicago, San Francisco, and Toronto.

III. For each of the following footnotes, write two subsequent parenthetical references (pp. 233–234). In each case, make your second reference more concise than your first.

[1]Thomas Mann, *Confessions of Felix Krull, Confidence Man* [*The Early Years*], trans. Denver Lindley (New York: Knopf, 1955), p. 18.

[2]Thomas Lindley, "Bichromate Printing," *Popular Photography,* Oct. 1973, pp. 124–25.

[3]Apicius, *The Roman Cookery Book,* trans. Barbara Flower and Elisabeth Rosenbaum (London: Peter Nevill, 1958), pp. 152–57.

[4]A. S. Neill, *Summerhill: A Radical Approach to Child Rearing* (1960; rpt. New York: Hart, 1964), p. xxiv.

[5]"Desperate Journey: The Story of the Mexican Alien," *Focus,* Sept. 1973, p. 11.

[6]Margaret Atwood, *Surfacing* (New York: Simon and Schuster, 1973), p. 84.

[7]Sheldon Renan, *An Introduction to the American Underground Film* (New York: Dutton, 1967), pp. 250–51.

[8]Sabrina Michaud and Roland Michaud, "Winter Caravan to the Roof of the World," *National Geographic,* 141 (Apr. 1972), 435–65.

[9]*Darwin: A Norton Critical Edition,* ed. Philip Appleman (New York: Norton, 1970), p. 39.

[10]Roy Huss and Norman Silverstein, *The Film Experience: Elements of Motion Picture Art* (New York: Delta, 1968), pp. 122–28.

IV. Make sample bibliographical entries for the items in Exercise II, placing the entries in normal bibliographical order (pp. 234–238).

NOTES

[1]J. M. Roberts, *History of the World* (New York: Knopf, 1976), p. 845.

[2]*A Manual of Style*, 12th ed. (Chicago: Univ. of Chicago Press, 1969).

[3]*The MLA Style Sheet*, 2nd ed. (New York: Modern Language Assn., 1970).

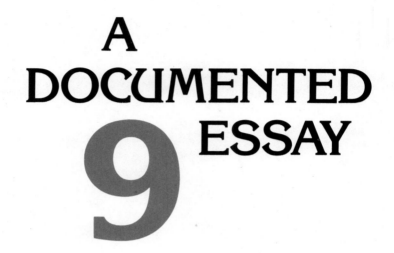

A
DOCUMENTED
9 ESSAY

Students sometimes approach the so-called research paper with unnecessary grimness. They feel that their main purpose should be, not
to write an interesting essay, but to prove that they've done a pun-
ishing amount of research. Thus the paper often has a fact-ridden,
gloomy air. Emphasis falls primarily on the footnotes, and readers
find themselves yo-yoing continuously between the text and the
notes. Students who let several sentences go by without a footnote
may feel they are losing the name of researcher and slipping back to
the primitive days when they had to write ''How I Spent My Summer
Vacation.''

A real research paper is simply an essay written on the basis of
materials the writer has sought out and examined. It should of course
have some notes, and it should also provide a bibliography at the
end, so as to indicate any sources that weren't directly quoted or
cited. But the essay itself needn't be dull or impersonal. Everything I
have said about lively prose applies as much to a research paper as to
other kinds of writing.

Perhaps the greatest risk you face in writing a documented essay is
the loss of your independent perspective. When you find a book or

article that seems impressive, you may be tempted to begin quoting it at great length, allowing it to dominate your ideas and distort the structure of your essay. The best way of ensuring that this doesn't happen is to choose a topic in which you've had a longstanding interest, or at least one which genuinely arouses your curiosity. The writer of the essay that follows, for example, though he didn't know in advance how he would explain W. C. Fields's humor, had followed Fields's movies for years and knew that he could come up with ideas of his own.

If you do find that a published work anticipates what you hoped to say, your first impulse may be to give up and begin from a completely new subject area. But this is usually a wasteful overreaction. The reading you've already done with one topic in mind will alert you to several closely related topics, one of which ought to prove satisfactory. As you take notes, then, you should keep exploring ways of shifting the topic, either to resolve unanticipated difficulties or to make room for new ideas and evidence you may want to include. Before settling finally on one topic, you should review all possibilities together, looking for the best way to be original, challenging, and convincing. The majority of good research essays are about topics slightly different from the writer's first idea.

Thus the author of the sample paper began by thinking he would write about the character and opinions of W. C. Fields, but as his research progressed he saw certain obstacles in his way. A recent book, he learned, cast doubt on the authenticity of many of the "facts" he had wanted to use; he had trouble finding a thesis that would have broad interest; and he gradually realized that a paper about Fields's personality wouldn't deal sufficiently with his comic art. Eventually, however, the writer found a way of including some of his biographical observations.

Here are some of the writer's notes comparing the several topics he had thought of choosing:

CHARACTER AND OPINIONS

Rich material, great quotes—but F's grandson questions many of the anecdotes. Can't get solid thesis. NB: F's *comedy* is what makes him interesting.

VAUDEVILLE AND FILM

Good topic for originality: many people are unaware that F. stole movie material from his own career as stage clown. Plenty of evidence in Ronald Fields's new book. But old Larson would probably say this is too cut-and-dried, just rehashing what R. Fields has turned up.

F'S IDEAS ABOUT COMEDY

Allows discussion of films, and there's enough material in Monti, R. Fields, and F's own writings—esp. "Anything for a Laugh." But this would just be retelling. I need a *problem*.

WHAT'S SO FUNNY ABOUT F?

Looks good. Draws on best evidence for other topics, and focuses on F's nastiness. (Good because that's what makes him different.) NB: F arouses wildly different reactions; make sure to bring this out.

WHY DO WE LAUGH AT W. C. FIELDS?

by

M. J. Kane

Professor Larson

Film Criticism 86D

The writer uses a topic outline (p. 41), showing the subordination of some ideas to others.

OUTLINE

Thesis: Fields's characterization as a doomed victim of American life allows us to laugh at his malice and cynicism.

I.   The Problem: How to Explain the Popularity of Such a Nasty Figure

    A. His popularity thrives

    B. Do we admire sheer aggression?

II. Evading the Problem: The Attempt to "Humanize" Fields

    A. Emphasis on his sympathetic roles

    B. Unsuccessful "proof" of his gentleness

III. The Record Is Clear: Fields as Cynic and Champion of Meanness

    A. Biographical testimony

    B. His remarks about comic appeal

    C. Sadistic episodes in his films

IV. The Problem Solved: We Laugh at a Ridiculous <u>Character</u>

    A. Distinction between isolated acts and a consistent character

    B. Fields as a defeated figure

        1. In appearance and manner

        2. In family and business

        3. In unfulfilled endings

    C. We laugh at Fields's pettiness, not his cruelty

    D. Fields gives us comic distance from his cynicism

WHY DO WE LAUGH AT W. C. FIELDS?

In San Francisco in 1973, a portly man wearing a long
checkered coat, spats, white gloves, and a top hat strolls
down Market Street, puffing on a cigar and twirling a cane.
He is not in fact W. C. Fields, who died in 1946, but one
Ted Allison, who makes a living entirely by impersonating
Fields in advertising stunts. Wherever he goes he is
"surrounded by the inevitable clusters of people, every age
group, every color seemingly mesmerized by the curious magic
he dispense[s]."[1] It is the same magic that prompts thousands
to stand in line for "W. C. Fields Film Festivals," to buy
enormous posters of their idol scowling behind a poker hand,
and to trade improbable tales about his offscreen antics.
W. C. Fields, it seems, is alive and well, not only in San
Francisco but across the United States.

This fact is by no means easy to explain. Fields was a
great slapstick comic, but he was only one among many performers
who successfully made the leap from burlesque to Hollywood. In
a contest of talent he would rank behind Charlie Chaplin and
not far ahead of Buster Keaton, Harold Lloyd, Laurel and Hardy,
or the Marx brothers. His comedy, furthermore, is offensive to

_____

[1]William Moore, "Following in W. C. Fields' Footsteps,"
San Francisco <u>Chronicle</u>, 23 July 1973, p. 14.

The essay begins with a
"baited opener" (pp.
189–192)—a story that
catches attention and
gradually leads us toward
the main argument.

Footnotes are placed at
the bottom of the page
where the reference
appears. They could also
have been placed
consecutively after the
end of the main text.
See pp. 60–61.

2

**Having caught our
interest, the writer poses
his problem.**

many people and puzzling even to his devoted fans. What is
funny about a pompous, malicious, disagreeable-looking fellow
whose half-inaudible gags, in the opinion of one critic,
combine "frustrated aggression" with "a hopeless expectation
of audience disapproval"?[2] Do we think that sheer nastiness
is funny?

**The next two paragraphs
consider, and reject, a
suggestion that the
problem doesn't exist.**

The problem of justifying Fields has been around for a
long time. Most people are reluctant to say that they enjoy
seeing vicious behavior even in a movie, and some of Fields's
commentators have denied that he usually appeals to such a
taste. Thus, in a 1939 review of You Can't Cheat an Honest
Man, Frank S. Nugent fumed: "Considering that he wrote it
himself, Mr. Fields seems singularly ignorant of the qualities
that have endeared him to his millions. His Larson E. Whipsnade,
circus proprietor, is completely unsympathetic. He is a scamp,
but not a loveable scamp; a blusterer who bullies for the
sake of bullying and not to conceal a tender heart."[3] Although
this in itself has a comical ring--surely, we tell ourselves,
"a tender heart" isn't something we should associate with Fields
--the reviewer was echoing a widely held belief that comic
figures should be appealing. Indeed, we now know that Fields

---

[2]Raymond Durgnat, "Subversion in the Fields," Films and
Filming, Dec. 1965, p. 43.

[3]Reprinted in Donald Deschner, The Films of W. C. Fields
(New York: Citadel, 1966), p. 137.

3

himself was at least passingly affected by this idea. He

complained to the producer of You Can't Cheat an Honest Man

that important scenes of "pathos" had been cut,[4] and he wrote

to Mae West that My Little Chickadee (1940) ought to present

"just the two of us at the end of the picture with no attempts

at comedy or wise cracks from either of us. I think it will

leave a nice human, homey feeling in the audience's mind."[5]

These revelations are provided by a new book which is

itself an unconvincing effort to solve the Fields problem by

declaring that no problem exists. Fields's grandson, in

introducing his collection of letters and scripts, claims to

be presenting us with "a gentle man, a proud father, and a

loving grandfather,"[6] and his editorial remarks imply that

Fields's audiences simply recognized the genius of "The Great

One." Skimming W. C. Fields by Himself, we could almost

imagine that we were dealing with an ordinary citizen who

happened to be very good at making people laugh. Yet the

documents themselves, when studied apart from Ronald Fields's

enthusiastic notes, make quite a different impression. The

"proud father" hardly ever saw his son, who grew up to despise

him, and the "gentle man" shows a disagreeable temper on page

---

[4]W. C. Fields by Himself, ed. Ronald J. Fields (Englewood
Cliffs, N.J.: Prentice-Hall, 1973), p. 322.

[5]Fields by Himself, p. 366.

[6]Fields by Himself, Introduction, p. xiv.

**Compare this note to the
bibliography entry for
the same book (p. 258).
Because a full reference
appears in the
bibliography, the
footnote is shortened.**

**A shortened second
reference (see pp.
233–234).**

4

after page. Fields may have wanted some pathos in his scripts,
but neither his grandson nor anyone else can convince us that
he projected "a nice human, homey feeling" either in his life
or in his art.

The next two paragraphs
rely heavily on quotation
to establish support for
the writer's view of Fields.

The Fields we see on the screen is, by and large, the one
we know from many biographical sources, and most reliably from
his mistress of fourteen years, Carlotta Monti. This Fields
is the pathologically suspicious, cynical man who once drawled
on election day, "Hell, I never vote _for_ anybody; I always
vote _against_."[7] It is the man who scorned the jury system
because, in his view, "It is impossible to find twelve fair
men in all the world."[8] Again, it is the man who once defined
business as "an establishment that gives you the legal, even
though unethical, right to screw the naive--right, left, and
in the middle."[9] The Fields we know is epitomized in Robert
Lewis Taylor's story about how the aging star performed his
old pool-hall routine in one last movie for wartime release
in 1944. After the shooting "several people thanked him for
his fine patriotic effort and said how much good the scene
would do. He shook their hands with self-conscious pleasure,

---

[7]Quoted by Robert Lewis Taylor, W. C. Fields: His Follies
and Fortunes (Garden City, N.Y.: Doubleday, 1949), p. 275.

[8]Quoted by Gene Fowler, Minutes of the Last Meeting (New
York: Viking, 1954), p. 173.

[9]Quoted by Carlotta Monti with Cy Rice, W. C. Fields and
Me (Englewood Cliffs, N.J.: Prentice-Hall, 1971), p. 134.

5

went to the cashier and collected the \$25,000 he had agreed
on, then shuffled off toward his car, whistling a soundless
tune, his eyes fixed on the distant horizon."10 Some of these
stories may be inaccurate, but there are dozens of similar
recollections that can't be dismissed.

When Fields wrote and talked about the nature of his
comedy, "homeyness" was the farthest thing from his mind. He
asked Carlotta Monti to remember that "everyone has a percentage
of the sadist in him, even though infinitesimal. If I hit you
over the head with a club in public . . . I'd be arrested. In
a comedy act, it draws laughter."11 Quarreling with script
writers (his favorite fish, he once said in reply to a question,
was "a piranha in a writer's bathtub"12) about whether he
should kick Baby Leroy in The Old-Fashioned Way (1934), he
remarked, "There is not a man in America who has not had a
secret ambition to boot an infant. They will love it."13
And in a magazine article Fields once had this to say:

> I know we laugh at the troubles of others, provided
> those troubles are not too serious. Out of that
> observation I have reached a conclusion which may be

For a long quotation, the writer omits quotation marks and indents the whole passage five spaces.

10Taylor, p. 85.

11Quoted by Monti, p. 66.

12Quoted by Monti, p. 68.

13Quoted by Alva Johnston, "Who Knows What Is Funny?",
Saturday Evening Post, 6 Aug. 1938, p. 43.

6

of some comfort to those accused of "having no
sense of humor." These folks are charming, lovable,
philanthropic people, and invariably I like them
--as long as they keep out of the theaters where
I am playing, which they usually do. If they get
in by mistake, they leave early.

The reason they don't laugh at most gags is
that their first emotional reaction is to feel sorry
for people instead of to laugh at them. . . .

I like, in an audience, the fellow who roars
continuously at the troubles of the character I am
portraying . . ., but he probably has a mean streak
in him and, if I needed ten dollars, he'd be the
last person I'd call upon.[14]

Turning to the films themselves, we find no shortage of

cruel, "sick" humor. The uncensored version of <u>The Dentist</u>

(1932), for example, contains an episode that looks provocatively

like a case of rape. In <u>The Fatal Glass of Beer</u> (1932) Fields,

alias the Northern trapper Snavely, notoriously announces that

he has eaten his lead-dog, who tasted "mighty good with mustard."

The movie ends with Mr. and Mrs. Snavely tossing their prodigal

son out into the Klondike snow, presumably to freeze. In <u>You</u>

<u>Can't Cheat an Honest Man</u> Fields knocks a woman down when no

one is looking and then tells her, for the benefit of the

gathering bystanders, that her husband should take her home

since he was the one who "got you drunk." And in <u>The Bank Dick</u>

(1940) Fields torments the bank examiner, J. Pinkerton Snoopington,

after he has made him sick with heavily spiked drinks, by

conjuring up pictures of the heaviest, greasiest fried foods

**Some of the research for
this essay consisted of
the writer's seeing old
movies. Although some
of the script lines were
verified in books about
Fields, no footnotes are
required for them.**

---

[14]W. C. Fields, "Anything for a Laugh," <u>American Magazine</u>,
Sept. 1934, p. 130.

7

he can imagine. The audience always howls with delight.

Thus we are brought back to our original question: if
Fields's sadism is undeniable, must we accept it as the
basis of his funniness? Perhaps so--yet I can't believe
that matters are so simple. Consider Fields's own example of
provoking laughter by hitting a woman over the head with a
club in a comedy act. In such a case would we be laughing
at a vicious assault, or rather at a ridiculous <u>figure</u> who
expressed his rage without any of the restraints we ourselves
would apply? Fields, we know, wasn't just a gagster but
a student of character who placed a high value on consistency.[15]
Although his fictional personality varies from one plot to
the next, he does have an increasingly well-defined "self"
that we hope and expect to meet in every film. It is this
total character, not a few instances of shocking cruelty,
that disposes us to laugh.

In order to define this character, let's begin by studying
Fields's celebrated appearance and manner. Unlike most of his
Hollywood contemporaries--Chaplin the tramp, Keaton the soulful
outsider, the mildly retarded Laurel and Hardy, the peasant
immigrant Marx brothers--he seems completely devoid of childlike

> **The writer restates his problem to indicate that he will now begin presenting his solution to it.**

----

[15]He told Carlotta Monti, for example, that although
Scrooge was his favorite Dickens character, "he fell from my
good graces at the end of the tale." Carlotta asked why. "He
reformed, that's what the blithering idiot did. He became
benevolent. That was Dickens' only mistake! He allowed Scrooge
to get out of character!" (Quoted by Monti, p. 40.)

> **A substantive footnote (see p. 226).**

8

innocence. He is not only grown up, but grown sarcastic as
well. His sarcasm, in fact, marks him as a more thorough
victim than any of his rival comedians: he is walking proof
that daily American life can strip away all illusions. His
shifty eyes indicate that he has long since learned not to
expect decent treatment. His bulbous nose identifies him as
a man who has been driven to drink. His spasmodic gestures
of self-defense, which prompted one critic to think of "the
crabbed helplessness of a teddy bear with arthritis,"[16] reveal
a frayed nervous system and a conviction that the worst is
yet to come. With his drinking Fields tries to blot out
humiliation; with his cheating he tries to compensate for the
bad hand he has been dealt by fate; and with his grandiose
fibs he tries to insulate himself in fantasy. What we laugh
at is the image of a man who has been made grotesque and
preposterous without losing his itch to settle the score.

Fields strikes us not only as a victim, but as a recognizably
American one who has to undergo the seemingly unbearable nuisances
of family and business life. Take the famous bedtime ritual in
The Fatal Glass of Beer, when mother, father, and long-lost son
exchange pseudo-helpful advice. "Good night, son, and don't
forget to open your window . . ." "I won't, Ma, and don't
forget to open your window . . . good-night, Pa, and you open

---

**This article has been
previously cited; hence
the shortened second
reference.**

[16]Durgnat, "Subversion in the Fields," p. 42.

9

your window too, Pa. . . ." The advice escalates as all
three characters begin speaking at once, until the din is
finally halted by the slamming of the son's door. Any
attempt at civility within the family, Fields seems to tell
us, is destined to backfire; after all, it can't possibly be
sincere in the first place.

Or again, consider what happens in The Pharmacist (1932).
There Fields, having cut through a large square of three-cent
stamps to get the one in the middle that his grouchy customer
has selected, wraps the stamp in a huge paper bag after the
customer has decided against having it "sent," gives it on
credit when the customer produces an unchangeable hundred-
dollar bill, and then remembers to present his latest sales
gimmick, a gigantic souvenir vase. Before the scene is over
Fields has given away three vases without having made a
genuine sale. He calls to our minds every small businessman
who has to abase himself, not in the ever more distant hope
of getting ahead, but simply because the customer is king.

Even though some of Fields's movies have conventional "happy
endings," there are limitations on the happiness that can be
imagined for a hero like Fields. Chaplin, Keaton, and Lloyd
regularly "get the girl" when their sufferings are over, but
the very thought of Fields on a honeymoon is wildly farcical.
In My Little Chickadee (1940) he reaches for Mae West in bed and
gets--a nanny goat. A typical fate is his reward in The Bank Dick:

a limp "heartiest handshake," a calendar of "Spring in Lompoc,"
a minor job, and a renewal of his life sentence of henpecked
marriage and parenthood. We begin to understand what Fields
meant when he welcomed the viewer "who roars continuously <u>at
the troubles of the character I am portraying</u>."

In short, then, Fields is an extraordinarily defeated
figure who invites a certain scorn. Unlike the typical comic
hero, who wins our sympathy and our permission to break a few
rules before achieving his rightful success and happiness,
Fields is going to keep mumbling and snarling forever. He
doesn't even <u>want</u> us to take his side in his quarrel with the
world; all apparent friends are really enemies in disguise.
What he wants is to be left in peace (an impossible hope) and
to win a few cheap victories over the people and animals who
get on his nerves.

Those victories are funny, not because of their cruelty,
but because of their extreme triviality: Fields is so helpless
that he can only pick on the weak, the infantile, the senile,
even the blind.[17] The supreme Fieldsian gesture occurs in

---

[17]Fields's movies contain more vendettas than a casual viewer
might think. Thus in <u>The Bank Dick</u> he stops to "help" an old lady
and her chauffeur with their stranded car, and after one turn of a
screw the engine drops onto the street--whereupon Fields tips his
hat and strolls briskly away. The scene looks like a funny
accident, but Fields, in Robert Lewis Taylor's words, "told a
friend that the automobile skit had been taken from his own life.
'People were always offering to help me out like that, with about
the same results,' he said" (Taylor, p. 328).

11

The Barber Shop (1932), after he has taken a giant safety pin
from a baby, warning him that swallowing the open pin could kill
him. But when the baby then socks Fields with his milk bottle,
Fields hands him back the pin, still unsheathed. It is a moment
either of mad fun or of appalling bad taste, depending on your
idea of how far comedy can go; but in any event it illustrates
Fields's absurdly defensive survival tactics toward everyone,
including the newborn. Although some--not all--of his actions
are sadistic, what they really show is a fear of assault from
every quarter.

  "A thing worth having," Fields intones in one of his movies,
"is worth cheating for."[18] The sentence is a marvelous reversal
of Ben Franklin wisdom. With one part of our minds we may
secretly agree with it, but if we openly agreed, the humor
would disappear. What Fields does for us is to portray such
a spiteful, self-absorbed, implausible character that we can
easily distance ourselves from his cynicism, taking it as a
joke instead of as a serious philosophy. Like every great
comedian, Fields finally has only one message, that life is a
laughing matter. The laugh, we have seen, is on him--and
that's exactly where he wanted it to be.

_____

  [18]Quoted in W. C. Fields, *Drat!*, ed. Richard J. Anobile
(New York: Signet, 1969), p. 53.

**A striking quotation
has been saved for
the concluding
paragraph.**

12

For bibliography form, see pp. 234–238.

BIBLIOGRAPHY

Agee, James. Agee on Film: Reviews and Comments. New York:
    McDowell Oblensky, 1958.

Deschner, Donald. The Films of W. C. Fields. Intro. Arthur
    Knight. New York: Citadel, 1966.

Durgnat, Raymond. The Crazy Mirror: Hollywood Comedy and the
    American Image. London: Faber and Faber, 1969.

_____. "Subversion in the Fields." Films and
    Filming, Dec. 1965, pp. 42–48.

Everson, William K. The Art of W. C. Fields. Indianapolis:
    Bobbs-Merrill, 1967.

Fields, W. C. "Anything for a Laugh." The American Magazine,
    Sept. 1934, pp. 73, 129, 130.

_____. Drat!: Being the Encapsulated View of Life by
    W. C. Fields in His Own Words. Ed. Richard J. Anobile.
    Intro. Ed McMahon. 1968; rpt. New York: Signet, 1969.

_____. Fields for President. Ed. Michael M. Taylor.
    1940; rpt. New York: Dodd, Mead, 1971.

_____. W. C. Fields by Himself: His Intended
    Autobiography. Ed. Ronald J. Fields. Englewood Cliffs,
    N.J.: Prentice-Hall, 1973.

Ford, Corey. The Time of Laughter. Boston: Little, Brown, 1967.

Fowler, Gene. Minutes of the Last Meeting. New York: Viking,
    1954.

Greene, Graham. Review of Poppy in The Spectator, 17 July 1936;
    rpt. Intellectual Digest, Apr. 1973, p. 29.

Johnston, Alva. "Who Knows What Is Funny?" Saturday Evening
    Post, 6 Aug. 1938, pp. 10, 11, 43, 45, 46.

Lahue, Kalton C. World of Laughter: The Motion Picture Comedy
    Short, 1910–1930. Norman: Univ. of Oklahoma Press, 1966.

Montgomery, John. Comedy Films, 1894–1954. 1954; 2nd ed.
    London: Allen and Unwin, 1968.

13

Monti, Carlotta, with Cy Rice. W. C. Fields and Me. Englewood
    Cliffs, N.J.: Prentice-Hall, 1971.

Moore, William. "Following in W. C. Fields' Footsteps." San
    Francisco Chronicle, 23 July 1973, p. 14, cols. 1-6.

Schickel, Richard. Movies: The History of an Art and an
    Institution. New York: Basic Books, 1964.

Sennett, Mack, with Cameron Shipp. King of Comedy. Garden
    City, N.Y.: Doubleday, 1954.

Taylor, Robert Lewis. W. C. Fields: His Follies and Fortunes.
    Garden City, N.Y.: Doubleday, 1949.

Zimmerman, Paul D. "The Great Debunker." Newsweek, 3 Apr.
    1967, p. 88.

4

    The Fields we see on the screen is, by and large, the one we know from many biographical sources, and most reliably from his mistress of fourteen years, Carlotta Monti. This Fields is the pathologically suspicious, cynical man who once drawled on election day, "Hell, I never vote for anybody; I always vote against."[7] It is the man who scorned the jury system because, in his view, "It is impossible to find twelve fair men in all the world."[8]

[7] Quoted by Robert Lewis Taylor, W.C. Fields: His Follies and Fortunes (Garden City, N.Y.: Doubleday, 1949), p. 275.

[8] Quoted by Gene Fowler, Minutes of the Last Meeting (New York: Viking, 1954), p. 173.

PART IV
BASICS

A REVIEW 10 OF GRAMMAR

Writers who want their prose to be effective—and who doesn't?—must obviously use the language in ways that other people consider "correct English." A personal style, with its own characteristic vocabulary and patterns of phrasing, can't afford to stray very far from the *usage,* or accepted contemporary practices, of *standard written English*, the kind of writing people expect to find in nearly all public communication. Later chapters will treat the problems that this expectation raises for a writer. First, however, we must recognize that standard usage rests squarely on a foundation of *general English grammar*—the formal, relatively stable features that distinguish the whole language from others.

As you write, you're likely to be consciously aware of *usage* questions, especially those on which good writers hold significantly different opinions: whether or not you should split infinitives in some circumstances, whether *hopefully* should be used in the sense of "it is hoped," and so forth. But meanwhile, without noticing that you're doing so, you're also practicing the rules of English *grammar*, such as the way nouns are made plural and possessive, the tense forms of verbs, and the placement of prepositions before their objects. Much of this practice is automatic, especially if you're a native speaker of standard English; for "good usage" in standard English is generally "good grammar" as well, and most grammatical rules have become second nature by an early age.

Nevertheless, a descriptive review of grammar has more than an academic claim on your interest. If your *dialect,* or group practice, differs from standard English in certain ways, you can spot the differences and then be watchful for them as you revise your drafts. Moving from conversation to writing, furthermore, is tricky even if you've spoken standard English since childhood. Difficulties that never come up in speech can't be avoided on paper — simple choices, for instance, between *its* and *it's* or *whose* and *who's,* and harder choices that call for a structural analysis of clauses. Which is the correct pronoun form, for example, in the following sentence?

He will read his poems to $\begin{Bmatrix} whoever \\ whomever \end{Bmatrix}$ will listen.

You can't be stumped by such puzzles if you're familiar with *sentence elements,* with the *parts of speech* and their characteristics, and with the *functions of phrases and clauses.* (The answer, by the way, is *whoever;* see p. 295.)

GRAMMATICAL UNITS

Every time you grasp the content of a sentence, you go through a surprising number of mental operations. In the first place, of course, you are perceiving single words. Their positions in the sentence, their changeable forms or *inflections,* and your awareness of their usual range of meanings all enable you to register their general types, or *parts of speech.* In *She squares the number,* for example, the position and ending of *squares* make it fit only as a verb, even though the word standing by itself would look like a noun. You may or may not be able to name the part of speech, but your mind "reads" it without hesitation.

Meanwhile, you are also perceiving *groups* of words as units of various types. In *He wanted to be free,* the three words *to be free* strike you as a unit, just as the single word *freedom* would. What did he want?

He wanted $\begin{Bmatrix} \text{freedom.} \\ \text{to be free.} \end{Bmatrix}$

In short, you read *to be free* as a *phrase*. At the same time, you grasp all five words *He wanted to be free* as a *clause*. You sense, not only that they form a unit, but that the unit contains the two essential parts of a clause, a *subject* (something spoken about) and a *predicate* (something said):

$$
\begin{array}{l}
\text{s} \quad\quad \text{PRED} \\
\end{array}
$$
• He wanted to be free.

Further, you recognize that this clause is of the type that can form a complete *sentence;* that is, it is *independent,* not *subordinate* (or *dependent*) like *when he wanted to be free* or *although he wanted to be free.* When you do find a subordinate clause, you expect an independent one to accompany it. You read—though you may not always write—with an understanding that *a sentence normally contains at least one independent clause,* and you know that independent clauses never begin with subordinating words like *when* and *although.*

Finally, you perceive various *sentence elements,* or working parts of sentences. Words, phrases, and subordinate clauses make grammatical sense to you only by serving as those parts. You might know, for example, that *tourist* and *safari* are both nouns, but unless you grasped the difference between subjects and direct objects, *The tourist takes the safari* and *The safari takes the tourist* would mean the same thing to you. Sentence elements, with which our review of grammar begins, are the building blocks of all statements; words, phrases, and clauses are the materials from which these blocks are made.

SENTENCE ELEMENTS

A sentence, we have said, must have a subject and a predicate. Since the minimum content necessary for a predicate is a verb, we can begin the review of sentence elements by saying that the *essential* elements are a *subject* and a *verb.* (Even a sentence like *Beware!* is assumed to have an implied subject, *You.*) Note that *verb* as a sentence element differs from *verb* as a part of speech. The parts of speech classify words by *type;* the sentence elements identify *function within a given sentence.* Conceivably, a word not usually recognized as a verb (part of speech) could serve as a verb (sentence element)—for instance, *skateboards* in *He skateboards well.*

subjects and verbs A root sentence might be:

$$
\begin{array}{l}
\text{s} \quad \text{v} \\
\end{array}
$$
• *Biff bites.*

A *subject* and a *verb* in an independent clause make a sentence.

Other sentence elements can be added to the base sentence:

S   V   D OBJ

direct objects   • *Biff bites* the *quarterback.*

The verb takes a *direct object,* something that the subject *acts upon* through the activity of the verb.

S   V   RET OBJ

etained objects   • *Biff is given* a *penalty.*

When the verb is made passive, changing the subject from the performer to the receiver of the verb's action, a word in the direct-object position is called a *retained object.*

S   V   IND OBJ   D OBJ

indirect objects   • *Biff gives* the *referee* an *argument.*

A sentence containing a direct object may also have an *indirect object,* the being, thing, or idea *for whom or which* or *to whom or which* the action of the verb is done. (Note that when *for* or *to* is actually used, we have a prepositional phrase instead of an indirect object: *for Biff, to the referee.* See pp. 283–284.)

S V   COMPL   S   V   COMPL

complements: • *Biff is* a sore *loser.*   *He has become bitter.*
predicate noun,
predicate   Now the verb, instead of sending an action from subject to
adjective   object, connects the subject to a *complement*—an element in the predicate that helps to *identify* the subject (Biff=loser) or *describe* the subject (Biff is bitter). We will see that the two major types of complements, illustrated here, are respectively a *predicate noun* and a *predicate adjective.*

S   V D OBJ   OBJ COMPL

objective   • *They call Biff* a sore *loser.*
complements
Biff has become a direct object, but once again it has *loser* as a complement. The complement of a direct object is called an *objective complement.*

M   M   M   S   M   V M   M   M   D OBJ

modifiers   • *The angry, vengeful fans energetically toss their dangerously heavy bottles.*

The sentence is crammed with *modifiers,* or elements that limit or describe other elements. We will see that the single-word modifiers here belong to different parts of speech: an *article*

(The), three *adjectives (angry, vengeful, heavy)*, two *adverbs (energetically, dangerously)*, and a *possessive pronoun (their)*.

appositives •

M   M   S   APP M M   V M M D OBJ   APP

The terrified referee Jones no longer scorns a gentler sport, badminton.

In this sentence *Jones* and *badminton*, though they may look at first like modifiers, are really *appositives*—elements whose sole function is to identify the preceding element. Whereas a modifier *limits* the modified word, an appositive is equivalent ("stands in apposition") to the noun, pronoun, or nounlike element it follows. You can test for an appositive by trying to *substitute it* for that element: *The terrified Jones no longer scorns badminton.* That makes sense; *Jones* and *badminton* are confirmed as appositives in the original sentence.

connectives •

CON   M   S   CON M   S   V CON   V   MOD D OBJ

Neither the coaches nor the players aid and comfort the referee.

Essential elements, the subject and the verb, are now *compound*, consisting of more than one item. They must be linked by *connectives: Neither . . . nor, and.*

These are the functioning parts of sentences, then: subjects, verbs, objects, complements, modifiers, appositives, and connectives. If you can recognize them where they appear, you have made a significant start toward comprehending English grammar—and toward ensuring that your own sentence elements will work together efficiently. The rest of this chapter will examine the three types of units that can serve *as* or *within* sentence elements: *words* in their various parts of speech, *phrases*, and *subordinate clauses*.

PARTS OF SPEECH

Full definitions of the parts of speech would have to include the *kind of meaning* a part of speech conveys; its *inflectional features* or changed forms, if any; and a list of all the *sentence positions* it can occupy. As a writer, however, you are probably more interested in recognition and effective use than in scientific classification. The following definitions will therefore concentrate on essentials.

Verbs

The heart of any sentence is its main *verb*, the word or set of words that tells what's going on:

$\overset{\text{v}}{ }$

You *are* a bore.

$\overset{\text{v}}{ }$

You *have exhausted* all my patience.

$\overset{\text{v}}{ }$

I *am leaving* now.

$\overset{\text{v}}{ }$ $\overset{\text{v}}{ }$

I *will* never again *listen* to your Folkways record, *Termite Mounds of Somaliland.*

Though the exact meaning of the concept *verb* is hard to pin down, the three tests of meaning, inflection, and position allow you to spot the verb or verbs in any sentence.

Meaning. If you can locate the subject of a clause, you can find the verb by spotting the word that either *sets up the characterization* of the subject or *transmits the action* of the subject to an object. Thus, in the first example above, which word sets up the characterization of *You* as a *bore?* The answer is the verb *are.* And in the second example, which word or words transmit the action from the subject *You* to the direct object *patience?* The answer is *have exhausted*—the verb or, since it consists of more than one word, the *verb phrase.* A verb, then, either *establishes a bridge between the subject and the subject's condition or identity* or *tells what the subject does.* Note that the verb itself is never a thing or idea, nor can it limit or *modify* another word.

Inflection. Verbs show inflection (altered form) for different *voices* (active and passive) and *tenses* or times:

active: You $\left\{ \begin{array}{l} \text{are} \\ \text{were} \\ \text{have been} \\ \text{had been} \\ \text{will be} \end{array} \right\}$ a bore.

passive: You $\left\{ \begin{array}{l} \text{are resented} \\ \text{were resented} \\ \text{have been resented} \\ \text{had been resented} \\ \text{will be resented} \end{array} \right\}$ for your indifference to Wanda.

Some verbs remain uninflected in certain forms: *They always beat* (present) *us, just as they beat* (past) *us yesterday.*

Position. Because a verb isn't a thing, it can't occupy *substantive* (nounlike) positions in a sentence. Thus *iron*, which might be either a verb or a noun, isn't a verb in these sentences:

- The iron is hot.
- He had a stomach of iron.

But it *is* a verb in *They iron their underwear;* only a verb could fill the sentence slot it occupies there. Again:

- She *is singing.*
- *Is singing* offensive?

The same two words appear in both sentences, but they constitute a verb only in the first, where they follow an apparent subject. Only a verb could fill the first sentence slot; only a nounlike element (in this case a gerund) could be the middle word in the second one. In the second sentence the verb is simply *Is*, standing where we would expect to find it in a question.

In the following passage the verbs are marked with v:

"I *have decided* to become a guru," *declared* Norbert. "Many years of study and self-denial *will be involved*, but the world *stands* in need of my services. Once certified as an adept, I *will bestow* advice upon everyone seeking enlightenment. People *will come* to know me as 'Norbert the Purified One of Daly City.'"

Note here that *become, certified, seeking,* and *know,* which resemble verbs, fail the tests of function and position. In this passage they are actually *verbals* (pp. 288–292) of different kinds.

A verb is the most complex, sensitively "tuned" part of speech. To appreciate all the communicative features of a verb in any given clause, you must observe not only its meaning, but also its *transitive, intransitive,* or *linking* function; its *person, number,* and *tense;* its *voice;* and its *mood.*

transitive, intransitive, and linking verbs   A verb appearing in any clause is either *transitive, intransitive,* or *linking.* A *transitive* verb *transmits* an action to a direct object—or, if the verb is passive (p. 271), to a retained object:

       S   TRANS V   D OBJ
- Norbert *burned* the incense.
       S   TRANS V   RET OBJ
- He *was given* a mantra from the phone book.

An *intransitive* verb expresses an action or state without reference to an object or complement:

       S   INTRANS V
- The incense *burned*.

A *linking* verb, like a transitive one, establishes a relation between the subject and part of the predicate. Instead of transmitting an effect, however, a linking verb allows the subject to be identified or modified by a *complement*. Where the subject is identified, the complement is a *predicate noun*:

      S   LV PRED N
- Norbert *is a fanatic*.

Where the subject is modified, the complement is a *predicate adjective*:

      S   LV PRED ADJ
- Norbert *is fanatical*.

By far the most frequently used linking verb is *be*. Others include *act, appear, become, feel, grow, look, loom, prove, remain, seem, smell, sound, taste*, and *turn*. Note, however, that you can't be sure you're reading a linking verb—or, for that matter, a transitive or intransitive one—without checking its relation to other words in the sentence. *Grew*, for instance, is by turns transitive, intransitive, and linking in these three sentences:

      S   TRANS V D OBJ
- Norbert *grew* lotuses in his window box.

    S INTRANS V
- He *grew* in spiritual strength.

      S   LV PRED ADJ
- Wanda *grew* impatient with his holy ways.

person and number Verbs "agree" in *person* and *number* with their subjects—even when the subjects are unstated, as in [*You*] *Come!* English uses three "persons," according to whether someone is *speaking (first person: I, we), being spoken to (second person: you)*, or *being spoken about (third person: he, she, it, they)*. The "numbers" are *singular (I, you, he, she, it)* and *plural (we, you, they)*. English verbs show little inflection for person and number, but the changes that do exist are important. *He go*, for example, strikes most readers as ungrammatical, since the standard third-person singular form of *go* is *goes*.

tenses The tense of a verb is the time it expresses. All tenses are based on one or more of the following forms of a verb:

the base or simple *infinitive* (without *to*):

>I go, she goes

the *present participle:*

>I am going, she is going

the *past* form:

>I went, she went

the *past participle:*

>I have gone, she had gone

and various forms of the verbs *be* and *have:*

>I have gone, she is going, I have been going, she will have been going, etc.

The base infinitive, past form, and past participle of a verb are known as its *principal parts*.

The most commonly recognized tenses are:

present (action happening now): *meditates*
present progressive (action ongoing in the present): *is meditating*
present perfect (past action regarded from the present): *has meditated*
present perfect progressive (past action continued into the present): *has been meditating*
past (completed action): *meditated*
past progressive (action that was ongoing in a previous time): *was meditating*
past perfect (action completed before another past time): *had meditated*
past perfect progressive (ongoing action completed before another past time): *had been meditating*
future (action to take place later): *will meditate*
future progressive (continued action to take place later): *will be meditating*
future perfect (action regarded as completed at a later time): *will have meditated*
future perfect progressive (continued action regarded as completed before a later time): *will have been meditating*

Perhaps the hardest problem in tense formation is getting the right past participle of *irregular* verbs — that is, verbs that don't simply add *-d* or *-ed* to form both the past tense and the past participle. Irregular verbs change more radically:

infinitive (base)	past tense	past participle
be	was	been
begin	began	begun
choose	chose	chosen
go	went	gone
lie	lay	lain
speak	spoke	spoken
throw	threw	thrown

The list could go on for many pages. When you hesitate between two forms, consult your dictionary, which gives the full principal parts of all irregular verbs.

voice The *voice* of a verb indicates whether the subject performs (is *active* in) or receives (is *passive* to) the action of the verb.

ACTIVE VOICE:
• Frankie *shot* Johnny.

PASSIVE VOICE:
• Johnny *was shot* by Frankie.

Observe that in these two sentences the actual performer of the action, *Frankie*, is the same. But only in the first sentence is *Frankie* the grammatical subject of the verb. In the second sentence the subject is *Johnny*, who is *acted upon* by the passive verb *was shot*. One peculiarity of the passive voice, you may notice, is that it can allow the performer of the action to go unmentioned: *Johnny was shot.*

Here are the *active* forms of a regular verb, *walk*, and an irregular verb, *go*. Of the twelve possible tenses, the eight most common ones are illustrated:

ACTIVE VOICE			
tense	person		
	I	*he, she, it*	*we, you (sing./pl.), they*
Present	walk	walks	walk
	go	goes	go
Present Progressive	am walking	is walking	are walking
	am going	is going	are going
Present Perfect	have walked	has walked	have walked
	have gone	has gone	have gone
Past	walked	walked	walked
	went	went	went
Past Progressive	was walking	was walking	were walking
	was going	was going	were going
Past Perfect	had walked	had walked	had walked
	had gone	had gone	had gone
Future	will (shall)* walk	will walk	will (shall) walk
	will (shall) go	will go	will (shall) go
Future Perfect	will (shall) have walked	will have walked	will (shall) have walked
	will (shall) have gone	will have gone	will (shall) have gone

*For the choice between *will* and *shall*, see page 427.

And here are the *passive* forms of a regular verb, *shock*, and an irregular verb, *take*, in the same eight tenses:

tense	PASSIVE VOICE		
	person		
	I	*he, she, it*	*we, you (sing./pl.), they*
Present	am shocked	is shocked	are shocked
	am taken	is taken	are taken
Present Progressive	am being shocked	is being shocked	are being shocked
	am being taken	is being taken	are being taken
Present Perfect	have been shocked	has been shocked	have been shocked
	have been taken	has been taken	have been taken
Past	was shocked	was shocked	were shocked
	was taken	was taken	were taken
Past Progressive	was being shocked	was being shocked	were being shocked
	was being taken	was being taken	were being taken
Past Perfect	had been shocked	had been shocked	had been shocked
	had been taken	had been taken	had been taken
Future	will (shall) be shocked	will be shocked	will (shall) be shocked
	will (shall) be taken	will be taken	will (shall) be taken
Future Perfect	will (shall) have been shocked	will have been shocked	will (shall) have been shocked
	will (shall) have been taken	will have been taken	will (shall) have been taken

Observe that the past participle is involved in all forms of the passive voice.

mood English verbs show certain other changes of form to indicate the *mood* or manner of a clause. If the clause is meant to be a statement or a question—by far the most common kinds of expression—its verb is in the *indicative* mood:

INDICATIVE:
• I *ate* a banana.
• *Did* you *eat* a banana?

The *imperative* mood is used for giving commands or directions, with or without the subject being named:

• You *eat* that banana!
• *Eat* that banana!

And for a variety of other, less common, uses, the *subjunctive* mood is called for:

SUBJUNCTIVE:
- If I *ate* the banana . . .
- If I *were* to eat the banana . . .

When should the subjunctive be used? Although at one time it was a flourishing part of daily usage, the subjunctive now survives only in limited kinds of statements:

1. Certain formulas such as:

as it were
be it known
be that as it may
come what may
God bless you
heaven forbid
long live the Queen
the devil take it
the taxpayers be damned

2. *That* clauses expressing requirements or recommendations:

- The IRS requires that everyone *submit* a return by April 15.

3. *Lest* clauses:

- Lest it *be thought* that I am neglectful of my duties . . .

4. Impossible or unlikely conditions:

- If I *were* on the moon now, I would tidy up the junk that has been strewn there.
- *Had he taken* that plane, he would be dead today.

Note that the writer of the first sentence isn't on the moon, and that the person mentioned in the second sentence didn't take that plane. The subjunctive constructions *If I were* and *Had he taken* show us these facts.

For uses 1–3, and for all verbs but *be*, the subjunctive forms are the same as the indicative ones, except that the third-person singular form loses its *-s* or *-es*. Thus:

	indicative	imperative	subjunctive
I	like		like
you	like	like	like
he, she, it	likes		**like**
we	like		like
you	like	like	like
they	like		like

Thus the one difference would show up in a sentence such as *I demand that he like me* — in contrast, say, to the indicative *I know that he likes me.*

For use 4, impossible or unlikely conditions, present and past verbs are made subjunctive as follows:

	indicative	subjunctive
present:	like	liked: If she liked me
past:	liked	had liked: If she had liked me; had she liked me

Be is made subjunctive as follows. For all *present* situations, use *were* or *be:*

If { I, you, he, she, it, we, you, they } *were* here   Lest { I, you, he, she, it, we, you, they } *be* here

For all *past* situations, use *had been:*

If { I, you, he, she, it, we, you, they } *had been* there

Analysis of verbs is further complicated by the existence of two special *kinds* of verbs, *auxiliaries* and *merged verbs.*

auxiliaries Certain words are called *auxiliaries* because they combine with, or "help," other verb forms. Unlike other verbs, the auxiliaries remain uninflected; but inserted before inflected verbs, they produce important changes in emphasis, obligation, and degree of likelihood. When used in that position, the following words are considered auxiliaries: *can, could, dare, do, may, might, must, need, ought, should,* and *would.* Note that a verb form immediately following an auxiliary is always a simple or base infinitive (lacking *to*): *could throw, must imagine.*

- He *could* throw harder.
- He *must* throw harder.
- He *should* throw harder.

merged verbs   A verb form combined with a preposition is sometimes called a *merged verb: check out, cave in,* etc. Note that merged verbs can easily be confused with verbs *followed by* a preposition. Compare:

- He *looked up* the number.
- He *looked up* the elevator shaft.

Or again:

- She *turned on* the switch.
- She *turned on* him in anger.

The first sentence in each pair contains a merged verb: *looked up, turned on.* In the other sentences, *up* and *on* are prepositions taking the objects *elevator shaft* and *him.* You can tell the difference either by observing the unity of meaning in a merged verb — in the first sentence *look* is incomplete without *up* — or by noting a difference in voice stress. In the merged verbs *look up* and *turn on,* the words *up* and *on* receive more stress than they do when used as prepositions.

Note too that in a merged verb the preposition can be moved without changing the sentence's meaning: *He looked up the number; he looked the number up. She turned on the switch; she turned the switch on.* Try this with the other sentences above and you'll see that they don't contain merged verbs.

Nouns

The traditional definition of a noun, while not completely adequate, provides a good start toward recognition of nouns in sentences: *a noun is the name of a person, place, or thing.* The "thing" can be an idea as well as a physical object. Thus *Harry, man, car, lemon, fraud,* and *Sing Sing* are all nouns.

A noun can occupy any sentence position where a "person, place, or thing" could be plausibly inserted. It can serve as:

a subject (pp. 264–265)
a direct object (p. 265)
a retained object (p. 265)
an indirect object (p. 265)
a subject complement (p. 265)
an objective complement (p. 265)
an appositive (p. 266)
an object of a preposition (p. 283)
a subject of an infinitive (pp. 288–289)
an object or complement of an infinitive (pp. 288–289)
an object of a participle (p. 291)
a subject of a gerund (pp. 291–292)
an object of a gerund (p. 291)
part of an absolute phrase (p. 293)
a possessive *(Harry's)*
a term in direct address (What do you plead, *Harry?*)
an adjectival or *attributive* noun (the *dictionary* meaning, a *Florida* sunset)

On the whole, the substance denoted by a noun is one that *acts or is acted on*, or one *about which* something is said.

Nouns are also identifiable by their inflections, or changes of form. With some exceptions, they can be made both *plural* and *possessive*. This distinguishes them from all other parts of speech except pronouns *(she, they)*; but while pronouns have a further inflection for *case (she, her; who, whom)*, nouns do not.

Nouns are usually made plural by the addition of *-s* or *-es*:

singular	plural
defect	two *defects*
shock absorber	three *shock absorbers*
toothless *clutch*	toothless *clutches*

But quite a few nouns, like *child (children)*, *thief (thieves)*, and *deer (deer)*, form irregular plurals; see pages 369–370 for details.

Nouns usually become possessive by the addition of *-'s*, but there are exceptions; see pages 366–369. Note that "possession" doesn't always mean ownership; the possessive form is also used for other relations, as in *a hard day's work, the country's beauty*. All possessives can be thought of as substitutes for an *of* construction: *the delights of the evening, the evening's delights*. But the process isn't always reversible: you wouldn't turn *the futility of it all* into *the all of it's futility*.

The most common error in writing nouns is the mixing up of plural and possessive forms. You must carefully observe the difference:

singular	plural	singular possessive	plural possessive
temple	temples	temple's	temples'
priest	priests	priest's	priests'
contribution	contributions	contribution's	contributions'

In the following passage, all nouns are marked by N:

N N N
Harry has an *answer* for everything. If a *customer* complains that his newly
 N N
purchased used *car* won't run, *Harry* says, "Think of what you're saving
 N N N N
on *gas*." If the *customer* says he has had to convert the *car* into a *garage*
 N N N N N
playhouse for his *children's recreation*, *Harry* replies, "*Convertibles* are hard
 N N
to find these *days*." And if the *customer* protests that he thought he was
 N N N
getting a *luxury model*, *Harry* tells him, "Your *dreamboat* just sits under the
 N N N N
house week after *week*. Now, that's what I call a *luxury*."

Note that *garage* in *garage playhouse* and *luxury* in *luxury model* are
attributive nouns—that is, nouns serving the function of adjectives.

Pronouns

Some, but not all, pronouns meet the old definition of a pronoun as *a word taking the place of a noun*. Pronouns serve so many functions, yet are so limited in number, that the best means of recognition is simply to memorize them. Even so, it is useful to know the *types* of pronouns and to understand their different grammatical features.

personal The *personal pronouns* stand for beings and objects. They consist of
pronouns all the *case forms* of *I, you, he, she, it, we,* and *they*—the words traditionally used in showing the tense forms of verbs (*I went, you went,* etc.). English has three *cases* to indicate different sentence functions: the *subjective* case (*I, we, they,* etc.), the *objective* case (*me, us, them,* etc.), and the *possessive* case (*my, mine; our, ours; their, theirs;* etc.). Among all words in the language, only personal pronouns and the relative pronoun *who* show inflection for *all three* cases. Nouns, you remember, don't change their form to show objective functions.

SUBJECTIVE:
• The *boy* went home.⎫
• *He* went home. ⎬ subject of verb

- He was the *boy.*⎫
- The boy was *he.*⎭ complement

OBJECTIVE:

- They punished the *boy.*⎫
- They punished *him.* ⎭ direct object of verb
- They taught the *boy* a lesson.⎫
- They taught *him* a lesson.   ⎭ indirect object of verb
- They taught it to the *boy.*⎫
- They taught it to *him.*   ⎭ object of preposition
- They wanted the *boy* to go.⎫
- They wanted *him* to go.   ⎭ subject of infinitive

POSSESSIVE:

- the *boy's* hat⎫
- *his* hat   ⎭ possession of noun
- the *boy's* departing⎫
- *his* departing   ⎭ subject of gerund

Here are all the personal pronouns aligned by person, case, and number:

SINGULAR			
	subjective	objective	possessive
First Person	I	me	my, mine
Second Person	you	you	your, yours
Third Person	he	him	his
	she	her	her, hers
	it	it	its
PLURAL			
First Person	we	us	our, ours
Second Person	you	you	your, yours
Third Person	they	them	their, theirs

Note especially the spelling of the "second possessive" forms: not *This kite is your's* but *This kite is yours;* not *The victory was their's* but *The victory was theirs.*

intensive These are *myself, yourself, himself, herself, itself, oneself, ourselves,*
and *yourselves, themselves* (never *theirself* or *theirselves*). These deriva-
reflexive tives of the personal pronouns are used either for emphasis (inten-
pronouns sive) or for indicating that the subject of a verb is also its object
(reflexive).

INTENSIVE:
- She *herself* will drive the truck.
- For *myself,* I want no part of it.

REFLEXIVE:
- He admires *himself* unreservedly.
- We have done *ourselves* very little good.

Note that an *intensive* pronoun is nothing more than an emphatic way of supplementing or replacing a personal pronoun. A *reflexive* pronoun, by contrast, *always serves as a direct or indirect object* (p. 265), and thus it can't be omitted or altered without completely changing the meaning of the sentence. In the reflexive examples above, *himself* and *ourselves* are essential parts of their sentences; you would never find intensive pronouns occupying those positions.

reciprocal These express mutual relation: *each other, each other's, one another,*
pronouns *one another's.* Although they always refer to at least two parties, they are always singular in form:

RIGHT:
- Wanda and Norbert compared *each other's* defects.

WRONG:
x Wanda and Norbert compared *each others'* defects.

indefinite Although some writers reserve *each other('s)* for two parties and *one*
pronouns *another('s)* for more than two parties, the terms are really interchangeable.

An *indefinite pronoun* leaves unspecified the person or thing it refers to. The indefinite pronouns are:

all	both	everything	nobody	several
another	each	few	none	some
any	each one	many	no one	somebody
anybody	either	most	nothing	someone
anyone	everybody	much	one	something
anything	everyone	neither	other	such

Some of the indefinite pronouns can become possessive, but none of them can be inflected in any other way. They are considered indefinite pronouns only when they are not used as modifiers. *Any* is an indefinite pronoun in *any of you,* but it is an adjective in *any coat.*

demon- *This, that, these,* and *those* are called *demonstratives* because they sin
strative gle out (or "demonstrate") what they refer to:
pronouns

- *These* are the good old days.
- I don't recognize *this* as your work.

Used adjectivally, these same words are called *demonstrative adjectives:*

- *These* days are the best we will ever see.
- *This* sculpture, consisting of a stack of soup cans on top of a motorcycle, is a powerful social statement.

relative The *relative pronouns* introduce *relative clauses* — that is, adjectival
pronouns subordinate clauses, *relating* the information they contain to an earlier sentence element, called an *antecedent:*

      ANT   REL PRO   REL CLAUSE
- *Tom, who is glad to have a working wife,* never misses an episode of "Search for Tomorrow."

Strictly speaking, a word in a sentence is a relative pronoun only if it meets three conditions. It must

a. introduce a subordinate clause (or follow a preposition that does so: *of whom you speak*),
b. serve a nounlike function, and
c. have an antecedent word or phrase in the same sentence.

Thus, in our example, *who* (a) introduces the subordinate clause *who is glad to have a working wife,* (b) serves a nounlike function as the subject of the verb *is,* and (c) has an antecedent, *Tom.* Some grammarians, however, also recognize an "indefinite relative pronoun" in sentences like these:

- He knows *who* he is.
- You are *what* you eat.

The relative pronouns include *who, whom, that,* and *which.* Since these same forms can serve other functions as well, you must apply the three-part test to see if they are relative pronouns in a given sentence. Note, incidentally, that some relative clauses are introduced by words other than pronouns:

- That was the time *when* he was needed.
- I know the woman *whose* dog is wearing the mink cape.

In these sentences *when* and *whose* would be called a *relative adverb* and a *relative adjective,* respectively. All adjectival clauses, by this reckoning, are relative clauses as well.

In restrictive (p. 294) clauses whose relative pronoun would serve as a direct object, that pronoun is often omitted:

- This modernistic Studebaker is the car [*that*] Bobo stole from Harry's lot.

interrogative pronouns *Who, whom, whose, which,* and *what,* when they introduce a question, are considered *interrogative* ("questioning") *pronouns:*

INT PRO
- *Who* could have predicted that Tom would put a set in every room?

Note that *whose, which,* and *what,* if followed by a noun, aren't pronouns but adjectives. Further, some interrogative forms, such as *why* and *when,* are considered either adverbs or conjunctions, but not pronouns, since they don't fill noun positions in their clauses. When *whose* introduces a question but is followed by a noun (*Whose idea was that?*), it's called an *interrogative adjective.*

Adjectives

Among the parts of speech, adjectives and adverbs are the chief *modifiers*—that is, words whose function is to limit or particularize the meanings of other words. Adjectives modify nouns, pronouns, and other nounlike elements:

    ADJ   N
- a *happy* viewer

    ADJ PRO
- *lucky* you!

        ADJ   GER (p. 291)
- his *outrageous* lying

Adjectives usually precede the words they modify, as in these examples, but a *predicate adjective* comes later: *The wind is strong.*

Most adjectives can be *compared,* or changed to show three *degrees* of coverage. The base form of an adjective is in the *positive degree: thin.* The *comparative degree* puts the modified word *beyond* one or more items: *thinner* (than she is; than everybody). And the *superlative degree* unmistakably puts the modified word beyond *all* rivals within its group: *thinnest* (of all).

The comparative and superlative degrees of adjectives are formed in several ways:

1. For one-syllable adjectives, add *-er* and *-est* to the root of the positive form: *wide, wider, widest.*
2. For one- or two-syllable adjectives ending in *-y,* change the *-y* to *-i* and add *-er* and *-est: dry, drier, driest; lazy, lazier, laziest.*

3. For all other adjectives of two or more syllables, put *more* and *most* or *less* and *least* before the positive form: *stupid, more stupid, most stupid; incredible, more incredible, most incredible.*
4. For certain "irregular" adjectives, supply the inflected forms shown in your dictionary. For example:

positive degree	comparative degree	superlative degree
bad	· worse	worst
good	better	best
far	farther, further	farthest, furthest
little	littler, less, lesser	littlest, least
many, some, much	more	most

Some words usually listed as adjectives can't be compared at all: adjectival *numbers* (*five* horses) and the pronounlike *demonstrative adjectives* (*those* horses). Nouns serving as adjectives (*horse* lovers) are called *attributive nouns.*

Adverbs

Adverbs are words that modify either verbs, adjectives, other adverbs, prepositions, infinitives, participles, phrases, clauses, or whole sentences. They typically express manner (*pleasantly*), degree (*very*), frequency (*seldom*), time (*now*), place (*there*), affirmation (*certainly*), negation (*not*), qualification (*however*), and logical relationship (*therefore*). While adjectives answer questions like *what kind* (*brown*) and *how many* (*few*), adverbs pose or answer questions like *how, when, where, why,* and *how often.*

Most single-word adverbs end in *-ly,* but some important ones do not:

> ahead
> down
> therefore
> well *(etc.)*

Some adverbs are identical in form to adjectives:

> better   late   much
> close   loud   slow
> fast   more   tight *(etc.)*

Thus you often have to distinguish an adverb from an adjective by its function alone. Remember: if a word that looks like an adverb isn't modifying a nounlike element, it *is* an adverb.

ADV
- He played *well.*

The adverb modifies the verb *played.*

ADV   ADJ
- He was a *much better* player than Ralph.

Here *better* modifies the noun *player,* and *much* modifies *better.*

ADV   ADV
- You are someone who buys *cheap* and sells *dear.*

The adverbs modify *buys* and *sells.*

ADV   ADJ
- He didn't want to go *slow* in that *slow* zone.

The first *slow* is an adverb modifying the infinitive *to go;* the second is an adjective modifying the noun *zone.*

Like adjectives, adverbs can be *compared: quickly, more quickly, most quickly.* Note that the *-ly* ending on most adverbs prevents them from being inflected when they are compared: not *sadlier* and *sadliest* but *more sadly* and *most sadly.* But some adverbs do have one-syllable forms *(hard, fast),* and they *are* inflected: He tried *harder;* She ran *fast-est* of all.

For the sentence positions an adverb can occupy, see pages 315–316.

Prepositions

Prepositions are rather shadowy words, hard to define but usually easy to recognize in a sentence. While they have no characteristic endings and no inflected forms, they always appear in the same kind of construction, a *prepositional phrase.* Though a prepositional phrase may contain various modifiers, its heart is a preposition and the *object* of that preposition:

PREP   OBJ PREP
- *without* much *fondness*

PREP   OBJ PREP
- *for* the finer *points*

PREP OBJ PREP
- *of grammar*

The most common objects of prepositions are nouns and pronouns, but other nounlike constructions can also serve:

PREP   OBJ PREP
- *about* the *deciding*

PREP OBJ PREP
- *of what people like*

In these last examples the two objects are a gerund (pp. 291–292), *deciding*, and a noun clause (pp. 293–294), *what people like*.

A word commonly recognized as a preposition (*by, for, of, onto, to, without,* etc.) isn't truly prepositional in a given sentence unless it has an object. Note how the presence or absence of an object affects the parts of speech marked in these examples:

PREP   OBJ PREP
- He looked *under* the *bridge.*

ADV
- He dived *under.*

PREP   OBJ PREP
- *Apart from* his *shyness,* nothing obstructed his career.

ADV
- He stood *apart.*

Some prepositions are *compound,* or composed of more than one word: *by means of, in front of, on account of, with respect to,* etc.

Conjunctions

Conjunctions are uninflected words that serve to connect other words, phrases, or clauses. Like prepositions, they express relationship; indeed, certain words — *after, before, but, for, than,* and *since* — can be either prepositions or conjunctions, depending on the words they join. Thus:

CONJ
- *Before* you leave, please give me your credit cards.

PREP OBJ PREP
- She will leave *before noon.*

CONJ
- She wanted to stay, *but* I said no.

PREP   OBJ PREP
- Everyone *but* her *lawyer* agreed with my decision.

In addition, various conjunctions share their form with adjectives, adverbs, and even pronouns:

PRO
- *That* is certain.

ADJ
- *That* idea is true.

CONJ
- I hope *that* she agrees.

Only in the last sentence is *that* a conjunction, joining two clauses.

Again:

ADJ
* *Either* alternative would be fine.

PRO
* Go ahead and choose *either.*

ADV
* I won't, *either.*

CONJ
* *Either* you go or I do.

The *either . . . or* formula joins two clauses, *you go* and *I do.*

The moral is that when you recognize a word as one that might be a conjunction, you can't be sure until you've made certain it has a connective function. The connected elements can be single words, phrases, clauses, or even whole sentences:

CONJ
* There may be difficulties ahead. *But* it is time to make a decision.

Since conjunctions are most likely to be confused with prepositions and adverbs, look to see if the word at issue *takes an object* or *modifies another word.* If it does either, it isn't a conjunction.

All conjunctions are either *coordinating, subordinating,* or *correlative:*

coordinating conjunctions			
and	or		
but	so		
for	yet		
nor			

subordinating conjunctions			
after	because	so (that)	when
although	before	than	whenever
as	how	that	where
as if	if	though	wherever
as long as	in order that	till	while *(etc.)*
as soon as	provided (that)	unless	
as though	since	until	

correlative conjunctions
both . . . and
either . . . or
neither . . . nor
not only . . . but also

The difference in function between coordinating and subordinating conjunctions is important to a writer aiming at precise statement (see pp. 131 – 141). Coordinating conjunctions are meant to join *grammatically like* elements, and they do so even-handedly, without turning one element into a modifier of the other:

- This is true, $\begin{Bmatrix} \text{and} \\ \text{but} \\ \text{or} \end{Bmatrix}$ you are crazy.

A subordinating conjunction, by contrast, joins *grammatically unlike* elements, turning one of them into a modifier and specifying its logical relation to the other:

$\left.\begin{matrix} \text{Although} \\ \text{Because} \\ \text{If} \\ \text{Provided} \\ \text{Since} \\ \text{Unless} \end{matrix}\right\}$ this is true, you are crazy.

Each of these subordinating conjunctions introduces a subordinate or dependent clause, modifying the main statement *you are crazy*. Note that the subordinate clause isn't necessarily less important in meaning than the independent one; but it is *grammatically* subordinate, in that it couldn't stand alone as a sentence.

Again, the difference in effect between coordinating and subordinating conjunctions can be illustrated by the versatile word *so* (which can also be an adverb, a pronoun, an interjection, and an adjective). As a coordinating conjunction, *so* conveys a rather half-hearted idea of cause and effect: *She is leaving, so I am staying.* Authorities dislike such uses of *so*, and you can see why; the construction *asserts* a dependence of one idea on the other (because she's leaving, I'm staying), but makes the two statements grammatically equivalent. As a subordinating conjunction — preferably followed by *that* — *so* has an entirely different meaning: *She is leaving so that I can stay.* Here the adverbial clause that tells why she is leaving modifies the verb *is leaving.*

Certain adverbs, when used to connect sentence elements, could also be regarded as conjunctions. The function of these *conjunctive adverbs* is intermediate between those of adverbs and conjunctions: they simultaneously modify a phrase or statement and indicate its logical relationship to a previous one.

conjunctive adverbs	
also	moreover
besides	nevertheless
consequently	nonetheless
furthermore	similarly
however	then
indeed	therefore
likewise	thus

Whether you call these words conjunctions or (as I would) adverbs is unimportant, but it's essential not to use them in place of *coordinating* conjunctions:

x She is leaving, however, I am staying.

Here a *comma splice* (p. 332) results from treating the conjunctive adverb *however* as if it were a word like *but* or *and*. (A semicolon instead of a comma after *leaving* would rescue the sentence.) Properly used, a conjunctive adverb keeps its intended function as a *modifier*:

          CONJ ADV
• It will be satisfying, *furthermore*, to throw all those cosmetics into the trash.

   CONJ ADV
• *Nonetheless*, I will miss her at breakfast time.

Note that these conjunctive adverbs, like many others, modify the whole preceding statement rather than anything in their own sentences.

Interjections

Interjections are certain familiar words that stand apart from other constructions in order to command attention or show strong feeling: *ah, damn, gosh, hurrah, O, oh, ouch, shh,* etc.

Note that an interjection is not the same thing as an *exclamation*. An exclamation is an outburst — an emphatic *statement,* not a part of speech. Though in fact an exclamation may consist of or contain an interjection, there's no necessary tie between the two. *O Henrietta Tittle, your hair is like peanut brittle* contains an interjection (the poetical *O*), but it isn't an exclamation; *Drop dead!* is an exclamation, but it contains only an imperative verb and an adjective.

Articles

The indicators (or "determiners") immediately preceding nouns, but showing none of the inflectional features of adjectives, are called *articles*. Articles are divided into *definite (the)* and *indefinite (a, an);* those three words compose the entire list. A definite article precedes the word for a specific item, whether singular or plural: *the report, the misstatements.* Sometimes a definite article precedes a modifier, as in *The bigger they are, the harder they fall.* An indefinite article precedes a general category, always singular, or a singular item not previously identified: *a report is due, an hour has passed, an idea of mine.*

A is used before consonant sounds, *an* before vowel sounds. When an initial *h* sound is distinctly pronounced, as in *historical,* most writers prefer to introduce it with *a: a historical inquiry,* not *an historical inquiry.*

VERBALS

Several forms derived from verbs are commonly grouped as *verbals,* but don't let the name mislead you. The three types of verbals — *infinitives, participles,* and *gerunds* — serve various functions, none of which is especially "verblike." Think of the three types separately as distinct parts of speech, each with its own typical function and sentence positions.

Infinitives

The base forms of verbs, customarily preceded by *to,* are called *infinitives: to love, to reconsider.* Within sentences, infinitives resemble verbs in that they can have *subjects, objects,* and *complements:*

SUBJECT:

             S INF INF
* Norbert asked *her to concentrate* on the One.

OBJECT:

                              INF   OBJ INF
* He was no longer concerned *to gratify her.*

COMPLEMENT:

             S INF   INF   COMPL INF
* He wanted *her to become enlightened.*

<pre>   INF   COMPL INF</pre>
* He wanted *to be* her *instructor.*

Note that both subjects and objects of infinitives, when they are pronouns, take the objective case form. You may wonder why this one kind of "subject" is always objective in case. The answer is that every subject of an infinitive is also an object (direct or indirect) of a preceding verb: *asked her to concentrate.* In the rare instance when the complement of an infinitive is a pronoun, it belongs in the objective case:

<pre>   COMPL INF</pre>
* She was glad not to be *him.*

Infinitives can correspond to several tenses and appear in either the active or the passive voice:

active voice	passive voice
to reconsider	to be reconsidered
to be reconsidering	
to have reconsidered	to have been reconsidered
to have been reconsidering	

Yet despite their similarities to verbs, infinitives never serve verb functions. Instead, by themselves or in strings of words called *infinitive phrases*, they do the work of *nouns, adjectives,* or *adverbs:*

NOUN FUNCTION:
<pre>   INF</pre>
* *To err* is human.

The infinitive is the subject of the verb *is.*

<pre>   INF</pre>
* Forgetting *to pay* taxes on time can be costly.

The infinitive phrase *to pay taxes on time* is the object of a gerund, *Forgetting.* (The complete subject of the sentence is *Forgetting to pay taxes on time.*)

ADJECTIVE FUNCTION:
<pre>   INF</pre>
* That was a meal *to remember.*

The infinitive modifies a noun, *meal.*

INF
- The hour *to gorge* themselves had arrived for Max and Bessie.

  The infinitive phrase *to gorge themselves* modifies the noun *hour*.

ADVERB FUNCTION:

INF
- They were eager *to start*.

  The infinitive modifies a predicate adjective, *eager*.

INF
- They chewed the celery too noisily *to hear* the waiter's questions.

  The infinitive phrase *to hear the waiter's questions* modifies an adverb, *noisily*.

Infinitives become harder to spot when the telltale *to* is omitted:

INF
- Everyone heard Max *tell* the waiter that "some jerk must have dropped an old piece of bread in this onion soup."

  Only the base-verb form of *tell* and its typical infinitive position reveal that it's an infinitive here.

Such *simple* or *base* infinitives are most usually found after auxiliaries: *should go, dare suggest, do know,* etc.

Participles

Participles are verbal forms used in the formation of certain tenses (pp. 269–271). They are true verbals, however, only when used as adjectives. In that capacity they can appear singly *(disrobing)* or in phrases *(savagely disrobing the lamb chops)*. They show several forms indicating tense and voice:

active voice	passive voice
shooting	being shot
shot	
having shot	having been shot

Since participles resemble gerunds, certain tense forms of verbs, and even an occasional noun, they must be recognized by their adjectival function:

> PART   GER
> • A person *owning* no property won't have much luck in *getting* the credit
>
>   N   PART   GER
> *rating needed* for *borrowing* money.

Here *owning, getting, rating, needed,* and *borrowing* all look like participles, but only *owning* and *needed* serve the necessary adjectival function. The participial phrase *owning no property* modifies the noun *person,* and the past participle *needed* modifies the compound noun *credit rating.*

Participles normally appear immediately before or after the words they modify: *the needed credit rating; the credit rating needed.* The same is true of participial phrases: *owning no property, a person . . . ; a person owning no property.* When a participle or participial phrase doesn't clearly modify a nearby nounlike element, it usually becomes subject to criticism as a *misrelated* or a *dangling modifier* (see pp. 315–317). An exception is made for *absolute* constructions (p. 293).

Gerunds

Gerunds look just like participles, but they or their gerund phrases are used only as nouns:

>   GER
> • *Meditating* is Norbert's favorite activity.

The gerund serves as the subject of the verb *is.*

>   GER
> • He loves *contemplating* the fact that all of nature worships him.

The gerund begins a *gerund phrase* containing an *object of the gerund (fact)* and a relative clause having that object as its antecedent. The entire gerund phrase is the direct object of the verb *loves.* (He loves what? *Contemplating the fact that* etc.)

>   GER
> • Norbert is weary of *having striven.*

The gerund is the object of the preposition *of.*

Gerunds and participles alike can take objects. Thus, if you see a phrase like *achieving perfection,* you can be sure that the *-ing* word is either a participle or a gerund; only its function in the sentence will tell you which it is. But the nounlike character of gerunds does give them some identifying features. Like nouns, they can be preceded by articles: *an achieving, the achieving.* If an *-ing* word *is* or *can be* preceded by an article, it isn't a participle. And like nouns, gerunds can be preceded by possessive forms, called the *subject of the gerund: Nor-*

bert's achieving perfection; his losing selfhood. When you have trouble deciding whether a certain word is a participle or a gerund, try inserting a possessive form before it. If the sentence still makes any grammatical sense at all, the word is a gerund:

GER
- [her] *Debating* with Norbert is futile.

PART
- [her] *Debating* with Norbert, Wanda drowned out his chants.

PHRASES AND CLAUSES

Familiarity with the parts of speech can help you to see which words in a sentence are its sentence elements, or main functioning parts. But sentence elements can also be formed by larger groupings of words, namely *phrases* and *clauses.* You can best understand the function of phrases and clauses if you think of them as usually standing in the place of single-word *subjects, objects, complements, modifiers,* and *appositives.*

A phrase, you recall, is a cluster of words, not containing a subject-predicate transaction, that functions as a single part of speech. If phrases act as parts of speech, and parts of speech can be sentence elements, then phrases too can be sentence elements. This is obvious if we think of simple *noun phrases* like *the ball,* in sentences like *Biff drops the ball;* the complete direct object isn't the single word *ball* but the phrase *the ball.* The same phrase-word equivalence holds for more complicated structures, namely *prepositional phrases, infinitive phrases, gerund phrases, participial phrases,* and *absolute phrases:*

- She worked
  - M *slowly.*
  - M *at a leisurely pace.*

A *prepositional phrase* is functioning as a *modifier* here—an alternative to an adverb, *slowly.*

- She disliked
  - D OBJ *haste.*
  - D OBJ *hurrying here and there.*

A *gerund phrase* becomes a *direct object.*

- M Toothless people
  M People *lacking teeth* smile less than others.

A *participial phrase* does the work of a *modifier* (an adjective) in this case.

$$
\text{• He rose from the negotiating table}
\begin{cases}
\overset{\text{M}}{\text{wearily.}} \\[1em]
\overset{\text{M}}{,\ \textit{his weary look a}} \\
\textit{sign of discouragement.}
\end{cases}
$$

An *absolute phrase* — one modifying nothing in particular — acts like an adverb, *wearily.*

As for clauses — clusters of words containing a subject and a predicate — they can serve as sentence elements only if they are *subordinate* or *dependent:*

SUB CLAUSE AS S
• *What you tell the committee* will be leaked to the press.

What you tell the committee is clearly a subordinate clause, since it contains a subject *(you)* and a predicate *(tell the committee what)* but makes no sense by itself. The whole clause serves as the subject of the verb *will be leaked.* A *noun clause,* it functions like a single-word subject such as *Testimony.*

SUB CLAUSE AS D OBJ
• The press always discovers *what you tell the committee.*

Our same noun clause is now the direct object of the verb *discovers.*

SUB CLAUSE AS IND OBJ
• The staff gives *what you tell the committee* a very critical reading.

The familiar noun clause is now performing the work of an indirect object. The staff gives a very critical reading *to* something, namely *what you tell the committee.*

SUB CLAUSE AS RET OBJ
• The staff is given *what you tell the committee.*

The same clause, occupying the direct-object position after a verb in the passive voice, is now a retained object.

SUB CLAUSE AS OBJ PREP
• Could you give us a general idea of *what you tell the committee* each day?

This time the whole noun clause serves as the object of the preposition *of.*

SUB CLAUSE AS COMPL

• The crucial thing is not what you actually did, but *what you tell the committee*.

Now the clause has become the complement of the subject *thing: The thing is x.*

SUB CLAUSE AS APP

• Your testimony, *what you tell the committee*, could get us all in trouble.

Finally, the same clause stands in apposition to a noun subject, *testimony*.

Just as a *noun clause* can act as any sentence element normally filled by a noun, so *adjectival* and *adverbial* clauses can act as *modifiers*. An adjectival clause does what an adjective would do; it modifies a noun, pronoun, or other nounlike element. And an adverbial clause acts like a single adverb, modifying a verb, an adjective, an adverb, a preposition, an infinitive, a participle, a phrase, another clause, or the rest of the sentence.

Here are some representative *adjectival* (or *relative*) clauses:

SUB CLAUSE AS ADJ

• Wratto, *who can make an entire poem out of zip codes*, deserves to be taken seriously by the critics.

The adjectival clause modifies the subject *Wratto*, just as *Clever* would in the sentence *Clever Wratto deserves to be taken seriously*. Note that adjectival clauses characteristically *follow* the words they modify.

SUB CLAUSE AS ADJ

• He is the bard *that America has been seeking*.

The whole clause modifies *bard*, a predicate noun.

One distinction among adjectival clauses is vital for a writer to grasp: the difference between *restrictive* and *nonrestrictive* clauses. A *restrictive* clause, as the name implies, serves to *restrict*—that is, to *establish the identity of*—its antecedent:

RESTR CLAUSE

• People *who can't climb as well as monkeys* should stay out of trees.

The restrictive clause *identifies* its antecedent, showing us that only certain people are meant.

A *nonrestrictive* clause, which should always be set off by commas, provides *information about* its antecedent, but doesn't *identify* it:

NONRESTR CLAUSE
- People, *who can't climb as well as monkeys,* should stay out of trees.

The commas show that all people are meant.

(See pages 336–337 for further discussion of nonrestrictive elements in general.)

Adverbial clauses are recognizable by the fact that they lack noun-like antecedents, or indeed any antecedents at all. They simply *modify* other parts of their sentences, or the entire rest of the sentence:

SUB CLAUSE AS ADV
- *Because you have never answered my letters,* Fannie Farmer, I am now corresponding with Betty Crocker.

The adverbial clause tells *why* something has happened; it modifies the verb *am corresponding.*

SUB CLAUSE AS ADV
- *However famous you may be as a sculptor,* that is an abominable snowman.

The adverbial clause is equivalent to a conjunctive adverb (p. 287) such as *nevertheless.*

SUB CLAUSE AS ADV
- I want it to melt *as soon as it can.*

This adverbial clause modifies an infinitive, *to melt.* Note that both clauses and phrases can be imbedded within larger structures that function as sentence elements.

All subordinate clauses, in fact, can be analyzed on two levels, for their *internal structure* and their *function in the whole sentence.* Recognizing this distinction, and knowing that *internal structure takes priority* in determining case forms, you can see why *whoever* was the right pronoun in our test sentence *He will read his poems to whoever will listen.* The *whole* subordinate clause *whoever will listen* is the object of the preposition *to;* within that clause, the verb *will listen* must have a subject in the subjective case.

Correct grammatical analysis, then, leads to "grammatical" sentence construction as well. And when you're confident about grammar, you have a sound basis for dealing with questions of *usage* — the subject of the following chapter.

EXERCISES

I. The italicized words in the following passage cannot be found in any dictionary. Nevertheless, each of them functions here as a *sentence element*—a subject, verb, direct object, retained object, indirect object, complement, modifier,
appositive, or connective (pp. 264–266). List the sentence element of each numbered word:

> Much needless *fragdoodle* [1] is written on the subject of threnkies. Are
> not *threnkies* [2] shy and harmless *fridclumpers* [3]? Unlike the fruit fly, a
> much less restrained *aerotomane* [4], the threnky *unsnops* [5] his or her
> *yumyodels* [6] quite *rendly* [7]. In this manner the whole *cosmonopoly* [8] is
> afforded a good *unctuation* [9]. Why, then, do some people call threnkies
> repulsive *ickles* [10]? Perhaps the nimble and *ambitendile* [11] threnky gives
> certain insecure *corsetchokers* [12] an acute *neuromaly* [13]. By criticizing
> threnkies, they merely *splot* [14] their own *parsonecherous* [15] *phlegmotility* [16].
> The threnky, a simple and innocent *thumpzinger* [17] *pok* [18] there ever was
> one, has outlasted many *crunchuglies* [19] in its million-year history, and
> will *mence* [20] be here when its human detractors are extinct.

II. List the *parts of speech* (pp. 266–288) of the twenty numbered words in
Exercise I.

III. Name the parts of speech of all the words in this sentence:

> "Hey, [1] Bessie," [2] shouted [3] Max [4] disbelievingly [5] as [6] he [7] stared [8] at [9] the [10] modern [11]
> painting, [12] "tell [13] me [14] what [15] squashed [16] that [17] poor [18] guy's [19] face." [20]

IV. Consider the following one-word sentence: *Choose!*

1. Do you regard *Choose!* as a complete sentence? Why, or why not? (See pp.
   263–264.)
2. Name the *person, tense, voice,* and *mood* of that verb (pp. 269–274).
3. Write a brief sentence using the same verb in a *different* person, tense,
   voice, and mood.
4. Identify the person, tense, voice, and mood of the verb in your sentence.
5. What part of speech is each word in your sentence?

V. Briefly discuss the grammatical differences between the italicized words in the following pairs of sentences:

    1. a. He charged *up* the field.
       b. He charged *up* the battery.
    2. a. She wants *alimony*.
       b. She wants *alimony* to be her largest source of income.
    3. a. They tried *harder*.
       b. It was *harder* than they expected.
    4. a. *Standing in the middle of the road*, Fido blocked traffic for hours.
       b. *Standing in the middle of the road* was Fido's idea of exercise.
    5. a. Norbert *himself* believes in immortality.
       b. Norbert believes *himself* to be immortal.

VI. List all the *verbals* (pp. 288–292) you find in the following sentences, and identify each one as either an *infinitive*, a *participle*, or a *gerund*:

    1. Having nothing better to do, Biff began choking his tackling dummy.
    2. He really wanted to take a nap on the Astroturf.
    3. Having won the big game while he was wearing his lucky socks, he decided never to put them in the laundry again.
    4. Roaring crowds made the only kind of music Biff liked to hear.
    5. Biff's teammates soon learned to refrain from borrowing his socks.

VII. Ten *phrases and clauses* (pp. 292–295) are italicized in the following passage. Name the *kind* of phrase or clause in each instance. Phrases will be either *prepositional, infinitive, participial,* or *gerund;* clauses will be either *independent* or *subordinate,* and, if subordinate, either *nounlike (nominal), adjectival,* or *adverbial.*

       Interviewed after practice,[1] Biff offered his opinion that *on any given*[2] *Saturday* one team would usually beat another. "Of course," he added, "they do have *to be playing each other*[3] on that day. Am *I right?*[4]" (Although *Biff is all business on the field*,[5] he has a great sense of humor.) *What he meant*[6] was that the better team is the one *that puts the most*[7] *points up there on the old scoreboard.* "I just think that *getting into the*[8] *end zone* is really an important part of the game," Biff said. "You can talk all you want about blocking, blitzing, and praying, but heck, I think the team *with the biggest score*[9] at the end is the one *you should*[10] *bet on.*"

VIII. Write five sentences, each containing one subordinate clause. Try to make the five subordinate clauses as similar as possible in content, repeating the same words wherever you can. But give those clauses five different functions:

1. a noun clause used as a subject;
2. a noun clause used as a direct object;
3. an adjectival clause modifying a direct object;
4. an adjectival clause beginning with an adverb;
5. an adverbial clause modifying the main verb of the sentence.

IX. Write three pairs of sentences in which the same words form a *restrictive* clause in the first sentence and a *nonrestrictive* clause in the second (pp. 294–295). Briefly indicate the difference of meaning in each case.

PROBLEMS OF
11 USAGE

To pass from grammar to usage is so short a step that many people wouldn't regard it as a change at all. They recognize no distinction between the *grammar,* or *formal features,* of English and its correct standard *usage* — that is, the *typical accepted practices* of speakers and writers. For them there is only "good grammar" and "bad grammar," as if all problems of usage could be referred to some binding code.

Writing would be a far less anxious business if this were so. In fact, however, the rules of grammar only begin to cover the tricky and ever-shifting area of correct standard usage. For usage often involves a choice between two forms that are equally "grammatical," such as *He saw that picture of Priscilla* and *He saw that picture of Priscilla's.* Both are proper English sentences, but only one would successfully convey your meaning in a given instance. What is acceptable in speech, furthermore, might provoke objections when written down. No grammatical rule can remove all doubt from the choice between writing *I know whom you mean* and *I know who you mean.* The first sentence might sound too stuffy in speech; the second, too informal for an essay. Questions of usage shade into questions of the *tone* and *level* (pp. 105–106, 146–148) you want to strike for a given audience and type of essay.

Nonetheless, certain broad principles of usage cover most of the problems you're likely to encounter:

1. Write complete sentences (below).
2. Match your subjects and predicates (p. 302).
3. Make your subjects and verbs agree in number (p. 304).
4. Place your verbs and verbals in consistent sequences (p. 307).
5. Match pronouns with their antecedents (p. 313).
6. Watch for misrelated and dangling modifiers (p. 315).
7. Use possessives where needed to show the performer of an action (p. 317).
8. Give parallel structure to elements that are parallel in meaning (p. 319).
9. Use comparative terms only where they are appropriate (p. 321).

COMPLETE SENTENCES

A sentence is a group of words that can stand alone because it is understood to constitute a complete thought. This normally requires a *subject* and a *verb* in at least one *independent clause:*

> s v
> She goes.
> IND CLAUSE

In the context of a preceding or following sentence, an *independent sentence fragment* is allowable:

> IND FRAG
> Whose stereo will be thrown overboard? *Certainly not mine!*

> IND FRAG
> And now for a closer look at the small intestine.

Such constructions are spared from sounding ungrammatical by the fact that they *function* as complete sentences. That is, readers perceive them as independent units, *stating something,* even though some of the ordinary makings of a statement aren't there. The lack of a subject and verb makes for a calculated informality or an effect of transition from one point to the next.

In many cases, however, sentence fragments are created by mistake. This is most clearly apparent when the fragment reads like a *continuation* of the sentence before it:

x He found himself unable to proceed to Vancouver. *Having forgotten his raincoat.*

The fragment is a participial phrase modifying *He* in the sentence before. The best correction would be to put it before the modified word: *Having forgotten his raincoat, he found himself unable to proceed to Vancouver.*

x In Clifford's best seller the talking sparrows decide to fly to the very top of
the sky. *Because they understand that every sparrow must strive to realize his or her most soaring dreams.*

The second "sentence" contains two sets of subjects and verbs, but the subordinating conjunction *Because* reveals that the whole construction is a subordinate or dependent clause. The fragment would be acceptable if the preceding sentence were a question such as *Why?* As it stands, however, it looks like a broken-off piece of one larger sentence. Try *In Clifford's best seller the talking sparrows, understanding that . . . dreams, decide . . . sky.*

Some writers try to justify haphazard sentence fragments by arguing that their meaning is easy to decipher. But this misses the point. Readers can't simultaneously piece together an intended statement and be swayed by its aptness. By making sure that each of your sentences contains an independent idea, you work *with* your reader's expectations instead of awkwardly pushing against them.

For the related problem of *run-on* sentences, see page 332.

PREDICATION

Predication—saying something about something—is the essence of all statement. Every complete sentence hinges on one of the three fundamental predicates: an intransitive verb *(turned)*, a transitive verb and its direct object *(turned the knob),* or a linking verb and its complement *(turned traitor, turned blue).* To work properly, of course, a hinge must be securely attached at both sides. If a subject and predicate are incompatible in meaning or structure, the sentence, instead of moving freely like a well-hinged door, becomes annoyingly jammed in its frame.

Take a simple example: *The meaning of the book deals with happiness.* The idea in this sentence is easy enough to grasp, but something's amiss with the predication. A *meaning* is said to *deal with* something. To do that, a meaning would have to be an *agent*, someone or something capable of action. In this case the agent could be the author or even the book itself, conceived as an extension of the author's intent:

- Clifford deals with happiness.
- The book deals with happiness.

But *meaning* isn't a subject of the same sort as *Clifford* or *book*. It's an *abstraction* — a concept, not an agent. If you wanted to keep *meaning* as the subject, you'd have to couple it with a linking verb and a complement:

                   S   LV   NOUN CLAUSE AS COMPL
- The *meaning* of the book *is that happiness lies within the reach of every courageous sparrow.*

                   S   LV ADJECTIVAL PHRASE AS COMPL
- The *meaning* of the book *is easy to determine.*

                   S   LV   PRED ADJ
- The *meaning* of the book *becomes* more *obvious* with each rereading.

In each of these examples the subject isn't represented as *doing* anything. Rather, it's being described or *characterized*. Every time you write a clause, whether you're consciously aware of the fact or not, you're choosing to treat the subject either as a performer of action or as something to be characterized. Where the subject can't plausibly fill its assigned role, as in *The meaning deals with* . . . , a fuzzy and unsatisfying effect results.

When authorities on usage complain about *The reason is because* . . . , they are objecting to faulty predication as well as redundancy. *Because* customarily introduces an *adverbial* clause, answering the adverbial question *Why?* Why did he write it? *He wrote it because he was hungry.* But in *The reason is because* . . . , the adverbial clause is awkwardly squeezed into a *nounlike* function:

            S   LV NOUN CLAUSE AS COMPL
x The *reason is because he was hungry.*

Once again the meaning is clear but the structure faulty. *Because* is for actions, but a *reason*, being an abstraction and not an agent, can't perform any action. As in all instances of faulty predication, two kinds of revision are available. You can either make the clause consistently "active" (*He wrote it because he was hungry*) or consistently "abstract" (*The reason is that he was hungry*).

Sometimes a mismatch of equated terms occurs entirely *within* the predicate of a sentence:

x Those sadistic dog trainers have changed the qualities that made the dog "man's best friend" into a demon.

> Here the subject *(dog trainers)*, transitive verb *(have changed)*, and direct object *(qualities)* are compatible, but the rest of the predicate falls apart. How can abstract *qualities* be changed into *a demon?* Try *Those sadistic dog trainers have changed man's best friend into a demon.*

Faulty predication is likely to result when a writer hurries past the actual words in a sentence, believing that the idea behind them is clear. Often it is. But readers must take in sentences before they can digest ideas, and a sentence whose parts aren't smoothly matched may be rejected before its content has been understood at all.

AGREEMENT OF SUBJECT AND VERB

In standard English, verbs are supposed to agree in number with their subjects: singular subject, singular verb; plural subject, plural verb. The rule is clear, but applying it can sometimes be tricky. Here are the main sources of doubt.

Collective Nouns

A collective noun is singular in form but possibly plural in meaning, since it refers to a *collection* of members: *administration, army, audience, band, class, committee, crowd, faculty, family, fleet, government, public, team,* etc. Because such words are technically singular, most choices should be settled in favor of a singular verb:

- The orchestra *is playing* better now that the conductor is sober.
- A strong, united faculty *is needed* to stand firm against the erosion of parking privileges.
- In Priscilla's opinion the middle class *is* altogether too middle-class.

But certain "numerical" words, such as *majority, minority, plurality, mass,* and *number,* take either a singular or a plural verb according to what's being discussed, the *totality* (singular) or the *items* (plural) that make it up. Thus:

TOTALITY (singular):
- The Democratic majority *is composed* of workers and shirkers.
- The mass of the two particles *was* difficult to measure.

SEPARATE ITEMS (plural):
- The majority of Democrats *are* staunchly *opposed* to local blackouts of the Game of the Week.
- The mass of men *lead* lives of quiet desperation.

Quantities

When the subject of a verb is a plural quantity such as *twenty-six miles,* ask yourself whether it's meant as a unit (singular) or as a number of items (plural):

AS A UNIT (singular):
- Twenty-six miles *is* the length of the race.

AS A NUMBER OF ITEMS (plural):
- Twenty-six difficult miles *lie* ahead of her.

When adding or multiplying, you can use either a singular or a plural verb:

- One and one *is (are)* two.
- Eleven times three *is (are)* thirty-three.

In multiplication, the singular is more common. But the plural is required when a multiplication is expressed without *times:*

- Eleven threes *are* thirty-three.

Use the singular for all subtraction and division:

- Sixty minus forty *is (leaves)* twenty.
- Six divided by three *is* two.

Troublesome Terms

<u>each</u>; <u>either</u>; <u>neither</u>   As pronoun subjects, these words are always singular, even when followed by a plural construction such as *of them:*

      S   V
- *Each* of them *has* her own way of doing things.

      S   V
- *Either* of those purple skateboards *is* good enough for me.

    S   V
- *Neither* of Clifford's novels *has been reviewed* in the zoology journals.

In the three sentences, *them, skateboards,* and *novels* are objects of prepositions, not true plural subjects.

Note that *each* sometimes appears in *apposition to* a plural subject. In this role it means *apiece* and doesn't affect the number of the verb:

```
      S   APP   V
```
- *They each have* their own favorite chapters to cry over.

here is (are); there is (are) These can't be regarded as subject-verb pairs. Rather, they are *anticipatory constructions,* signaling that the real subject will follow. The number of the verb *(is* versus *are,* or *was* versus *were)* is determined by the number of the delayed subject:

```
       V      S
```
- Here *is* his *agent.*
```
       V      S
```
- Here *are* his *contracts.*
```
       V           S
```
- There *were* many *celebrities* at the party honoring Clifford's book.
```
       V           S
```
- There *was* enough stuffed *pheasant* for all the guests.

none The number of *none* should be determined by its meaning within a given sentence. If you mean *none* in the sense of *not a single one,* make the verb singular:

```
    S           V
```
- *None* among us *is* likely to agree with Stanley's proposal to smash racism by blowing up Kentucky Fried Chicken.

But if you mean *all are not,* you can use a plural verb:

```
    S        V
```
- *None* of us *are* enthusiastic about Operation Fingerlicker.

In doubtful cases you would do well to stick to the singular verb, preferred by purists.

or; either . . . or; neither . . . nor When these conjunctions link the parts of a compound subject, the verb should be governed, not by the sum of the parts, but only by the *nearest* (the last) item in that subject. Thus, if the last item is singular, the verb too should be singular:

```
                                 LAST ITEM IN S    V
```
- Neither apple pie nor roller skating nor her neglected *guppy collection holds* the slightest interest for Priscilla any more.

But don't strain this rule by putting a singular item after a plural one:

x Neither Priscilla's old high-school *teachers* nor her *mother understands* a word she says on her vacations from college.

It would be better to take a few extra words and say *Priscilla's old high-school teachers don't understand . . . , and neither does her mother.*

along with; as well as; in addition to; together with These and other *compound prepositions* (p. 284) shouldn't be mistaken for *conjunctions*. In other words, they don't make a singular subject plural:

> Stanley's *mimeograph machine*, along with his bullhorn and spray paint, gives him a sense of comradeship with working people everywhere.

The prepositional phrase *along with his bullhorn and spray paint* doesn't affect the number of the verb.

Inverted Syntax

When a subject comes after its verb, make sure you don't allow an earlier noun to control the number of the verb. That error occurs here:

> x Immediately after the light rains of early November have dampened the woods *come* the *time* when Melody can be found gathering certain prized mushrooms.

The writer has mistaken *woods*, the direct object of *have dampened*, for the subject of *come*. The verb must be *comes*, in agreement with the singular subject *time*.

Subjects Consisting of Phrases or Clauses

A phrase or clause acting as a subject takes a singular verb, even if it contains plural items:

> PHRASE AS S
> *Having the numbers of several bail bondsmen is* useful in an emergency.
> NOUN CLAUSE AS S
> *That none of his customers wanted to buy a matching fleet of De Sotos was* a disagreeable surprise for Harry.

SEQUENCE OF TENSES

The first verb in a sentence establishes a time frame for the rest of that sentence, affecting the tense of any later verb, infinitive, participle, or gerund. A reader will be jarred if one of those later forms unexpectedly drops out of the frame:

PAST   PRESENT
ˣ When he *phoned* her, she *tells* him to leave her alone.

The second verb must be *told*, to conform with the past frame established by *phoned*.

Although this principle looks clear enough, applying it consistently can become difficult in certain cases:

Verbs

past perspective on a prior time   If your main verb is in the past tense and you want to relate it to *a still earlier time,* the verb expressing that earlier time should be in the *past perfect* tense:

PAST   PAST PERFECT
• Philo *discovered* that he *had made* a mistake in giving Priscilla a pink teddy bear.

past perspective on a later time   If your main verb is in the past tense and you want to look forward from that time to a later one, use the auxiliary *would* plus the base (infinitive) form of the verb:

PAST   AUX BASE V
• He *knew* that he *would have* some explaining to do.

action to be completed before a future time   If your sentence looks forward to a time when a certain action *will have been completed*, combine the present and future perfect tenses:

PRESENT   FUTURE PERFECT
• When Philo *sees* her next week, she *will have exchanged* the teddy bear for tickets to the harpsichord recital.

hypothetical conditions   Some sentences describe what *would* be true, or *would have been* true, in certain imagined circumstances. For circumstances imagined as *present*, use the present subjunctive (p. 274) in the "condition" clause and *would* plus a base verb form in the "consequence" clause:

PRES SUBJV   AUX BASE V
• If Philo *phoned* Priscilla now, he *would get* an icy reception.
    CONDITION CLAUSE   CONSEQUENCE CLAUSE

For circumstances imagined as *past*, use the past subjunctive (p. 274) in the "condition" clause and *would have* plus a past participle in the "consequence" clause:

> PAST SUBJV   AUX   PAST PART
> * If he *had phoned* her then, he *would have gotten* an icy reception.
>   CONDITION CLAUSE   CONSEQUENCE CLAUSE

Note that you can use an alternative subjunctive form for *present* hypothetical conditions: *If he were to phone* etc. But for past hypothetical conditions, stay with the subjunctive form that's identical to the past perfect:

> PAST SUBJV   AUX   PAST PART
> * If he *had called,* she *would* have *said,* "Priscilla is not at home. This is her teddy bear speaking. Leave your message at the sound of the tone."

A common mistake is to allow *would* to enter both clauses: *If he would have called, she would have said* etc. Remember that *would* always belongs with the consequence, not the condition.

indirect discourse   Reporting what was said, instead of directly quoting it, is known as *indirect discourse.* Observe what happens to tenses in shifting from quotation to indirect discourse:

		quotation	indirect discourse
present verb in quotation		"I find it difficult to remember your name," she said.	She said that she *found* it difficult to remember his name.
past verb in quotation		"Your interest in bowling gave cause for alarm," she revealed.	She revealed that his interest in bowling *had given* cause for alarm.
present perfect verb in quotation		She protested, "I have never encouraged your crude advances."	She protested that she *had* never *encouraged* his crude advances.
past perfect verb in quotation		"Until then," she reflected, "I had never known how barbarous a male could be."	She reflected that until then she *had* never *known* how barbarous a male could be.
future verb in quotation		She added, "You will do better to bestow your 'date,' as you choose to call it, for the 'demolition derby' on some companion more keenly appreciative of such cultural gatherings than myself."	She added that he *would do* better to bestow his so-called "date" etc.

In short, indirect discourse

makes a *present* verb *past;*
makes a *past* or *present perfect* verb *past perfect;*
leaves a *past perfect* verb *past perfect;* and
turns a *future* verb into *would* plus a base (infinitive) form.

You can deduce other tense changes in indirect discourse from these basic ones; *will have refused* becomes *would have refused, has been refusing* becomes *had been refusing,* etc.

discussion of literature — Although most literary works are narrated in the past tense (*Mike poured Brett a triple martini*), you should shift the action to the present tense when you write about it: not *poured* but *pours.* In other words, treat the action of the story, novel, poem, or play as if it were unfolding in a continuous present time.

You may be tempted to break this rule when you're quoting as well as summarizing the literary work, for the quotations are likely to contain verbs in the past tense. Don't allow such past forms to influence your own verbs, as this writer does:

> PRESENT
> x Lawrence *describes* Cecilia as "a big dark-complexioned, pug-faced young
>   PAST   PAST
> woman who very rarely *spoke* . . ." When she *did* speak, however, her
> PAST
> words *were* sharp enough to kill her aunt Pauline.

> Everything is fine here until the second sentence, where the writer, confused by the past *spoke* in his quotation from Lawrence, shifts his own verbs to the past tense. Correct: *When she does speak, however, her words are sharp enough. . . .*

Matters are complicated even further by the fact that there can be tense sequences within the reporting of the action. A certain event in the plot *follows* certain developments and *anticipates* others that you may want to mention. In such a case, use the present tense for the action being immediately discussed, and the past and future for the preceding and following times:

>   PAST   PAST
> • When Dimmesdale *wrote* the sermon he *believed* he would be setting sail
>   PAST
> secretly for England with Hester on the day after he *delivered* it. By the
>   PRESENT
> time he *enters* the pulpit, however, he has changed his mind. He now
> PRESENT   FUTURE
> *knows* that after the sermon he *will mount* the scaffold and confess his guilt
> before the assembled populace.[1]

Note, finally, that an author has two kinds of relation to his or her completed work. First there is a past, or *historical,* relation, reflecting the fact that the writing and publishing of the work have taken place once and for all:

HISTORICAL RELATION:
- Hawthorne wrote the novel feverishly.
- He published it in 1850.

Second, a quite different, *continuing* relation also exists. No matter how long ago it was written, the work addresses us in an unfolding present as we read it. Thus, when you're discussing what the author "says to us" through the work, you should use the present tense:

CONTINUING RELATION:
- Hawthorne *gives* us little insight into his hero's mind.
- He *does* everything he can to heighten the suspense.

Verbals

The tenses of infinitives, participles, and gerunds must be changed to show different relations to the indicated time of action.

infinitives   No matter what tense the controlling verb is in, use a *present* infinitive to show action *at the same time as,* or *later than,* the indicated time:

SAME TIME:
PRES INF
- Bobo tried *to read* the obituaries every day.

LATER TIME:
PRES INF
- He hopes *to offer* protection to wealthy widows.

Use a *past* infinitive to show action *earlier than* the indicated time:

EARLIER TIME:
PAST INF
- Bobo expected the police *to have become* more cooperative than they had so far.

participles and gerunds   Whatever the tense of the controlling verb, use *present* participles and gerunds to show action *at the same time as* the indicated time:

SAME TIME:
PRES PART
- *Expressing* her outlook on life, Priscilla asserted that she would rather be a snob than a slob.

PRES GER
* *Displaying* her emotions in public had never been one of her aims.

Use *past* participles and gerunds to show action *earlier than* the indicated time:

EARLIER TIME:
PAST PART
• *Having entitled* her essay "Some Things Are Surely Less Vulgar Than Others," she began to worry about the scarcity of good examples.

PAST GER
* *Having written* a high-school paper on "Good Citizenship" didn't help her a bit with this project.

PRONOUN PROBLEMS

Choice of Case

overcorrection   The choice between subjective *(she)* and objective *(her)* case forms of pronouns causes misery for many writers. Knowing that nonstandard speakers tend to use objective forms where standard English calls for subjective ones (x *Him and me are friends*), they automatically "overcorrect" in certain situations:

D OBJ   D OBJ
x They appointed *she* and *I* to a subcommittee.

> As direct objects, the pronouns must be *her* and *me*. Nothing should be changed by the fact that there are two direct objects instead of one.

OBJ PREP   APP
x Parking is a tragic dilemma for *we* professors.

> An appositive following a pronoun shouldn't influence its case. Since you wouldn't write *for we*, don't write *for we professors*.

Observe that the way to decide between two pronoun forms is *not* to choose the one that sounds like "better English," but to see which grammatical function is being performed. If you identify a pronoun as a direct or indirect object, an object of a preposition, a subject of an infinitive *(gave her to understand)*, an object of an infinitive *(to meet her)*, or a complement of an infinitive *(to be her)*, make it objective in case.

pronoun complements In speech, pronoun complements are often heard in the objective case *(That's him; It's them)*. In standard English writing, the same policy would raise some eyebrows. Should you, then, write *That is he* and *It is they*? Yes—if you don't mind sounding like a fussy purist. It would be better to duck the problem: *He is the one; I meant them;* etc.

who versus whom Most worries over pronoun case have to do with the relative and interrogative forms *who* and *whom*. The advice already given suggests that (1) you shouldn't use one form where the other is strictly correct, and (2) you shouldn't use either of them if the "right" form sounds like a forced attempt at "good English."

1. Wherever you find yourself using *who* as the *subject of a clause*, go ahead and do so—even though the whole clause may have an objective function in its sentence:

> s
> • Stanley had no doubt about *who* would be elected Minister of Defense.

> The whole clause *who would be elected Minister of Defense* is the object of the preposition *about*. But *who*, as a pronoun *within* that clause, must remain subjective; it is the subject of the verb *would be elected*. Remember that case is always determined by the function *within the clause*, not by the function *of* the clause.

2. Wherever the "correct" form makes a strained effect, recast the whole sentence. Thus, if *Whom did you see there?* sounds overformal, don't write *Who did you see there?* Find an alternative: *Who was it? Who was there? Who was it that you saw?* etc.

Pronoun Reference

Personal, relative, demonstrative, and some indefinite pronouns usually stand in relation to *antecedents*—words for which they are substitutes. *Pronoun reference* has to do with the two key relations between a pronoun and its antecedent. First, is the antecedent immediately recognizable? And second, does the pronoun agree with its antecedent in number and person?

identification of antecedent As a rule, the antecedent of a pronoun is a noun or nounlike element in the same sentence or the one just before. Sometimes a personal pronoun, such as *she* or *they*, is so clearly identified that it can appear in several sentences in a row without repetition of the antecedent. A whole paragraph without an antecedent, however, would exhaust your pronoun credit; the first sentence in a paragraph is an especially important place to remind readers of a continuing antecedent.

An antecedent ought to be explicitly stated, even when the reader could supply it. The following sentences don't measure up:

PRO
x The peanut jar was empty, but Bobo was tired of nibbling *them* anyway.

There are no *peanuts* here to serve as the antecedent of *them*.

x He was opposed to gun control because he felt that every citizen should
PRO
have *one* in case the cops staged a surprise raid.

The word *gun* appears in the sentence, but only as an attributive (adjectival) noun. A phrase like *control of guns* would put things right.

Even when an explicit antecedent is present, make sure it can be easily spotted. If a reader has to study the context in order to see which of two nounlike elements is the antecedent, the sentence should be clarified:

ANT?   ANT?   PRO
x Because Biff now loved *Suzie* better than *Alice*, he made *her* return his souvenir faceguard.

After some reflection, a reader might see that *Alice* must be the intended antecedent. But why not make the meaning clear at once? Try *he made Alice return* etc., or rewrite the sentence: *Because he had decided to split up with Alice, Biff made her return* etc.

agreement with antecedent Personal pronouns agree with their antecedents in *number* and *person*, but not necessarily in case. Shifts of number or person, although often heard in speech, should be avoided in writing:

ANT   PRO
x Melody learned that if a *person* has a hang-loose attitude, *they* will get fired from the lingerie department.

The plural pronoun *they* disagrees in number with the singular antecedent *person*.

ANT   PRO
x If *one* asks the customers for spare change, *you* should expect complaints.

The shift from third person *(one)* to second person *(you)* is awkward. Keep to *one*, or use another appropriate third-person pronoun — in this case *she* (see p. 113).

MODIFIERS

Misrelated Modifiers

A *misrelated* modifier is one with a flawed relation to the term it modifies. Either the modified term is hard to identify, or the modifier unnecessarily interrupts another construction, or there's too much distance between the modifier and what it modifies.

squinting modifiers

Beware of sandwiching a modifier between two sentence elements that might compete to serve as the modified term. This becomes a *squinting* modifier—one that seems to be looking in two directions at once:

SQ MOD
x How Harry silenced the transmission *completely* amazes me.

Does *completely* modify *silenced* or *amazes*? In saying the sentence aloud, a speaker would control the meaning by pauses and stresses, as you can see if you speak each of the possible versions in turn. Again:

SQ MOD
x Priscilla was confident *on Tuesday* she would receive a divine signal.

Was she confident on Tuesday, or would she receive the signal on Tuesday? A timely *that*, placed either before or after *on Tuesday*, would make everything clear.

split infinitives

Much nail-biting over adverbs can be traced to the taboo of the *split infinitive*—the most discussed, but by no means the most important, point of debate among commentators on usage. A split infinitive is one containing an adverb between *to* and the next verb form: *to thoroughly understand*. Most writers would now indulge in an occasional split infinitive, but only where every alternative position for the adverb would make for even more awkwardness:

• Harry always made it a point to *clearly* state that his cars carried a twenty-minute, thirty-mile guarantee.

A writer in terror of splitting an infinitive might have written *clearly to state* or *to state clearly*. But the trouble with these alternatives, especially the first, is that they would have called attention to the writer's discomfort. It's better to split and have done with it than to sound overfastidious.

Although opinion is divided about the importance of avoiding split infinitives, everyone agrees that adverbial constructions of more than one word make an ugly effect in the split-infinitive position: *I want to soberly and patiently analyze the problem.* Rephrase: *I want to analyze the problem soberly and patiently* or *I want to make a sober and patient analysis.* . . .

hidden modified terms Modifiers should come immediately before or after the words they modify. Don't allow other nounlike elements to stand where a reader would expect to find the modified term:

>   M
> _____   MODIFIED TERM
> **x** *Head of the Fingerlickers from the start,* they naturally looked to *Stanley* for ideological guidance.

> The pronoun *they* stands where the modified term ought to be. Possible revision: *All the Fingerlickers looked to Stanley, their leader from the start, for ideological guidance.*

Again:

>   M
> _____
> **x** *Thinking that a Snoopy sweat shirt would win Priscilla over,* it only remained
> MODIFIED TERM
> for *Philo* to choose an appropriate greeting card.

> Here the anticipatory pronoun *it* stands where the modified term ought to be. Revise: *Thinking . . . over, Philo turned his attention to the choice of an appropriate greeting card.*

Dangling Modifiers

If the modified term is altogether absent, the modifier is called *dangling.* These faulty sentences illustrate the problem:

>   M
> _____
> **x** *Embracing the astonished Priscilla,* a rash erupted behind Philo's left knee.

> The possessive form *Philo's* can't serve as the modified term; its function is adjectival, and one adjectival element can't modify another. Revise: *Embracing etc., Philo felt a rash erupting etc.*

>   M
> _____
> **x** *Anticipating every taste,* it was decided to advertise the car as "an oversexed, pulse-quickening respecter of environmental quality."

Nobody is doing the anticipating here. Try *Anticipating* etc., *they decided* etc.

Note that *absolute phrases* (p. 293) look like misrelated or dangling modifiers, but aren't held accountable to the usual requirement of having a nearby modified term:

ABS PHRASE
* *Generally speaking,* Melody's memory is rather smoky.

ABS PHRASE
* *The Gauls having been defeated,* Caesar sat down to practice his declensions.

We read these constructions as if they were sentence adverbs, modifying the entire rest of the sentence.

POSSESSIVES

Care is required for the correct formation of ordinary possessives (pp. 276–278). In addition, problems arise over *double possessives* and *subjects of gerunds.*

Double Possessives

The possessive or genitive relation is usually indicated *either* by an -'s inflection *(Lindbergh's)* or an *of* construction *(of Lindbergh).* Sometimes, however, the two forms can be meaningfully combined. Observe the difference between these sentences:

* She remained unmoved by any thought $\begin{cases} \text{of Philo.} \\ \text{of Philo's.} \end{cases}$

These are two distinct statements. The top one deals with a thought *about* Philo; the bottom one, with a thought *proposed by* Philo — it is *his.*

Note that although some grammarians frown on double possessives, everyone uses them with pronouns: *a peculiarity of hers, that nasty habit of his.* You can use them just as easily with nouns: *a book-keeping trick of Harry's, that sawed-off shotgun of Bobo's.*

Subjects of Gerunds and Gerund Phrases

The subject of a gerund is usually written in the possessive case:

S GER GER
- Biff didn't know why everyone laughed at *his saying* he would like to be an astronaut and see all those steroids going by.

But the rule is hard to apply in many instances. For example, if the gerund's subject is separated from the gerund by other words, that subject goes in the objective case instead of the possessive:

S GER   GER
- People were surprised at *him,* a veteran speaker on many campuses, *having* no ready reply when Stanley seized the microphone and called him an irrelevant murderer.

Again, when the subject of a gerund is an abstract or inanimate noun, it can appear in a nonpossessive form:

S GER   GER
- We cannot ignore the danger of *catastrophe striking* again.

DOUBLE NEGATIVES

Although they were accepted for centuries as imparting extra emphasis to denials, double negatives are now regarded as *canceling* those denials and forming roundabout affirmations. Thus, *I don't intend to tell you nothing* would be read either as a nonstandard sentence or as a confusing way of saying *I intend to tell you something.*

Certain phrases that are fairly common in speech are widely disapproved in writing:

negatives with shouldn't wonder; wouldn't be surprised; etc. In a sentence like *I shouldn't wonder if it didn't rain,* the negative sense is unnecessarily doubled and thus made doubtful. *Didn't rain* should be *rained.*

cannot help but Many readers would consider this a double negative, since *not* and *but* are separate forms of denial. You can satisfy everyone by changing *cannot help but wonder,* for example, to *cannot help wondering.*

can't hardly; can't scarcely; etc. Since a negative sense is already contained in *hardly* and *scarcely,* the verb should be left in affirmative form: *Bobo can hardly wait to get his finger on the trigger.*

doubt but what; no doubt but that Both *doubt* and *but* have a negative force; thus in combination they make a double negative. In every case where *doubt but what* or *no doubt but that* comes to mind, try *doubt that:*

* I don't *doubt that* fleas and mosquitoes will one day inherit the earth.
* There is no *doubt that* this is so.

PARALLELISM

Parallelism, or the giving of equivalent structure to two or more parts of a sentence, is a fundamental resource of prose. It is present wherever words, phrases, or whole clauses are joined by coordinating conjunctions such as *and* or *but;* where items are linked in a series; where alternative possibilities are matched through correlative conjunctions such as *neither* and *nor;* where structures like *not only . . . but also* add one item to another; where items are compared through words like *more than* or *equal to;* or where the same order of sentence elements recurs, with or without repeated words. The principle behind all parallelism is that form should follow meaning. If terms x and y are being compared or contrasted or added or affected by the same agent, then x and y should receive parallel emphasis: *both x and y; not x but y; the impact of x and y; x or y; neither x nor y; more x than y; not only x, but y as well.*

Whether you use parallelism seldom or often, elaborately or inconspicuously, you should take care to ensure that the matched terms — words, phrases, or whole clauses — are structurally equivalent. In a series, for example, the elements being placed in sequence must be of the same kind — verbs matched with verbs, nouns with other nouns or nounlike elements, objects of prepositions with other objects of prepositions, and so forth. Compare:

x Fido's whole ambition in life was *to eat, to play,* and *sleeping.*
* Fido's whole ambition in life was *to eat, to play,* and *to sleep.*

> In the first sentence, two infinitives are awkwardly matched with a gerund. In the second, the three infinitives form a grammatically symmetrical parallelism.

Again:

x In this modern success story, the hero decides to *give up* making sand candles, *leave* his commune, and *goes* to New York to become an IBM executive.

> The verb *decides* and the infinitive marker *to* prepare us for a parallelism of three infinitives: *decides to x, y,* and *z.* Instead, the "z" turns out to be a verb. Change *goes* to *go.* Or, if *goes* conveys what you mean, take it out of the parallel series:

* . . . the hero decides to give up making sand candles and leave his commune. Eventually, he goes to New York etc.

Note that if you begin repeating any word within a series, you should do so consistently until the series ends:

• He never misses *his* sandals, *his* yogurt, *his* goat, and *his* compost heap.

> Once the second *his* appears, the writer is committed to supplying the other two.

• The hope of the world, he now realizes, must lie *in* software, *in* semiconductors, and *in* systems analysis.

> The second *in* makes the third necessary. Note that *in software, semiconductors, and systems analysis* would be equally right.

In *not only . . . but also* constructions, remember that a key element appearing after *not only* must have a counterpart after *but also*. Often a writer forgets to duplicate a verb:

> v
X He not only *broadens* his outlook, but also his waistline.

> To repair the faulty parallelism, the writer can do either of two things: place a second verb after *but also,* or move *broadens* outside the *not only . . . but also* construction: *He broadens not only his outlook, but also his waistline.*

In *not . . . neither* constructions, make sure the first negation doesn't warp the meaning of the second one:

X The Marquis de Sade was not an agreeable man, and neither are his novels.

> The complement *man* makes the sentence appear to say that the novels were not an agreeable man. Try *The Marquis de Sade was not agreeable, and neither are his novels.*

Beware also of compound verbs involving a change of tense:

X Melody *can,* and indeed *has been, hitchhiking* in both directions at once.

> The way to check such sentences is to read them without the interruption: *Melody can hitchhiking* etc. To save the present form of the sentence, write *Melody can hitchhike, and indeed has*

been hitchhiking, in both etc. But that sounds clumsy. A better solution is to get rid of the compound verb: *Melody has been hitchhiking* etc.

And similarly, note that "suspended" comparisons like the one below often end in a tangle:

ˣ Melody likes total strangers *as much,* if not *more than,* her closest friends.

The sentence says that Melody likes strangers *as much her friends. As much as* would make the parallelism technically correct, but it would still be cumbersome. Try *She likes total strangers at least as much as her closest friends.*

COMPARISONS

As we have just seen, comparing one item with another sometimes involves difficulties of parallel structure. Other problems to be alert for are the absence of a compared term, comparison of incomparable things, misuse of the superlative degree, and comparison of absolutes.

Missing Term

At least two terms should be explicitly present if a comparison is to be made. This seems obvious, but it is blurred by the influence of advertising style: *Get 23 percent less emphysema!* It's true, to be sure, that some normal expressions contain incomplete comparisons: *I feel better today, It is best for you to leave, You have been most helpful,* etc. No one would regard these sentences as erroneous; either the rest of the comparative word is being used merely as an intensifier (*most* = "very"). The problem sentences are those in which we wait for the second shoe to drop:

ˣ Biff learned that it was *more* important for a pro athlete to be able to shave in front of a TV crew without snickering.
ˣ *Fewer* grapefruit-eaters are now wearing goggles.

More important than what? Fewer now than when? Once this information has been promised by the comparative words *more* and *fewer,* it ought to be supplied.

Comparing the Incomparable

Don't allow your language to imply a comparative relation between items of completely different types:

x The accuracy of Bobo's shooting was greater than his tax return.

> The sentence appears to compare *accuracy* to a *tax return*. Revise: *greater than that of his tax return*.

Misuse of the Superlative

When comparing *only two* things, don't use the superlative degree of an adjective (*most, least,* etc.):

x Sluggo and Bobo had a playful little fight to see who would pick up the check. Bobo, the survivor, proved the *strongest* of the two.

> Change *strongest* to *stronger*, the comparative form of the adjective.

Many readers object to the "gushy" use of superlatives when no comparison is intended:

x Biff has the *oddest* complexion since he started taking those shots.

Comparison of Absolutes

Words like *complete, equal, infinite, perfect*, and *unique* are sometimes called *absolutes;* that is, they are regarded as not lending themselves to qualification. If something isn't altogether unique, it isn't unique at all. But does this mean that such words should never be modified or compared? When you look at sentences one by one you find that matters aren't so simple. Thus the comparison of *perfect* sounds normal enough in this sentence:

• Our purpose in founding this institute in Zurich is to form a *more perfect* Jungian.

Or again:

• The inclusion of his early letters to Santa Claus makes this the *most complete* edition of Dickens ever published.

But compare:

x The sands of Lake Havasu City are *less infinite* than those of the Sahara.

Here the dictionary meaning of *infinite* is being violated: the word can't be applied to any number or size smaller than the greatest. *Perfect* and *complete,* by contrast, have allowable secondary meanings of *excellent* and *thorough,* and this is why they can be used more flexibly.

For other problems in forming comparisons, see the Index of Usage entries for *compared with* versus *compared to; fewer* versus *less; like* versus *as; more . . . rather than;* and *other than that.*

EXERCISES

I. Each of the following numbered items contains a *sentence fragment* (pp. 301–302). Even though they lack the usual makings of a sentence, some of the fragments are of the "independent" variety that readers generally accept. Others would be perceived as unacceptable, "unintentional" sentence fragments. Write a brief evaluation of each of the five fragments. Explain what causes you to regard each one as acceptable or unacceptable. For the unacceptable ones, make the revisions necessary to form complete sentences.

1. This stock is selling at a price below its book value. What a bargain!
2. Its price-earnings ratio is 1:0. Which is hard to beat.
3. The market for laser death rays is expected to become firmer in the 1980's. Unless the peaceniks get control of the White House again.
4. Why do you suppose it's listed as an under-the-counter stock? To attract the small investor, perhaps?
5. Although he happens to be in jail at the moment. The chairman of the board has high hopes for General Catastrophe.

II. Correct any instances of *faulty predication* (pp. 302–304) in these sentences:

1. The reason Crazy Hoarse is a star is because he listens carefully to his research staff.
2. He is always changing the wording of his lyrics into a song with greater appeal.
3. His latest musical idea treats thirteen-year-old would-be lovers with special sympathy.
4. Purchases made by thirteen-year-old would-be lovers, it has been learned, buy more popular records than all other groups combined.
5. Crazy Hoarse's definition of success is when a person has three gold records about being broke, lonely, and out of luck.

III. For each sentence, choose the verb form that makes for *subject-verb agreement* **(pp. 304–307):**

1. It is their own secret vices that *(allows, allow)* people to tolerate the vices of others.
2. Neither of them *(remembers, remember)* who ran for President against Harry Truman.
3. Above the wealthiest section of Rio *(stands, stand)* some of the world's most miserable slums.
4. Baseball, along with all other sports, *(strikes, strike)* Priscilla as utterly meaningless.
5. There *(is, are)* four candidates in this election.
6. A number of people *(dislikes, dislike)* mushroom pizza.
7. Each of them *(is, are)* equally certain of being right.
8. Any idea for improving this company's profits *(is, are)* welcome.
9. A majority of votes *(is, are)* all you need to be elected.
10. Neither age nor illness *(prevents, prevent)* her from laughing at the world's follies.

IV. Locate any mistaken uses of *tense* **(pp. 307–312) in the verbs and verbals, and revise each faulty sentence to remove the error:**

1. He knew she stopped smoking five years before.
2. She had wanted to have quit even earlier.
3. Forster publishes *A Passage to India* in 1924.
4. At the beginning of the novel, Aziz has no idea that he will be the defendant in a notorious trial.
5. If I would have known Marilyn Monroe, I would have treated her respectfully.
6. She had always wanted to be named Mother of the Year, but she was not altogether pleased when the quintuplets had been born.
7. He announced that he will take the plane to Miami.
8. Going to a good high school was of considerable use to her in college.
9. She will have completed the paper by next Tuesday.
10. We concluded by saying that we have never had such a thoroughly enjoyable time.

V. Locate any problems of *pronoun reference* **(pp. 313–314) in these sentences. Explain the flaw and propose a suitable revision in each instance.**

1. I want to drum some statistics into your heads which are concrete.
2. His father always told him what to do, but sometimes he wasn't familiar enough with the facts.
3. Although she was worried at first, it diminished after a while.
4. A woman who turns in their friend to the police isn't going to be very popular.
5. If your goldfish won't eat its food, feed it to the canary.

VI. Locate any *misrelated* **or** *dangling modifiers* **(pp. 315–317) in these sentences, and propose suitable revisions:**

1. He knew by Friday he would soon be free.
2. Before going to bed, the false teeth should be removed for maximum comfort.
3. If you want to quickly, safely, and pleasantly make your way through the dense jungle at Disneyland, a native guide is necessary.
4. His coach, though he was still very inexperienced, believed he detected some athletic promise in the eight-foot Elbows Lodgepole.
5. He paid the penalty for his crimes in prison.

VII. Correct any mistaken use (or absence) of *possessives* **(pp. 317–318) in these sentences:**

1. That plan of Stanley is one that even his closest friends can't endorse.
2. He being there came as a shock to everyone.
3. Philo didn't enjoy thinking of Priscilla's, his beloved's, spurning him.
4. They all rejected that idea of the Senator's.
5. Stanley leaving town was suspiciously hasty.

VIII. Correct any faulty handling of *parallel structure* **(pp. 319–321):**

1. He is not an outstanding swimmer, and neither is his running.
2. Harry can, and indeed always has, succeeded in his Halloween midnight clearance sale.
3. George couldn't remember whether Susan had asked him to buy low-fat milk, condensed milk, defatted, reconstituted, or evaporated milk.
4. Stanley writes leaflets, makes underground broadcasts, tape recordings, and paints warnings on police-station walls.
5. Not only is he skilled in sabotage, but in psychological warfare as well.

IX. Correct any awkward or faulty *comparisons* **(pp. 321–323):**

1. The chemical structure of smog is entirely different from cigarette smoke.
2. Melody wears the sweetest smile all day long.
3. She is more totally carefree now than ever before.

4. He is certainly the best member of that pair.
5. Heating systems for neocolonial-Elizabethan tract homes are harder to install than large apartment buildings.

NOTE

[1]Henry Nash Smith, "Some Patterns of Transcendence in Hawthorne and Howells," *English Studies Today*, 6 (1975), 437.

12
PUNCTUATION

The ideal of correct punctuation may appear at first to be a very small matter. No one, after all, is likely to exclaim that you punctuate like an angel, or to single out your brackets and quotation marks for special praise. In writing, however, small matters count; that is, they count against you if you botch them. After you've decided just what to write and have gotten it down in pointed, well-formed phrases and clauses, one little comma or dash in the wrong place can sabotage your sentence. Punctuation marks are like railroad switches. Their job is the inconspicuous one of allowing sentences to go where a writer intends; if they're noticed at all, it's because something has just plunged off the track.

Punctuation, it is sometimes said, is a writer's way of trying to substitute for pauses in speech. That may be so, but marks of punctuation can be much more exact and revealing than pauses. Often we can't tell whether a speaker has finished a sentence at all, much less how its parts are related. But with such subtly graded devices as commas, parentheses, brackets, dashes, colons, semicolons, and periods, writers can offer us a total, continuing grasp of their logic and emphasis. Even when, as sometimes happens, writers "listen" for a pause to tell whether punctuation is called for, they must still decide which of several marks to choose. Only an understanding of the unique function of each punctuation mark can resolve such questions.

Some of the dos and don'ts of punctuation are rather complex, but you shouldn't allow them to distract you from the main general principles. If you master the following five rules, you'll be able to avoid the mistakes that occur most frequently.

1. Don't separate *parts* of sentences as if they were full sentences (below), or punctuate two sentences as one (p. 332).
2. Separate independent clauses *either* with a comma and a coordinating conjunction (p. 331) *or* with a semicolon (p. 341).
3. Use commas to separate items in a series (p. 334), introductory modifying clauses and phrases (p. 335), and nonrestrictive elements, including those which are parenthetical (p. 336).
4. Don't insert needless punctuation between main sentence elements, compound elements, or terms of comparison and preference (p. 333).
5. Use the same marks at both ends of parenthetical elements (p. 337).

PERIOD ●

End of Sentence

A period signifies a full stop, not a pause. The normal place for a period is at the end of a complete sentence — one containing at least one independent clause. Independent sentence fragments (p. 301) can also end with periods:

- Did Betsy want to become a gardener? *Yes, Ava Gardner.*

Beware, however, of writing unacceptable sentence fragments, those that clearly belong within the preceding sentence:

x Biff wanted to sell his talents to the highest bidder. *Either the AAU or the NCAA.*

For this important difference between independent and unacceptable fragments, review the discussion on pages 301–302.

Indirect Questions

A sentence constituting an indirect question should end with a period, not a question mark:

WRONG:

x He asked me whether I could go?

RIGHT:

• He asked me whether I could go.

Abbreviations

Abbreviations such as *Mr., Dr., Jr.,* and *N.Y.* require periods, but some common abbreviations and acronyms (p. 437) often appear without periods: *UAW, NOW, SST,* etc.

Note that when an abbreviation ends a sentence, one period does the work of two:

• Send the money directly to Lincoln Dollar, M.D.

QUESTION MARK **?**

Direct Questions

Question marks follow direct questions wherever they occur in a sentence:

• Can a camel pass through the eye of a needle?
• I know that many strange things are possible, but can a camel really pass through the eye of a needle?
• It was just fifteen years ago today—remember?—that the camel got stuck in the eye of the needle.
• "Can a needle," asked the surrealist film director when he met the Arab veterinary surgeon, "pass through the eye of a camel?"

Indications of Doubt

A question mark within parentheses expresses doubt:

• Saint Thomas Aquinas, 1225(?)–1274

Some writers unwisely use such question marks as a form of sarcasm:

x The President expects to make four nonpolitical (?) television speeches in the month of October.

The sentence is momentarily in contradiction with itself. First it offers the "straight" assertion that the speeches will be nonpolitical; then it negates that idea through the parenthetical question. By eliminating the question mark and putting quotation marks around *nonpolitical,* the writer would get the desired effect without inconsistency.

Questions Within Questions

When a sentence asking a question also *contains* a question at the end, one question mark will serve the purpose:

- Why didn't he stop and ask himself, "Is it wise to invest *all* my money in pet rocks?"

EXCLAMATION POINT

Exclamation points should be used sparingly to punctuate outbursts or statements requiring extraordinary emphasis:

- "My geodesic dome! My organic greenhouse! My Tolkien collection! When will I ever see them again?"
- Standing in the bread line, he had a moment of revelation. So *this* was what his economics professor had meant by structural unemployment!

Frequent use of exclamation points dulls their effect. Be especially slow to use sarcastic exclamation points in parentheses:

x The General told them on Monday that the battle had to be completely won (!) by Wednesday afternoon.

COMMA

Independent Clauses

When you write two independent clauses in a row, you must separate them either with a semicolon (p. 341) or with a comma and a coordinating conjunction *(and, but, for, nor, or, so, yet):*

- George was lonely at first, but after a while he came to like having the whole house to himself.

But when the first independent clause is short, the comma can usually be omitted:

- He ate constantly but he still couldn't get enough food to satisfy his cravings.

The comma can also be omitted to show that one independent clause logically belongs with another one:

- George's reliance on prepared foods was total, for Susan had left him and she had taken her cookbooks with her.

> The omission of a comma after *him* helps to show that everything from *for Susan* to the end of the sentence constitutes a single explanation of the first clause.

run-on sentences Failure to join independent clauses properly results in a *run-on sentence* — that is, the punctuating of two sentences as if they were one. Run-on sentences come in two varieties, either of which can turn your prose into a leaking faucet. For a slow leak there is the *comma splice*, a comma without the necessary coordinating conjunction:

comma splices

x George's health was now much improved, his diet was rich in preservatives.

> Without a conjunction such as *for* after the comma, the two clauses become separate sentences unnaturally presented as one.

fused sentences And for an all-out, unstoppable flow there is the alarming *fused sentence,* in which the independent clauses run together with no punctuation at all:

x He put the television set right on the table he never took his eyes off the game.

> Run-on sentences are among the most common and serious errors a writer must avoid. Comma splices in particular may plague you unless you fully grasp the difference in function between commas and semicolons. Note that inserting a sentence adverb like *however* or *furthermore* between comma-spliced clauses does *not* solve the problem:

x He turned the oven dial to the "Clean" position, however, the dishes seemed dirtier than ever when he took them out.

> Since *however* isn't a coordinating conjunction, it has to be preceded by a semicolon, not a comma.

emphatic sequence of clauses   You can sometimes omit a coordinating conjunction when presenting several brief, tightly related independent clauses in a sequence:

* He saw the frozen tamale pie, he yearned for it, he stuffed it eagerly into the shopping cart.

> Here the lack of a conjunction before the third clause helps to bring out the rapidity and compulsiveness of the activities described.

Separation of Compound Elements

Elements consisting of two parts joined by a coordinating conjunction should generally *not* be separated by commas. The following sentences are correct:

         a   b
* Both *sodium nitrate* and *sodium nitrite* have been suspected of causing cancer.

         a   b
* *Either you are wrong about that or I have forgotten everything I knew.*

                 a   b
* Sterno has been called *a killer drug by some people* and *a modest depressant*
  b
by others.

> Commas after the *"a"* elements would be inadvisable. But try to avoid very lengthy compound elements that might strain the rule.

Comparisons and Statements of Preference

When comparing two terms or expressing a preference for one over the other, don't allow commas to come between them. These sentences follow the rule:

         a   b
* She felt more *wistful and nostalgic* than *resentful.*

> *She felt more a than b;* a comma after *nostalgic* would interrupt the comparative structure.

                           a
* Wellington's mother preferred *the mathematical elegance and understatement*
  a   b
of Bach to *the thunderous thumping of Berlioz.*

> She *preferred a to b;* even though the *"a"* term is lengthy, it shouldn't be followed by a comma.

Members of a Series

Items in a series should be separated by commas, with a coordinating conjunction before the last item: *a, b, and (or) c.*

- Every night Rupert had wild, passionate dreams about *mag wheels*[a], *bucket seats*[b], *and rally stripes*[c].

omission of final comma It is also acceptable to omit the final comma, provided you do so consistently; don't mix styles of punctuation. But the *a, b and (or) c* formula may not always allow your meaning to come through clearly. Consider:

x The returning knight had countless tales to tell of *adventure*[a], *conquest of hideous monsters*[b] *and helpless damsels in distress*[c].

> Did he conquer the damsels as well as the monsters? A comma after *monsters* would remove all doubt. If you keep to the traditional *a, b, and (or) c* method, such problems won't arise.

series without commas If all the members of a series are connected by conjunctions, no commas are needed:

- From listening to Rupert you might gather that the universe consisted entirely of *Chargers*[a] *and Pacers*[b] *and Cutlasses*[c].

Coordinate Modifiers

Coordinate adjectives or adverbs, if not separated by coordinating conjunctions, must be separated by commas:

- George fixed himself a *delicious*[ADJ], *nutritious*[ADJ] dinner of Gatorade and Chun King Chop Suey.

> Here *delicious* and *nutritious* are coordinate, for they both modify the same noun, *dinner.*

But note that some paired modifiers aren't coordinate:

- He wolfed down his *typical*[ADJ] *American*[ADJ] meal.

> Here *American* modifies *meal*, but *typical* doesn't; it modifies

American meal. A comma after *typical* would wrongly imply that *typical* and *American* modified the same word.

To determine whether you have a coordinate series, try shifting the order of the terms. Truly coordinate items can be reversed without affecting their meaning: *a nutritious, delicious dinner.* Noncoordinate items look all wrong when reversed: *an American typical meal.*

Modifying Clauses and Phrases

modifier preceding main clause   Modifying clauses and phrases are usually set off by commas if they *precede* the main clause:

- *After Susan left,* George spent a few evenings reading Dr. Lincoln Dollar's helpful book of advice, *The Aerobic Kama Sutra.*
- *In order to prove that he wasn't narrow-minded,* Rupert decided to buy a trail bike and a snowmobile.

But you can omit the comma if the clause or phrase is brief and its grammatical distinctness from what follows is clear:

- *When Susan came back* she found George sitting in the lotus posture and eating a Ho-Ho.
- *Until that moment* she hadn't appreciated the spiritual side of his nature.

> Commas after *back* and *moment* would also be correct. When in doubt, supply the comma instead of omitting it.

Never omit a comma if the sentence would become even momentarily ambiguous without it:

- *Although Susan begged,* George said that she could go live with Julia Child for all he cared.

> Without the comma, we might think at first that the sentence says *Although Susan begged George . . .*

modifier following main clause   When a modifying clause or phrase *follows* a main clause, ask whether it *completes the meaning* of that main clause (no comma) or *adds something new* (comma required). In reading the sentence aloud, you can tell a modifier of the first type by the lack of a pause before it:

- An apple a day was all Betsy allowed herself *until the diet was completed.*

> The modifying clause limits the time of the action described in

the main clause. Because it affects the meaning of that main clause, we tend to read it without a break.

* She would dip the apple in chocolate *to improve the flavor.*

    The modifying phrase gives us essential information about the purpose of the action described in the main clause. A comma after *chocolate* would obscure this fact and distort the normal pace of reading.

A clause that adds something new, without affecting the meaning of the main clause, is preceded by a pause in speech and a comma in writing:

* Betsy's apple a day required great self-control, *for which a few evening milk shakes seemed a fitting reward.*

    Notice that the meaning of the main clause is complete with or without the italicized modifier.

Restrictive Versus Nonrestrictive Elements

The foregoing discussion suggests an important principle that applies to all modifiers and to all appositives as well. They can all be regarded as either *restrictive* or *nonrestrictive* — that is, as necessary or unnecessary to *identification* of the term they refer to.

restrictive: no commas   Restrictive, or identifying, elements should *not* be set off on both sides by commas:

* The union leader *John L. Lewis* was not amused by the headline *"Lewis Drops Union Suit."*

    The two italicized elements are restrictive appositives, necessary to identify who the union leader was and what the headline said.

* The task *to be performed* requires great concentration.

    The passive infinitive *to be performed* tells us which task is meant.

* The discipline *that George had recently adopted* was called Transcendental Weight-watching.

    A restrictive adjectival clause, identifying the discipline in question, is presented without commas.

Nonrestrictive, or nonidentifying, elements *should* be set off on both sides by commas (except of course if they come at the beginning or end of a sentence):

* A union leader, *a man like John L. Lewis,* led a dangerous life back in those days.

    The nonrestrictive appositive gives an instance of a *leader,* but doesn't restrict its meaning to one name.

* The task, *to be performed adequately,* requires great concentration.

    It is clear that *The task* has already been identified in a previous sentence. The nonrestrictive modifier tells something *further* about a known subject.

* Transcendental Weight-watching, *which George had adopted as his newest discipline,* struck Betsy as a promising idea.

    The subject is fully identified before we reach the nonrestrictive modifying clause, which must therefore be set off by commas.

Parenthetical Elements

A parenthetical element is a word or group of words that interrupts the main flow of a sentence. It could be a modifying phrase or clause, a sentence adverb like *moreover,* an appositive (p. 266), a name in direct address (you, *Andrew Marvell*), or an inserted question or exclamation. What makes it parenthetical (as in "parentheses") is that the elements before and after it fit together grammatically:

* A diet, *she believed,* called for strong discipline during the sleeping hours.

    The sentence is perfectly coherent without the parenthetical clause *she believed.*

Being interruptions, parenthetical elements are by definition *nonrestrictive,* and as such they must always be set off by punctuation marks *on both sides;* otherwise they would "leak" into the elements surrounding them. Extreme breaks such as whole statements, questions, or exclamations demand parentheses, brackets, or dashes, but commas are preferred for milder interruptions:

* Reindeer droppings on the roof, *to be sure,* count as strong evidence for Santa's existence.
* Congress, *it appears,* has little interest in closing tax loopholes.

- You, *George,* have been chosen by the computer to be Betsy's mate.
- The computer, *an antique Univac,* is badly in need of repair.

testing for parenthetical elements To be considered parenthetical, a modifier must meet two conditions: it must be nonrestrictive in meaning and it must come *between* essential parts of a statement. Compare:

- But *without hesitating for a moment,* Betsy enrolled in the autohypnosis course.

  The italicized modifier comes before the modified statement has properly begun. A comma after *But* would be optional here.

- No one was surprised when, *without hesitating for a moment,* Betsy enrolled in the autohypnosis course.

  No one was surprised by a certain event, to be identified in the *when* clause. But *after that clause has begun,* we must pause to consider the modifier, which thus becomes a parenthetical interruption. The commas on both sides are necessary.

Conjunctions Versus Conjunctive Adverbs

conjunctions: no comma follows Conjunctions (*and, but, since,* etc.) that aren't followed by parenthetical elements should never be followed by commas. Beware especially of starting a sentence with a conjunction and comma:

x *Yet,* Wellington's mother tried to be forgiving toward the vulgar nineteenth century.

  The comma serves no purpose and should be removed.

conjunctive adverbs: set off with commas The frequency of this mistake derives from confusion between *conjunctions* and *conjunctive* (or *sentence*) *adverbs,* those words that modify a whole statement by indicating its relation to another statement (p. 287). Words like *furthermore, however,* and *moreover,* not being true conjunctions, *should* be set off by commas:

- She taught her son, *however,* that the arts had begun decaying when artists no longer sought wealthy patrons.

  Like all other conjunctive adverbs, *however* is parenthetical here and must therefore be isolated by commas.

Separation of Main Sentence Elements

don't
separate:

Unless you are setting off modifiers or appositives, don't allow commas to come between main sentence elements such as subject and verb, verb and direct object, or verb and complement. The following sentences are wrongly punctuated:

subject and
verb

        S   V
x *Betsy, found* it difficult at first to chant through the dinner hour.

The subject *Betsy* is mistakenly separated from the verb *found*.

verb and
direct
object

     AUX   V   D OBJ
x She *could* not altogether *forget,* her chocolate-covered *apple.*

The verb phrase *could forget* shouldn't be cut off from its direct object *apple.*

verb and
complement

                       LV   COMPL
x Earthly thoughts *proved, hard to suppress.*

The comma wrongly blocks the linking verb *proved* from its complement *hard to suppress.*

Note that the rule *don't separate main sentence elements* can be hard to follow if a subject or verb is *compound,* consisting of more than one item:

- A delightful drive through the Holland Tunnel, an exquisite hour on the Pulaski Skyway, and a whiff of the fragrant North Jersey marshlands were Gertie's idea of a fine outing.

  Although this sentence is correctly punctuated, some writers would be tempted to put a comma after *marshlands.* Keep to the rule—but also try to avoid constructions that put the rule in conflict with natural pauses.

direct object before subject: comma allowed   In one unusual situation you *can* separate main sentence elements. When a direct object *precedes* the subject and verb, you may want to put a comma after it to show that it isn't the subject:

                    D OBJ
- *That Walt Whitman is nothing less than a cosmos,* few readers would accept without question.

The comma marks off the direct object, a noun clause, and thus warns us that it won't be the subject of the sentence.

Quotations

To decide whether a quotation should be enclosed in commas, disregard the quotation marks and think of the quoted matter as an ordinary part of the sentence. A quotation that fits readily into the syntax of a clause or phrase needn't be set off by commas:

• Macbeth expresses the depth of his despair when he describes life as "a tale told by an idiot."

A comma after *as* would wrongly separate the preposition *as* from its object *tale.*

But a quotation that doesn't form part of a phrase or clause in the rest of the sentence should be introduced by either a comma or a colon:

• When asked what he thought of Western civilization, Gandhi smiled and replied, "I think it would be a very good idea."

A colon after *replied* would be equally correct.

Conventional Uses

Commas occur routinely in certain contexts:

numbers of more than four digits   Commas should separate every three digits of a number consisting of more than four digits: *109,368,452.* In four-digit numbers the comma is optional: *6083* and *6,083* are both correct.

No commas separate the digits of years *(2001),* telephone numbers, zip codes, serial numbers, and other figures meant to identify an item or place. Such figures are sometimes divided into segments by hyphens.

dates   A comma should separate the day of the month and the year if the month is given first: July 4, 1934. If the sentence continues after the date, the year too should be followed by a comma: *She was born on July 4, 1934, in Peralta Hospital.* But if the day is given first, no punctuation is necessary: *4 July 1934.*

When only the month and the year are stated, a comma separating them is optional. Both *July 1934* and *July, 1934,* would be considered correct.

addresses   New York, New York
7713 Radnor Road, Bethesda, Md. 20034
Department of Economics, Simon Fraser University, Burnaby 2, B.C.,
   Canada

titles and degrees following names   Herbert Moroni, Ph.D.
Adlai Stevenson, III

But *Adlai Stevenson III* would also be acceptable.

SEMICOLON ;

To Join Independent Statements

Use a semicolon to join independent statements that are closely related. When one statement *explains* the other, for example, a semicolon
allows you to get them both into the same sentence:

- Wellington bade farewell to his tutors; he revealed that he was being sent
  off to boarding school "for graduate study."
- He wasn't easily persuaded to leave home; his little polo pony, he feared,
  would die of heartbreak.

There is nothing wrong with following a semicolon with either a
conjunction *(and, but)* or a conjunctive adverb and a comma
(nevertheless, likewise). But it *is* wrong to put an independent statement on one side of the semicolon and a fragment on the other:

x Wellington invited the headmaster to tea; knowing how important it is to
  make a good impression on the first day of school.

There is no independent clause after the semicolon.

To Show Main Divisions in a Series

When members of a series are subdivided into parts separated by
commas, it may be hard to tell where each member ends and the next
begins. The solution is to use semicolons at the *main* points of separation:

- Wellington first decided that he couldn't bear to live without his mother,
  who wrote to him every day; then that he might be able to stand his loneliness until Thanksgiving vacation; and finally that if she continued to pes-
  ter him with mail and telegrams, he would have to get himself a lawyer
  and seek an injunction.

The semicolons help to show where each of the three items ends; otherwise the commas would be too confusing. Note that the items *in a series* punctuated by semicolons don't have to constitute independent clauses.

If you pepper your first drafts with semicolons as a way of keeping one thought in mind while struggling with the next, look back to see if the connected statements really belong together. Remember that the basic unit of communication is the one-statement sentence, not a string of statements looped together by semicolons. Abundant semi-colons can tax a reader's patience.

COLON ⁚

To Introduce a Statement or Figure

A colon marks a formal introduction:

- Wellington began cultivating a new passion at Lordover: terrorizing the weakest boys in the lower grades.

colon versus semicolon A colon implies a symmetry or equivalence between items on either side. Something is to be presented: here it is. If you don't mean to insist on the equivalence, you may want a semicolon rather than a colon. A semicolon announces development of, or relationship to, what has just been stated; a colon delivers the thing itself in different terms. Don't use a colon unless you could plausibly insert *namely* or *that is* immediately after it.

Note that a colon is inappropriate when you want to interrupt the main flow of a sentence and then pick it up again. For this function you need dashes or parentheses — marks, that is, that can be closed off at both ends.

Don't allow a colon to wall off sentence elements that belong to-gether, such as a verb, preposition, or infinitive and its object:

x Wellington asked his mother to send him: two pairs of knickers, a croquet set, and a new polo helmet.

The colon wrongly separates the infinitive *to send* from its ob-jects, the items listed. Use a colon only when you have a genuine *stopping*-point: *These are the things Wellington asked for: two pairs* etc.

Colons are normally used to introduce figures:

* The results of the poll were surprising: 7 percent in favor, 11 percent opposed, 82 percent no opinion.

To Introduce a Quotation

A quotation that can be suitably introduced by a comma (p. 340) can also be introduced by a colon. The difference is that the colon makes for a more formal pause, a greater separation between your own prose and the quotation:

* Wellington clarified his position: "Either you invite *all* the fellows to spend Christmas vacation with us this year or I won't come home at all."

As usual, you should choose the punctuation by disregarding the quotation marks and treating all the words in the sentence as your own. If no punctuation is called for *without* the quotation marks, none is called for *with* them:

* Wellington's postcard reported that "the fellows and I could use some extra funds for our trip to Bermuda."

   A comma or colon before the quotation would wrongly separate the subordinating conjunction *that* from the rest of its clause.

* The Mayor at the freeway opening urged the assembled dignitaries to "reason not the need."

   This is correct. A comma or colon placed after *to* would wrongly interrupt an infinitive, *to reason.*

Other Uses

A colon should be used between hours and minutes in time references, and after the salutation of a business letter:

* 10:15 p.m.
* Dear Mr. Green:

Subtitles of books and articles are also introduced by colons:

* *Hemingway: The Inward Terrain*
* "Windward Oahu: Last Stand Against the Developers?"

DASH —

A dash signifies an abrupt break in thought. If the main sentence doesn't resume after the break, only one dash is used:

- The Senator stood ready to remedy any grievances — for a price.

If the main sentence resumes, a second dash is needed:

- The Senator stood ready — for a price — to remedy any grievances.

Don't allow a comma to substitute for the second dash, and be sure that your sentence would make complete sense if the portion within dashes were omitted. Sentences like this are all too common:

x Although Betsy took up massage — somebody told her it would increase her human potential — but she soon discovered that she was too ticklish.

> The material between dashes has caused the writer to forget the presence of *Although. But* has to be deleted.

A dash can serve as a less formal equivalent to a colon:

- At least Betsy had accumulated some souvenirs — a black eye from Encounter, bruised ribs from Rolfing, and a whiplash from Aikido.

Dashes can be used to mark the beginning and end of a series which might otherwise get confused with the rest of the sentence:

- The people who knew Betsy most intimately — her doctor, her pharmacist, and her lawyer — were eager to know what she would try next.

Dashes are also used to mark the interruption of a sentence in dialogue:

> "Run, Jane, run!" yelled Dick. "I see the principal and he's coming toward us with—"
>
> "It's too late, Dick, it's too late! The curriculum enrichment consultants have blocked the gate and—"
>
> "Oh, Jane, oh, Jane, whatever will become of us?"

Dashes shouldn't be combined with other punctuation marks. A comma and a dash together are redundant; a period and a dash are contradictory.

As a stylistic matter you should be frugal with dashes, or you'll make a scatterbrained impression. Don't fall into the careless habit of using the dash as an all-purpose punctuation mark.

PARENTHESES ( )

Parentheses mark a gentler interruption than dashes do. The material enclosed is parenthetical (p. 337) in both cases, but parentheses have the effect of *subordinating* it, so that the reader is less distracted from the rest of the sentence. Parentheses can be used either to set off incidental information such as numbers, dates, and references or to signal a digression from the main thought:

- Your furniture will be repossessed in thirty (30) days.
- The article appears in *National Geographic*, 149 (June 1976), 755–785.
- Julia Moore (revered in her lifetime as "the Sweet Singer of Michigan") offered the memorable observation that "Literary is a work very difficult to do."

No mark of punctuation should ever *precede* a parenthesis, but you can supply punctuation *after* the closing of the parenthesis if necessary. The rule is that the parenthesis shouldn't affect the punctuation of the main statement. If the main statement calls for a comma but a parenthesis intervenes, the comma is delivered at the end of the parenthesis:

- After she had tried Primal Jogging and I'm-O.K.-You're-Not-O.K. (she still hadn't met any interesting men), Betsy resolved to become a Hatha Backpacker.

Similarly, if no comma would have been required without the parenthetical material, none is required with it:

- Betsy discovered (though not with true surprise) that swarms of mosquitoes were no remedy for loneliness.

When a parenthetical statement is placed between complete sentences, it too should be punctuated as a complete sentence. The end-punctuation comes within the parenthesis, not after it:

- Betsy soaked her feet in the river and reached into her backpack for a book. (It was *Think Your Blisters Away*, by Dr. Lincoln Dollar.) Becoming absorbed in her reading, she absent-mindedly swallowed three granola bars, countless handfuls of chocolate chips, and a packet of Bushwack Buster Oyster Purée.

Try to avoid situations in which parenthetical material occurs *within* parenthetical material, but if you can't, use brackets for the inner set. The problem arises most often in footnotes:

[8]It may be difficult to imagine why anyone would want to challenge the idea of insanity. (See, however, D. L. Rosenham, "On Being Sane in Insane Places," *Science,* 179 [19 Jan. 1973], 250–58.)

> The date would normally have gone into parentheses, but brackets are useful because they distinguish this material from the larger parenthesis.

Like dashes, parentheses should be regarded as a stylistic luxury. If your prose is full of them, you will annoy your reader:

x The "King of Swing" (I use quotation marks because in my judgment this was a misnomer from the first) thought he had to have a concert (?) in Carnegie Hall (where else?) before he could be accepted by the mass public.

> To read a sentence like this is comparable to being poked in the ribs several times by a drunken jokester.

BRACKETS [ ]

Brackets, which are often confused with parentheses, have a special function. They set off an insertion of your own words into a quotation:

• "My personal idols," said the forty-four-year-old defendant, "are Jerry [Rubin] and Abbie [Hoffman]."

Note that parentheses in place of brackets would imply a parenthetical remark *by the speaker,* not by the writer. Brackets are necessary to indicate that the quotation is being interrupted.

The bracketed, italicized word *sic* (Latin 'thus') is used to signal that a peculiarity occurs in the original and therefore isn't an error of your own. A misspelling, for instance, could be marked this way:

• "Beachcombbing [*sic*] no longer appeals to me," Wellington wired. "Send money."

But don't abuse this device to get a cheap advantage over an opponent:

x The Republican nominee, who describes himself as a "statesman" [*sic*], wouldn't know that World War Three had started if they didn't print it on the sports page.

ELLIPSES   ● ● ●

Material Omitted from Quotations

brief
omissions
The ellipsis mark, consisting of three periods separated by single spaces, is used to signify that something has been omitted from a quotation:

- President Clearance declared that he had "nothing . . . to hide," and that "secrecy in University affairs is . . . contrary to all my principles."

If an ellipsis occurs within a sentence, type three spaced periods preceded and followed by a space, as in the example above. If the ellipsis occurs just after the end of a sentence, retain the end-punctuation of the sentence and then add the ellipsis:

- Clearance was lavish in his praise for the University: "Everything is fine. . . . We're tooled up to turn out a real classy product."

Similarly, use four periods when omitting material that contains a period:

- "I resent the implication that nerve gas is being developed. . . . Besides, every safety precaution has been taken."

longer
omissions
If you are omitting a whole line or more of verse, or a whole paragraph or more of prose, mark the ellipsis by a complete line of spaced periods:

What have U done fer yr poets O Amerika?
I'm sitting here waiting fer a call from the Nash
Ional Endowment fer the Arts and Humanities.
Is it arty to keep me waiting Amerika?
Is this yr crummy idea of a humanity?
. . . .
How much longer must I borrow & steal?
O Amerika I hold U responsible fer this hole in the seat of my Levis!

quoting
sentence
fragments
When quoting a fragment of a sentence, introduce it with a clause or phrase that fits it into your own sentence structure. In that way you can avoid *beginning* the quotation with an ellipsis:

- Is Wratto referring to his high vocation when he writes that he is "waiting fer a call"?

Dialogue

Ellipses sometimes occur in dialogue to indicate incomplete or interrupted statements or thoughts:

- "You may be right," she said pleadingly, "but I don't really see why you can't . . ."
  "Oh, stop your infernal whining, will you?"

Weak Use of Ellipses

Some writers abuse ellipses as a semiapologetic way of getting from one topic to another. In the following example the ellipses don't indicate omitted material, but simply a trailing-off of thought:

x Wratto goes beyond the achievements of Olson and Creeley in many ways. . . . Listing them would probably be too tedious . . .

And some writers use ellipses as all-purpose punctuation marks, for example to punctuate the items of a series:

x Yogurt improves your morale . . . releases your inhibitions . . . postpones death . . .

APOSTROPHE   ,

Apostrophes are used chiefly in the formation of possessives (pp. 276, 317–318), certain plurals (pp. 370–371), and contractions (*won't, didn't, havin' fun*, etc.). The apostrophe also marks the omission of one or more digits of a number: *the winter of '65.* In dates expressing a span of time, however, the apostrophe is usually dropped: *1847–63.* And when page numbers are shortened, the apostrophe is never used: *pp. 207–91.*

In addition, apostrophes are used to form the past participles of certain verbs derived from nouns:

- Frazier was K.O.'d in the second round.
- Young parents these days are so Spock'd and Gesell'd that they hardly trust their own feelings about how a child should be raised.

In forming contractions, think of the two original words that are being joined. If you recall that *doesn't* comes from *does not*, for example, and that an apostrophe signifies a missing *letter* and not a missing *space,* you won't commit the spelling error *does'nt.*

HYPHEN -

A hyphen sets off certain prefixes, separates the parts of certain compound words, connects the parts of compound modifiers and the words in certain compound phrases, and indicates that an uncompleted word at the end of a line will be completed at the beginning of the next line. Problems of hyphenation are considered under spelling (see pp. 371–375).

QUOTATION MARKS 66 99

Quotation marks, which are usually double (" ") in American English, set off direct speech in dialogue, quoted material, certain titles, definitions and translations, and words given certain special emphases. (Single quotation marks are normal in British usage.) Whether single or double, quotation marks must come in pairs. Don't leave your reader wondering where a quotation really begins or ends.

Dialogue

Direct speech in dialogue is usually enclosed in quotation marks:

- "You get away from those chocolate chips right now, you nasty old bear!"

If a character's speech extends for more than a paragraph, put quotation marks at the beginning of each paragraph, but at the end of only the final paragraph. (This is the only exception to the rule that quotation marks must come in pairs.)

Quoted Material

When you are quoting material other than dialogue, you have to be aware that there are two ways of doing so. *Short* quotations — prose passages of less than about a hundred words or verse passages of a line or two — should be placed within quotation marks and integrated into your main text:

- "Take a loftier view of your blisters," writes Dr. Dollar. "Regard them as so many lucky opportunities to expose the real inner you."

Longer quotations should be *indented* so that they stand apart from your text; they are *not* enclosed in quotation marks.

A verse passage of two lines could be quoted in either of the standard ways:

- The poet tells us, "Ain't got my food stamps yet this month, & wonder if / Maybe this is fascism at last."
- The poet tells us:
      Ain't got my food stamps yet this month, & wonder if
      Maybe this is fascism at last.

   The virgule, or slash, in the first version indicates a line ending. It's necessary only in verse quotations.

When you do indent a quotation, reproduce it exactly, including any quotation marks it may already contain. But when you run a quotation into your own text and put it within quotation marks, any quotation marks already in the passage must become *single:*

- "The concluding lines of Wratto's 'Ode to Amerika,' " observes Pieper in *The Defenestrated Imagination,* "rest on an ingenious paradox."

In general, quotations-within-quotations require single marks. In the rare case in which a third set of marks must be boxed in, they become double (" ' "   " ' "):

- Orwell's friend Richard Rees informs us that "when Socialists told him that under Socialism there would be no such feeling of being at the mercy of unpredictable and irresponsible powers, he remarked: 'I notice people always say "*under* Socialism." They look forward to being on top — with all the others underneath, being told what is good for them.' "[1]

Certain Titles

The titles of essays, poems, articles, stories, chapters, and other units smaller than a whole volume are indicated by quotation marks:

- Joyce's story, "The Dead"
- Keats's poem, "To Autumn"
- Robert Alter, "The New American Novel," *Commentary*, Nov. 1975, pp. 44–51.

Note that this rule applies only to titles *being cited or discussed.* When you write an essay and supply a title for it (pp. 43–44), no quotation marks or italics should be added (except of course for *titles mentioned in your title*). Except in newspapers, where italics are generally not used, you should italicize (underline) the titles of whole volumes, without including quotation marks (see p. 392). If a poem occupies a whole volume, it should be italicized: *Paradise Lost, The Prelude, Paterson.* Names of newspapers, magazines, and journals are also italicized rather than placed in quotation marks:

* Biff felt sure that marijuana would soon be legalized when he spotted an article in the *Reader's Digest* called "I Owe My Life to L-Dopa."

Definitions and Translations

When a word or phrase is cited in italics and defined or translated, the definition or translation should be put within quotation marks:

* *Benevolent,* which means "desiring to do good to others," should be kept distinct from *beneficent,* which means "doing good to others."
* The German term for "a little" is *ein wenig.*

When a foreign word is immediately followed by a translation, you can put the translation in single quotation marks without intervening punctuation:

* *ein wenig* 'a little'
* They call the Fiat 500 *Topolino* 'Little Mouse.'

Special Emphasis

Quotation marks call attention to the words they enclose. Some writers use them in place of italics to indicate that a word is being treated *as* a word, not as the thing it stands for:

* The term "Iron Curtain" was coined by Winston Churchill.

It may be necessary now and then to put a word within quotation marks to show that you don't share a certain attitude:

* Nero's solution to "the Christian problem" also helped to cut the monthly budget for lion food.

But like several other devices (sarcastic capitals, derisive exclamation points and question marks, and bracketed *sic*'s), such quotation marks can become a bad habit. Some writers, for example, use them to slander anything they can't understand:

x Proust's "novel" consists of nothing but endless, tedious reminiscences narrated in a tone of pure snobbery.

Try to do without free rides; let your reasoning make its own case.

Quotation Marks Combined with Other Punctuation

In British usage quotation marks generally go inside other punctuation, but American usage is more complicated. You have to know the following conventions:

1. *Commas* and *periods* should be placed *inside* the closing quotation marks in all circumstances. You don't have to consider whether the comma or period is part of the quotation, or whether the quotation is short or long. Just routinely put the comma or period inside the closing quotation marks:

- Quoth the Raven, "Nevermore."
- "Nevermore," quoth the Raven.

2. *Colons* and *semicolons* are just as rigidly placed as commas and periods. They always go *outside* the closing quotation marks:

- "Nevermore": that's what the daffy bird said.
- Once again the bird said "Nevermore"; and I said, "Why do you always have to take such a negative attitude?"

3. *Question marks, exclamation points,* and *dashes* go *either inside or outside* the closing quotation marks, depending on their function. If they are punctuating the quoted material itself, they go *inside:*

- "Is it helpful to sit there all day and nag, nag, nag?"

The same marks go *outside* the closing quotation marks if they aren't part of the quotation:

- Do you think the Raven could be taught to say "I'll think it over and let you know in the morning"?

4. When the quotation must end with a question mark or exclamation point and your own sentence calls for a period at that point, the period vanishes:

- Grandpa used to listen to Walter Cronkite every evening and constantly scream, "Horsefeathers!"

5. Otherwise, the end-punctuation of the quotation makes way for your own punctuation. If the quoted passage, for example, ends with a period but your own sentence doesn't stop there, you should drop the period and substitute your own punctuation, if any:

- "I wonder why they don't impeach newscasters," said Grandpa.

    The quoted passage would normally end with a period, but the main sentence calls for a comma at that point.

6. In general, a closing quotation mark can be accompanied by only one other mark of punctuation. But an exception can be made for the rare case in which extra punctuation rescues a sentence from ungrammaticality:

- When the Dow-Jones Index fell through 600 — the market analysts had the nerve to call it a "technical adjustment"! — Stanley decided to become a revolutionary again.

   The quotation marks, exclamation point, and dash after *adjustment* each serve a necessary function.

7. When a quotation is accompanied by a footnote number, the footnote number should come *after* all other punctuation except a dash that may resume your own part of the sentence:

- Burgess finds "no substance to these charges."[2]

- Burgess finds "no substance to these charges"[2] — and I emphatically agree with him.

8. When a quotation is integrated into your text (without indention) and is followed by a parenthetical citation (pp. 233–234), the parenthesis should come *after* the final quotation marks but *before* a comma or period — even if the comma or period occurs in the quoted passage:

- Dr. Dollar says, "No modern home should be without a queen-sized trampoline" (*Aerobic Kama Sutra*, p. 217).

9. But if the quotation ends with a question mark or an exclamation point, you should include it before the closing quotation marks and add your own punctuation after the parenthesis:

- "Should we in the education industry," Clearance asked, "allow ourselves to lag behind in the vital areas of packaging and promotion?" (*Times* interview, p. 18, col. 2).

10. When, finally, a quotation is indented and set apart from your text, the parenthetical citation follows *all* punctuation and is customarily given either in a footnote or on a separate line:

- I'm just sittin here washing television
washin telvsn
wshn t.v.
(yeah!)
wshn *teee veeee.*
             ("Ode to Amerika," ll. 13–17)

Fuller advice about citation is given in Chapter Eight.

VIRGULE /

A virgule or slash is used chiefly to separate alternatives *(the moon and/or the stars; the who/whom controversy)* and to indicate line divisions in brief poetic quotations that aren't set apart:

- Wratto informs us that he is "just sittin here washing television/washin telvsn . . ."

The virgule may replace a dash to show a time period covering parts of two successive years:

- During the 1980/81 school year Gertie began her study of the glass harmonica.

The virgule symbolizes the word "per" in expressions like *km./hr.* (kilometers per hour) and *ft./sec.* (feet per second).

PUNCTUATING BY TYPEWRITER

To see how the punctuation marks are normally typed and spaced, examine the typescript essay on pages 247–259. In addition, note the following points:

1. Place punctuation marks directly next to the punctuated word, without leaving a space. The one exception is an ellipsis in the middle of a sentence; leave one space before typing such an ellipsis *(hardly any . . . secrets)*.
2. Leave two spaces after each period, question mark, exclamation point, semicolon, and colon.
3. Leave one space after commas, closing parentheses, closing brackets, and closing quotation marks, unless other punctuation immediately follows the mark in question. In that case, put the two marks together without a space between.
4. Leave no space before or after dashes, hyphens, and apostrophes, unless the apostrophe ends a word and is followed by no other punctuation.
5. Dashes come in three lengths, depending on their function. A dash separating numbers is typed as a hyphen: *pp. 432–39.* As the sign of a break in thought, a dash is typed as two hyphens

with no space between: *Try it – – if you dare.* A dash standing in place of an omitted word should be longer. Use four unspaced hyphens: *He refused to disclose the name of Ms. – – – – .*

6. If your typewriter lacks keys for brackets, improvise by either
   a. typing slashes (/) and completing the sides with underlinings
      [ ].
   b. typing the slashes and adding the lines later in ink; or
   c. leaving blank spaces and doing the brackets entirely in ink.
7. Leave one space after each of the periods making up an ellipsis; but leave two spaces after the last period if you're beginning a new sentence.
8. Don't begin a line with any mark that punctuates a *preceding* word, and don't carry an ellipsis from one line to the next.

EXERCISES

I. Correct any errors in the use of periods and question marks (pp. 329–331):

1. Aunt Sophia was disoriented by the family reunion. Never having played frisbee with thirty-five people before.
2. He wondered if I would like to shoot the rapids with his novelist friend?
3. I am not sure—will you correct me if I'm wrong—that porpoises are more intelligent than raccoons.
4. She wanted her psychiatrist to tell her whether it was possible to get seasick in Iowa?
5. His fellow workers at the car wash did not seem very impressed by his Ph.D..

II. Correct any *comma splices* and *fused sentences* that you find (p. 333):

1. Henry James was fond of Italy, in fact, he wrote a whole book about its civilized pleasures.
2. This surprised Biff he had thought that Henry James spent all his time playing the trumpet.
3. Betsy studied hard, she hypnotized herself, she forgot to go to the exam.
4. She repeatedly tried but failed to keep her eyes open.
5. Finally she consulted a specialist in trance-breaking, however, after several interviews he decided she would be better off as she was.

III. Make any necessary improvements in the use of commas (pp. 331–341):

1. Animals, vegetables, and minerals, all get involved in the exciting game of "Twenty Questions."

2. September 1939 was a bad time to be in Europe.
3. But without a broad-brimmed hat or an umbrella, no one can go out in this tropical sun.
4. Airline passengers seem to prefer a safe trip with armed guards, to an unsafe trip without them.
5. They won't lower the taxes, merely because people complain.
6. Did you know that, the first baseball game played under electric lights occurred in 1883?
7. Whether the earthquake was caused by fault slippage, or by excessive drilling, couldn't be determined.
8. The nutrition expert voiced some doubts about a generation of American children raised on, "Crazy Cow, Baron Von Redberry, Sir Grapefellow, Count Chocula, and Franken-Berry."
9. One good reason for moving to San Antonio is that it's the cleanest city in the United States.
10. Every person, no matter how incompetent he or she may be at everything else is the world's greatest expert at deciphering his or her own handwriting.
11. The issue of 16 October, 1975 contained some of the finest prose he had ever read.
12. What Shaw called the most licentious of institutions, other people call holy matrimony.
13. Statisticians, who are slavishly admired by some people, and criticized as frivolous by others, have discovered that the taste for dill pickles declines after age sixty-five.
14. Most Americans it seems, suffer from aching feet.
15. Homemakers agree that soyburgers are the best, low-cost, high-protein, food to serve these days.
16. A porcupine has approximately 30,000 quills for your information.
17. As the press had expected the President announced on Friday that the price of steak, not gold, would henceforth define the value of the dollar.
18. In a house work is more tedious than in an office.
19. The one mystery, that I can't explain, is why Greg and Cher had to call it quits.
20. You Gertie are a woman of taste and sensitivity.

IV. **Correct any errors in the use of colons and semicolons (pp. 341–343):**

1. A penny saved is a penny earned: but rich people, I've noticed, tend to put their pennies into shrewd investments.
2. The planning commissioner said that in his judgment the new skyscraper had: "all the earmarks of an eyesore."
3. Special sunglasses have now been devised for skiers, some of whom suffer acutely from glare; for people who want to wear only one pair of glasses in sun and shade; and for others who, for whatever reason, don't want their fellow citizens to catch sight of their eyes.

4. The robber asked for only two things; her money and her life.
5. Biff told his teammates to watch out on the next play for one of the following: a quarterback sneak; a statue of liberty play; or a drop-kick field goal.

V. Correct any errors in the use of dashes, parentheses, brackets, and ellipses (pp. 344–348):

1. "Joe (Morgan) and Johnny (Bench) hit the long ball for us," said Sparky.
2. It is simply untrue, — and nothing you can say will convince me — that trees make wind by waggling their branches.
3. Although some researchers blame LSD use for damage to chromosomes, others (knowing that people who take LSD tend to consume other drugs as well), are now focusing their suspicions on marijuana.
4. He didn't want to accuse her of being forward with other suitors — after all, women were supposed to be more independent nowadays, but he couldn't help wondering why she had a toll-free telephone number.
5. The banker assured the judge that his trip to Switzerland with the missing $2,000,000 had resulted from "an unfortunate . . . . oversight."
6. Stanley issued an ultimatum which gave the world twenty-four [24] hours to get out.
7. "Since I want to try a mountain gig anyway," wrote Melody on her application form — "I might as well pick up some bread being a counciler (sic)."
8. She enjoyed sitting around the campfire ring . . . watching the smoke rise . . . after everyone else had gone to bed . . . and the fire had gone out.
9. Melody told the campers in her tent to be careful with matches, (she remembered her own early troubles) especially if they hadn't learned how to roll paper properly.
10. Every morning — because the camp director insisted on it, — she inspected each bed, but she hardly ever found anything she could use.

VI. Correct any errors in the use of quotation marks (pp. 349–353):

1. "We want a "G" rating for this movie," said the director, so I'd like you to stab her only in the throat and stomach."
2. Is it true that the witness said, "I refuse to answer on the grounds that my answer might tend to incinerate me?"
3. Stanley's most secret communiqués were signed *El Macho* 'the masculine one.'
4. The poet tells us a good deal about his life when he writes,
   "Counted up Fri. and saw I still got
   Four lids and two caps,
   One lovin' spoonful,
   Three buttons from Southatheborder,

Some coke but no Pepsi,
And a bottle of reds.
O Amerika we can still be friends fer a few more weeks."

5. Since he hoped to become a dog trainer when his football career was over, Biff was especially eager to read the article in "National Geographic" called *Sikkim*.

NOTE

[1]Richard Rees, *George Orwell: Fugitive from the Camp of Victory* (London: Secker and Warburg, 1961), p. 153.

PART V
FOR
REFERENCE

SPELLING 13

Misspelled words, like faulty usage and punctuation, can chip away at the trust you've earned through sound planning and persuasive reasoning. Some misspellings leave a reader wondering which word the writer intended; was it *affect* or *effect*, *council* or *counsel*, *loose* or *lose?* Others are clear enough in meaning, but still disagreeable to run across. Every reader—even one whose own spelling is fanciful in the extreme—expects writers to spell correctly and holds it against them if they don't. That, in brief, is why spelling should be of concern to you.

Though you may currently be having trouble with spelling, you mustn't think of yourself as doomed to being a bad speller. If you always look up doubtful words and keep a list of those that fooled you, you can gradually narrow the area of difficulty. Be conscious of spellings that look strange in magazines and books, and check them as soon as you can get to your dictionary. If the author was right and you were wrong, put that word on your list and come back to it from time to time. Even if you haven't finally mastered a word, you can recognize it as an item from your list and look it up there before using it. Test yourself periodically against the list, and adopt any tricks you can think of to memorize correct spellings.

Some words can be spelled correctly in more than one way. In general you can assume that the first spelling offered by your (American) dictionary is the one to use. Avoid British spellings (*centre, cheque, civilise, connexion, labour, programme,* etc.) and out-of-date spellings (*draught, mediaeval, encyclopaedia,* etc.) unless they occur in titles or names: *The Encyclopaedia Britannica.*

PREFIXES AND SUFFIXES

Most of the uncertainties about whether words have single or double letters *(withold? withhold?)* pertain to words consisting of a *root* plus a *prefix* or *suffix*. The root is the base: *hold.* A prefix consists of one or more letters that can be attached before the root to make a new word: *with.*

PREFIX + ROOT = NEW WORD
with   + hold = withhold

A suffix is one or more syllables appended after a root:

ROOT   + SUFFIX = NEW WORD
sincere   + ly   = sincerely
fool   + ish   = foolish
contagious + ness   = contagiousness

Note that a word can have both a prefix and a suffix:

PREFIX + FOOT + SUFFIX = NEW WORD
pre   + fix + es   = prefixes

Common Prefixes

If you know the meaning and spelling of commonly used prefixes, you have a head start toward correct spelling:

prefix	meaning	example
ab-, abs-	away from	abrupt, abstract
ad-	toward, to	adore
ante-	before	antecedent
anti-	against	antiperspirant
bene-	well	beneficent
bi-	two	bisect
bio-	life	biological

co-, col-, com-, con-, cor-	with	cooperate, collect, compact, consent, correlate
contra-	against	contradict
de-	down	descend
dia-	through	dialogue
dis-	apart, opposite	displease
dys-	ill, bad	dyspeptic
epi-	upon	epitaph
ex-	out of, from	exclude
extra-	beyond	extravagant
for-	away, off	forbid
fore-	before	forehead
il-, im-, in-, ir-	not	illogical, imprecise, inexact, irreplaceable
im-, in-	in	immerse, incarnation
inter-	between	intercept
intra-	within	intravenous
intro-	within	introspection
meta-	beyond	metaphysics
mis-	ill, wrong	mispronounce
non-	not	nonscheduled
ob-	against	obstinate
para-	beside, beyond, against	parachute
per-	through	perfect
peri-	around	periphery
post-	after	postpone
pre-	before	prefix
re-	again, back	regenerate
sub-	under	submarine
super-	above	supernatural
sym-, syn-	together	symphony, synthesis
trans-	across	transport
un-	not	unequal
with-	against	withstand

Common Suffixes

Suffixes are generally found on verbs, nouns, adjectives, and adverbs:

Verb suffixes: -ate, -en, -fy, -ise, -ize.
Noun suffixes: -acy, -age, -an, -ance, -ancy, -ant, -ary, -ate, -cy, -dom, -ee, -eer, -ence, -ency, -ent, -er, -ery, -ess, -ette, -hood, -ice, -ier, -ism, -ist, -ite, -ity, -ive, -ment, -mony, -ness, -or, -ory, -ship, -ster, -tion, -tude, -ty, -ure, -y, -yer.
Adjective suffixes: -able, -al, -ary, -ate, -ent, -er, -escent, -ful, -ible, -ic, -ical, -ile, -ish, -less, -like, -ly, -ory, -ous, -some, -ty, -ulent, -wise, -y.
Adverb suffixes: -ally, -fold, -like, -ly, -ward, -ways, -wise.

inflections as suffixes Most of the *inflections,* or changes of form that a word can take without losing its identity, may also be considered suffixes: *-ing, -ed, -en, -er, -est,* etc.

SOME RULES OF SPELLING

Since modern English derives from many languages, no rule can tell you with certainty how a given word is spelled. The best course by far is to tackle your errors one by one. As you list them, though, you may notice family resemblances among some of them: failure to double letters, extra *-e*'s in participial forms *(writeing)*, confusion between *-ie* and *-ei,* etc. When you find such a pattern, you should memorize the principle you've been violating and try to apply it self-consciously until it becomes second nature. Below are some of the most common principles. For now, just check the examples under each rule and see if they typify your own mistakes; there's no need to memorize the reason for something you're already doing right.

Single Versus Double Letters

words like address When the last letter of a prefix is the same as the first letter of a root *(ad + dress),* retain both letters:

col + league = colleague
con + note = connote
dis + similar = dissimilar
mis + speak = misspeak
re + enlist = reenlist
un + noticed = unnoticed

words like fitting and regretful If a word ends in a single accented consonant preceded by a vowel *(fit, defer, regret),* the final consonant is usually doubled when *a suffix beginning with a vowel* is added:

fit + ing = fitting
defer + al = deferral
regret + able = regrettable

But in those same roots, the final consonant is not doubled when the suffix *begins with a consonant:*

fit + ful = fitful
defer + ment = deferment
regret + ful = regretful

words like
bigoted and
handi-
capped

If the last syllable of a word is *not* accented, don't double a final consonant before a vowel suffix:

bígot + ed   = bigoted
démocrat + ic = democratic
quárrel + ing = quarreling
rívet + er   = riveter

But even a minor accent on the final syllable can call for a double consonant:

hándicáp + ed   = handicapped
oútfít + ed   = outfitted
sándbág + ed   = sandbagged

You can see the point of the rule if you try pronouncing the words without the double consonant: *handicaped*, etc.

words like
brutally

When *-ly* is added to words ending in *-l*, the *-l* is retained, making a double *-l:*

brutal + ly   = brutally
cynical + ly   = cynically
hypothetical + ly = hypothetically

words like
cleanness

Words ending in *-n* retain the *-n* before *-ness:*

clean + ness = cleanness
even + ness = evenness
open + ness = openness
plain + ness = plainness

words like
artful

The correct suffix is *-ful*, not *-full:*

artful
beautiful
rightful
wonderful

Change of Final -e, -ie, and -y

words like
giving and
courageous

Except for words ending in *-ce* or *-ge*, most words that end in a silent *-e* drop the *-e* when adding a vowel suffix:

give + ing = giving
note + able = notable
stare + ing = staring

In most words ending in *-ce* or *-ge*, the *-e* is retained:

courage + ous = courag*e*ous
peace + able = peac*e*able
singe + ing   = sing*e*ing

> Note how these spellings keep the -*c*'s and -*g*'s "soft" in pro-
> nunciation, like -*s*'s and -*j*'s. If the -*e* were dropped, the words
> would be pronounced "peakable," "singing," etc.

words like Most words ending in one or more consonants plus a silent -*e* (*haste,*
wasteful *late*) retain the -*e* when adding a suffix beginning with a consonant:
and
abridgment waste + ful   = wast*e*ful
shame + less = sham*e*less
vile + ly   = vil*e*ly

In American English, however, when -*dg* precedes the final silent
-*e*, the -*e* is usually dropped before the suffix -*ment:*

abridge + ment   = abridgment
acknowledge + ment = acknowledgment
judge + ment   = judgment

words like Most verbs ending in -*ie* change the -*ie* to -*y* when taking -*ing:*
dying

die + ing = d*y*ing
lie + ing = l*y*ing
tie + ing = t*y*ing

words like When one or more consonants precedes a final -*y* (*beauty, fly*) and
beautiful further letters are added, the -*y* usually becomes -*i:*

beauty + ful   = beaut*i*ful
crazy + ness   = craz*i*ness
fly + er   = fl*i*er
prettify + ed   = prettif*i*ed
rectify + cation = rectif*i*cation

> But note that *busyness* retains the -*y* so as to remain distinct
> from *business.*

words like When the first added letter is -*i*, a final -*y* is retained:
flying

fly + ing   = fl*y*ing
rectify + ing = rectif*y*ing

-c Versus -ck

Most words ending in -*c* add -*k* when an additional syllable beginning with -*e*, -*i*, or -*y* is added:

bivouac + ed = bivouacked
picnic + ed   = picnicked
mimic + ing = mimicking
panic + y   = panicky

Note how the -*k* in each case prevents a mispronunciation.

-*ie* Versus -*ei*

Remember the old jingle:

I before E
Except after C
Or when sounded as A
As in *neighbor* and *weigh*.

Thus:

I BEFORE E:
• achieve, believe, chief, field, fiend, niece, piece, shield, thief, wield, yield

EXCEPT AFTER C:
• ceiling, conceive, perceive, receive

OR WHEN SOUNDED AS A:
• freight, inveigh, obeisance, reign, sleigh, veil, weight

But note these exceptions among others: *either, financier, foreign, heifer, height, leisure, seize, weird.* The rule, then, can only jog your memory of a correct spelling; it can't tell you for certain whether a given word contains -*ie* or -*ei*.

FORMATION OF POSSESSIVES

Singular Nouns

Singular nouns usually become possessive by the addition of -'*s*, whether or not the noun ends in an -*s* sound:

• a *day's* work
• *Camus's* novels
• *Keats's* verse

optional -s But the -*s* after the apostrophe is optional when it might not be pronounced:

pronounced -*s*	unpronounced -*s*
Dickens's	Dickens'
Demosthenes's	Demosthenes'

You can follow either of these practices, provided you do so consistently. Meanwhile, you should automatically add -'*s* to all *one*-syllable words: *Jones's, Snopes's, Sis's, Wes's.*

unusual Even if you intend to make all singular nouns possessive by using
singular -'*s*, you should recognize certain exceptions. Where an -'*s* would
posses- make for three closely bunched -*s* sounds, the apostrophe alone can
sives be used: *Moses', Ulysses', Xerxes'.* And certain fixed expressions violate the -'*s* rule: *for conscience' sake, for goodness' sake, for Jesus' sake.* Some writers even omit the apostrophe in these phrases.

Of course, singular nouns can also be made possessive by a preceding *of: the work of a day, the novels of Camus, the verse of Keats.* Be careful not to add an apostrophe in such cases. (For "double possessives" in which *of* and an apostrophe *are* combined, see p. 317.)

Plural Nouns

Plural nouns normally become possessive either by a preceding *of* (*the views of Americans*) or by the addition of an apostrophe alone:

the Americans' views
several days' work

posses- But plural nouns that do not end in -*s* become possessive in the same
sives of way that singular nouns do:
irregular
plurals the children's room
those deer's habitat
three mice's tails
the alumni's representative

When such a plural possessive sounds awkward, change it to the *of* form: *the tails of three mice.*

Plural Possessives of Time

There is a growing tendency to drop the apostrophe in plural possessives of time: *two years parole, a six weeks holiday.* For the present, however, it might be wise to write *two years' parole, a six weeks' holiday.* The apostrophes serve a function in showing that the modified nouns in these phrases are *parole* and *holiday.*

Compound Possessives

In compound possessives, only the final name takes the possessive form:

Bradley, Beatty, and Long's anthology
Laurel and Hardy's comedies

But note that this applies only when the possession is truly collective. Compare:

• Bradley's, Beatty's, and Long's efforts were pooled in the task of compiling and editing the book.

The possessive forms are correct here because three separate *efforts* are being discussed.

Possessives in Titles

In some titles the expected possessive form is lacking: *The Authors Guild, The Merchants Bank, Finnegans Wake*. Don't "improve" such titles by adding an apostrophe.

Possessives of Pronouns

Pronouns that are already possessive in meaning take no apostrophe: *his, hers, its, ours, yours, theirs, whose* (see the chart on p. 278). Note especially the treacherous *it's*, which is the correct form for the contraction of *it is* but a blunder for the possessive *its*.

Some indefinite pronouns form the possessive in the same manner as nouns: *another's, nobody's, one's, somebody's*, etc. But some other indefinite pronouns can only be made possessive in the *of* form: *of each, of all*, etc.

Awkward Possessives

Certain problems of spelling possessives can't be satisfactorily resolved at all. For example, how should you form the possessive of a noun that's followed by a parenthesis? Is it *Mrs. Jones (née Davis)'s coat, Mrs. Jones's (née Davis) coat*, or what? All possible versions are awkward, except possibly *the coat of Mrs. Jones (née Davis)*.

Again, don't try to form the possessive of a word followed by quotation marks: *"The Dead" 's symbolism*. Resort to the *of* form: *the symbolism of "The Dead."*

And finally, watch out for unnatural separation of the *-'s* from the word it refers to. You can write *someone else's problem* or *the Queen of Sheba's tuba*, but you shouldn't write *the house on the corner's roof*. In that phrase the *-'s* is just too far away from the word that "possesses" it, *house*. Once again, a timely recourse to *of* can rescue you: *the roof of the house on the corner*. And note that inanimate (nonliving) nouns often make awkward possessives. Instead of *the page's bottom*, write *the bottom of the page*.

FORMATION OF PLURALS

Regular and Irregular Plurals

Most nouns become plural by the addition of *-s* or (if the plural form is pronounced with an extra syllable) *-es: hats, dishes*. Some nouns don't follow either pattern:

a. *-en plurals:* children, oxen;
b. *unchanged plurals:* deer, fish, mink, series, sheep, swine;
c. *vowel-changing plurals:* feet, geese, lice, men, mice, teeth, women.

Nouns Ending in a Vowel plus -y, a Consonant plus -y; Names Ending in -y

Nouns ending in a vowel plus *-y* usually form the plural by adding *-s: bays, boys, keys, trays*.

Nouns ending in a consonant plus *-y* usually form the plural by changing *-y* to *-i* and adding *-es: berries, constabularies, emergencies, companies*.

But names ending in *-y* become plural by adding *-s: Bundys, Connallys, Kennedys, Rubys*. A few names of places do change *-y* to *-ies: Alleghenies, Rockies*.

Nouns Ending in -o

Nouns ending in a vowel plus *-o* become plural by adding *-s: patios, studios*. Most nouns ending in a consonant plus *-o* become plural by adding *-es: potatoes, vetoes*. But some words flout the rule (*solos, pianos, tyros, sopranos*), and some others have alternative plurals: *cargos, cargoes; zeros, zeroes*. Where your dictionary lists two forms, adopt the first.

Compound Nouns

Most compound nouns—that is, nouns consisting of more than one word—form the plural by adding *-s* to the final word: *cross-examinations, fire fighters, head starts*. But when the first word is the most significant one, it takes the plural form: *mothers-in-law, men-of-war, secretaries-general, senators-elect.*

Nouns Ending in *-ful*

These become plural by adding *-s* to the end: *cupfuls, shovelfuls, spoonfuls.*

Nouns with Foreign Plural Forms

A number of words taken from foreign languages, especially from Greek and Latin, retain their foreign plural forms. Some have also acquired English plural forms, and thus have two plural spellings. The rule for deciding which plural to use is: look it up! Even so, the dictionary can't settle your doubts in all cases. It won't tell you, for example, that the plural of *appendix* is *appendixes* if you're referring to the organ, but either *appendixes* or *appendices* if you mean supplementary sections at the end of books. Similarly, alphabetical guides are always *indexes*, but abstract indicators such as the rate of unemployment are sometimes *indices*. A bug has *antennae* but television sets are usually said to have *antennas. Formulas* are proposed for peace and integration, but chemists devise either *formulas* or *formulae. Mediums* who chat with the departed sometimes make guest appearances on the *media.* You have to trust your sense of current usage in making such choices.

When in doubt, you should lean toward the English plural. It's likely to sound less pretentious, and it won't risk an embarrassing mistake. Thus you can always write *apparatuses*, but if you want to get fancy and write *apparati* you will regret it. There's no such form; the Latin plural is *apparatus.* The same caution applies to *afflatus, conspectus, hiatus, impetus, nexus, prospectus,* and *status. Cactuses, curriculums, maximums, minimums, radiuses, sanatoriums, sanitariums,* and *syllabuses* are acceptable for all purposes. But we do still speak of social *strata*, spinal *vertebrae, data* (the singular should be *datum*), *criteria* (the singular must be *criterion*), and *phenomena* (the singular must be *phenomenon*). A few words that look plural are in fact singular; *kudos*, for example, is singular and shouldn't be used in a plural sense at all.

Greek and Latin derivatives ending in *-is* do show a high consistency. They regularly change *-is* to *-es: analyses, crises, parentheses, theses.*

Letters and Figures

Letters and figures usually become plural by the addition of *-'s:*

• Hester was rapidly losing whatever fondness she might once have felt for capital *A*'s.

- Now that the postal rates have gone up again, do you think we can expect a closeout sale on 11's?

Some writers omit the apostrophe and give the plurals as *As, 11s*. But this can make for confusion; *As*, for example, looks too much like a two-letter word. It's better to use *-'s* consistently.

Words Considered *as* Words

Whole words can be given the plural form *-'s* if you're trying to indicate that they *are* words:

- I hired you as my yes man, but in this memorandum of yours I find four *no*'s.

   Note how the italicizing of the isolated word, but not of the *-'s*, helps to make the writer's meaning clear.

HYPHENATION

Only your dictionary can tell you whether, and at what point, many terms should be hyphenated. However, the following survey of problems offers some general guidelines:

Word Division at the End of a Line

In a manuscript or typescript, where right-hand margins are uneven, the problem of hyphenation can be dodged. Just end each line with the last word that you can *complete*. Your reader will never know or care whether you are someone who finds it hard to divide words at the right junctures. But if you find that you must divide a word, do so only at one of the syllable (speech segment) breaks as marked in a dictionary.
   Observe these further conventions:

1. Never divide a one-syllable word, even if you might manage to pronounce it as two syllables (*rhythm, schism*).
2. Don't leave one letter stranded at the end of a line (*o-ver, i-dea*), and don't leave a solitary letter for the beginning of the next line (*Ontari-o, seed-y*).
3. If a word is already hyphenated, divide it only at the fixed hyphen. Avoid *self-con-scious, ex-Pre-mier*.
4. You can anticipate what the dictionary will say about word division by remembering that:

    a. Double consonants are usually separated: *ar-rogant, inef-fable*.

    b. But when the double consonants come just before a suffix, the division falls *after* the double consonants: *stall-ing, kiss-able*.

    c. When a word has *acquired* a double consonant in adding a suffix, the second consonant belongs to the suffix: *bet-ting, fad-dish*.

Prefixes

Hyphens are used to separate certain prefixes from the root words to which they are attached:

all-, ex-, self-

Words beginning with *all-, ex-,* and *self-,* when these are prefixes, are hyphenated after the prefix:

all-powerful
ex-minister
self-motivated

Note that in *selfhood, selfish, selfless,* and *selfsame* the accented syllable *self* isn't a true prefix, and no hyphen is called for.

prefixes with names

Prefixes before a name are always hyphenated:

pro-Carter
un-American
anti-Chinese

words like anti-intellectual and cooperate

Prefixes ending with a vowel sometimes take a hyphen if they are followed by a vowel, especially if the two vowels are the same:

anti-intellectual
co-op
semi-invalid

The hyphen prevents ambiguity and mispronunciation, as in *coop*.

But prefixed terms that are very common are less likely to be misconstrued, and many double vowels remain unhyphenated:

cooperate
coordinate
preempt
reeducate

You will find good dictionaries in some disagreement with each other about such words. Some dictionaries prefer hyphens in most double-vowel situations; some have all but abolished the convention; and some recommend a dieresis mark over the second vowel to show that it's separately pronounced: *reëducate.* In contemporary prose, however, you won't come across many instances of the dieresis.

hyphenate to avoid confusion

Certain words are sometimes hyphenated because they would otherwise look identical to very different words:

- If you don't *re-sort* the laundry, I'll have to resort to buying new underwear at the resort.
- Mystic Mandala Village, an authentic *re-creation* of a hippie commune, is being advertised as a future center of recreation.
- Having run in the Olympics, she had a *run-in* with the Rules Committee about pep pills.

constructions like pre- and postwar

When a modifier occurs with two alternative prefixes, the first prefix often stands alone with a hyphen.

- There was quite a difference between *pre-* and postwar prices.
- *Pro-* and antifascist students battled openly in the streets of Rome.

Note that the first prefix takes a hyphen even if it wouldn't have one when joined to the root word.

Compound Nouns

Many compound nouns (nouns formed from more than one word) are hyphenated: *bull's-eye, city-state, poet-philosopher, point-blank, secretary-treasurer,* etc. Many others, however, are written as separate words (*fire fighter, head start, ice cream, oil spill,* etc.) or as single unhyphenated words (*earring, milkmaid, scofflaw, scoutmaster, underwriter,* etc.). As compound terms become familiar with long use, they tend to drop their hyphens. The dictionary can guide you in individual cases of doubt—though dictionaries themselves will differ somewhat over various words.

Among the compound nouns that are hyphenated, many contain prepositions: *good-for-nothing, jack-in-the-box, man-of-war, mother-of-pearl, son-in-law,* etc. The hyphenation shows that the prepositional phrase is part of the thing named, not part of the rest of the sentence. Compare:

- She had a *son-in-law.*
- She had a daughter in medicine and a *son in law.*

Compound Modifiers

A compound modifier (containing more than one word) is usually hyphenated if it *precedes* the modified term:

before modified term: well-trained

a *well-trained* philosopher
an *out-of-work* barber

The hyphens are useful because they shift attention to the real noun: not a *well*, but a *philosopher*.

after modified term: well trained

But no ambiguity is likely when a compound modifier *follows* the modified term, and in this position the hyphen usually disappears:

- The philosopher was *well trained.*
- A barber *out of work* is bound to resent people who cut their own hair.

modifiers like barely suppressed

When a compound modifier contains an adverb in the *-ly* form, it doesn't have to be hyphenated in any position. The adverb, clearly identifiable *as* an adverb, does the hyphen's work of signaling that the real noun comes later:

a barely suppressed gasp
an openly polygamous chieftain
the hypocritically worded note of protest

modifiers like fast-developing

Adverbs lacking the *-ly* form are another matter: *the fast-developing crisis, a deep-boring bit,* etc.

modifiers with fixed hyphens

If a modifier is hyphenated in the dictionary, it remains hyphenated in all positions:

- She was an *even-tempered* instructor.
- She was *even-tempered.*

Compound Numbers

hyphenate numbers twenty-one to ninety-nine

Numbers twenty-one to ninety-nine, when written out, are hyphenated, even when they form part of a large number:

- Her waist was a perfect *forty-eight.*
- Two hundred *seventy-five* years ago there was an Indian burial mound on the site of this beautiful Texaco station.

Note that *and* isn't a recognized part of any whole number. Strictly speaking, *two hundred and seventy-five years ago* would be incorrect.

fractions with and without hyphens Fractions are hyphenated when they're used as modifiers, otherwise not:

AS MODIFIER:
• The jug of Thunderbird was *seven-eighths* empty at the end of the party.

Seven-eighths modifies *empty.*

NOT AS MODIFIER:
• *Seven eighths* of all adults have experimented with such dangerous drugs as nicotine, caffeine, and alcohol.

The fraction serves as the subject of the verb *have experimented.*

But many people ignore this rule, and by now it's debatable whether the commoner fractions such as *two thirds* and *one quarter* ever need to be hyphenated.

hyphens with compound fractions Don't add an extra hyphen to compound fractions such as these:

three seventy-thirds
twenty-one forty-sevenths

Hyphens after *three* and *twenty-one* would blur the distinction between the numerator and the denominator in each case.

Connection of Numbers

Hyphens are used to connect numbers expressing a range:

pages 136–198
the period September 11–October 4

In such cases the hyphen means *between.* It's therefore redundant to write *the period between September 11–October 4.*

COMMONLY MISSPELLED WORDS

The following list contains many of the words most frequently misspelled by college students. Take some time to scan it. If you never misspell any of these words, you're a remarkably good speller. Any spellings that do look unfamiliar to you should be added to your own list and reviewed from time to time. The abbreviation *cf.* means "compare."

abridgment

absence

absorption

academy

accelerate

accept *(take), cf.* except

access *(availability), cf.* excess

accessible

accident, accidentally

accommodate

accompaniment

accumulate

accustom, accustomed

achieve, achievement

acknowledgment

acquire

acquit, acquitted

address

advice (noun), advise (verb)

affect (verb, *influence*), *cf.* effect

aggravate, aggravated

aggress, aggressive, aggression

aging

alcohol

all right

allege

alley *(passage), cf.* ally

allude *(refer), cf.* elude

allusion *(reference), cf.* illusion ·

ally *(associate), cf.* alley

almost

already

altar (of a church), alter *(change)*

altogether

always

analysis, analyses (plural)

analyze

angel *(spirit),* angle (in geometry)

anonymous, anonymity

apiece

apparent

appreciate, appreciation

appropriate

approximate

aquatic

argue, arguing

argument

arithmetic

ascent *(climb), cf.* assent

assassin, assassination

assent *(agreement), cf.* ascent

assistant, assistance

athletic, athletics

attendance

bachelor

balloon

barbiturate

bare *(naked),* bear *(carry)*

beautiful

beggar

beginner, beginning

belief, believe

benefit, benefited, benefiting

besiege

biased

bigoted

biscuit

born *(brought into being),*
    borne *(carried)*

boundary

bourgeois, bourgeoisie

breadth *(width),* breath (noun),
    breathe (verb)

bridal *(of a bride),* bridle *(of a horse)*

bulletin

buoyant

bureau

bureaucracy, bureaucratic

burglar

bus

business *(job),* busyness *(being busy)*

cafeteria

calendar

camouflage

cannon *(gun),* canon *(law)*

canvas *(fabric),* canvass *(solicit)*

capital *(city),* capitol *(state house)*

careful

carriage

category

ceiling

cemetery

censor *(forbid publication),*
    censure *(criticize)*

certain

changeable

characteristic

chastise

chief

chimneys

choose *(select)*, chose (past tense)
chord *(tones)*, *cf.* cord
cite *(mention)*, *cf.* sight, site
climactic *(of a climax)*,
  climatic *(of a climate)*
coarse *(rough)*, *cf.* course
cocoa
coconut
collaborate
colonel
colossal
column
commit, commitment
committee
competent
competition
complementary *(matching)*, *cf.*
  complimentary
complexion
complimentary *(flattering)*, *cf.*
  complementary
concede
conceive, conceivable
concomitant
condemn
conferred
confidant *(recipient of secrets)*,
  confidante *(female confidant)*,
  confident *(assured)*
conqueror
conscience
conscientious
conscious
consensus
consistent, consistency
consummate
control, controlled, controlling
controversy
coolly
cord *(rope)*, *cf.* chord
corollary
correlate
corroborate
counterfeit
course *(direction)*, *cf.* coarse
courtesy, courteous
criticism, criticize
curiosity
currant *(raisin)*, current *(flow, present)*

cylinder
dealt
debatable, debater
deceive
defendant
defense
definite, definitely
democracy
dependent
descendant *(offspring)*, descendent
  (going down)
descent *(lowering)*, *cf.* dissent
desirable
despair
desperate, desperation
destroy
develop, development
die, dying *(expiring)*, *cf.* dye
dilapidated
dilemma
diminution
disappear
disappoint
disastrous
discernible
disciple
discipline
dispensable
dissent *(disagreement)*, *cf.* descent
dissipate
divide
divine
doctor
dominant
drunkenness
dual *(double)*, duel *(fight)*
duly
dye, dyeing *(coloring)*, *cf.* die
echoes
ecstasy
effect (verb, *accomplish;* noun, *result)*,
  cf. affect
efficient
eighth
elicit *(draw forth)*, *cf.* illicit
eliminate
elude *(evade)*, *cf.* allude
emanate
embarrass, embarrassed,
  embarrassing

embodiment
enemy
enthusiasm, enthusiastic
envelop (verb), envelope (noun)
environment
equip, equipped, equipment
equivalent
especially
evenness
everybody
evidently
exaggerate
exceed
excellent, excellence
except *(omit, omitting)*, *cf.* accept
excerpt
excess *(too much)*, *cf.* access
excruciating
exercise
exhaust
exhilarate
existence
exorbitant
expel
expense
experiment
extraordinary
fallacy
familiar
fascinate
fascist
faze *(daunt)*, *cf.* phase
February
fiend
fiery
finally
forbear *(refrain)*, forebear *(ancestor)*
forehead
foreign
foresee, foreseeable
foreword *(preface)*, *cf.* forward
forfeit
forgo
forward *(ahead)*, *cf.* foreword
friend
fulfill
fulsome
fundamental
futilely
gases

gauge
genealogy
germane
ghost
glamour, glamorous
goddess
government
governor
grammar, grammatically
greenness
grievance, grievous
gruesome
guarantee
guard
guidance
handkerchief
hangar (for airplanes), hanger
  (for coats)
harangue
harass
height
heroes
hindrance
hoping
hundred
hygiene
hypocrisy
idiosyncrasy
ignorance, ignorant
illicit *(unlawful)*, *cf.* elicit
illusion *(deception)*, *cf.* allusion
imagery
immediate
impel
inadvertent
inasmuch as
incidentally
incredible
independent, independence
indestructible
indispensable
infinitely
inflammable
influential
innuendo
inoculate
insistence, insistent
insofar as
intelligence, intelligent
interference, interfered, interfering

interpretation

interrupt

intramural

intransigence, intransigent

inveigh

irrefutable, irrefutably

irrelevant

irreparable, irreparably

irreplaceable, irreplaceably

irresistible, irresistibly

its *(belonging to it)*

it's *(it is)*

jeopardy

judgment

knowledge, knowledgeable

laboratory

laid

languor

lead (noun, *metal;* verb, *conduct*),
  led (past tense of verb *lead*)

legitimate

leisure

length

lessen *(reduce),* lesson *(teaching)*

liaison

library

license

lightening (participle), lightning (noun)

likelihood

lily, lilies

lineage

loath *(reluctant),* loathe *(despise),*
  loathsome

loneliness

loose *(slack),* lose *(mislay)*

lying

maintenance

maneuver

mantel *(shelf),* mantle *(cloak)*

manual

marriage

marshal (verb and noun), marshaled,
  marshaling

material *(pertaining to matter),*
  materiel *(supplies, especially military)*

meant

medicine

mediocre

melancholy

memento

merchandise

metaphor

millennium

millionaire

mimic, mimicked

miner *(digger),* cf. minor

miniature

minor *(lesser),* cf. miner

minute

mischief, mischievous

missile

misspell, misspelled

moral *(ethical),* morale *(confidence)*

moratorium

mortgage

mucus (noun), mucous (adjective)

muscle (of the body), mussel
  (mollusk)

naval *(nautical),* navel *(bellybutton)*

necessary

nerve-racking

nickel

niece

ninety

noncommittal

noticeable, noticing

occasion

occur, occurred, occurring,
  occurrence

omit, omitted, omitting, omission

opportunity

oppose

optimist

paid

pain *(agony),* cf. pane

pair *(set of two),* cf. pare

pajamas

pane *(glass),* cf. pain

parallel, paralleled

paralysis, paralyze

pare *(peel),* cf. pair

parliament

particular

passed *(went by),* past *(previous)*

pastime

patent

peace *(tranquillity),* cf. piece

peaceable

peal *(ring),* peel *(strip)*

pejorative

perceive
perennial
perfectible, perfectibility
perform, performance
permanent
permissible
personal *(individual)*, personnel
  (employees)
perspiration
persuade
phase *(period)*, *cf.* faze
phony
physical
physician
physiology
piece *(part)*, *cf.* peace
plain *(level land; clear)*, plane (noun,
  level; verb, *smooth)*
playwright
pleasant
pleasurable
poison, poisonous
politician
pore *(scrutinize; small opening)*, *cf.*
  pour
portentous
possess, possession
pour *(spill)*, *cf.* pore
practically
practice
pray *(implore)*, *cf.* prey
precede, *cf.* proceed
precinct
predominant
prefer, preferred, preferring
preference
prejudice
prescribe
pretense, pretension
prevalent
prey *(victim)*, *cf.* pray
principal (adjective, noun, *chief)*,
  principle (noun, *rule)*
privilege
probably
proceed, procedure, *cf.* precede
professor
pronunciation
propaganda
propagate

prophecy *(prediction)*, prophesy
  (predict)
prostate (gland), prostrate *(prone)*
psychiatry
psychology
pumpkin
pursue, pursuit
putrefy
quizzes
rack *(framework)*, *cf.* wrack
rain *(precipitation)*, *cf.* reign, rein
raise *(lift)*, *cf.* raze
rarefied
rarity
raze *(destroy)*, *cf.* raise
realize
really
recede
receipt
receive
recipe
recognizable
recommend
refer, referred, referring
regretted, regretting
reign *(sway)*, *cf.* rain, rein
rein *(restrain)*, *cf.* rain, reign
relieve
remembrance
reminisce
repellent
repentance
repetition
resemblance
resilience, resilient, resiliency
resistance
restaurant
rhetoric
rhyme
rhythm
ridiculous
rigmarole
roommate
sacrifice
sacrilegious
said
satellite
satire *(ridicule)*, satyr *(woodland
  deity)*
schedule

secretary
seize
sense
sentence
separate
sergeant
severely
sheriff
shriek
siege
sieve
sight *(vision), cf.* cite, site
significance
similar
simultaneous
site *(locale), cf.* cite, sight
skeptic, skepticism
skiing, skis
smooth
soliloquy
sophomore
source
sovereign, sovereignty
specimen
sponsor
stationary *(still),* stationery *(paper)*
steely
straight
strength
strictly
stupefy
subtlety
succeed, success
succinct
succumb
suffrage
superintendent
supersede
suppose
suppress
surprise
symbol
symmetry
sympathize
synonym, synonymous
tariff
technique
temperament
temperature
tendency

testament
than
their *(possessive), cf.* there
then
there *(at that place), cf.* their
therefore
thinness
thorough
threshold
through
to *(toward), cf.* too, two
tobacco
too *(also), cf.* to, two
track *(path),* tract *(area)*
traffic, trafficked, trafficking
tragedy
tranquil, tranquillity
transcendent, transcendental
transferred, transferring
tries, tried
truly
two *(one plus one), cf.* to, too
tyranny, tyrannically
unanimous
unmistakable, unmistakably
unnecessary
unshakable
unwieldy
vacillate
vacuum
valuable
vegetable
vengeance
venomous
vice
vilify, vilification
village
villain
waive *(relinquish),* wave *(movement)*
weather *(state of the atmosphere), cf.*
 whether
Wednesday
weird
were (past of *to be*), we're *(we are)*
whether *(if), cf.* weather
whole
wield
wintry
withhold
woeful

worldly, unworldly   wreak *(inflict)*, wreck *(ruin)*
worshiped, worshiping   your *(belonging to you)*,
wrack *(ruin), cf.* rack   you're *(you are)*

EXERCISES

I. Spell each new word that is made with the indicated roots, prefixes, and suffixes (pp. 361–363):

1. un + natural	10. cat + ing	19. fudge + ing
2. mis + state	11. final + ly	20. outlie + ing
3. clan + ish	12. moral + ly	21. try + ing
4. bet + ing	13. wan + ness	22. pacify + er
5. hit + ing	14. wrath + ful	23. ply + able
6. cat + like	15. live + ing	24. bite + ing
7. wit + less	16. compose + ition	25. cut + throat
8. erotic + ally	17. debate + able	
9. pivot + ing	18. late + ly	

II. Spell the following words, inserting *ie* or *ei* in each case (p. 366):

1. p__rce	5. s__ge	8. c__ling
2. conc__t	6. y__ld	9. n__ce
3. sl__gh	7. s__ve	10. f__nd
4. h__r		

III. Give the alternative possessive form for each of the following (pp. 366–369):

1. of the victor
2. of the bystanders
3. for the sake of goodness
4. of a Pisces
5. of the children
6. of the louse
7. a journey of four days
8. the wives of the Yankee pitchers
9. the partnership of John, Paul, George, and Ringo
10. the fault of somebody

IV. Give the plural forms of the following words (pp. 369–371):

1. ox	6. woman	11. wrong turn
2. ax	7. alloy	12. chairman-elect
3. datum	8. ferry	13. forkful
4. radio	9. Murphy	14. phenomenon
5. wish	10. tomato	15. psychoanalysis

V. If it were necessary to hyphenate these words at the end of a line, where would breaks be appropriate (pp. 371–372)?

1. overripe
2. ex-Republican
3. passionate
4. butted
5. penning

VI. Correct any errors of hyphenation you find in the following (pp. 371–375):

1. selfsufficient
2. antiAmerican
3. semi-incapacitated
4. redesign
5. pre and postinflationary
6. suicide leap
7. father-in-law
8. an ill schooled student
9. The doctor was poorly prepared.
10. Teachers are under-paid.
11. a bad looking thunderhead
12. a finely-tuned violin
13. sixty-five days
14. a hundred-thirty-one times
15. a three sixteenths opening
16. four-elevenths of those people
17. forty-three eighty-ninths
18. a delay of between 8–10 hours
19. between pages 45–50
20. a completely unsettling experience

VII. Find and correct any misspellings in this passage:

In order to accomodate the widespread public desire for a crackdown on vise, the Police Department last year finaly undertook a vigorous program to supress some of the more noticable violations. One result was announced today by Cheif Paola, who reported the arrest of Clem Foster, seventy two year old café owner, alledged to have payed real money to pinball winners on his premisses. It was Fosters bad fortune to be placed under survaillance by Officer John Beck, himself recently aquitted of agravated assault in connection with his under cover impersonation of a Hells Angle.

Beck's asignment was to frequent Foster's Friendly Oasis in plane clothes, remaining on the look out for illegal occurences. The roll was an easy one for the immaginative and enthousiastic Beck, a life long pinball athalete, to assume. Before many months had past, Beck suceeded in inviegling Foster into giveing him a nickle for each free game on the "Hubba Hubba Hula Girl" machine — where upon Officer Beck removed his camoflage and effected the necesary arrest. Released on $5,000 bale, Foster now awaits trial, while Officer Beck is believed to have allready asumed a new disguise to protect the citizens of his precint.

14 OTHER CONVENTIONS

CAPITALS

---

first letter of sentence The first letter of every sentence or independent sentence fragment should be capitalized:

- *Are* you a Pisces? *Certainly* not! *Too* bad.

sentences within sentences Sentences within sentences customarily begin with capitals:

- Max asked Bessie, "*Why* don't we skip the tourist spots and just hang around American Express today?"
- I wondered, How am I ever going to finish this book?

But once in a while, words that might be construed as sentence openers are left uncapitalized:

- Max was curious. Who had invented that awful French coffee? *when? and* why?

By leaving *when* and *and* in lower case, the writer emphasizes that Max was asking a three-part question, not three distinct questions. Capitals would have been equally correct and more usual.

Note that indirect questions aren't capitalized:

- I wondered *how* I was ever going to finish that book.

sentences Sentences contained within parentheses should begin with capitals
within only if they stand between complete sentences:
parentheses

CAPITALIZED:
- Max and Bessie had a fine time in Moscow. (*They* especially liked shopping for used blue jeans and drinking Pepsi with Herb and Gladys.) But in Bulgaria Max missed the whole World Series because no one would lend him a short-wave radio.

UNCAPITALIZED:
- Dr. Dollar's best seller, *Be Fat and Forget It* (*the* publisher decided on the title after a brainstorming session with his advertising staff), has freed millions of Americans from needless anxiety.

statement Some writers capitalize the first letter of a complete independent
following statement following a colon, but some readers regard this as an error.
colon Play it safe and keep to the lower case:

- Dr. Dollar faced this dilemma: *should* he or shouldn't he appear on television and let people see that he weighed only 113 pounds?

quotations Capitalize the first letter of a quotation only if (a) it was capitalized in the original, (b) it represents the beginning of a complete remark, or (c) it begins your own sentence:

- Ben Jonson believed that "*Memory* of all the *powers* of the mind, is the most *delicate* and *fraile*; it is the first of our *faculties* that Age invades."

Neither *Memory* nor *Age* would ordinarily be capitalized in the positions they occupy here, but the writer wants to reproduce Jonson's text exactly.

- What Shelley considered immortal was "Thought/Alone, and its quick elements . . ."

The capitals are found in Shelley's poem.

- Bessie told Max, "*There's* nothing like a good American cup of freeze-dried coffee."

The beginning of Bessie's sentence must be capitalized, even though it doesn't begin the writer's own sentence.

- *"Citizen's* band radio" was the phrase Max kept muttering to himself as he walked through Paris, wondering how a civilization could have survived so long without the bare necessities of technology.

Max's phrase isn't a complete statement, but it begins the *writer's* sentence.

uncapital- When a quotation doesn't meet any of the three tests for capitaliza-
ized tion, leave its first letter in the lower case:
quotation

- Bessie said that she didn't mind the coffee's tasting like lentil soup, *"if only they would make it hot."*

The quotation is a subordinate clause, not a full statement.

titles In citing titles written in English, you should capitalize the opening
of works letters of the first word, the last word, and other important words. If articles, conjunctions, and prepositions don't occur in the first or last positions, they are usually left in the lower case. But prepositions of more than five letters (*through*, for instance) are usually capitalized:

- *Dr. Dollar Raps with the Newborn*
- *Eternal Youthfulness Through Organ Transplants*

The same rules hold for subtitles in English. Note also that the first letter of a subtitle is always capitalized:

- *Working Within the System: A Guide to Sewer Repair*

Foreign titles tend to follow different conventions; if you don't translate the title, use the capitalization as you find it on the title page.

names Names of people, places, businesses, and organizations are capitalized:

- William Wordsworth
- Louisville, Kentucky
- Marvelous Max's Junktiques
- American Broadcasting System

historical Specific events, movements, and periods are often known by capi-
terms talized names:

- the Bronze Age
- the Civil War
- the War Between the States
- the Romantic poets
- the Depression

adjectives
derived
from names

Most adjectives derived from names are capitalized:

- Shakespearean
- American
- Maoist
- the French language

times

Days, months, and holidays are capitalized, but seasons usually aren't:

- next Tuesday
- May, 1975
- Christmas
- Columbus Day
- next winter

ranks and
titles

A rank or title is capitalized when joined to a name or when it stands for a specific person, but it is often left uncapitalized in other circumstances:

CAPITALIZED:
- General R. R. Junket

UNCAPITALIZED:
- Two *generals* and a *colonel* were reprimanded for mislaying the B-52's.

Note, however, that some high offices are uniformly capitalized: *the Queen of England, the President of the United States, Secretary of Defense, Chief Justice of the United States.* (There's no such office as *Chief Justice of the Supreme Court.*)

groups
versus
groupings

Organized groups and nationalities require capitals, but looser groupings don't:

CAPITALIZED:
- Christian
- Hungarian
- Republican
- Women for Peace

UNCAPITALIZED:
- the upper class
- the underprivileged
- the peace movement

abbrevi- Abbreviations after a name are usually capitalized: *M.A., Ph.D.,*
ations *M.D., Esq., U.S.N. (Ret.).* There is no consensus, however, as to
whether *Jr., Sr., a.m.,* and *p.m.* require capitals.

directions Geographic directions are left uncapitalized, but specific places take
versus capitals. When faced with a word like *northwest,* think whether it
places refers in this case to a compass point *(northwest of here)* or to a fixed
place or route *(Northwest Territories, Northwest Passage).*

CAPITALIZED:
- Southeast Asia
- the winning of the West

UNCAPITALIZED:
- southeast of Tucson
- go west until you meet the oily surf

specific Specific institutions are capitalized, and so are their formal sub-
institutions divisions:

- Museum of Modern Art
- University of Chicago
- the Department of Business Administration
- Franklin High School

Subsequent, shortened references to the institution or department
are sometimes left uncapitalized:

- She retired from the *university* last year.

But *University* would also be correct here.

Note that articles, brief prepositions, and conjunctions are left in
the lower case, as they are in titles of publications.

general Institutions meant in a general sense aren't capitalized:
institutions
- a strife-torn *museum*
- Every *university* is threatened by anarchy.
- His *department* fired him because the students were too fond of him.
- He dropped out of *high school* to give all his time to chess.

sacred Sacred names are conventionally capitalized, whether or not the
names writer is a believer:

* the Old Testament
* the Bible
* God
* the Lord
* He, Him, His [pronouns of the Judeo-Christian deity]
* the Virgin Mary
* the Koran
* the Upanishads

courses Specific courses of study are capitalized, but general branches of
versus learning aren't:
branches of
learning
CAPITALIZED:
* Physics 1A
* Social Welfare 203

UNCAPITALIZED:
* He never learned the rudiments of *physics.*
* Her training in *social welfare* didn't prepare her for this.

family Family relations should be capitalized only when they are part of a
relations name or when used in direct address:
versus
names
CAPITALIZED:
* Everyone has seen posters of *Uncle Sam.*
* Oh, *Mother,* you're so old-fashioned!

UNCAPITALIZED:
* My *uncle* Sam wasn't the same man after the Dodgers moved to Los
  Angeles.
* You're the only *mother* on this block who objects to pierced noses.

different Sometimes a word has quite different meanings in its capitalized
meanings forms:

* The Pope is a *Catholic.* [He belongs to the Church.]
* Marjoe has *catholic* tastes. [His tastes are wide-ranging.]
* He became a *Democrat* after the President declared a national day of prayer
  for the Redskins. [He joined the party.]
* Tocqueville saw every American farmer as a *democrat.* [He believed that
  they all supported the idea of equality.]

ITALICS

Ordinary typeface is known as *roman*, and the thin, slightly slanted typeface that stands apart from it is called *italic*—as in *these three words*. In manuscript or typescript, underlining is the equivalent of italic type. The conventional symbols *rom* and *ital*, when used in correction of a manuscript or typescript, mean respectively "do not underline" and "underline."

Italics are used for certain titles, foreign words, scientific names, names of ships, words considered *as* words, and words bearing a special rhetorical emphasis.

titles   Titles of books, plays, films, newspapers, magazines, journals, and other works that form complete publications are usually italicized:

- *Mademoiselle*
- *The Golden Notebook*
- *A Streetcar Named Desire*
- The Philadelphia *Inquirer*
- *Paradise Lost*

Note that:

a. in the names of newspapers, the *place* of publication is usually left in roman type.
b. a single poem, if it was first published as a whole volume, is named in italics; if it formed only part of the volume, it is named in roman type, within quotation marks. This applies to the titles of chapters, essays, and short stories as well.
c. a work that was first published in a magazine may later be expanded into a whole book; or, if the book is itself a collection, it may bear the title of the story, article, or poem. Remember that when you print the title in italics (i.e., underline it on your typewriter) you are always referring to the complete volume, not to the item that gave the volume its title.
d. newspapers and magazines have their own conventions for identifying titles. Some publications use italics sparingly or not at all. If you *know* that your writing will be printed by a given magazine or newspaper, follow its own rules. Student papers, scholarship, and writing that may be submitted to various publications should observe the rules given here.
e. the Bible and its divisions are left in roman type: the Bible, the Old Testament, Leviticus.

foreign versus "domesticated" terms   Foreign words that have not yet been adopted as routine English expressions should be italicized:

- Dr. Dollar's *Weltanschauung* was a mixture of Dale Carnegie and P. T. Barnum.

• After four best sellers he was assured of *la dolce vita*.

But compare the following borrowed words, which are familiar enough to be printed in roman:

ad hoc	de facto
bourgeois	genre
cliché	junta
debutante	

Consult your dictionary for doubtful cases. Use foreign terms sparingly; they often sound affected.

Latin abbreviations Latin abbreviations are often italicized, but the tendency is now to leave them in roman. There's no need to italicize the following, for example:

cf.	i.e.
e.g.	q.v.
et al.	viz.
f., ff.	vs.

See pages 394–395 for the meanings of these and other abbreviations.

translations When translating foreign words, it's customary to put the foreign term in italics and the English one in quotation marks:

• The Italian term for "the book" is *il libro*; in French it is *le livre*.

See also page 351 for the use of single quotation marks in translation.

scientific names Technical scientific names should be italicized:

• Don't mess around with the threadtailed stonefly *(Nemoura venosa)*.

ships Names of ships are italicized: *Queen Elizabeth, Cristoforo Colombo.*

words as objects Words considered *as* words are often italicized:

• Bessie couldn't think of the Spanish word for *indigestion*.

Quotation marks serve this function equally well.

emphasis Italics can be used to impart emphasis to a word or group of words, but this device, if used too frequently, becomes a form of shouting. Try to resort to emphatic italics only when clarity demands them.

ABBREVIATIONS

Abbreviations are useful devices for saving space. Knowing their meaning, however, is only half the battle; you must also know where they do and don't belong.

main text   The words for certain things are generally *not* abbreviated in the main body of an essay:

a. titles: *the Reverend, the Honorable, Senator, President, General.*
b. given names: *George, Richard, Martha.*
c. months, days of the week, and holidays: *October, Monday, Christmas.*
d. localities, cities, counties, states, and countries: *Point Reyes National Seashore, Philadelphia, Westchester, Alabama, Bangladesh.*
e. *Street, Lane, Avenue, Boulevard,* etc.
f. courses of instruction: *Botany, Physical Education.*
g. units of measurement: *inches, meters, pounds, hours, pints.*

citations   Certain abbreviations do frequently appear in essays, but only in footnotes, parenthetical references, and bibliographies. These abbreviations are tools for referring to consulted works in the briefest space:

abbreviation	meaning
anon.	anonymous
b.	born
bibliog.	bibliography
©	Copyright
ca. or c.	about (with dates only)
cf.	compare (not *see*)
ch., chs.	chapter(s)
d.	died
diss.	dissertation
ed., eds.	editor(s), edition(s), edited by
e.g.	for example (not *that is*)
esp.	especially
et al.	and others (people only)
etc.	and so forth (not interchangeable with *et al.*)
f., ff.	and the following (page or pages)
ibid.	the same (title as the one mentioned in the previous note)
i.e.	that is (not *for example*)
introd.	introduction
l., ll.	line(s)

loc. cit.	in the place cited (in the same passage mentioned in a recent note)
MS, MSS	manuscript(s)
n., fn.	note, footnote
N.B.	mark well, take notice
n.d.	no date (in a book's imprint)
no., nos.	number(s)
op. cit.	in the work cited (in a recent note; but the page number here is different; cf. *loc. cit.*)
p., pp.	page(s)
pl., pls.	plate(s)
pref.	preface
pt., pts.	part(s)
q.v.	see elsewhere in this text (literally *which see*)
rev.	revised, revision; review, reviewed by (beware of ambiguity between meanings; if necessary, write out instead of abbreviating)
sc.	scene
sec., secs.; sect., sects.	section(s)
ser.	series
st., sts.	stanza(s)
trans.	translator, translation, translated by
viz.	namely
vol., vols.	volume(s)
vs.	verse, versus

Note that *passim,* meaning *throughout,* and *sic,* meaning *thus,* are full Latin words and are not followed by a period. (For the use and abuse of *sic,* see p. 346.) Exceptions: it's customary to use abbreviated units of measurement if they're preceded by figures *(986 m.p.h.,* but not *I want to know how many m.p.h.).*

acceptable in main text Some other abbreviations, however, are considered standard for any piece of writing, including the main body of an essay:

a. *Mr., Mrs., Dr., Messrs., Mme., Mlle., St.,* etc., when used before names. Some publications now refer to all women as *Ms.,* and this new title has rapidly gained favor as a means of avoiding designation of marital status.

b. *Jr., Sr., Esq., M.D., D.D., D.D.S., M.A., Ph.D., LL.D.,* etc., when used after names.

c. abbreviations of, and acronyms for, organizations that are widely known by the shorter name: *CIA, FBI, ROTC, CARE, NATO, UNESCO,* etc. Note that very familiar designations such as these are usually written without periods between the letters.

d. *B.C., A.D., a.m., p.m.* These abbreviations should never be used apart from numbers *(in the p.m.). B.C.* always follows the year, but *A.D.* usually precedes it: *252 B.C.,* but *A.D. 147.*

titles with names   In abbreviating titles attached to people's names, watch for two problems. First, beware of redundancy. You can write *Dr. Lincoln Dollar* or *Lincoln Dollar, M.D.,* but don't write *Dr. Lincoln Dollar, M.D.;* that says the same thing twice. And don't allow the abbreviation to stray from the name it is supposed to accompany:

x There were two famous Jameses, Henry and *Wm.*

x As the collection plate was being passed, the *Rev.* described how misers are everlastingly chained to the burning lake.

technical terms   Abbreviations of complex technical terms, or of terms that will be used many times in one essay, can spare monotony. *ACTH* is better in every way than *adrenocorticotropic hormone,* provided it's been sufficiently identified. It's customary to give one full reference before relying only on the abbreviation:

• The best investment Dr. Dollar ever made was in Holiday International Tours (HIT). The corporate philosophy of HIT agreed with his own views in several respects.

spacing   When the letters of abbreviations are separated by periods *(M.D.),* no space should be left between a period and the next letter. The one exception is the initials of a name *(F. H. Bradley).*

NUMBERS AND FIGURES

numbers versus figures   No universally applicable rules govern the choice between written-out numbers *(sixty-seven)* and figures *(67).* In scientific and technical writing, figures are generally preferred; newspapers customarily use figures for all numbers higher than ten; and in nontechnical books and journals, the usual rule is that figures are to be used only for numbers that can't be expressed in one or two words or a brief phrase. For your own essays, this last rule is the best one to follow. Thus you should write *forty-three pounds of lard,* but not *seventy-one dollars and twenty-eight cents ($71.28).* There may be *eighteen counties* and *sixty-eight precincts* involved in an election, but the winning candidate's tally shouldn't be given as *two hundred ten thousand three hundred ninety-seven votes (210,397 votes)*.

Note, however, that a mixture of figures and written-out numbers can be confusing if they all refer to quantities of the same thing. If *any* figures are necessary in such circumstances, *all* the numbers should be expressed in figures:

- The initial orbit was 39–125 miles from the surface of the earth.
- The astronauts' heart rates varied between 55 and 120.
- It was later discovered that they had hidden between 25 and 347 trinkets in the capsule for later sale as souvenirs.

A number beginning a sentence should always be written out. But if the number is a long one, find a way of recasting the sentence so that the number comes later; then it can be stated as a figure.

normal uses Figures are regularly used for the following:
of figures

    a. apartment numbers, street numbers, and zip codes: *Apt. 17C, 544 Lowell Ave., Palo Alto, Calif. 94301.*

    b. tables of statistics.

    c. numbers containing decimals: *7.456, $6.58, 52.1 percent.*

    d. dates (except for extremely formal communications such as wedding announcements): *October 5, 1974; 5 October 1974; October 5th.*

    e. hours, when they precede *a.m.* or *p.m.*: *8 a.m., 12 p.m., 2:47 p.m.* Whole hours, unmodified by minutes, are usually written out before *o'clock*, *noon*, and *midnight*: *eight o'clock, twelve noon.* Don't write *twelve-thirty o'clock.*

    f. page numbers: *page 76, p. 76, pages 76–78, pp. 76–78.* All these forms are correct, but the abbreviated ones should be saved for footnotes and parenthetical references.

    g. volumes, books (e.g., of the Bible), acts, scenes, and lines. (See p. 234.)

plurals Figures can be made plural by the addition of either *-s* or *-'s*, but the latter form is more common: *two 7's, many 10's.* Note that no apostrophe is used when the number is written out: *many tens.*

Roman In general, the only reason for using Roman numerals (*XI, LVIII*) is
numerals that together with Arabic numerals (*11, 58*) they can distinguish one set of numbers from another. (See p. 234 for typical situations.) Lower-case Roman numerals are also used to indicate page numbers preceding the main text of a book (*Preface, p. xi*).

The following list will remind you how Roman numerals are formed:

1	I	10	X	50	L	200	CC
2	II	11	XI	60	LX	400	CD
3	III	15	XV	70	LXX	499	CDXCIX
4	IV	19	XIX	80	LXXX	500	D
5	V	20	XX	90	XC	900	CM
6	VI	21	XXI	99	XCIX	999	CMXCIX
7	VII	29	XXIX	100	C	1000	M
8	VIII	30	XXX	110	CX	1500	MD
9	IX	40	XL	199	CXCIX	3000	MMM

cardinal versus ordinal numbers Numbers like *one, two,* and *three (1, 2,* and *3)* are called cardinal numbers; numbers like *first, second,* and *third (1st, 2nd,* and *3rd)* are called ordinal numbers. The choice between the cardinal and ordinal systems is usually a simple one, but differences between written and spoken usage do arise. You say *Louis the Fourteenth* but should write *Louis XIV;* you say *July seventh, 1962,* but should write *July 7, 1962,* or *7 July 1962.* When the year is omitted, however, you should write the date as an ordinal number: *July 7th* or, preferably, *July seventh.*

Note finally that ordinal numbers can serve as adverbs without the addition of *-ly:*

• Let me say, first, that . . . . Second, . . .

The *-ly* forms aren't incorrect, but they're unnecessary. The only plainly wrong choice would be a mixture of forms: *Firstly, ... Second, . . .*

EXERCISES

I. Correct any errors of capitalization (pp. 386–392):

1. Our most musical president was Harry Truman, who, after reading a review of one of his Daughter Margaret's concerts, threatened to beat up the critic.
2. Each year the Pelicans fly south to build their nests near the outfall pipe.
3. Realizing that her marriage was in trouble, Rose went straight to the lingerie department and asked if she could try on a Freudian slip.
4. She wondered Whether it was really necessary for the management to frisk people who lingered near the meat counter.
5. Stanley believed that the People, guided by himself and a few trusted friends, knew more about their true interests than any politician did.

6. Above the Sun and Moon (So the natives believed) lay a god who had been suffering from heartburn for a thousand years.
7. Harry was always hoping they would turn world war two into a movie.
8. It was in home economics 145 that she learned the difference between a pancake and a waffle.
9. For Christmas Rose gave her Mother doctor Dollar's latest volume, *Wit And Wisdom For The Terminal Patient.*
10. Bobo's idea of summer fun was to drain a trout stream so that there would be plenty of fish for the whole gang.

II. Correct any errors in the use of italics, abbreviations, and numbers (pp. 392– 398):

1. Most drunk drivers would find it difficult to count backward from 135 to twenty-one by threes.
2. He had only one reason for not wanting to ride — e.g., he was afraid of horses.
3. 40 dollars will buy an adequate dinner for 1 at that restaurant.
4. Four six'es are twenty-four.
5. The attack was planned for precisely 7:42 o'clock.
6. "Gone with the Wind" was the film that introduced profane language to the Hollywood screen.
7. Alimony was never an issue for the ex-wives of king Henry the VIIIth.
8. *The Falmouth Enterprise* is a typical small-town newspaper.
9. You can still get a sporty sedan, fully equipped with roll bars, seat belts, impact-absorbing bumpers, and collision insurance, for five thousand eight hundred forty-four dollars.
10. Melody thought that *A Midsummer Night's Dream* was the most realistic play she had ever seen.
11. She made an appointment with Dr. Calvin Gold, D.D.S.
12. The Titanic at its launching was the world's largest, and soon thereafter the world's wettest, ocean liner.
13. Over the loudspeaker came an urgent and repeated request for a dr.
14. Criminals are treated leniently in Rome if they committed their offenses during lo scirocco, the hot, dry wind that supposedly makes people behave irrationally.
15. He won the primary election on June 8th, 1976.

III. The following paragraph contains errors in the use or absence of capitals, italics, abbreviations, and numbers. Find the errors and make a list of your corrections.

No piece of criticism has ever been harsher, or funnier, than Mark Twain's essay, *Fenimore Cooper's Literary Offenses*, which can be found in a vol. called "Selected Shorter Writings Of Mark Twain." Twain asserts that Cooper, in novels such as *the Deerslayer*, *The Last of the Mohicans*, et al., has committed one hundred fourteen offenses against literary art out of a possible 115. "It breaks the record," says Twain. He proves that Cooper's Natty Bumppo, the indian Chingachgook, etc., perform physically impossible deeds and speak wildly different kinds of english from 1 page to the next. The attack is hilarious, but on a 2nd reading it can also be taken as seriously indicating Twain's allegiance to the literary realism of the later XIXth Century.

AN INDEX OF

15 USAGE

Important as they are, general rules of usage can't resolve many of the choices a writer must make between rival expressions. You may know, for example, that a verb should agree in number and person with its subject, but suppose you aren't sure whether the word in question — *research*, let's say, or *critique* or *author* — should be used as a verb at all. No rule, such as "Don't turn nouns into verbs," can settle the issue for you; standard written English is under constant pressure to admit new terms and habits that have arisen in popular speech, and many an accepted verb took its origin from a noun. You have to know how a typical educated reader would regard the *particular* instance at hand.

It isn't always easy to find such information. If you consult authorities on usage, you will find some of them distinctly more "liberal" than others in welcoming new practices into the written language. Some, for example, feel that the use of *data* as a singular term, or of *disinterested* to mean *uninterested*, or of *hopefully* to mean *it is hoped*, is now so widespread that further protest would be futile; others remain unswervingly opposed. What you want to know, of course, is not what pleases a would-be guardian of purity, but what the actual readers of your prose expect to find. Unfortunately, not even the most recent and objective dictionary of usage can keep pace with all such expectations.

The following Index of Usage copes with this fact in several ways. In the first place, the Index is largely based on a study of various dictionaries of usage, including one dictionary that systematically compares the judgments of the others: Roy H. Copperud's *American Usage: The Consensus.* (You can check that book for expressions not covered here.) Second, instead of always offering a simple *do* or *don't,* the Index occasionally alerts you to divisions of opinion. Third, its advice tends to be rather conservative, on the principle that a word offensive to no readers is always better than a word offensive to some. But fourth, the Index recognizes that there's such a thing as straining too hard to avoid a blunder. Where the "right" form sounds wrong to educated readers, you are urged to choose a completely different expression. The point of the Index is not to dictate eternal correctness, but to steer you away from mistakes and needless controversy.

Since the Index is meant for writers wondering chiefly whether to *use* or *avoid* certain forms, its labels are simple. Informal, colloquial, and slang words are all marked *colloq.,* meaning "Don't use in standard written English" *(S.E.).* Some entries, however, include references to the kind of jargon (pp. 109–111) illustrated.

The abbreviations on the following page appear in the Index.

adj.	adjective, adjectival
adv.	adverb, adverbial
ambig.	ambiguous, having more than one possible meaning
awk.	awkward
bureauc.	bureaucratese (pp. 110–111), bureaucratic
colloq.	colloquial, to be avoided in standard written English
compl.	complement
conj.	conjunction
coord.	coordinating
inf.	infinitive
intrans.	intransitive; the verb takes no object
jarg.	jargon (pp. 109–111)
jrn.	journalese (p. 110)
n.	noun
neg.	negative
obj.	direct object
p.p.	past participle
part.	present participle
plu.	plural
prep.	preposition, prepositional
pro.	pronoun
redt.	redundant, conveying the same meaning twice
S.E.	standard written English
sing.	singular
subj.	subject of a verb
subord.	subordinating
syn.	synonym, a word having the same meaning as another
trans.	transitive; the verb takes an object
v.	verb
x	marks an illustration of a typical mistake or awkward construction

a, an   Use *a* before words beginning with consonants or pronounced with initial consonants: *a usual day.* Use *an* before vowels: *an orange.* Words with initial pronounced *h*'s can be preceded by either *a* or *an*, but *an* sounds affected to many readers and often causes an unnecessary change in pronunciation of the next word. Write *a humble man,* not **x** *an humble man.* Unpronounced *-h* words take *an: an hour.*

Watch out for an extra *a* or *an* where it isn't justified, as in **x** *What kind of a hat is that?* In this sentence the *a* is wrong because *hat* refers to hats in general, not to the individual hat.

above (n., adj.)   Pedantic or legalistic in phrases like **x** *in view of the above* and **x** *the above reasons.* Wherever possible substitute *therefore, for these reasons,* etc.

absolute, absolutely   Too frequently used

as meaningless intensifiers: **x** *He is absolutely the greatest poet I have ever read.* The effect is insincere. Save *absolute* to mean *utter, unrestricted: an absolute monarch.* When you're tempted to write *I am absolutely certain,* ask yourself whether *I am certain* doesn't sound more confident.

A.D. Should precede the date: *A.D. 1185.* Note that it's redt. to write *in the year A.D. 1185,* since *A.D.* already says "in the year of our Lord."

adapt, adopt To *adapt* something is to *change* it *for a purpose: He adapted the Constitution to his own ends.* To *adopt* something is to *take control or possession* of it: *He adopted the Constitution as his code of ethics.*

admit, confess Save the latter for serious charges. A suspect *admits* that he's the hunted man, but may not be willing to *confess* having committed the crime.

affect, effect (v., n.) As a v. to *affect* is to *influence: This affected the whole subsequent course of events.* To *effect* is to *bring about: She effected a stunning reversal.*
    As a n. *affect* is a technical word for *feeling: The patient was flooded with affect during his anxiety attacks. Effect* is *result: The effect of the treatment was slight.*

afraid See *frightened.*

again, back Redt. after *re*-prefixed words that already contain the sense of *again* or *back: rebound, reconsider, refer, regain, reply, resume, revert,* etc. Don't write **x** *refer back.*

aggravate, aggravating Some readers object to these words in the sense of *annoy, annoying:* **x** *I had an aggravating day today.* Strictly speaking, you can only *aggravate* a condition that's already disagreeable; the v. means to *make worse.* Don't write **x** *You really aggravate me.*

aggression Beware of using this abstract term as a plu. sum of feelings: *get rid of my aggressions.* Keep *aggression* sing., and ask yourself whether you don't mean *hostility* or *ill will* anyway. People feel *hostile* toward specific others, but their *aggression* is either a hostile *act* or a general disposition to take the offensive, regardless of the opponent or goal.

ain't Colloq. for *isn't* or *aren't.*

all, all of Use *all of* only when items are involved: *All of the skillets were sold.* When there are no items to be counted, use *all* without *of: All her enthusiasm vanished; He was a hermit all his life.*

all . . . not; not all *All . . . not* constructions are often ambig.: **x** *All the tea in China is not worth exporting.* Does this say that *none* of the tea, or *only some* of it, is worth exporting? Try to do without *all . . . not.* For the meaning *only some,* you can use *not all: Not all the tea* etc.

all right, alright Only the first is S.E.

all that Colloq. in sentences like **x** *I didn't like her all that much.*

allusion, illusion, delusion The first is a *glancing reference: an allusion to Shakespeare.* An *illusion* is a *deceptive impression: the illusion of reality in laser photography.* A *delusion* is a *mistaken belief,* usually with pathological implications: *the delusion of thinking he was Napoleon.* Don't confuse *elusive* (evasive) with *allusive* (containing allusions) or *illusory* (deceptive).

along the lines of See *in terms of.*

alot A mistaken form of the two words *a lot,* which in turn are usually colloq.; see *lot.*

also Don't use as a coord. conj.: **x** *She had two cars, also a stereo.*

altogether, all together *Altogether*

means *entirely: She is altogether convinced. All together* means *everyone assembled: They were all together at the reunion.*

a.m., p.m. Shouldn't be used as nouns: **x** *at six in the a.m.* And they shouldn't be accompanied by *o'clock,* which is already implied.

among, between *Among* is appropriate when there are at least three separable items: *among his friends, among all who were there.*

Between can be used for any plu. number of items, though some purists think it should be reserved for two items (also see *between).* The real difference is that *among* is vaguer and more collective than *between,* which draws attention to each of the items:

• They hoped to find one good person *among* the fifty applicants.
• The mediator saw a basis for agreement *between* management and the union.

amoral, immoral Not syns. An *amoral* act stands outside the categories of moral judgment. Logic and actuarial statistics, for example, are *amoral,* i.e., unaffected by moral considerations. *Immoral* means *violating moral principles: His destruction of the files was thoroughly immoral* [not *amoral*].

amount, number If the items are countable, *number* is right: *a small number of crabs.* Reserve *amount* for total quantities that aren't being considered as units: *the amount of the debt, a large amount of trash.* The common error here is to use *amount* for *number,* as in **x** *The amount of people in the hall was extraordinary.*

analyzation A mistake for *analysis.*

and who, and which Don't use unless the sentence contains an earlier *who* or *which:* **x** *Everyone is impressed by Bobo, a*

man of action, and who can protect you from random violence in your neighborhood. A parallel structure (p. 319) is needed: *a man who acts decisively, and who can* etc.

angry See *mad.*

ante-, anti- The first prefix means *before,* the second *against: ante-bellum, ante-date; anti-Ford, antifascist.*

any more, anymore Only the first is S.E. Don't write **x** *They don't make disposable diapers the way they used to anymore.*

anybody, any body; nobody, no body; somebody, some body The first member of each pair is an indefinite pro.: *Anybody can see . . .* The others are adj.-n. pairs: *Any body can be dissected.*

anyway, any way, anyways *Anyway* is an adv.: *There's no hope, anyway.* Don't confuse this with the two words *any way: I haven't found any way to do it. Anyways* is always colloq.

anywheres Colloq. for *anywhere.*

apprehend, comprehend When you *catch the meaning* of something, you *apprehend* it: *I think I apprehend what you're driving at.*

When you *understand thoroughly,* you *comprehend: After years of study I still don't comprehend transformational grammar.* Note that an *apprehension* always occurs in a single moment, but a *comprehension* is usually more enduring.

apt, liable, likely Close in meaning. But some people reserve *liable* to mean *exposed* or *responsible* in an undesirable sense: *liable to be misunderstood; liable for damages. Likely* means *probably destined: She is likely to succeed. Apt* is best used to indicate habitual disposition: *Miss Fuller's cow is apt to kick over the pail.*

area See *field.*

argue, quarrel They can be syns., but *argue* has a special meaning of *make a case,* and this meaning has no overtones of quarrelsomeness.

around As a syn. of *about, around* is considered all right by some authorities and condemned by others. To stay on the safe side, write *about five months.*

as (conj., prep.) The subord. conj. *as* in the sense of *because* is often ambig.: **x** *As she said it, I obeyed.* Does *as* here mean *because* or *while?* Use *because* if that's what you mean.

Don't use *as* to mean *whether* or *that:* **x** *I can't say as I do.*

as, like *As* is usually a conj. introducing an adv. clause, and *like* is usually a prep. introducing a prep. phrase:

CONJ:
• As the *Maine* goes, so goes the nation.

PREP:
• Like General MacArthur, Melody was fond of wading.

In speech, many people use *like* as a conj. You'd do well to avoid it in writing, though: **x** *Like he said, . . .*

Note that when *as* is a prep., it differs in meaning from *like:*

• He works like a fool.
• He works as a fool [for the King].

as, such as Not syns. Don't write **x** *Santa's bag contained many toys, as ray guns, cluster bombs, and torture kits. Such as* would be appropriate.

as far as . . . is concerned If you're going to use this formula at all, it must be completed. Don't write **x** *As far as money, I have no complaints.*

as good as, as much as Colloq. when used for *practically:* **x** *He as good as promised me . . .*

as if, as though Equally proper. When they introduce a clause stating a condition contrary to fact, the v. ought to be subjunctive: *As if she weren't already busy enough, . . .*

aspect A much overworked term. Literally, an *aspect* is a *view from a particular vantage.* Moving around the object, you see different *aspects* of it. As a cliché, though, *aspect* has lost any sense of this physical basis and become a syn. of *consideration: the following eight aspects; The problem has many aspects.*

Aspect may be impossible to do without, but you should try to use it with at least a shadow of concreteness: *When the issue is regarded from this perspective it shows a wholly new aspect.*

assure, ensure, insure To *assure* is to *promise, give assurance: I assure you that I mean well. Ensure* and *insure* can be considered variant spellings of the same word, meaning *make certain.* Because *insure* has become associated with the selling of insurance policies, though, many writers prefer to use only *ensure* to mean *make certain: He ensured his family's security by insuring his life for $50,000.*

at the same time that Wordy for *while.*

at this (that) point in time Wordy for *now* or *then.*

author (v.) Widely used, but also widely condemned as colloq.: **x** *She has authored four novels.* Use *wrote* instead, and keep *author* as a n.

average, mean, median An *average* is reached by dividing the sum of quantities by the number of items. Four neckties priced at $3, $5, $7, and $9 have an *average* price of $6 ($24 divided by 4).

A *mean* is a *midpoint*. The *mean* between 10 and 20 is 15. (If there are only two figures, the mean and average are the same.)

A *median* is a *point having an equal number of items above and below it*. If the *median* income of American families is $10,000, the same number of people have incomes smaller and larger than $10,000.

Some writers object to *average* as a syn. of *ordinary:* **x** *He's just an average person.*

awake, wake, waken   The choice between these verbs is difficult. Try using *awake* to mean *become awake; wake* in the trans. sense of *wake* [somebody else] *up;* and *waken* in passive uses: *I was wakened at six.*

awhile, a while   *Awhile* is an adv.: *I worked awhile. While* is a n. in *a while ago.* The adv. is wrongly substituted for the n. in **x** *awhile ago* and **x** *worked for awhile.*

background   Overused as a syn. of *origin, reason, credentials.* In constructions like **x** *Give me some background on this,* it's outright bureauc. Try to use the word sparingly, and if possible with some sense of its concrete pictorial meaning in contrast to *foreground.*

bad   Don't use as an adv. meaning *badly* or *severely:* **x** *It hurt so bad I wanted to cry.*

basically, essentially, ultimately   These advs. all have legitimate uses, but all are overworked as vague means of emphasis. Delete them from sentences like **x** *Basically, he supports the Tigers;* **x** *Essentially, she didn't know what to say next;* **x** *Ultimately, we have to begin somewhere.*

basis, on the basis of   Overworked and often redt. **x** *She admired it on the basis of clarity* should be *She admired its clarity.*

being (part.)   Often redt.: **x** *The city is di-*vided into three districts, with the poorest being isolated from the others by the freeway. Either *with* or *being* should be dropped.

being as, being that   Colloq. for *because, since.*

bemused   Doesn't mean *amused,* but *bewildered.*

beside, besides   *Beside* means *at the side of; besides* means *in addition to. Besides her father and the groom, no one stood beside Susanna at the altar.*

better than   Colloq. as a syn. of *more than:* **x** *Better than half an hour remained.*

between   Can be used for more than two items (see *among*), but does require *at least* two. This rule is violated, for example, in **x** *Hamlet's conflict is between his own mind* and in **x** *The poems were written between 1956–58.* In the second sentence *1956–58* is one item, a period of time. The sentence should read *The poems were written between 1956 and 1958.*

Between always requires a following *and,* not *or.* Don't write **x** *The choice is between anarchy or civilization.*

between each, between every   Because *between* implies at least two items, it shouldn't be joined to sing. adjs. like *each* and *every:* **x** *He took a rest between each inning.* Try *after every inning* or *He rested between innings.*

between you and I   A mistake for *between you and me.* The prep. *between* requires an objective pro.

bi-   A treacherously ambig. prefix. It always means *twice;* but what is being doubled, e.g., in *biweekly?* If the weeks are doubled, *biweekly* means *every two weeks;* if the times are doubled, *biweekly* means *twice a week.* There's no way of deciding which sense a writer intends.

Consequently, you'd do better to find another phrase: *every other week, twice a week.*

bias Don't use as an adj., as in **x** *They were extremely bias.* The correct adj. is *biased.*

bored Followed by *with* or *by*, not *of.* Don't write **x** *He was bored of skiing.*

born, borne The first has to do with birth, the second with carrying. But note that pregnancy is itself a form of carrying: *She had borne six children.*

both Beware of redt. phrases such as *both alike, both agree, both together:* **x** *Both alike were upset.* Try *Both were upset* or *Both of them were upset.*

When two items are connected by *both,* the companion word is *and*, not *as well as: Both Ralph and* [not *as well as*] *Linda were upset.*

breakdown S.E. in the sense of *collapse.* But it's bureauc. in the sense of *itemization* or *analysis: a breakdown of the statistics.* Wilson Follett issued the classic warning about the possible ambiguity of *breakdown* and its derivatives; his example was **x** *This was a report on the population of the U.S. broken down by age and sex.*

bring, carry, take You *bring* something from one place to a nearer one. You *carry* something in any direction. And you *take* something from a nearer place to a farther one.

broke (adj.) Colloq. in the sense of *penniless.*

bunch, crowd (n.) A *bunch* is a dense collection of *things;* a *crowd,* of *people* or *animals.* Don't write **x** *a bunch of my friends.*

burglar, robber, thief A *burglar* breaks and enters in order to steal. A *robber* takes money from people by threatening or harming them in person. A *thief* is someone who steals, usually without the victim's knowledge. A dishonest bank teller, for example, may be a *thief* without being either a *burglar* or a *robber.*

but however, but nevertheless, but yet Redt. Don't write **x** *But yet I intend to resign.* Either *but* or *yet* would be appropriate alone.

but that, but what These are awk. equivalents of *that* in clauses following an expression of doubt: **x** *I don't doubt but that you intend to remain loyal.*

calculate See *figure.*

calculated See *designed.*

can, may Both are now acceptable to indicate permission. *May* has a more polite and formal air: *May I leave?*

can not, cannot Unless you want to italicize *not*, always prefer *cannot.*

case, instance Often used in a needlessly roundabout way: **x** *Who was to blame in the case of the plane crash?* Write *Who was to blame for* etc.

cause, reason Not syns. A *cause* is what produces an effect: *The earthquake was the cause of the tidal wave.* A *reason* is someone's *professed motive or justification: He cited a conflict of interest as his reason for not accepting the post.*

cause is due to Redt. Write *The cause was poverty,* not **x** *The cause was due to poverty.*

censor, censure (n.) A *censor* is an official who judges whether a publication or performance will be allowed. *Censure* is vehement criticism. *The censor heaped censure on the play.*

center around Since a center is a point, not a circle, *center around* is imprecise.

Center on or *center upon* would be better: *The investigation centered on tax evasion.*

character Often redt. **x** *He was of a studious character* means, and should be, *He was studious.*

childish, childlike Both mean *like a child,* but *childish* is usually scornful: *Why are you acting in this childish way? Childlike* emphasizes the better aspects of childhood: *a childlike innocence.*

class (v.) *Classify* is preferable. Don't write **x** *He classed the documents under three headings.*

climactic, climatic *Climactic* means *pertaining to climaxes, decisive: a climactic encounter. Climatic* means *pertaining to climate: climatic conditions.*

coed (n.) Why should there be a second-class word to describe female students? You can write that a college is *coeducational,* but *coed* is jrn. Note also that the word is technically misused when applied to students in an all-female college.

commence Almost always pompous for *begin, start.*

communication Pompous when used for *letter, note,* or *memorandum.*

compare, contrast *Compare* means either *make a comparison* or *liken.* To compare something *with* something else is to make a comparison between them; the comparison may show either a resemblance or a difference. To compare something *to* something else is to assert a likeness between them. (See also pp. 321–323.)

To *contrast* is to emphasize *differences: He contrasted the gentle Athenians with the warlike Spartans.* As a v., *contrast* should always be followed by *with.*

comprise, compose, constitute *Comprise* means *embrace, include: The curriculum comprises every field of knowl-* edge. *Compose* and *constitute* mean *make up: All those fields together compose [or constitute] the curriculum.* The most common mistake is to use *comprise* as if it meant *compose:* **x** *The parts comprise the whole. Is comprised of,* though frequently seen, is open to criticism: **x** *The whole is comprised of the parts.* Try *The whole comprises the parts* or *The parts compose the whole.*

concept, conception, idea The broadest of these terms is *idea,* and it should be the preferred term unless you're quite sure you mean *concept* or *conception.* A *concept* is an abstract notion meant to characterize a class of particulars: *the concept of civil rights.* A *conception* is a particular idea, often carrying a sense of error: *She had an odd conception of my motives.* Note that *idea* would have been suitable even in these examples.

concern (v.) Sometimes used fuzzily, as in **x** *The problem concerns how to win the election.* By changing the v. to *is* you can express the true relation between the subj. and compl.

concur in, concur with You concur *in* an action or decision: *He concurred in her seeking a career.* But you concur *with* a person when you agree with him or her: *He concurred with her in her decision.*

conscious, aware Almost syns., but you can observe a difference. A person is *conscious* of his or her own feelings or perceptions, but *aware* of events or circumstances.

consensus Don't use this n. unless you mean something very close to unanimity. And beware of the redt. *consensus of opinion* and *general consensus. Opinion* and *general* are already contained in the meaning of *consensus.*

considerable Colloq. in the sense of *many* (items): **x** *Considerable dignitaries were there.*

consist of, consist in Something *consists of* its components: *The decathlon consists of ten events. Consist in* means *exist in* or *inhere in: Discretion consists largely in knowing when to remain silent.*

contemptible, contemptuous Very different. *Contemptible* means *deserving contempt. Contemptuous* means *feeling or showing contempt.*

continual, continuous *Continual* means *recurring at intervals. Continuous* means *uninterrupted.*

contributing factor See *factor.*

convey Always trans. Don't write **x** *They conveyed that they were unhappy.*

convince, persuade Often treated as syns., but you can preserve a valuable distinction by keeping *convince* for *win agreement* and *persuade* for *move to action.* If I *convince* you that I'm right, I may *persuade* you to do what I recommend.

Observing this distinction, you'll have to avoid writing *convince to,* as in **x** *I convinced him to come.* Make it *persuaded.*

cope Somewhat colloq. when used without *with* and its obj.: **x** *He just couldn't cope.*

correspond to, correspond with *Correspond to* means *match; correspond with* means *exchange letters with.*

council, counsel, consul A *council* is a governing or advisory board: *the city council. Counsel* means *advice* or *attorney: The defendant's counsel gave him counsel.* A *consul* is a foreign-service officer stationed abroad: *the British consul.*

couple, pair *Couple* refers to two things that are united; it's colloq. when nothing more than *two* is intended, as in **x** *I have a couple of questions to ask you.* When you do use *a couple of,* be sure not to drop

the *of,* as in **x** *a couple reasons.*

Pair refers to two things that are inseparably used together: *a pair of skis. The Joneses are a couple, but they aren't much of a pair.*

Pairs tends to prevail over *pair* in the plu.: *three pairs of shoes.*

Verbs governed by *couple* and *pair* are generally plu., although a sing. v. might be appropriate in rare cases: *A couple becomes a trio when the first child is born.*

criteria Always plu.: *these criteria.* The sing. is *criterion.*

critique (v.) Some readers consider this bureauc. Instead of **x** *She critiqued the proposal,* try *She criticized . . . .* or *She wrote a critique of . . . .*

crucial Often used wrongly to mean *important.* Something is *crucial* only if it presents a decisive, momentous choice. Think of *important, critical,* and *crucial* as representing increasing degrees of urgency, and use *crucial* only when the milder terms won't do.

cute Colloq. for *pretty* or *clever:* **x** *a cute idea.*

data Opinion is divided over the number of *data.* You would do well to keep *data* plu.: *these data,* not *this data.* The sing., rarely seen, is *datum; fact* or *figure* would sound more natural.

deduce, deduct Both form the same n., *deduction,* but *deduce* means *derive* or *infer* and *deduct* means *take away* or *detract.*

defect, deficiency A *defect* is a *fault* or *imperfection;* a *deficiency* is an *incompleteness.* If someone is *deficient,* it's in relation to certain standards: *His spelling was deficient.* A *defect* is a more permanent flaw: *His main defect is his stubbornness.*

definite, definitive Often confused. *Defi-*

nite means *clearly defined* or *exact* or *positive: There were definite limits to her patience. Definitive* means *final* or *conclusive: a definitive edition.*

denotation, connotation A word's primary, or dictionary, meanings are its *denotations.* Its *connotations* are its overtones, the associations it calls up in our minds. Lightning *denotes* a luminous electric discharge in the atmosphere, but it *connotes* speed, inspiration, terror, etc.

depend Don't omit *on* or *upon,* as in **x** *It depends whether the rain stops in time.* And don't use *it depends* without specifying a reason; **x** *It all depends* is incomplete.

desert, dessert The former is the barren place where you see mirages of the latter.

designed, calculated Misused in passive constructions where no designing agent is envisioned: **x** *The long summer days are designed to expose your skin to too much sunlight.* It's doubtful that this is what the Creator had in mind. Again, don't write **x** *This medicine is perfectly calculated to turn you into an addict.*

desperation, despair Not syns. *Desperation* means *readiness to take extreme measures because of despair or urgency: He showed his desperation by leaping from the train. Despair* is a state of *hopelessness: He fell into despair and confessed everything to the police.*

device, devise In common uses the first is always a n., the second a v. You *devise devices.*

dialogue Means *conversation* (among any number of characters) *in a literary work.* Overused in the extended, bureauc. sense of *exchange of ideas:* **x** *Let's get some dialogue going with the ghetto.*

differ from, differ with To differ *from* someone is to *be different* from him; to differ *with* him is to *express disagreement.*

different Often used unnecessarily, as in **x** *I have five different reasons for refusing to comply.* If they weren't different they'd be one reason.

different from, different than Some experts regard *different than* as an error in every instance. When in doubt, therefore, lean toward *different from.* But most people wouldn't object to *different than* when it results in a saving of words: *The outcome was different than I expected.* The safe alternative would be *from what I expected.*

discreet, discrete The first means *prudent* or *judiciously reticent,* the second *separate. She was discreet about revealing the three discrete meanings of the hieroglyph.*

disinterested, uninterested Many writers use both to mean *not interested,* but in doing so they lose the unique meaning of *disinterested* as *impartial: What we need here is a disinterested observer.*

distinctive, distinguished Something *distinctive* is *different, readily identified: a distinctive cauliflower ear. Distinguished* means *eminent* or *having an air of importance: a distinguished statesman.*

don't Colloq. when used with the third person sing.: **x** *He don't care;* **x** *Don't she ever take a bath?* Use *doesn't.*

doubtless(ly) *Doubtless* is already an adv.; the *-ly* is excessive.

drastic Once meant *violent,* and still retains a sense of harshness and sacrifice. Don't write **x** *a drastic improvement.*

dubious, doubtful An outcome or a statement may be *dubious;* the person who calls it into question is *doubtful.* The distinction is useful, though not observed by all good writers.

due to Criticized by some authorities

when it's used in the sense of *owing to* or *because of:* **x** *Due to his absence, the team lost the game.* Here *Due*, an adj., isn't modifying any n. No one would object to *due to* in *The loss was due to his absence.*

due to the fact that Wordy for *because, since.*

duo, trio, quartet, etc. Imply a formal connection. It's wrong to say **x** *A trio of jaywalkers were arrested yesterday,* unless perhaps the three had locked arms in solidarity against traffic laws.

during the course of Can always be *during.*

each other, one another Form the possessive by adding *-'s,* with a plu. following n.: *George and Marsha admired each other's belts.* But an exception is made for abstract nouns that don't easily accept plu. forms: *one another's bravery.*

economic, economical *Economical* always means *thrifty* or *avoiding waste: an economical use of words. Economic* can bear the same meaning, but it usually means *pertaining to economics* or *finances: Keynes's economic theory.*

effect See *affect.*

e.g., i.e. Often confused. *E.g.* means *for example;* it can only be used when you're *not* citing all the items you have in mind. *I.e.* means *that is;* it can only be used when you're giving the *equivalent* of the preceding term. Except in footnotes and parenthetical references, use the written-out equivalents *for example* and *that is.* Don't write **x** *I am utterly faithful to my loved one, i.e., Marsha, who has many charms, e.g., her nose.*

Once you've written *e.g.,* don't add *etc.,* as in **x** *They saw many cities, e.g., Davenport, Biloxi, Portland, etc.* The idea of unlisted further examples is already present in *e.g.*

egoism, egotism Not syns. *Egoism* is a philosophical position emphasizing the central importance of the self; it can also mean an attention to one's own interests. *Egotism* is what's popularly called "conceit." It's an unwarranted puffing-up of one's self-estimation. A widespread error is the use of *egoism* or *egoist* in this derogatory sense.

elicit, illicit Sometimes confused. *Elicit* is a v. meaning *draw forth: His performance elicited applause. Illicit* is an adj. meaning *unlawful: illicit entry.*

emigrate, immigrate Describe the same action, but from different vantages. The action is travel from one's native country to another where one hopes to reside. In *emigrating,* one *leaves* the first country; in *immigrating,* one *arrives* at the second country. If an Englishman moves to Mexico, he is *emigrating* from the standpoint of England and *immigrating* from the standpoint of Mexico.

eminent, imminent *Eminent* means *prominent: He had become eminent through decades of service. Imminent* means *about to happen: The outbreak of war was imminent.*

emote Acceptable only as a derogatory term characterizing bad acting. Don't use it to mean *show emotion.*

endeavor Usually pompous for *try.*

enhance Doesn't mean *increase,* as in **x** *I want to enhance my bank account.* It means *increase the value or attractiveness of,* as in *He enhanced his good reputation by making further sacrifices.* In order to be enhanced, something should already be valued to some degree. Note that it's the quality, not the person, that gets enhanced. Don't write **x** *She was enhanced by receiving favorable reviews.*

enormity Doesn't mean *vastness* or *enormousness;* it means *atrocious wicked-*

ness. Don't write **x** *the enormity of his feet.*

enthuse Widely condemned, even though it looks like a plausible substitute for *show enthusiasm.* Don't write **x** *He enthused over the performance.*

epic (adj.) Cheap when applied to forward passes, talkathons, press conferences, etc. If you take the exploits of Hercules or Aeneas as your standard of what's *epic,* you'll give this adj. a needed rest.

equally as Always redt. Wherever you feel inclined to write *equally as,* you'll find that *equally* can be dropped. *It was [equally] as far to Denver as to Colorado City.*

escalate An inaccurate cliché when the meaning is simply *increase,* as in **x** *The price of meat has escalated.* Used properly, *escalate* means *increase in magnitude by calculated stages.* Military leaders *escalate* hostilities when they deliberately intensify their actions to a certain degree, "raising the ante" in order to force the enemy to match the intensification or give in.

escape (v.) When used with an obj., it should mean *elude,* as in *They escaped punishment.* **x** *They escaped the jail* is wrong. Make *escaped* intrans. here: *They escaped from the jail.*

especially, specially Significantly different. *Especially* means *outstandingly: an especially interesting idea. Specially* means *for a particular purpose, specifically: This racket was specially chosen by the champion.*
    Watch out for meaningless uses of *special:* **x** *There are two special reasons why I came here.* This just means *There are two reasons,* not *Two of the reasons are special ones.*

et al. Means *and other people,* not *and other things.* It belongs in footnotes and parenthetical references, not in your main text.

etc. Means *and other things,* and shouldn't be extended to mean *and other people. Et al.* is available for that purpose.

eventhough Should always be *even though.*

everyday, every day *Everyday* is an adj. meaning *normal, habitual: an everyday practice.* Don't use *everyday* where the two words *every day* are called for: *They did it every day.*

everyone, every one *Everyone* means *everybody.* It shouldn't be used in place of *every one,* as here: **x** *Everyone of your arguments is false.*
    As sing. pros., *everyone* and *everybody* take sing. verbs: *Everyone is away.*

everywheres Colloq. for *everywhere.*

exact Don't use *exact* as an adv.: **x** *the exact same symptoms.* Write *exactly the same.*

exceeding(ly), excessive(ly) *Exceeding* means *very much; excessive* means *too much.* It's no criticism to call someone *exceedingly rich.*

except Shouldn't be used as a conj., as in **x** *She told him to leave, except he didn't want to.* Keep *except* as a prep. meaning *excluding: He remembered everything except his toothbrush.*

exist Often meaningless, as in **x** *among all the problems that exist today. Among all current problems* says the same thing with no leakage of energy.

expect Mildly colloq. in the sense of *suppose, believe:* **x** *I expect I won't be able to get there.*

expensive Because *expensive* already means *high-priced,* you shouldn't combine it with *price* or *prices:* **x** *The price was expensive.* That's like writing *The heat was* *hot.* The item being sold is what's *expensive.*

express When followed by a reflexive pro., *express* takes *as:* not **x** *He expressed himself amazed* but *He expressed himself as amazed.* Of course *He expressed amazement* would be better yet.

Note that *express* isn't a syn. of *say.* Don't write **x** *She expressed that she would be there.* Always use an obj. with the trans. v. *express.*

facet A facet is one of the surfaces of a gem; thus it comes into view as the gem is turned. A sentence containing *facet* should retain some idea of this shift in perspective: *An unexpected facet of the problem appears when we adopt the Indians' point of view.* The danger is that *facet* will become a syn. of *part:* **x** *The problem has four facets.*

fact, fact that Can't be used with untrue statements, as in **x** *The fact that the moon is inhabited was vigorously denied by the astronomer.* Once *fact* is used, the statement is presumed to be true; a *true fact* is redt.

The fact that can often be deleted for economy: **x** *I appreciate the fact that you are helping me* should be *I appreciate your help.*

factor A *factor* is a *contributing element helping to produce a given result.* All too often it's misused to mean *item* or *point:* **x** *I want to emphasize four factors in this lecture.* Another sign of the word's recent abuse is the redt. **x** *contributing factor.* If a factor isn't already contributing, it isn't a factor. The word is used properly in sentences like *In seeking the cause of the riot, they overlooked several important factors.*

fail Use only in the context of an actual attempt. Don't write **x** *Lincoln failed to agree with Douglas.* Was Lincoln trying?

famous, notorious *Famous* means *possessing fame,* usually in a positive sense: *a*

famous victory. Notorious means *possessing fame in an unfavorable sense: a notorious cheater.*

fantastic Should mean *fanciful, imaginary.* It's colloq. as an all-purpose term of enthusiasm: **x** *He had a fantastic swim.*

farther, further *Farther* usually refers to distance, but *further* is often used in all possible senses. Many careful writers, however, restrict *further* to its abstract meaning: *I would like to make one further remark.* This has the advantage of leaving *farther* free to cover all occasions when physical distance is involved.

Farthest, furthest are the superlatives (not *fartherest, furtherest*).

fatal, fateful Something *fatal* leads to death; something *fateful* is *momentous,* whether or not the outcome is *fatal.*

feedback Bureauc. for *response,* as in **x** *She wanted feedback from her father.* Don't stray from the several technical senses of *feedback* given in your dictionary.

few, little *Few* refers to things or persons that can be counted; *little* refers to things that can be measured or estimated, but not itemized. *Few people were on hand, and there was little enthusiasm for the speaker.*

fewer, less, lesser, least *Fewer* refers to numbers, *less* to amounts: *fewer members, less revenue. Lesser* is an adj. meaning *minor* or *inferior: The lesser emissaries were excluded from the summit meeting. Least* is the superlative of *little;* as an adj. it should only be used when more than two items are involved.

Fewer in number is redt.

field *The field of* is often wordy, as in **x** *He majored in the field of astronomy.* Write *He majored in astronomy.* The same goes for *subject* and, worst of all, *area.*

figure, calculate These verbs are colloq.

for *think, suppose,* or *believe:* **x** *I figure she will be here by the fifteenth.*

final Often redt., as in **x** *final conclusion, final result, final outcome.*

finalize Bureauc. for *complete.*

flaunt, flout Widely confused. To *flaunt* is to *display arrogantly: They flaunted their superior wisdom.* To *flout* is to *defy contemptuously: They flouted every rule of proper behavior.*

flunk Colloq. for *fail: She failed* [not *flunked*] *the course.*

for It's all right to begin a sentence with a conj., but *for* is tricky. Often it can be taken as either a conj. or a prep., as in **x** *For many days passed uneventfully.* The first three words look at first like a prep. phrase. Don't begin a sentence with *for* unless the next word makes clear what part of speech *for* is.

for free Should be *free.*

for the purpose of Usually wordy: **x** *He came to the city for the purpose of getting rich* should be *He came to the city to get rich.*

for the simple reason that Should be *because.*

former, latter These formal-sounding terms should be used only when there are two items and when the reader will have no difficulty identifying them; you shouldn't use them after intricate constructions. Note that each item can be plu.: *The admirals and generals flatly disagreed; the latter prevailed.*

When *former* means *ex-,* don't combine it with *ex-* (**x** *a former ex-nun*) or use it with a past v. (**x** *She was a former nun*) if the person is still alive.

formulate Usually pompous for *form.* Save *formulate* for the sense of *state sys-*

tematically: He formulated a new theory of solar storms. In **x** *I formulated my plans for the summer,* the v. should be *formed.*

fortuitous Means *by chance,* whether or not an advantage is implied. Don't use it to mean simply *favorable* or *auspicious.*

framework Fast becoming a bureauc. cliché, as in **x** *Consider this problem in the framework of factor analysis.* A *framework* is properly a *skeletal structure designed to support or enclose something.* Thus, metaphorically, you could say that a person's religious beliefs provide the framework for his or her day-to-day behavior. Compare this with the abstract and meaningless use in the first example.

free, freely *Free* is both an adj. and an adv., meaning, among other things, *without cost.* People who suspect that *free* can't be an adv. are inclined to use *freely* in its place: **x** *I give it to you freely.* But this is ambig.: *freely* means *liberally, unreservedly.* Don't be afraid to write *I give it to you free* if you mean *without charging you.* If you mean *unreservedly,* write *I freely give it to you.*

frightened, scared, afraid You're *frightened* or *scared by* an immediate cause for alarm; you're *afraid of* a more persisting danger. The erroneous *frightened of* and *scared of* jumble the two senses.

fulsome Doesn't mean *abundant;* it means *offensively insincere.*

fun Colloq. as an adj.: **x** *a fun affair.*

function (v., n.) Overused as a v. meaning *work, operate:* **x** *I function best in the morning.* The term always has a mechanical air about it. A body *functions,* but people *act, behave, conduct themselves,* etc.

As a n., *function* is often pretentious for *event* or *occasion.* Use it only when the event has a certain importance and formality: *a diplomatic function. Function* also has a precise mathematical sense which is sometimes pretentiously extended: **x** *My character is a function of my up-bringing.* Try *result.*

funny Colloq. for *odd:* **x** *That's a funny mistake for a mathematician to have made.* Substitute *odd, strange,* or *peculiar.*

gap A cliché in phrases like *communications gap, credibility gap.*

gay Now so common for *homosexual* that you must watch out for ambiguity when you mean to use the word differently.

gender Reserve for grammar, not sex. Don't write **x** *He went to Sweden to have his gender changed.* And genders are always *masculine* and *feminine*, never *male* and *female*.

general public Redt. for *public.*

get The p.p. is either *got* or *gotten. Gotten* is more usual in American English.
   Some phrases containing *get* are common in speech but colloq. in writing:

x The smell of that sewer gets me.
x You get on my nerves.
x She got him fired.

Try *The smell . . . offends me; You annoy me; She had him fired.*

good, well *You look good tonight* means that you're attractive. *You look well tonight* means that you don't look sick.

had better Don't shorten to *better,* as in **x** *You better pay attention.*

had ought Should be *ought to have,* as in *They ought to have listened.* Don't write **x** *They had ought to listen.*

half a Don't precede *half a* with a redt. *a,* as in **x** *He was there for a half an hour.*

hanged, hung Criminals aren't *hanged* very often now, but grammarians still insist on this p.p. While the distinction lasts, you should observe it: *hanged* is for executions, *hung* for all other uses of *hang.*

hang-up Colloq. for *inhibition, problem, reservation, perversion.* All these terms can be used precisely; *hang-up* can't, because it calls up all of them at once.

hard, hardly Both of these can be advs. Fear of using *hard* in its legitimate adv. sense sometimes leads to ambiguity: **x** *I was hardly pressed for time.* This could mean either *I was rushed* or *I had plenty of time,* with a presumption for the latter. Hyphenation can be helpful: *I was hard-pressed for time.*

hardly . . . than An error for *hardly . . . when.* Don't write **x** *Hardly had she finished composing the letter than the telephone rang.*

has reference to Rarely preferable to *means* or *refers to.*

head up (v.) Colloq. for *head, direct,* as in **x** *She headed up the string quartet.*

high, highly Remember that *high* can be an adv. as well as an adj., and is preferable in such phrases as *he jumped high; a high-flying pilot.* An antique vase may be *highly prized* and therefore *high-priced* at an auction.

historic, historical *Historic* means *history-making, figuring in history: Marx's carbuncles may have had historic importance. Historical* means *pertaining to history: There is a historical controversy about Marx's carbuncles* (that is, historians quarrel about their significance).

hopefully Many people resent the use of *hopefully* to mean *it is hoped;* they remember that until recently it meant only *in a hopeful manner.* A majority of readers do accept the new meaning, but you should keep the others in mind.

host (v.)   Jrn. as a v.: **x** *She hosted four-teen guests.* Try *She entertained.*

house, home   A *house* is a residential structure that may or may not be some-body's *home,* depending on whether any-one lives there.

how   Don't use in place of *that*, as in **x** *I told her how I wouldn't stand for her sar-casm any more.*

how ever, however   Distinct terms. *How ever are you going to tie that knot? You, however, know more about it than I do.* The same distinction applies to *what ever* and *whatever.*

However is correct in the sense of *in whatever manner: However you consider it, the situation looks desperate.*

human history   Redt. for *history.*

humanism, humanity, humaneness, hu-manitarianism   *Humanism* is a doctrine emphasizing the central importance of mankind; *humanity* is human kind or the possession of *humaneness,* that is, sympa-thy and compassion; *humanitarianism* is a deliberate devotion to charitable public causes.

To call someone a *humanist* is to say nothing about his character; it means ei-ther that he's an advocate of the philoso-phy of humanism or that he's a student of the humanities, the "liberal arts."

-ics   Words ending in *-ics* that refer to a body of knowledge (*mathematics, dynam-ics,* etc.) are sing. if the whole field or dis-cipline is meant: *Mathematics is difficult.* But some *-ics* words should be treated as plu. when the *practical application* of the field is meant: *Her politics are dif-ferent now.*

identify, relate   These verbs are increas-ingly used in a reflexive sense without re-flexive pros.: *I identify [myself] with John Wayne; He can't relate [himself] to the Army point of view.* To include the reflex-ives sounds stuffy, but to exclude them may be risky. Look for alternatives: *feel an identity with, accept,* etc.

i.e.   Means *that is;* see *e.g.*

if and when, when and if   Clichés. Usually you can do without one of the paired words.

if not   Dangerously ambig., as in **x** *There were good reasons, if not excellent ones, for taking that step.* A reader has no way of knowing whether this means that the rea-sons decidedly weren't excellent or that they may have been excellent after all.

ignorant, stupid   Often confused. To be *ignorant* of something is not to know it: *Newton was ignorant of relativity.* An *igno-rant* person is one who has been taught very little. A *stupid* person is mentally una-ble to learn: *The main cause of his igno-rance was his stupidity.*

imaginary, imaginative   *Imaginary,* mean-ing *unreal* or *imagined,* is sometimes wrongly displaced by *imaginative,* which means *showing imagination:* **x** *I reject your idea as totally imaginative.* Substitute *imaginary.*

immortal   Public-relations jarg. for *mem-orable.* Not being mortal in the first place, artistic works can't become *immortal.* Nei-ther can touchdowns, melodies, or politi-cal speeches.

implicit, explicit, tacit   *Implicit* can cause ambiguity, for it means both *implied* (left unstated) and *not giving cause for investi-gation.* In the sentence **x** *My trust in her was implicit,* both interpretations are pos-sible. Was the trust beyond question, or was it left unstated? Wariness is advised whenever you feel like using *implicit* to mean *unshakable* or *profoundly clear.*

Explicit is the opposite of *implicit* in one

of its senses: *In his will he spelled out the explicit provisions that had previously been left implicit. Tacit* is close to *implicit* but means *silent, unspoken;* its reference is not to expression in general but to speech.

imply, infer Widely confused, with *infer* often used where only *imply* would be right. To *imply* is properly to *leave* an implication; to *infer* is to *take* one. *She implied that she was still loyal to him, but he inferred otherwise from her embarrassed manner.*

in a very real sense Pointless verbiage. Your statements are presumed to have a very real sense already; this cliché can only stir up suspicion that they don't.

In all probability, in all likelihood Always wordy for *probably.*

in case Can usually be improved to *if: If* [not *In case*] *you don't like this model, we will refund your money. In case* should be saved for *in the event: This sprinkler is provided in case of fire.*

in connection with See *in terms of.*

in excess of Invariably wordy for *over* or *more than.*

in number, in length, in size, in volume, in area, etc. Can almost always be deleted with profit: *The plot was two acres* [*in area*].

in spite of (despite) the fact that Can always be *although* or *though,* either of which is preferable on grounds of brevity.

in terms of, along the lines of, in connection with These vague bureauc. phrases are subject to the same abuse as *regarding, in regard to,* etc. When your sentence says **x** *In terms of prowess, Tarzan was unconquerable,* see how much you can lop off. *Tarzan was unconquerable* says

the same thing with fewer than half the words. Similarly, **x** *He was pursuing his studies along the lines of sociology* should be simply *He was studying sociology.*

in the affirmative, in the negative Pompous for *yes* and *no.*

in the event that Means, and should always be, *if.*

in the form of Usually excess baggage, as in **x** *His Christmas present arrived in the form of a necktie.* Would the present have changed its form in any circumstances? Save the phrase for sentences like *The witch appeared in the form of his aunt Grace.*

in the neighborhood of Wordy when it means *about* or *approximately. There were approximately* [not *in the neighborhood of*] *80,000 people on hand.*

in the worst way Colloq. for *extremely.* Besides, it can be ambig.: **x** *She loves him in the worst way.* Should she find a better way?

in this day and age A wordy cliché for *now.*

in to, into *In to* is distinct from *into: we went into Cleveland; we went in to do some shopping.* The chief danger is that *into* will be used where *in to* is required, as in **x** *The guilty sorcerer's apprentice confessed his crime and turned himself into the sorcerer for punishment.*

   Also watch out for the colloq. use of *into* in sentences like **x** *I'm into ceramics.*

in view of the fact that Wordy for *because, since,* or *considering that.*

incidence, incident, instance Sometimes confused. *Incidence* means *rate of occurrence: the incidence of crime.* An *incident* is *one occurrence.* Thus it's wrong to write **x** *An incidence of murder happened yesterday.*

Note also that *incident* has become jrn. for *serious disorder,* as in **x** *The students heckled the speaker, but there were no incidents.* Every reported event, however peaceful, is an incident.

An *instance* is an *example,* something instanced. *In the instance of,* like *in the case of,* is almost always unnecessary and cumbersome. And *often* is preferable to *in many instances.*

include Shouldn't be used loosely to mean *are,* as in **x** *The Marx brothers include Groucho, Harpo, Chico, and Zeppo.* Only when at least one member is unnamed, as in *The Marx brothers include Chico and Zeppo,* should you write *include.* Note also that *include* is wrong after a limitation has already been indicated: **x** *A few of my reasons for saying this include. . .*

incredibly Overused as a vague intensifier: **x** *an incredibly believable alibi.*

individual (n.) Often pompous for *person:* **x** *He was a kind-hearted individual.* When you use *individual* as a n., keep in mind its sense as an adj.: *personal, not general. Our laws respect the individual* illustrates the n. in its correct use; the individual is implicitly contrasted with the collectivity.

inevitable, inevitably Don't use these words unless you really mean *unavoidable, unavoidably.* The mere fact that something has happened doesn't mean that it was *inevitable.* **x** *Inevitably, Hamlet succeeds in killing Claudius.* Really? The whole play casts doubt on this *inevitably.*

input, output Both (especially *input*) are brutally overworked clichés. Restrict them to their mechanical sense *(the computer handles input),* and abandon such bureauc. as **x** *Let's get more input into our thinking.*

inside of Can always be *inside;* and some people regard *inside of* as ungrammatical. For metaphorical uses, *within* is preferable, anyway: *within twenty minutes.*

involved Stale in the sense of *socially concerned:* **x** *I admire Hannah because she's so involved.* Since *involve* means *envelop, wrap in,* it's important to supply an obj.

irony, ironic Use only when there's a significant contradiction between a statement and its real import, or between an expectation and a result. It's *ironic* if a plane crashes into the home of the director of the Civil Aeronautics Board, but not if a person tries unsuccessfully to get rich; there's got to be a twist.

is when, is where Often involved in false predication: **x** *A war is when opposing countries take up arms;* **x** *Massage is where you lie on a table and . . .* Match *when* only with times, *where* only with places: *When she was ready, she went where she pleased.* Most predication problems can be solved by changing the verb: *A war occurs when* etc.

-ize New verbs made from nouns plus *-ize* continually appear, and some of them will eventually be accepted as S.E. This has already happened to *editorialize, hospitalize,* and *socialize,* for example. Others, like *finalize* and *randomize,* are used widely in certain quarters but are regarded as jarg. elsewhere. Stay away from them in essay prose, and don't invent *-izes* of your own.

join together Can always be *join,* since things are never joined apart.

just exactly Redt., as in **x** *This is just exactly what I meant to say.* Delete one word or the other.

kind of, sort of, type of When used at all, these expressions should be followed by the sing.: *this kind of woman.* But *such a woman* is preferable.

   Sort of and *kind of* are awk. in the sense of *somewhat*, and they sometimes appear in the unnecessary form *sort of a, kind of a:* **x** *He was an odd sort of a king.* Don't use *sort* and *kind* unless your sentence needs them to make sense. If *He was an odd king* will do, there's no reason to drag in *sort* or *kind.* A legitimate example is *This kind of bike has been on the market for only three months.*

lack, need, want   A *lack* is a *shortage* or *absence;* a *need* is the *condition arising from a lack;* and a *want,* in the pertinent sense, is a *lack of necessary things and an awareness of that lack:*

• There was a lack of power reserves.
• The people had a need for emergency shipments of food.
• The people felt the want of bread and rice.

Note that *lack* and *want* are neg. ideas. Don't write **x** *He possessed a lack of intelligence.* That would be like saying *The absence was present.*

lack for   Should be *lack: Oregon does not lack* [not *lack for*] *rain.*

large   Can be an adv., as in *loom large.* Don't "improve" the phrase to **x** *loom largely.*

large part, large portion, large share, large number of   These formulas are often wordy for *many* or *much:* **x** *a large number of people,* **x** *a large share of the explanation.* Try *many people, much of the explanation.* The same holds for other adjs. of size or amount: **x** *a small number of deer* should be *few deer.*

leave, let   Have different senses in clauses like *leave him alone* and *let him alone.* The first means *get out of his presence;* the second means *don't bother him* (even if you remain in his presence).

lend, loan   Some writers prefer to keep *lend* as a v. and *loan* as a n.; but *loan* can also be a v. *Loan* as a v. is most often seen in past forms: *I loaned it to her.*

let's   Don't follow with the pro. *us,* as in **x** *Let's us talk it over. Let's* already says *let us.*

level   (n.)   Overworked in the colorless, indefinable sense illustrated by **x** *at the public level;* **x** *on the wholesale level.* Use only when the idea of degree or ranking is present: *He was a competent amateur, but when he turned professional he found himself beyond his level.*

lie, lay   If nothing more than repose is intended, the intrans. *lie* is the right word: *lie down.* The trans. *lay* means, among other things, *set: lay it here.*

   The past forms of these verbs are troublesome. All of the following sentences are correct:

• I lay down. [present is *lie*]
• I laid down my cards. [present is *lay*]
• I have lain in bed all day. [present is *lie*]
• I have laid down my cards. [present is *lay*]

like   See *as.*

likely   Weak as an unmodified adv.: **x** *She likely had no idea what she was saying.* Some readers would also object to **x** *Very likely, she had . . . .* Try *probably* or even *in all likelihood.*

likewise   An adv., not a conj. You can write *Likewise, Myrtle failed the test,* but not **x** *Jan failed the test, likewise Myrtle.*

literally   Means *precisely as stated, without a figurative sense.* If you write **x** *I literally died laughing,* you must be writing from beyond the grave. Many writers wrongly use *literally* to mean *definitely* or *almost* or even its opposite, *figuratively.*

live, alive Both can be adjs., but only *live* should precede a n. You can write *He was really alive,* but don't write **x** *He is an alive man at a party.* The right term here would be *lively.*

lot, lots Some people find *a lot* and *lots* colloq. in the sense of *a great many* or *a good deal:* **x** *I could give you lots of reasons. Many* would be a safer choice. *A lot* and *lots* make colloq. advs. as well: **x** *She pleases me lots.* Try *very much* instead.
   See also *alot.*

loud Can be an adv. as well as an adj. *He played loud* is just as "good English" as *He played loudly.*

mad, angry *Mad* means *insane,* but many writers also use it as a syn. of *angry: She was mad at me.* If you use *mad* in this sense, you can expect complaints.

majority Often used pretentiously where *most* is all that's meant. Don't write *majority* unless you have in mind a contrast with *minority.* And make sure that the majority consists of individual members. *The majority of the group* makes sense; **x** *the majority of the time* does not.

many, much *Many* refers to quantity, *much* to amount: *Many problems make for much difficulty.* Don't reverse these senses and write **x** *There were too much people in the line.*

marginal Widely misused for *small. Marginal* means *near the lower limits, at the threshold;* the word should only be used for degrees that barely qualify or barely fail. A test score is *marginal* if it just manages to pass, and *marginally failing* if it almost passes. Don't say **x** *His talents were marginal* if you mean *He had very little talent.*

massive Stale for *large, extensive:* **x** *a massive crusade against littering;* **x** *massive cleanup efforts.* Give this jarg. a

vacation, and use the word only in its literal sense of *bulky: a massive landslide.*

may, might In hypothetical or past conditions, the auxiliary should be *might,* not *may: If I had known this, I might* [not *may*] *have acted differently. If you could see her now, you might* [not *may*] *not believe your eyes.*
   Many writers use *might* for simple conditions, as in **x** *I might visit you tomorrow.* Strictly speaking, *might* should be *may* here.

means Always plu. when it means *money: Her means were exhausted.* In other senses *means* may be either sing. or plu.: *Harry's means of operation is/are to quote an attractive price and then count the tires as options.*

media Always plu. Don't write **x** *The media is to blame.* The sing. is *medium.*

mental attitude Almost always redt. for *attitude. Mental* would be meaningful only if a contrast, e.g., with *spiritual,* were implied.

methodology A *methodology* is a *system or theory of methods,* not a *single method.* Nearly every choice should be settled in favor of *method.*

mighty Colloq. as an adv. meaning *extremely:* **x** *a mighty big job.*

militate, mitigate Often confused. To *militate* is to *have an adverse effect;* it's followed by *against,* as in *His poor eyesight militated against his chances of becoming a pilot.*
   Mitigate means to *reduce an unpleasant effect;* it takes an obj., as in *The doctor's cheerful manner mitigated the pain.*

more preferable Redt. for *preferable.*

more . . . rather than; prefer(able) . . . than These are faulty structures:

x Stanley said the dean was more like a Gestapo officer, rather than a liberal administrator.

Correct to *more like a Gestapo officer than . . . .*

x Priscilla preferred staying home than exposing herself to microbes and viruses at the party.

Correct to *preferred staying home to exposing . . . .*

In short, follow through with the structures *more x than y* and *prefer x to y.*

most Colloq. as an adv. meaning *almost:* **x** *We were most dead by the time we got there.*

motive, motivation A *motive* is a psychological cause for a specific action: *the motive for the crime; my motive in leaving. Motivation* is a more general term, referring either to the whole topic of motives or to the state of being motivated: *I am interested in human motivation; His motivation was weak.* A common error is use of the general word *motivation* where the specific sense of *motive* is intended: **x** *I never learned his motivation for running away.* The plu. *motivations* is always awk.

much less Use only in neg. contexts, as in *He hasn't even appeared, much less begun his work.* Watch out for affirmative senses: **x** *Skiing is difficult, much less surfing.*

muchly Always wrong for *much.*

must As a n., *must* has become acceptable to most readers: *Conservation is a must.* But it's still disapproved as an adj.: **x** *This is a must game for us.*

myself Don't use the intensive pro. *myself* as a free substitute for *I* or *me:* **x** *The other Fingerlickers and myself will stop at nothing in our terrorism against Colonel Sanders.* Keep *myself* for emphatic or reflexive uses: *I myself intend to do it; I admire myself.*

nature Often unnecessary: **x** *Books of this nature offend me.* Try *Such books . . . .* The same observation holds for *kind, sort,* and *type.*

near future, not too distant future Wordy in sentences like **x** *He hopes to see her again in the not too distant future.* Try *soon* or *before long.*

no sooner . . . than The right formula. *No sooner . . . that* and *No sooner . . . when* are mistakes, as in **x** *No sooner had I left when my typewriter was stolen.*

not so much . . . as The right formula. Avoid *not so much . . . but* and *not so much . . . but rather.* **x** *She was not so much selfish, but rather impulsive* illustrates the mistake. *She was not so much selfish as impulsive* is better.

not too, not that Colloq. when used to mean *not very:* **x** *I'm not too sure about that;* **x** *He's not that interested in sailing.*

nothing like, nowhere near These shouldn't be used in place of *not nearly,* as in **x** *I am nothing like* [or *nowhere near*] *as spry as I used to be.*

now As an adj., *now* is hip jarg.: **x** *Brautigan is a now writer.* Keep *now* an adv. in your writing.

nowheres A mistake for *nowhere.*

numerous Properly an adj., not a pro. meaning *a number of.* Don't write **x** *Numerous of his debts remain unpaid.*

occur, take place *Take place* is the narrower term; it should be used only with *scheduled* events. Don't write **x** *The storm took place last Wednesday.*

-odd Redt. with *about, some,* or *approxi-*

mately: **x** *some eighty-odd immigrants.* When you do use *-odd,* be sure to retain the hyphen so as to prevent ambiguity. Don't write **x** *Thirty odd friends of mine came to the party.*

of between, of from   Avoid pairing preps.: **x** *an estimate of between thirty and forty-five people.* Try *an estimate of thirty to forty-five people.*

off of   Should be *off* or *from: She jumped off [from] the bridge,* not **x** *She jumped off of the bridge.*

oftentimes   Should always be *often.*

old-fashioned   The correct form, not *old-fashion.*

on, upon, up on   *On* and *upon* are interchangeable in most uses, but you should save *upon* for deliberately formal effects: *She swore upon her word of honor . . .* Note that *up on* is different in meaning from *upon: He climbed up on the ledge.*

on account of   Never preferable to *because of.*

on the one hand . . . on the other hand Once you've written *on the one hand,* you've committed yourself to dropping the second shoe, *on the other hand.* But *on the other hand* can be used alone when you want to introduce a qualification; it doesn't always have to be preceded by *on the one hand.*

on the order of   Change to *about* or *approximately* when estimates of quantity are involved.

on the part of   Wordy when it means *by, among,* or *for:* **x** *Strong objections were voiced on the part of welfare mothers. By* would be proper here.

other than that   A weak substitute for *otherwise* or *apart from that:* **x** *Other than*

that, I can follow your reasoning. The problem is that the adj. *other* is being forced into an adv. function.

other times   Shouldn't be construed as a complete adv., as in **x** *Other times she felt depressed. At other times* is what you want.

otherwise   Keep as an adv. and do not extend to supplant the adj. *other.* In **x** *He loved old buildings, Victorian and otherwise,* the adj. *Victorian* is being forced into parallelism with an adv. If *other* sounds odd, recast the sentence.

ourself   Should be *ourselves.*

outside of   Should be simply *outside.* In metaphorical uses (**x** *Outside of these reasons*) it should be replaced by *except for.*

overall (adj.)   Sounds precariously like the sing. of *overalls.* You'd do better to choose a syn.: *total, comprehensive, general, complete.* Note also that in some sentences the word conveys nothing at all: **x** *The overall outcome was that the Dodgers won.* Look for opportunities to delete.

owing to the fact that   Wordy for *because, since.*

part, portion   A *part* is a *fraction of a whole;* a *portion* is a *part allotted to some person or use.* Thus you shouldn't write **x** *A large portion of the sea is contaminated.*

partial, partially   Can be ambig., since they mean either *incomplete(ly)* or *biased, in a biased manner. A partial survey* could be a survey that lacks completeness or one that lacks objectivity. Let your reader see which sense you intend. Where *partially* means *incompletely,* it can be replaced by *partly.*

particular   Serves no purpose in phrases like **x** *no particular purpose.*

party   Has a legalistic sense when it's a n.

meaning *person*. Don't use it this way unless you want the person to be conceived abstractly as a litigant, defendant, or other formal participant in an action or relationship. In **x** *Four parties refused to go,* the n. should be changed to *people.*

Party as a v. is colloq.: **x** *We partied all night.*

past history, past experience, past record, etc.   *History, experience,* and *record* already refer to the past. Thus *past* can and should be dropped.

per   Sounds excessively technical where *a* or *an* would do: **x** *twice per month,* **x** *fifty miles per hour. As per* is bureauc. for *in accordance with:* **x** *as per your letter of the fifteenth.* Don't use *per* to mean *by,* as in **x** *She sent it per first-class mail.*

percent, percentage   Both *percent* (sometimes written *per cent*) and *percentage* mean *rate per hundred. Percent* should be used with numbers (whether written-out or numerals): *twenty percent. Percentage* appears without numbers: *a high percentage.*

Don't use either *percent* or *percentage* where you simply mean *part.* And don't assume that a percentage is always small, as in **x** *Only a percentage of them agreed.* A *percentage* could be any part less than 100 percent.

persecute, prosecute   To *persecute* is to *single out for mistreatment;* to *prosecute* is to *bring to trial.*

personal, personally   Often meaningless, as in **x** *my personal preference* and **x** *personally, I would say . . .* Since you are obviously the person making the statement, the extra word conveys nothing. Use *personal* only as the opposite of *impersonal* or *general.*

phenomenon   The only correct sing. form. Don't write **x** *this phenomena.* The more common plu. is *phenomena,* not *phenomenons.*

philosophy   Widely misused to mean *belief, idea, practice:* **x** *Here is my philosophy about refunds.* A *philosophy* is a *whole system of doctrine: Kant's philosophy; the philosophy of pragmatism.* The plu. *philosophies* sounds especially ridiculous in sentences like **x** *I have come to this college to develop and extend my philosophies.*

place   Some readers consider words like *any place, no place,* and *some place* to be colloq. It's safer to write *anywhere, nowhere, somewhere. Go places* is colloq. in the sense of *make progress:* **x** *Now we're really going places.*

plan   The v. is followed by *to,* not *on: He plans to run,* not **x** *He plans on running.* Note that *plan* implies a future action, so that it's never necessary to write **x** *plan ahead* or **x** *future plans.*

plenty   As an adj., *plenty* must be followed by *of.* Don't write **x** *She has plenty reasons for her opinion.*

plus   Not a coord. conj. (**x** *He was sleepy, plus he hadn't studied*) or a conjunctive adv. (**x** *She enjoyed her work; plus, the hours were good*). *Plus* is also somewhat colloq. as a n.: **x** *It was an important plus.* Use it chiefly as a prep. with numbers: *Two plus two is four.*

point of view   See *standpoint.*

poorly   Colloq. in the sense of *ill* or *sick:* **x** *I feel poorly.* Of course *poorly* is acceptable in the more common meaning: *She performed poorly.*

popular   Implies favor with a large number of people. Don't use it when only a few people are meant: **x** *The hermit was popular with his three visitors;* **x** *That idea isn't very popular with me.*

possible, possibly   Don't use *possible* as an adv.: **x** *a possible missing airliner.* Substitute *possibly.*

Watch for redt. phrases like **x** *can possibly*, **x** *may possibly*, and **x** *possible likelihood*. These should be *can, may,* and *likelihood* alone.

precede See *proceed.*

preclude Always takes the thing being prevented as its obj. Don't write **x** *This law precludes children from working.* That would imply that the children themselves were being prevented. Try *This law precludes child labor.*

predominate, predominant Keep these separate. The v. is *predominate,* the adj. *predominant.* Don't write **x** *a predominate idea.*

prefer(able) See *more . . . rather than.*

prejudice Not always bias *against;* it can also be bias *for: She was prejudiced in favor of all radical measures.*
Note that the adj. is *prejudiced,* not *prejudice.* Don't write **x** *She was prejudice.*

present (adj.) Redt. in **x** *the present incumbent,* cumbersome in **x** *at the present time* (try *now*), and stuffy in **x** *the present writer (*use *I).*

pressure Hasn't gained full acceptance as a v.: **x** *He pressured us to agree.* Try *pressed.*

pretty Colloq. when it means *rather,* as in **x** *He was pretty fond of camping. Pretty nearly,* as in **x** *He was pretty nearly exhausted,* should be *almost.*

previous to, prior to Never better than *before.*

proceed, precede To *proceed* is to *go forward;* to *precede* is to *go ahead of. The king preceded his courtiers as they proceeded toward the castle.*
Proceed is pompous if all you mean is *go:* **x** *He proceeded to the supermarket.*

Use *proceed* only in the sense of a continued action.

prophecy, prophesy, prophesize *Prophecy* is a n.: *I make this prophecy. Prophesy* is a v.: *I prophesy this outcome.* There is no such word as *prophesize.*

proportion Often involved in wordy formulas: **x** *the greater proportion* for *most,* **x** *in greater proportion* for *many.*
Some authorities object to *proportions,* a mathematical term of *relationship,* when all that's meant is *dimensions* or *size.*

proposition (n., v.) Inaccurate as a syn. of *project, undertaking,* etc. A *proposition* is an *offer of terms,* a *statement of plan,* or, in logic, a *statement affirming or denying something.*
As a v., *proposition* is colloq. for *propose sexual relations.* You'll be sorry if you try to make it mean *propose* in the wider sense.

prosecute See *persecute.*

question of whether, question as to whether Wordy. Shorten **x** *The question as to whether they will go remains unsettled* to *It isn't known whether they will go.*

quote (n.) Widely used to mean *quotation,* as in *quotes* for *quotation marks.* But this sounds colloq. to many readers, and you'd be safer using the longer forms in your writing.

raise, rise As a v. *raise* is trans.: *raise the arm. Rise* is intrans.: *rise and shave.* Don't use these terms interchangeably.
As a n., *raise* is now accepted S.E.: *a raise in pay.*

rarely ever Redt. for *rarely.*

rather than This formula gets involved in difficulties of parallelism: **x** *She wanted to ride rather than walking. Walking* should be *walk,* since it's parallel to the inf. *ride.* Again: **x** *Rather than risking a new war, the*

President decided to compromise. Risking should be *risk.*

real Colloq. as an adv., as in **x** *I am real interested in finishing this book.* Try *very.*

reason is because The idea of *because* is already contained in *reason;* the phrase is therefore redt. Write *the reason is that.*

reckon Colloq. for *suppose, think:* **x** *I reckon I'll come.*

regarding, in regard to, with regard to, with respect to, relating to, relative to These are flourishing elements of bureauc. *On, about,* and *concerning* are almost always preferable. See also *in terms of.*

Note that *regards* is wrong in **x** *in regards to;* keep to the sing. if you must use the phrase.

relate See *identify.*

relation, relationship Overlap in meaning, and many writers use *relationship* for all possible senses. *Relation,* however, is correct and preferable when an abstract connection is meant: *the relation of wages to prices.* Save *relationship* for connections of mutuality: *his relationship with Susie; the President's relationship with the press.*

relevant Meaningless without a following n.: **x** *The course was extremely relevant.* To what?

replace See *substitute.*

research Widely accepted as a v.: *She researches her dissertation.* But a significant number of writers consider this ugly and would take the trouble to write *She does research on. . . .*

respective(ly) Use only where absolutely needed for clarity. In **x** *The teams returned to their respective dugouts* the word re-*spective* is unnecessary. Would anyone have imagined that the teams returned to *each other's* dugouts?

reticent Doesn't mean *reluctant,* as in **x** *They were reticent to comply.* It means *disposed to be silent,* as in *Reticent people sometimes become talkative after a few drinks.*

rob, steal *Rob* takes as its obj. the person or institution robbed; *steal* takes as its obj. the thing stolen: *He robbed the store, stealing eight television sets.* Don't write **x** *He robbed eight television sets.*

same, the same Don't use these as pros.: **x** *He raced for the train and caught same.*

scarce, scarcely *Scarce* makes an ugly adv., as in **x** *I had scarce finished speaking when . . .* The genuine adv. *scarcely* should be substituted. Note that *scarcely* should be followed by *when,* not *than.*

Watch for double negs. (pp. 318–319) with *scarcely:* **x** *He didn't scarcely mind;* **x** *She didn't do scarcely enough.* Try *He scarcely minded* and *She did scarcely enough* or *She didn't do nearly enough.*

scared See *frightened.*

scene Colloq. in several recent senses: **x** *the drug scene,* **x** *making the scene,* etc. Try to stay near the literal sense of the locale of a specific action: *the scene of the crime; a scene of havoc.*

sensual, sensuous Widely confused. *Sensual* means *carnal, voluptuous,* or *having to do with sex: a sensual thrill. Sensuous* means *pertaining to the senses, showing a general receptivity of the senses: The baby was delighted by sensuous impressions.*

shall, will Except in questions *(Shall I come?), shall* has been falling into disuse. You can still use *shall* in the first person *(I shall go),* but this makes a formal effect.

shape (n.) Colloq. for *condition:* **x** *in good shape.*

-ship Plu. words like *leaders, readers, members* shouldn't be replaced by *leadership, readership, membership:* **x** *The membership disapproved* should be *The members disapproved.* Save the *-ship* forms for abstract uses: *The membership dropped again last year; We train young men in leadership.*

show (v.) Colloq. for *appear:* **x** *Nobody showed. Showed up* is better but still questionable. Try reserving *show* for trans. uses.

   The p.p. of *show* can be either *showed* or *shown,* but *showed* sounds like an error to many readers. You'd better write *shown* every time: *I have shown it.* The past tense is always *showed: I showed it.*

similar Means *resembling,* not *same.* Thus it's wrong to write **x** *Ted died in 1964, and Alice suffered a similar fate two years later.* The writer doesn't mean to assert any difference between one death and the other, but *similar* implies both likeness and unlikeness.

   Don't use *similar to* as an adv. meaning *like:* **x** *This steak smells similar to one I had last Tuesday.* Substitute *like.*

since If you use *since* to mean *because,* watch for ambiguity: **x** *Since she left, he has been doing all the housework.* Here *since* could mean either *because* or *from then until now.*

sit, set With few exceptions, *sit* is in-trans.: *She sat. Set* is usually trans.: *She set the table.* You can of course write *She sat her baby in the high chair* and *The sun set,* but don't write **x** *I set there sleeping* or **x** *I want to sit these weary bones to rest.*

situation, position These words, useful in their place, tend to get inflated in bureauc. prose, especially when urged on by the catchall connectives *regarding, with respect to,* etc. (see *regarding*). **x** *With respect to our position regarding the dangerous situation* should be *About our response to the danger.* And don't use *situation* without naming particular circumstances.

something Do not use as an adv. meaning *somewhat,* as in **x** *He is something under six feet tall.* Note also that *something* can be ambig.: **x** *She smells something like a dead fish.* And **x** *She smells something awful* is both ambig. and colloq.

sometime, sometimes, some time *Sometime* means *at an unspecified time: Let's get together sometime. Sometimes* means *now and then: We sometimes quarrel. Some time* is *a span of time: It has been some time now since the last snowfall.*

somewheres Should be *somewhere.*

sort of See *kind of.*

special, specially See *especially.*

standpoint, viewpoint, point of view, perspective, angle These terms can be used metaphorically, but they easily become clichés, as in **x** *He considered the consumer angle* or **x** *She likes it from an ecology standpoint.* The problem is that none of the literal meaning of *standpoint* or *angle* survives in these examples. When you use such a word, try to carry through its consequences: *Regarded from the standpoint of ecology, the project looks very different; The chairmanship gave him the perspective needed to see both sides of the debate.* Your sentences should show an awareness that a particular point of view alters the way the viewed object is perceived.

state (v.) A formal, official-sounding word meaning *make a declaration.* Don't use it when *say* will do: **x** *They stated that they liked the party.*

structure (v.) Overused as a syn. of *order, arrange, construct,* one of which is always preferable: *Give me a moment to* *arrange* [not *structure*] *my thoughts.* Many readers prefer to keep *structure* a n.

subject (n.)   See *field.*

substitute, replace   *Substitute* takes as its obj. the new item that is supplanting the old one: *She substituted margarine for butter. Replace* takes as its obj. the item being abandoned: *She replaced the butter with margarine.* Note that these sentences are describing the same act.

such   When it precedes an adj. clause, *such* should be followed by *as,* not *that: He took such belongings as he could save from the fire.*

Don't use *such* as an unqualified intensive: **x** *They had such a good time.* Complete the idea with an adj. clause: *They had such a good time that they decided to buy season tickets.*

suppose   Beware of writing *suppose* where *supposed* is necessary: **x** *We are suppose to finish early.*

sure   Colloq. as an adv.: **x** *She sure likes muffins.* But *surely* would sound too stiff; try *certainly.*

sympathy for, sympathy with, sympathize with   To feel *sympathy for* someone is to experience compassion: *She has sympathy for the people of Bangladesh. Sympathy with* is a *feeling of kinship or identity: Her sympathy with Mary Wollstonecraft made her a feminist.* To *sympathize with,* however, is once again to experience compassion: *She sympathized with the poor.*

than, as (conjs.)   A pro. following *than* or *as* can be either subjective or objective in case, depending on the meaning. Supply any missing parts of the clause to see the function of the pro.:

- Biff tackled Otto harder than [he did] *me.*
- He is stronger than *I* [am].
- He is as tall as *they* [are].

Since the "right" choices often sound strained, however, you may prefer to include the missing sentence elements: *He is stronger than I am,* etc.

that, which (relative pros.)   *That* is always restrictive (pp. 294–295); *which* can be either restrictive or nonrestrictive. Many careful writers recognize this difference by keeping *that* for restrictive functions only and *which* for nonrestrictive functions only:

RESTR
- This is the evidence *that* I mentioned.

NONRESTR
- This evidence, *which* I mentioned yesterday, can now be presented.

Beware of using *that* as an unexplained demonstrative adj.: **x** *He didn't have that much to say.* How much is *that much?*

Again, watch for unnecessary doubling of *that:* **x** *She told him that, after all they had been through, that she would certainly keep his ring.* The second *that* is redt.

theirselves   A mistake for *themselves.*

those kind, type, etc. Should be *that kind, type,* etc.

thusly   A mistake for *thus.*

till, until, til, 'til, 'till   *Till* and *until* are interchangeable; suit yourself. The other forms, *til, 'til,* and *'till,* are all inappropriate in prose.

to all intents and purposes   Tiresome for *in effect, practically.*

to the contrary, to the contrary notwithstanding   The first of these phrases is an illegitimate shortening of the second. But both are awk. Change **x** *Burke to the contrary notwithstanding,* . . . to *Despite what Burke says,* . . .

together   Resist the trend that makes

together an adj.: **x** *Wally is really a together person.*

too Don't use *too* as a syn. of *very:* **x** *I'm not too happy today.*

totally Means *entirely, wholly.* It is especially appropriate when the idea of a total sum or amount is involved: *His savings were totally exhausted.* The word is abused when it simply means *very,* as in **x** *We had a totally marvelous experience.*

toward, towards Interchangeable, but *toward* is somewhat more common in American English. Choose whichever form you please, but don't mix it with the other.

type Colloq. in place of *type of:* **x** *You are a headstrong type woman.* In technical contexts *type* is sometimes acceptable as part of a hyphenated compound: *a rotary-type engine.* But in all contexts *type* can usually be omitted with profit: *a headstrong woman, a rotary engine.* Don't try to turn a n. into an adj. by adding *-type:* **x** *an athlete-type person.*

underwater, under water Keep distinct. *Underwater* is an adj. or adv.: *an underwater adventure; he stayed underwater for fifteen minutes. Under water* is a prep. phrase: *Place the boiled eggs under water.*

undue, unduly Often redt., as in **x** *Undue haste isn't called for* or **x** *You shouldn't worry unduly.* Both statements are absurd truisms which might become meaningful if the offending word were dropped.

usage, use Widely confused. Save *usage* for contexts implying *convention* or *custom: English usage; the usages of our sect.* Don't write **x** *He discouraged the usage of cocaine* or **x** *Excessive usage of the car results in high repair bills.* Substitute *use* in both sentences.

Even where *use of* is technically right, ask yourself whether it's needed at all. Thus, **x** *By his use of symbolism Ibsen establishes himself as a modern playwright* could be condensed to *Ibsen's symbolism establishes him . . . .*

use, utilize; use, utilization *Utilize* and *utilization* are almost always bureauc. for *use.* To *utilize* is to *put to use* or to *turn a profit on,* and it makes sense when coupled with an abstraction: *to utilize resources.* Because *utilize* and *utilization* have a depersonalizing effect, they sound especially odd when applied to people. **x** *The underutilization of women,* for example, was coined to give a name to sex discrimination in jobs, but it makes the writer or speaker sound exploitative.

use to In an affirmative past construction, be sure to write *used,* not *use: They used to think so.*

Past neg. constructions always sound awk: **x** *Didn't she use to take the bus?* Try something like *She used to take the bus, didn't she?*

verbal, oral *Verbal* means *in words,* whether or not the words are spoken. *Oral* means *by mouth.* Choose *oral* when you mean spoken: *an oral* [not *verbal*] *presentation.*

violently Don't use as a syn. of *strongly:* **x** *I violently oppose your program.* Actual violence causes physical damage.

way, ways Don't use *ways* in the sense of *distance:* **x** *It was only a short ways.* The correct form is *way.*

what ever, whatever See *how ever.*

where . . . at Redt. and colloq., as in **x** *She didn't know where he was at.*

will See *shall.*

-wise Acceptable when it means *in the manner of,* as in *clockwise* and *lengthwise,* and when it means *having wisdom: penny-wise and pound-foolish; a ring-wise boxer.* But most authorities protest coinage by adding *-wise* in the sense of *with respect* to: **x** *taxwise,* **x** *agriculturewise,* **x** *conflict resolutionwise.* These terms do save space, but the feeling against them is strong. Look for concise alternatives: not **x** *the situation taxwise* but *the tax situation;* not **x** *America's superiority agriculture-wise* but *America's superiority in agriculture* or *America's agricultural superiority.*

would like for Colloq. in sentences like **x** *They would like for me to quit.* Try *They want me to quit.*

Appendix:
The Examination Essay

All the skills you are learning in a composition course will help you in answering so-called "essay questions" on examinations. Obviously, though, the high-pressure exam situation calls for certain adjustments of method. Having little time to plan an essay and even less time to revise it, you must make quick, sensible decisions and abide by them. Also, you should bear in mind that the grader of your blue book will be reading rapidly, looking not for subtleties but for signs that you have *grasped the relevant material* and *stated a coherent, well-supported position*. If the subtleties are there to be perceived, so much the better; but your first job is to ensure that the grader can't miss your main ideas.

Here, then, are ten essential principles, the first of which can be put into operation weeks before the exam:

1. *Try to anticipate questions.* Students who consistently write successful examination essays don't just get lucky when they see what the question is. Throughout the term they have been reading, listening, and notetaking with attention to broad patterns of meaning, and they arrive at the exam with ideas that *tie together* the assigned material. Some of those ideas inevitably prove useful, for in

part they reflect the instructor's own notion of what deserves emphasis.

2. *Read the question with care.* Pressure, haste, and a wish to make use of memorized information can mislead you into writing answers to questions that weren't asked. You *must* pause and study the wording of the question. If it asks you to contrast X with Y, don't give ninety percent of your emphasis to X. If it tells you to state the relationship between A and B, don't throw in C for good measure. If you're required to analyze the content and style of a quoted passage, don't suppose that a double effort on content alone will gain you full credit. Break the question into its natural parts and attend to all of them.

3. *Gauge your available time.* Every question on an exam has a point value which can be quickly translated into a time value. A 30-point question in a 50-minute, 100-point exam shouldn't take much more of your time than 15 minutes (30 percent of 50). If you find yourself running over, stop and leave some blank space while you get something written on *all* other questions.

4. *Plan your essay.* For longer answers, take the necessary time to draw up a scratch outline (p. 39), and check the outline against the question to make sure it covers the required ground. This will enable you to write confidently and quickly.

5. *Don't waste time restating the question.* A grader can only be annoyed by a hollow introductory paragraph that merely announces your willingness to address the topic. He or she is already looking for *ideas.*

6. *State your thesis in the opening paragraph.* Fairly or unfairly, graders tend to decide after one or two paragraphs whether a student has a clear thesis to present. Perhaps a negative impression will be erased later—but don't count on it. Rather, use the opening paragraph to *announce your main point* and *establish the structure of everything that follows.* Don't fear that your strategy will be made too obvious. The more obvious the better, provided your thesis *directly answers* the question that has been posed.

7. *Keep to the point.* Digressions, or passages that stray from the case being made, are of questionable value in any essay. In an examination essay you simply have no time for them. Don't, for example, try to befriend your grader with humorous asides, pleas for sympathy, or reflections about the swift hands of the clock. If you can imagine the mental state of someone who has been reading, say,

fifty consecutive essays on the same topic, you will realize that this is no one to be trifled with.

8. *Be emphatic.* Your ideas may be complex, but your way of presenting them should be direct and plain. Don't shrink from underlining your leading points to ensure that they won't be overlooked.

9. *Support your generalizations.* Most essay questions are broad enough to allow for a variety of "right" answers. An experienced grader will be looking, not for a single, all-important idea, but for evidence that you have done the reading and have thought about it carefully. Your own ideas, *backed by detailed references to the assigned material*, will be much more impressive than unsupported statements taken directly from lectures and textbooks.

10. *Read through your completed answer.* If time permits, go over your exam essay *as if you were the grader*, and try to catch inconsistencies, incoherent sentences, illegible scribbles, and mistaken predictions about what follows. Don't hesitate to cross out whole paragraphs if necessary, or to send your grader to an extra page in the back of the blue book.

GLOSSARY
OF TERMS

The glossary offers simple definitions of terms used in this book. Words appearing in **boldface** have separate entries which you can consult if the term is unfamiliar. The abbreviation *cf.* means "compare"—that is, note the difference between the term being defined and another. And *e.g.* means "for example."

abbreviation   A shortened word, with the addition of a period to indicate the omission *(Dr.).* Cf. **acronym.**

absolute (n.)   An **adjective** or **adverb** that doesn't easily lend itself to qualification or comparison, since it already contains an idea of the highest degree: *infinite, uniquely,* etc. Since something *unique* stands by itself, it would be illogical to write *the most unique experience* or *She performed more uniquely than ever.*

absolute phrase   A **phrase** that, instead of modifying a particular word, acts like an **adverb** to the rest of the sentence in which it appears:

ABS PHRASE
• *All struggle over,* the troops lay down their arms.

ABS PHRASE
• *Time out having been called,* four commercials were shown.

Absolute phrases are not considered mistakes of usage. Cf. **dangling modifier** and **misrelated modifier.**

abstract language   Words that make no appeal to the senses: *aspect, comprehensible, enthusiasm, virtuously,* etc. Cf. **concrete language.**

acronym   A word formed from the initial letters of words in a name—e.g., *NOW,* formed from the National Organization for Women. Cf. **abbreviation.**

active voice   See **voice.**

ad hominem argument   **Reasoning** that appeals to prejudice or emotion instead of addressing the merits of the case. Most commonly, the user of ad hominem reasoning seeks to discredit a position by scorning the person, party, or interest that supports that position.

adjectival clause   See **clause.**

adjective   A **modifier** of a **noun, pronoun,** or other **nounlike element**— e.g., *strong* in a *strong contender.* Most adjectives can be compared: *strong, stronger, strongest.* See **degree.**

adverb   A word **modifying** either a **verb,** an **adjective,** another adverb, a **preposition,** an **infinitive,** a **participle,** a **phrase,** a **clause,** or a whole **sentence:** *now, clearly, moreover,* etc. Any one-word **modifier** that isn't an **adjective** or an **article** must be an adverb.

adverbial clause   See **clause.**

agreement   In **grammar,** the matching of **subjects** and **verbs** in **number** and **person.** In *I stumble,* e.g., the verb *stumble* "agrees with" the subject *I;* both are singular and first-person in form. Cf. **pronoun reference.**

alliteration   Conspicuous repetition of a **consonant** sound within a group of words: *humble house, potential power play,* etc.

allusion   A passing reference to a work or idea, either by directly mentioning it or by borrowing its well-known language. Thus, someone who writes *She took arms against a sea of troubles* is alluding to, but not mentioning, Hamlet's most famous speech. Shakespeare is directly alluded to in the sentence *He did it with Shakespearean flair.* Allusion differs from **plagiarism** in that readers are expected to notice the reference.

ambiguity   Uncertainty of meaning between two or more possible interpretations. The sentence *He wants nothing more than fame* is ambiguous. Is fame *all* he wants, or does he want fame more than he wants other things?

analogy   In general, a similarity of features or pattern between two things: *The nearest analogy to human speech may be the songs of whales.* In **rhetoric,** an analogy is an extended likeness drawn between two things, purporting to show that a feature or pattern in one is also present in the other. Thus, someone who disapproves of people leaving their home towns might devise this analogy: *People, like trees, must find their nourishment in the place where they happen to grow up; to seek it elsewhere is as fatal as removing a tree from its roots.* Like most analogies, this one starts with an obvious resemblance and proceeds to a more debatable one.

analysis   Close examination of a thing, issue, or text, to uncover its features, parts, or structure.

annotated bibliography   A **bibliography** including brief comments on the content and value of the separate entries.

antecedent   The word for which a **pronoun** stands:

ANT   PRO
* *Jane* was here yesterday, but today *she* is at school.

ANT PRO
* *John, who* is twenty-one, . . .

anticipatory construction   The words *here is, here are, there is,* or *there are,* when used in **sentences** with a delayed **subject:** *Here are my ideas.* The **verb** *are* agrees with the delayed subject *ideas,* not with the "expletive" *Here.*

antonym   A word opposite, or nearly opposite, in meaning to another word: *hard,* an antonym of *soft.*

aphorism   A memorably concise **sentence** conveying a very general assertion: *If wishes were horses, beggars would ride.* Aphoristic and **epigrammatic** are close in meaning.

appositive   A word or phrase whose only function is to identify an immediately preceding **noun, pronoun,** or **nounlike element:**

APP
* Mike *the butcher* is quite a clown.

APP
* We *the people* hope to keep the government in check.

APP
* What she wanted, *a cheetah purse,* would be hard to acquire.

Arabic numerals   Numerals like *1, 5,* and *12,* as opposed to **Roman numerals** like *I, V,* and *XII.*

argumentative essay (argument)   See **essay.**

article   An indicator or determiner immediately preceding a **noun** or **modifier.** Articles themselves may be considered modifiers, along with **adjectives** and **adverbs.** The *definite article* is *the;* the *indefinite articles* are *a* and *an.*

attributive noun   **A noun** serving as an **adjective:** *Massachusetts* in *the Massachusetts way of doing things,* or *gun* in *a gun lover.*

auxiliary   A **verb** form, usually lacking **inflection,** that combines with other verbs to express possibility, likelihood, necessity, obligation, etc. The commonly recognized auxiliaries are *can, could, dare, do, may, might, must, need, ought, should,* and *would,* as in *She can succeed* and *He could become jealous. Is, have,* and their related forms act like auxiliaries in the formation of **tenses:** *He is coming; They have gone.*

balance   A **parallelism** of sentence structure in which the related parts are given equal weight, creating an effect of symmetry: *the wrongs of the defeated and the rights of the victors; He expressed his love, though timidly, and she believed him, though reluctantly.*

base form of verb   An **infinitive** without *to: see, think,* etc. Base forms appear with **auxiliaries** (*should see*) and in the formation of present and future **tenses** (*I see, I will see*).

begging the question   Treating a debatable idea as if it had already been proved. Someone who asserts, in an essay favoring national health insurance, that only the greedy medical lobby could oppose such an obviously needed program, is begging the question; he is assuming the rightness of his position instead of establishing it with evidence.

bibliography   A list of consulted works presented at the end of a book, article, or **essay.** Also, a whole book devoted to listing works within a certain subject area.

bureaucratese   The inflated, important-sounding language often used in government reports — e.g., *finalize* for *complete.*

card catalog   An alphabetical index of a library's holdings, with a separate card for each entry.

cardinal numbers   Numbers like *one (1), two (2), and three (3).* Cf. **ordinal numbers.**

case   The **inflectional** form of **nouns** and **pronouns** indicating whether they designate actors (*subjective* case: *I, we, they*), receivers of action (*objective* case: *me, us, them*), or "owners" of the thing or quality modified (*possessive* case: *his* toy, *their* indecision, *Biff's* endorsement). **Personal pronouns** also have **second possessive** forms: *mine, theirs,* etc. See also **double possessive.**

catchall explanation   The ascribing of one cause to phenomena that may have many causes — for example, claiming that unemployment is due entirely to the unreasonable demands of union leaders.

circular reasoning   Argument that **begs the question** by reasserting an assumption instead of supporting it. Suppose you wanted to show that prayer in public schools is really constitutional, despite recent Supreme Court decisions to the contrary. If you wrote, *The fact that school prayer doesn't violate the Constitution shows that the Supreme Court has been wrong on this issue,* you'd be engaging in circular reasoning — using the point to be proved as evidence for a further contention.

circumlocution Roundabout expression — e.g., *when all is said and done* in place of *finally.*

classification The placing of a subject within a larger group or category, thus fixing its relation to other subjects — e.g., putting "1918 flu" in the category of "epidemics." Cf. **division.**

clause A cluster of words containing a **subject** and a **predicate.** All clauses are either independent or subordinate (dependent). An *independent* clause makes a complete statement and thus can stand alone: *Biff held the cologne in front of the camera.* A *subordinate* clause, which doesn't make a complete statement, can't stand alone: *before I go out on the field.* In *I splash myself with this he-man preparation before I go out on the field*, the subordinate clause modifies the main **verb** *splash.*

Among subordinate clauses, an *adjectival* clause serves the function of an **adjective**:

ADJ CLAUSE
* The model, *who was gorgeous,* pretended to faint in ecstasy.

The adjectival clause modifies the noun *model,* as in *the gorgeous model.*

An *adverbial* clause serves the function of an **adverb**:

ADV CLAUSE
* She swore at Biff *when he tried to help her up.*

The adverbial clause modifies the verb *swore,* as in *she swore then.*

And a *noun* clause serves the function of a **noun**:

NOUN CLAUSE
* *That a little cologne could cause such extreme reactions* surprised him.

The noun clause serves as the subject of the verb *surprised,* as in *reactions surprised him.*

cliché A trite, stereotyped, overused expression: *an open and shut case; a miss is as good as a mile.* Most clichés contain **figurative language** that has lost its vividness: *get the lead out, bring the house down,* etc.

collective noun A **noun** that is singular in form but designates a group of members: *band, family,* etc.

comma splice See **run-on sentence.**

common gender The intended sexual neutrality of **pronouns** used to indicate an indefinite party. Traditionally, indefinite (*one*) and masculine personal (*he*) pronouns were used, but feminine personal pronouns are now frequently added to ensure the neutral effect: *A candidate must file his or her application without delay.*

comparative degree   See **degree**.

complement   Usually, an element in the **predicate** that identifies or describes the **subject**. A single-word complement is either a *predicate noun* or a *predicate adjective:*

```
   S     PRED N
```
* He is a *fool.*

```
   S     PRED ADJ
```
* He is *foolish.*

In addition, a **direct object** can have a complement, known as an *objective complement:*

```
           D OBJ  OBJ COMPL
```
* They consider him *unteachable.*

Infinitives, too, can have complements:

```
              INF COMPL INF
```
* They beg him to be *serious.*

complex sentence   A **sentence** containing only one independent **clause** and at least one subordinate clause: *Although they loved the book, they found the movie puzzling.*

compound (adj.)   Consisting of more than one word, as in a *compound noun (ice cream),* a *compound preposition (in spite of),* or a *compound subject* (He and she were there).

compound-complex sentence   A **sentence** containing at least two independent **clauses** and at least one subordinate clause: *They were happy when they checked in, but soon they began to quarrel.*

compound sentence   A **sentence** containing at least two independent **clauses** but no subordinate clauses: *The tornado arrived, but the town was spared.*

concession (conceding)   In argument, the granting of an opposing point, usually with the purpose of showing that it doesn't overturn one's own **thesis.**

conclusion   In **logic**, an **inference** either **deduced** from **premises** or **induced** from a set of examples. The conclusion is the point that was to be demonstrated.
    In an **essay**, the conclusion is the final segment, which ideally leaves the reader with a sense of completion.

concrete language   Words describing a thing or quality appealing to the senses: *purple, car, buzz, dusty,* etc. Cf. **abstract language.**

conjunction   An uninflected function word that connects other words, **phrases,** or **clauses**: *and, although,* etc. Unlike a **preposition,** a conjunction is not itself the opening word in a phrase.

A *coordinating conjunction* joins grammatically similar elements, without turning one into a **modifier** of the other: *and, but, for, nor, or, so, yet.*

A *subordinating conjunction* joins grammatically dissimilar elements, turning one of them into a modifier and specifying its logical relation to the other—e.g., *Although* in *Although you are sad, I am cheerful.*

Correlative conjunctions are matched pairs with a coordinating function: *either/or, neither/nor,* etc.

conjunctive adverb (sentence adverb)   An **adverb** that also serves to indicate a logical connection between the modified **clause** or a whole **sentence** and a previous statement—e.g., *therefore* in *He took the job; therefore, he had to resign his fellowship.*

connotation   An association that a word calls up, as opposed to its **denotation** or dictionary meaning. Thus, the word *exile* denotes enforced separation from one's home or country, but it *connotes* loneliness, homesickness, and any number of other, more private, thoughts and images.

consonant   A speech sound involving the blockage or diverting of breath: *b, c, d, f, g,* etc. The consonants consist of all the letters of the alphabet that are not **vowels.**

contraction   The condensing of two words to one, with an apostrophe added to replace the omitted letter or letters: *isn't, don't,* etc.

coordinating conjunction   See **conjunction.**

coordination   The giving of equal grammatical value to two or more parts of a **sentence,** usually connected by a coordinating **conjunction:** *Apples and eggs are scarce; He tried, but he failed.* Cf. **subordination.**

correlative conjunction   See **conjunction.**

dangling modifier   The **modifier** of a term that has been wrongly omitted:

                    DM
x *Not wishing to be bothered,* the telephone was left off the hook.

    The person who didn't wish to be bothered goes unmentioned, and is thus absurdly replaced by *telephone.*

Cf. **misrelated modifier** and **absolute phrase.**

dead metaphor   See **metaphor.**

declarative sentence   A **sentence** that makes a statement: *Lambs are woolly.*

deduction   In **logic,** the process of **reasoning** from **premises** to **conclusions.** Thus, the conclusion is *deduced* in the following chain of reasoning:

PREMISE:
Every red-blooded citizen loves hot dogs.

PREMISE:
Priscilla despises hot dogs.

CONCLUSION:
Priscilla is not a red-blooded citizen.

definite article   See **article.**

degree   The form of an **adjective** or **adverb** showing its quality, quantity, or intensity. The ordinary, uncompared form of an adjective or adverb is its *positive* degree: *quick, quickly.* The *comparative* degree is intermediate, indicating that the modified term surpasses at least one other member of its group: *quicker, more quickly.* And an adjective or adverb in the *superlative* degree indicates that the modified term surpasses all other members of its group: *quickest, most quickly.*

Note that the three degrees show increasing extremeness or coverage, but not necessarily increasing size or value: *little, less, least; bad, worse, worst,* etc.

demonstrative adjective   A **demonstrative pronoun** form serving as a **modifier** — e.g., *those* in *those laws.*

demonstrative pronoun   A **pronoun** that singles out what it refers to: *this, that, these,* or *those,* when not used as a **modifier.** *Those* is a demonstrative pronoun in *Those are the laws.* Cf. **demonstrative adjective.**

denotation   The primary, "dictionary," meanings of a word. Cf. **connotation.**

dependent clause   See **clause.**

descriptive essay   See **essay.**

diction   The choice of words, especially insofar as they contribute to different **tones** or occupy different *levels:*

FORMAL	MIDDLE	INFORMAL
impecunious	bankrupt	broke
appellation	name	handle
deranged	crazy	nuts
livelihood	job	racket

Extremely informal diction of a faddish character is called *slang: a together dude, blow your cool,* etc.

direct object   A word naming the item directly acted upon by a **subject** through the activity of a **verb:**

   S   V   D OBJ
* She hit the *jackpot.*

Cf. **indirect object, retained object,** and **object of preposition.**

division   In composition, the breaking up of a **topic** or **subject area** into its logical parts — e.g., breaking "epidemics" into "bubonic plague," "yellow fever," etc. Cf. **classification.**

double possessive   A possessive form (see **case**) using both *of* and *-'s*: *an idea of Linda's.*

either/or reasoning   Depicting one's own position as the better of an artificially limited and "loaded" pair of alternatives — e.g., asking readers to favor a certain air-pollution measure as the only possible way of avoiding mass asphyxiation.

ellipsis   The three or four periods used to indicate material omitted from a quotation: *"about the . . . story."* Longer rows of ellipses are used to indicate omission of lines of verse.

endnote   A **footnote** placed in a consecutive series with others at the end of an article, chapter, or **essay.**

epigrammatic   Ingeniously concise and pointed in phrasing. Professor Spooner's famous slip, *Work is the curse of the drinking classes,* accidentally struck an epigrammatic note.

essay   A fairly brief (usually between three and twenty typed pages) piece of nonfiction that tries to make a point in an interesting way.
   The standard modes of the essay are *description,* in which the writer tries to acquaint the reader with a place, object, character, or group; *narration,* recounting something that has happened; *exposition,* presenting information or explaining something; and *argument,* attempting to convince the reader that the writer's position on a certain issue is well-founded.

euphemism   A vague or "nice" expression used in place of a more direct one; e.g., *rehabilitation facility* for *prison,* or *disincentive* for *threat.*

evading the question   Avoiding the issue at hand, usually by shifting to a related point that is easier to maintain. Thus, someone who favors sharply limiting the number of immigrants to the United States is evading the question if he dwells on the government's right to pass immigration laws; that right isn't the point being contested.

evidence   Facts and informed opinions tending to support a **thesis**. One statement can be used as evidence for another only if there is a high likelihood that readers will accept it as true.

expletive   See **anticipatory construction.**

expository essay (exposition)   See **essay.**

extension   In **reasoning,** the exaggeration of an opposing idea in order to make it easier to **rebut.** Someone who opposed curfews for minors would be engaging in extension if he depicted the rival argument as calling for an end to all constitutional rights. Cf. **straw man.**

extracted quotation A quoted passage set apart from the writer's own text. Long prose quotations (c. 100+ words) and poetic quotations of more than two lines are customarily extracted. Such passages are **indented**, and quotation marks at the beginning and end are dropped.

fallacy A formal error or illegitimate shortcut in **reasoning**. See **ad hominem argument, begging the question, catchall explanation, either/or reasoning, extension, faulty generalization,** and **straw man.**

faulty generalization The drawing of a general **conclusion** from inadequate **evidence**—e.g., concluding from one year's drought that the world's climate has entered a long period of change.

figurative language **Metaphorical** expression, lending imaginative coloration to the thing described—e.g., *the hungry maw of the grave* for *death,* or *the budding springtime of life* for *youth.* Cf. **literal language.**

footnote In general, any citation or comment set below or after a main text. More narrowly, a note at the bottom ("foot") of a page. Cf. **endnote.**

formal diction See **diction.**

funnel paragraph A **paragraph** beginning with a broad assertion and gradually narrowing to a specific subject.

fused sentence See **run-on sentence.**

gender The concept of sexual classification determining the forms of masculine (*he*), feminine (*she*), and neuter (*it*) **personal pronouns** and the feminine form of certain **nouns** (*actress*). Cf. **common gender.**

general language Words that are not **specific**: *suburbia,* as opposed to *Chestnut Hill; bird,* as opposed to *scarlet tanager.*

gerund A **nounlike** form derived from a **verb**—e.g., *Skiing* in *Skiing is dangerous.* Gerunds take exactly the same form as **participles**, and they are capable of having **subjects** (usually possessive in **case**) as well as **objects:**

```
   S      GER    OBJ GER
• Nancy's making the putt was unexpected.
```

gerund phrase See **phrase.**

grammar The formal features of a language; also, the rules for fashioning "grammatical" or technically correct sentences in that language. Cf. **usage.**

identity, signals of Signs that something already mentioned is still under discussion: chiefly **pronouns, demonstrative adjectives,** repeated words and **phrases**, and omissions based on words previously supplied. In *That is what I meant*, e.g., *That* is a signal of identity with something in the sentence before. Cf. **transition, signals of.**

imperative mood See **mood.**

implied subject A **subject** not actually present in a **clause**, but nevertheless understood: [*You*] *Watch out!*

indefinite article See **article**.

indefinite pronoun A **pronoun** that leaves unspecified the person or thing it refers to: *anybody, one*, etc.

indefinite relative pronoun An apparent **relative pronoun** lacking an **antecedent**—e.g., *what* in *She says what she thinks.*

indention The setting of the first word of a line in from the left margin, as in a new **paragraph** or an **extracted quotation.**

independent clause See **clause.**

independent sentence fragment See **sentence fragment.**

indicative mood See **mood.**

indirect discourse Reporting what was said, as opposed to directly quoting it. Not *She said, "I am tired,"* but *She said she was tired.*

indirect object A word designating the person or thing *for whom or which*, or *to whom or which*, the action of a **verb** is performed. Note that an indirect object never appears without a **direct object** occurring in the same **clause:**

```
            IND OBJ           D OBJ
• She sent him a discouraging letter.
```

Note that when a seeming indirect object is preceded by a **preposition**, it is in fact an **object of a preposition:**

```
                          OBJ PREP
• She sent a discouraging letter to him.
```

indirect question The reporting of a question without use of the question form—not, e.g., *She asked, "Where should I turn?"* but *She asked where to turn.*

induction The process of deciding that a number of examples, all leading toward the same **conclusion**, do in fact justify that conclusion. Thus someone who sees many dead, oil-covered birds on a beach might *induce*, without being able to prove conclusively, that an oil spill has occurred at sea. Cf. **deduction.**

inference   A **conclusion** drawn by means of either **deduction** or **induction**. You *infer* one statement from others that imply it (deduction) or from an array of evidence that makes it plausible (induction).

infinitive   The **base form of a verb**, usually but not always preceded by *to*: *win, to win; prove, to prove.*

infinitive phrase   See **phrase.**

inflection   A change in the ending or whole form of a word, without turning it into a new word. Thus, *he* can be inflected to *his*, *George* to *George's, go* to *went*, etc. The word is recognizably the same, but the inflection has placed it in a new state.

informal diction   See **diction.**

intensive pronoun   A **pronoun** like *myself* or *themselves*, when used for emphasis: *I myself disagree with that.* Cf. **reflexive pronoun.**

interjection   A word that stands apart from other constructions in order to command attention or show strong feeling: *aha, hey, wow*, etc.

interrogative adjective   An **interrogative pronoun** form serving as a **modifier** that introduces a question—e.g., *Whose* in *Whose socks are these?*

interrogative pronoun   A **pronoun** serving to introduce a question: *who, whom, whose, which,* and *what*, as in *Which is it?*

intransitive verb   A **verb** expressing an action or state without connection to an **object** or a **complement:** *They complained.* Cf. **transitive verb** and **linking verb.**

invalid reasoning   See **reasoning.**

inverted syntax (inversion)   Reversal of the normal order of **sentence elements:** *Naked I came into the world; His goal he clearly perceived.* Cf. **suspended sentence.**

irony   A sharply incongruous effect, as when an advocate of holy poverty is found to have been collecting Rolls-Royces.
   In **rhetoric**, irony is the saying of one thing in order to convey a different or even opposite meaning: *Let us continue this noble war, by all means; when the best young men of their generation have all been killed or maimed, the rest of us can congratulate ourselves on having upheld the national honor.* Cf. **sarcasm.**

irregular verb   A **verb** that doesn't simply add *-d* or *-ed* to form its past **tense** and its past **participle:** *go (went, gone), swim (swam, swum)*, etc.

italic type (italics)   The thin, slightly slanted typeface of *these three words,* represented in typing and handwriting by underlining: good, *good.* Cf. **roman type.**

jargon   Technical language used in inappropriate, nontechnical contexts—e.g., *upwardly mobile* for *ambitious, positive reinforcement* for *praise, paranoid* for *upset.*

journalese   **Jargon** borrowed from the language of newspapers—e.g., *gets the nod* for *wins the decision, the blaze rages* for *the fire is out of control.*

level of diction   See **diction.**

linking verb   A **verb** connecting its **subject** to an identifying or **modifying complement**:

* They *were* Mormons.
  L V

* She *became* calmer.
  L V

Cf. **transitive verb** and **intransitive verb.**

literal language   Words that factually represent what they describe, without poetic embellishment: *dog, car, landscape.* Cf. **figurative language.**

logic   The principles governing the means of drawing reasonable **inferences** or **conclusions;** the use of those principles.

lower case   The ordinary, uncapitalized form of letters, as in *hello.*

merged verb   A **verb** combined with a **preposition** to make a new unit— e.g., *knock down,* as in *He knocked down the challenger.*

metaphor   An implied comparison, whereby the thing at hand is **figuratively** asserted to be something else: *He was a tower of strength.*
   A *dead metaphor* is one that has become so common that it usually doesn't call to mind an image: *a devil of a time, rock-bottom prices,* etc. When overworked, a dead metaphor becomes a **cliché.**
   A *mixed metaphor* is one whose elements clash in their implications: *Let's back off for a closer look; He's a straight arrow who shoots from the hip.*

meter   The alternation of stressed and unstressed syllables according to a fixed pattern: *My heárt leaps up when I behóld.* Cf. **rhythm.**

middle diction   See **diction.**

misrelated modifier   A **modifier** that might modify either of two terms, or that stands too distant from its modified term, or that unnecessarily interrupts another construction:

MOD TERM? MM MOD TERM?
✗ The proposal that he rejected *utterly* amazes me.

   MM   MOD TERM
✗ *Laughing* so hard, it was extremely difficult for Alice to keep control of the wheel.

           MM
✗ They chose to *finally and decisively* end their relationship.

See also **split infinitive** and **squinting modifier.** Cf. **dangling modifier.**

mixed metaphor   See **metaphor.**

modifier   A word, **phrase,** or **clause** that limits or describes another element:

    M
* the *gentle* soul

    M
* *When leaving,* turn out the lights.

     M
* *Before you explain,* I have something to tell you.

mood   The manner or attitude that a speaker or writer intends a **verb** to convey, as shown in certain changes of form. Ordinary statements and questions are cast in the *indicative* mood: *Is he ill? He is.* The *imperative* mood is for commands: *Stop! Get out of the way!* And the *subjunctive* mood is used for certain formulas *(as it were),* unlikely or impossible conditions *(had she gone), that* **clauses** expressing requirements or recommendations *(They ask that she comply),* and *lest* clauses *(lest he forget).*

narrative essay (narration)   See **essay.**

nominal   See **nounlike element.**

nonrestrictive element   A **modifier,** often a **phrase** or **clause,** that doesn't serve to identify ("restrict") the modified term:

               NONRESTR EL
* That woman, *whom I met only yesterday,* . . .

               NONRESTR EL
* The man, *brushing the dust from his suit,* . . .

Cf. **restrictive element.**

note   See **footnote.**

noun   A word like *house, Jack,* or *Pennsylvania,* usually denoting a person, place, or thing, capable of being **inflected** for both plural and possessive forms (*houses, house's, houses'*), and of serving a variety of sentence functions (see p. 276).

noun clause See **clause.**

nounlike element (nominal, substantive) A word or group of words having the same function as a **noun** — e.g., *what you mean* in *He knows what you mean.* The nounlike **clause** *what you mean* serves as a **direct object,** a typical noun function.

noun phrase See **phrase.**

number In **grammar,** the distinction between *singular (boat)* and *plural (boats)* words.

object A **noun, pronoun,** or **nounlike element** representing a receiver of an action or relation. See **direct object, indirect object,** and **object of preposition.** In addition, **infinitives, participles,** and **gerunds** can take objects:

> OBJ INF
- to hit the *ball*

> OBJ PART
- Hitting the *ball,* he heard the bat crack.

> OBJ GER
- Hitting the *ball* is gratifying.

object of preposition A **noun, pronoun,** or **nounlike element** following a **preposition** and completing the prepositional **phrase** — e.g., *November* in *throughout November,* or *siesta* in *during a long siesta.*

objective case See **case.**

objective complement See **complement.**

ordinal numbers Numbers like *first (1st), second (2nd),* and *third (3rd).* Cf. **cardinal numbers.**

outline A concise, consecutive list of the points an **essay** will make, usually with **indention** and sets of numbering and lettering to show the relation of major to minor points.

A *scratch outline* simply lists the points to be made in order, without use of categories and subcategories. A *topic outline* is one whose headings are words or **phrases.** In a *sentence outline,* the headings — except perhaps for the most general ones — are full **sentences.**

paradox A seeming contradiction that may nevertheless be true: *That country is the richest — and the poorest — in the world.* (Perhaps the country has the highest per-capita income but the poorest mass of peasants.)

paragraph One or more **sentences** marked as a unit, usually by the **in-**

dention of the first line. A typical effective paragraph develops one central idea in a consistent manner.

paragraph block A group of **paragraphs** addressing the same part of a **topic**, with strong continuity from one paragraph to the next.

parallelism The giving of equivalent structure to two or more parts of a sentence—e.g., the words *Utica, Albany,* and *Rye* in the sentence *He went to Utica, Albany, and Rye,* or in the three equally weighted **clauses** that begin this sentence: *That he wanted to leave, that permission was denied, and that he then tried to escape—these facts only became known after months of official secrecy.* Cf. **coordination** and **balance.**

paraphrase Sentence-by-sentence restatement of the meaning of a passage.

parenthetical citation A page reference to a work, given not in a **footnote** but in parentheses within a main text—e.g., *(Meyers, pp. 241–75).* Parenthetical citations are usually given only after a full footnote citing the same work has been supplied.

parenthetical element A word or group of words that interrupts the main flow of a **sentence:**

PRTHL EL
• You, *alas,* are not the one.

participial phrase See **phrase.**

participle An adjectival form derived from a **verb**—e.g., *Showing* in *Showing fear, he began to sweat.* Participles can be *present (showing)* or *past (having shown),* and *active* or *passive (being shown, having been shown).* Like **gerunds,** they can also have **objects** (*fear* in the sentence above), but they do not generally have possessive-case **subjects,** as in *George's showing fear.* Cf. **gerund.**

part of speech Any of the major classes (**noun, verb, conjunction,** etc.) into which words are customarily divided, depending on their dictionary meaning and their **syntactic** functions in sentences. Since many words belong to several parts of speech, you must analyze the sentence at hand to see which part of speech a given word is occupying.

passive voice See **voice.**

past participle See **participle.**

periodic sentence See **suspended sentence.**

person In **grammar,** a characteristic of **pronouns** and **verbs** indicating whether someone is speaking *(first person: I go, we go),* being spoken to *(second person: you go),* or being spoken about *(third person: he, she, it goes; they go).*

personal pronouns The **pronouns** traditionally used in the conjugation (tense formation) of **verbs**—*I, you, he, she, it, we,* and *they*—plus the objective and possessive forms of those pronouns: *me, my, mine, your, yours,* etc.

phrase A cluster of words functioning as a single **part of speech** and lacking a **subject–predicate** transaction.

A noun and its modifiers are sometimes called a *noun phrase (the elliptical billiard balls),* and a verb form consisting of more than one word is sometimes called a *verb phrase (had been trying).* But the types of phrases most commonly recognized are prepositional, infinitive, participial, gerundive, and absolute.

A *prepositional phrase* consists of a **preposition** and its **object**, along with any **modifiers** of those words:

PREP   M   M   M OBJ PREP
• *among the many fine things*
⎵⎵⎵⎵⎵⎵⎵⎵⎵⎵⎵⎵⎵⎵⎵⎵
      PREP PHRASE

An *infinitive phrase* consists of an **infinitive** and its **object,** along with any **modifiers,** and it may also include a **subject** of the infinitive:

            S INF INF M   M   M OBJ INF
• They asked *John to hit the tiny red target.*
          ⎵⎵⎵⎵⎵⎵⎵⎵⎵⎵⎵⎵⎵⎵⎵⎵
              INF PHRASE

A *participial phrase* consists of a **participle** and its **object** and/or **modifiers:**

   M   PART   M   M   OBJ PART
• *Quickly reaching the correct decision,* he pressed the button.
⎵⎵⎵⎵⎵⎵⎵⎵⎵⎵⎵⎵⎵⎵⎵⎵
      PART PHRASE

A *gerund phrase* consists of a **gerund** and its **object,** along with any **modifiers,** and it may also include a **subject** of the gerund:

S GER   GER OBJ GER M
• *Their sending him away* was a bad mistake.
⎵⎵⎵⎵⎵⎵⎵⎵⎵⎵⎵⎵
      GER PHRASE

An *absolute phrase* may be of any of the listed types. It differs from them not in form but in its modifying function. See **absolute phrase.**

Phrases are often confused with clauses; cf. **clause.**

plagiarism The taking of others' thoughts or words without due acknowledgment.

plural See **number.**

positive degree See **degree.**

possessive case See **case.**

predicate In a **clause,** the **verb** plus all the words belonging with it:

PRED
• He *had a serious heart attack.*

Cf. **subject.**

predicate adjective See **complement.**

predicate noun See **complement.**

predication The selection of a **predicate** for a given **subject.** The problem of *faulty predication* appears when subjects and predicates are mismatched in meaning: *The purpose of the film wants to challenge your beliefs,* etc.

prefix One or more letters that can be attached before the root or base form of a word to make a new word: *pre-, with-,* etc. Cf. **suffix.**

prejudgment Making up one's mind about an issue before sufficient **evidence** has been presented; forming a prejudice.

premise One of the statements ("propositions") from which a **conclusion** is deduced in logical **reasoning.** See **deduction.**

preposition A function word introducing a **prepositional phrase**—e.g., *to* in *to the lighthouse.* Cf. **conjunction.**

prepositional phrase See **phrase.**

principal parts The **base** or simple **infinitive** form of a **verb,** its past **tense** form, and its past **participle:** *walk, walked, walked; grow, grew, grown.*

pronoun One of a small class of words, mostly used in place of **nouns** for a variety of purposes. See **personal pronoun, intensive pronoun, reflexive pronoun, reciprocal pronoun, indefinite pronoun, indefinite relative pronoun, demonstrative pronoun, relative pronoun,** and **interrogative pronoun.**

pronoun reference The matching of **pronouns** with their **antecedents,** with which they should agree in **number, person,** and **gender.** Thus, in the sentence *When they saw Bill, they gave him a warm welcome,* the pronoun *him* properly refers to the singular, third-person, masculine antecedent *Bill.* Cf. **agreement.**

psychologese Psychological **jargon**—e.g., *superego* for *conscience, schizophrenic* for *undecided.*

punctuation marks Marks used to bring out the meaning of written **sentences.** They are:

period .	parentheses ( )
question mark ?	brackets [ ]

exclamation point !	ellipses . . .
comma ,	apostrophe '
semicolon ;	hyphen -
colon :	quotation marks " "
dash —	virgule (slash) /

reasoning   The process of drawing **inferences,** either through **deduction** or **induction;** moving from **evidence** to **conclusions** about that evidence.
   Reasoning that avoids formal errors or **fallacies** is said to be *valid,* whether or not the conclusion reached is true. (A valid inference from mistaken **premises** may be false.) Fallacious reasoning is *invalid,* even if, by chance, the conclusion happens to be true. The aim of reasoning is to reach true conclusions by drawing valid inferences from true premises.

rebuttal   An opposing argument, intended to overturn an argument already made by someone else. Rebuttals don't always succeed; cf. **refutation.**

reciprocal pronoun   A **pronoun** expressing mutual relation: *each other, each other's, one another, one another's.*

redundancy   The defect of unnecessarily conveying the same meaning more than once; also, an expression that does so—e.g., *retreat back, ascend up.*

reference works   Books that survey a field of knowledge and tell how to locate materials within that field.

reflexive pronoun   A **pronoun** like *myself* or *themselves,* used to indicate that the **subject** of a **verb** is also its **direct** or **indirect object:** *They killed themselves; I gave myself a treat.* Cf. **intensive pronoun.**

refutation   The disproving of an argument already made. Cf. **rebuttal.**

relative adjective   An **adjective** serving to introduce a relative or adjectival **clause**—e.g., *whose* in *the one whose picture you saw.*

relative adverb   An **adverb** serving to introduce a relative or adjectival **clause**—e.g., *where* in *the place where he lives.*

relative clause   In this book, any adjectival **clause.** (Some grammarians would say that only a **relative pronoun** can introduce a relative clause.)

relative pronoun   A **pronoun** introducing a relative or adjectival **clause**—e.g., *that* in *This is the one that he chose.* Relative pronouns have **antecedents**, such as *one* in the example above. But see also **indefinite relative pronoun.**

restrictive element   A **modifier,** often a **phrase** or **clause,** that "restricts" or establishes the identity of the modified term:

RSTR EL
- The woman *whom I met* has disappeared.

RSTR EL
- The man *in the black suit* is following you.

Cf. **nonrestrictive element.**

retained object   A word in the **direct object** position, but receiving the action of a *passive* **verb:**

RET OBJ
- They were shown the *hall.*

rhetoric   The strategic placement of ideas and choice of language, as in *His rhetoric was effective* or *His ideas were sound but his rhetoric was addressed to the wrong audience.* Note that the unmodified noun *rhetoric* needn't mean *deception* or *manipulation.*

rhetorical question   A question posed for effect, without expectation of a reply: *How often have we seen this same pattern of betrayal?*

rhyme   Identity in sound between the closing letters of words: *road/toad; elect/select,* etc.

rhythm   The pattern of rising and falling emphasis of sound in a unit of writing, whether or not regular **meter** is apparent.

Roman numerals   Numerals like *I, V,* and *XII.* Cf. **Arabic numerals.**

roman type   The ordinary typeface of printed words, equivalent to what is produced by the keys of most typewriters. Cf. **italic type.**

run-on sentence   A **sentence** in which two or more **independent clauses** are improperly joined. One type of run-on sentence is the *comma splice,* in which independent clauses are joined with a comma but without a coordinating **conjunction:** *She likes candy, she eats it every day.* The other type of run-on sentence is the *fused sentence,* in which independent clauses are joined without any punctuation or conjunction: *She likes candy she eats it every day.*

sarcasm   Abusive ridicule of a person, group, or idea, as in *What pretty phrases these cold-hearted traitors speak!* Cf. **irony.**

scratch outline   See **outline.**

second possessive   The **case** forms of possessive **pronouns** used when the **modified** term doesn't immediately follow the pronoun: *mine, yours, ours, theirs,* as in *The blame is ours.*

self-evident thesis   A **thesis** saying little or nothing more than is already implied in the meaning of its terms — e.g., *If we fail to solve our transportation problems, congested traffic will continue to plague us.*

sentence   A complete unit of thought, usually containing at least one **independent clause**, beginning with a capital letter, and ending with a period, question mark, or exclamation point. See also **sentence fragment.**

sentence adverb   See **conjunctive adverb.**

sentence element   One of the functional parts of a **sentence: subject, direct object,** etc.

sentence fragment   A set of words punctuated as a **sentence,** but lacking one or more of the elements usually considered necessary to a sentence:

> SENT FRAG
> x *When they last saw her.*

In general, sentence fragments are regarded as blunders. But an *independent sentence fragment* — one whose context shows that it is a shortened sentence rather than a dislocated piece of a neighboring sentence — can sometimes be effective:

> IND FRAG
> • How much longer can we resist the enemy? *As long as necessary!*

sentence outline   See **outline.**

series   A set of **coordinated** items in a **sentence:**

> SERIES
> • He gave it to *her, them, and us.*

simile   An explicit or open comparison, whereby the object at hand is **figuratively** asserted to be *like* something else: *She ran like the wind; It happened as if in a dream.* Cf. **metaphor.** Both similes and metaphors are called metaphorical or figurative language. Also cf. **analogy.**

simple sentence   A **sentence** containing one independent **clause** and no subordinate *clauses*: *The empire toppled.*

slang   See **diction.**

sociologese   **Jargon** taken from sociology — e.g., *peer group* for *friends.*

specific language   Words dealing in particulars — e.g., *the 200-meter high hurdles,* as opposed to *the race.* Cf. **general language.**

split infinitive   An **infinitive** interrupted by at least one **adverb:** *to firmly stand.* When such an adverb makes an awkward effect, it is considered a **misrelated modifier.**

squinting modifier   A type of **misrelated modifier** sandwiched between sentence elements, either of which might be regarded as the modified term:

SQ M
. Why he collapsed *altogether* puzzles me.

standard English The most widely accepted dialect, or group practice, in English **usage**.

straw man A weak, often absurd argument opposing one's own position, invented in order to be easily **refuted.** The straw man's only function is to topple: *Some people will tell you that America should give up its precious freedoms and invite the Kremlin to rule us as a colony. But I say . . .* The obviously contrived nature of straw-man reasoning makes it generally ineffective. Cf. **extension.**

subject The part of a **clause** about which something is **predicated:**

S
. *Ernest* shot the tiger.

The subject alone is called the *simple subject.* With its modifiers included it is called the *complete subject* — e.g., *The only thing to do* in the sentence *The only thing to do is compromise.*
   Not only **verbs,** but also **infinitives** and **gerunds** can have subjects:

S INF
. They wanted *him* to be king.

S GER
. *His* refusing upset them.

subject area A wide range of concerns, from which the **topic** of an **essay** may be extracted. Cf. **topic, thesis.**

subjective case See **case.**

subjunctive mood See **mood.**

subordinate clause See **clause.**

subordinating conjunction See **conjunction.**

subordination In general, the giving of minor emphasis to minor elements or ideas. In **syntax,** making one element grammatically dependent on another, which the subordinate element limits or supports or explains — e.g., in *They were relieved when it was over,* the **subordinate clause** *when it was over* limits the time in which the verb *were relieved* is in effect.

substantive See **nounlike element.**

suffix One or more letters that can be added at the end of a word's root or base to make a new word: *-ship, -ness,* etc. Cf. **prefix.**

superlative degree See **degree.**

suspended comparison   A comparison proposing two possible relations between the compared items, and in which the second item is stated only at the end of the construction: *Taco Bell is as good as, if not better than, the Pizza Hut.*

suspended sentence   A sentence, usually rather long, in which an essential grammatical element is withheld until the end: *In every encounter with her supervisors, whether in the office or at company picnics and parties, what Trudy seemed destined to experience was a fundamental lack of understanding.* Cf. **inverted syntax.**

synonym   A word having practically the same meaning as another word —e.g., *car, auto.* Cf. **antonym.**

syntax   The pattern of word order in a **sentence.**

tense   The time a **verb** expresses: present *(see),* future *(will see),* etc. See pages 269–270.

thesis   The point, or one main idea, of an **essay.** Cf. **subject area, topic.**

thesis statement   A one-**sentence** statement of the **thesis** or main idea of an **essay.** Also called a *thesis sentence.* Cf. **topic sentence.**

tone   The quality of feeling conveyed by something. Words like *factual, sober, fanciful, urgent, tongue-in-cheek, restrained, stern, pleading,* and *exuberant* may begin to suggest the range of tones found in **essays.**

topic   The specific subject of an **essay;** the ground to be covered or the question to be answered. Cf. **subject area, thesis.**

topic outline   See **outline.**

topic sentence   The **sentence** in a **paragraph** that conveys its main idea. Not to be confused with the **thesis statement** of a whole **essay.**

transition, signals of   Signs that a previous statement will be expanded or qualified in some way—e.g., words like *therefore, in the second place,* and *to be sure.*

transitive verb   A **verb** transmitting an action to a **direct** or **retained object:**

      TR V
• They *cast* the dice.

      TR V
• She *was given* the prize.

Cf. **intransitive verb** and **linking verb.**

trial thesis   A possible **thesis** or main idea, considered before a final thesis has been chosen.

usage   The practices of word choice and sentence formation typically accepted by a group of speakers and writers. Cf. **grammar, standard English.**

valid reasoning   See **reasoning.**

verb   A word or words like *goes, saw,* or *was leaving,* serving to convey the action performed by a **subject,** to express the state of that subject, or to connect the subject to a **complement.** See pages 267 – 275 for other features of verbs.

verb phrase   See **phrase.**

verbal   A form derived from, but different in function from, a **verb.** Verbals are either **infinitives, participles,** or **gerunds.**

voice   The form of a **verb** indicating whether the **subject** performs (*active* voice: *we strike*) or receives (*passive* voice: *we are struck*) the action.

vowel   An unblocked speech sound, marked by one of the letters *a, e, i, o, u,* or *y* as in *try* (not as in *yellow*). Cf. **consonant.**

Note: Page numbers in boldface type **(436–459)** indicate main entries in the Glossary of Terms.

A

E

G

H

had better, 417
had ought, 417
half a, 417
handwritten essay, form for, 260
hanged vs. *hung,* 417
hang-up, 417
hard, -ly, 417
hardly . . . than, 417
has reference to, 417
head up, 417
here are, is, number of, 306
high, -ly, 417
high offices, capitalization of, 389
historic, -al, 417
historical terms, capitalization of, 388–389
history, reference books to, 212–213
home vs. *house,* 418
hopefully, 417–418
host (v.), 418
house vs. *home,* 418
how, 418
how ever vs. *however,* 418
human history, 418
humanism vs. *humanity, humaneness, humanitarianism,* 418
Humanities Index, 209
hung vs. *hanged,* 417
hyphen, 349; at line ending, 371–372; in compound modifiers, 374; in compound nouns, 373; in compound numbers, 374–375; in connection of numbers, 375; in spelling, 371–375; spacing with, 354; with prefixes, 372–373
hypothetical conditions: and sequence of tenses, 308–309; and subjunctive, 273, 274

I

-ics, 418
idea vs. *concept, conception,* 410
identify, relate, 418
identity, signals of, 175–179, **446**
i.e. vs. *e.g.,* 413
if and when, 418

if not, 418
ignorant vs. *stupid,* 418
illicit vs. *elicit,* 413
illusion vs. *allusion, delusion,* 405
imaginary vs. *imaginative,* 418
immigrate vs. *emigrate,* 413
imminent vs. *eminent,* 413
immoral vs. *amoral,* 406
immortal, 418
imperative mood, 272, 449
implicit vs. *explicit, tacit,* 418–419
implied subject, 264, 269, 272, **446**
imply vs. *infer,* 419
in a very real sense, 419
in addition to, effect on number of verb, 307
in all probability, likelihood, 419
in case, 419
in connection with, 419
in excess of, 419
in number, length, size, volume, area, etc., 419
in regard to, 427
in spite of the fact that, 419
in terms of, 419
in the affirmative, negative, 419
in the event that, 419
in the form of, 419
in the neighborhood of, 419
in the worst way, 419
in this day and age, 419
in to vs. *into,* 419
in view of the fact that, 419
inanimate noun, possessive of, 369
incidence vs. *incident, instance,* 419–420
include, 420
incredibly, 420
indefinite article, 288, 438
indefinite person, gender of, 113
indefinite pronoun, 279, **446**
indefinite relative pronoun, 280, **446**
indention, 445, **446**; of long quotations, 251, 350; of poetry, 353
independent clause, 264, 301, 331–333, 440; punctuation between, 331–333
independent sentence fragment, 301, 329, 456
indexes, periodically issued, 208–210
indicative mood, 272, 449
indicator, 288
indirect discourse, **446**; tenses in, 309–310

S

W

Y

ABOUT THE AUTHOR

Frederick Crews, Professor of English at the University of California, Berkeley, received the Ph.D. from Princeton University. Throughout a distinguished career he has attained many honors, including a Guggenheim Fellowship, appointment as a Fulbright Lecturer in Italy, and recognition from the National Endowment for the Arts for his essay, "Norman O. Brown: The World Dissolves." His writings include highly regarded books on Henry James, E. M. Forster, and Nathaniel Hawthorne, the best-selling satire *The Pooh Perplex*, and a recent volume of his own essays entitled *Out of My System*. Professor Crews has published numerous articles in *Partisan Review*, *New York Review of Books*, *Commentary*, *Tri-Quarterly*, and other important journals. He is currently Chairman of Freshman Composition in the English Department at Berkeley.